Wonderful Wooden Toys

 Sterling Publishing Co., Inc. New York
By arrangement with the British Broadcasting System

BLIZZARD'S
WONDERFUL
WOODEN TOYS

Richard Blizzard

The plans for the toys and models
were drawn by Peter F Farley and
Mervyn Hurford

The black and white and colour
photographs were taken by
Stanley Dutton of How Professional

The running headings and diagrams in the
tools section were drawn by Alan Burton

The guide to building a basic tool kit on
page 220 is reproduced by kind permission
of Bahco Record Tools Ltd

The photograph on the front cover shows
completed models of a Scania 142E V8
truck and a Hyster fork lift truck

This book accompanies the BBC Television
series *Blizzard's Wonderful Wooden Toys,*
first broadcast in Spring 1983

Series produced by Peter Ramsden

Library of Congress Cataloging in Publication Data

Blizzard, Richard E.
  Blizzard's Wonderful wooden toys.

  Includes index.
  1. Wooden toy making. I. Title. II. Title:
Wonderful wooden toys.
TT174.5.W6B583 1983   745.592   83-5080
ISBN 0-8069-7798-1

CONTENTS

Throughout the book metric measurements are given first,
followed by imperial measurements in brackets

It would have been impossible to write this book and create this series on wooden toys without the help, advice and encouragement of many talented men and women. I don't think of this book as mine but ours, something we have all contributed to. I should like to thank:

Peter Ramsden, Ann Curtis and Paula Gilder who had such imaginative and practical suggestions to make. Without their professionalism and full involvement the series would not have taken place

Charles Elton of BBC Publications whose encouragement and patience was inexhaustible while waiting for the last few chapters

Norman Brownsword who planned and designed the book

Peter F Farley and Mervyn Hurford who were responsible for the plans and cutting lists

Stanley Dutton for imaginative photography

Pamela and Lynne Ratley for typing the book script

I should also like to acknowledge all those companies who assisted with drawings, photography and vehicles for the wooden models section

Bob Cartwright and Christine Hollinshead of Rolls Royce Motors who spirited the Silver Ghost onto location for filming. Bob Bruce who built the miniature radiator

My chauffeur Steve for many miles of happy motoring

Ken James and Don Green of Land Rover who taught me how to drive a Land Rover over rough terrain, and made my hair stand on end!

Dermott Bambridge and Birgitta Hjerpe of Scania who provided a magnificent truck for me to drive and researched the 1902 Scania lorry

Philip Edmonds of Hyster Europe Limited who made it possible for us to photograph these giant fork lifts at work

Several companies helped with the supply of tools and made it possible for me to have two complete workshops, one at home and the other in the studio

Roger Cottle and Roger Pitchfork of Bahco Record Tools Ltd who provided the majority of hand tools used

John Costello of Black and Decker Ltd who helped with electric tools and machines

Ken Stalker of Makita Electric Ltd for the use of an electric screwdriver

Peter King of Evode Ltd for Mole Rack cramps

John Hunter Connolly Brothers (Carriers) Ltd for the supply of leather for the Rolls Royce Silver Ghost

Last but by no means least my wife Valerie who listened patiently to all the difficulties and did a great deal of work behind the scenes; Edward, Joy and Christopher who 'played around'

Richard Curtis and Paz for such a splendid and happy introductory piece of music

Ingrid Bennett – Graphics Design Department Bristol who painted the toys so very beautifully.

Mr A. H. J. Kennett, Headmaster of Bussage Primary School, for allowing us to use the school for the colour photographs.

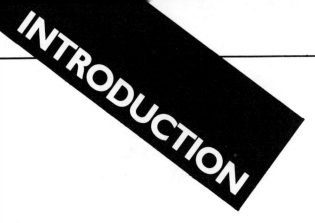

Foreword

'Yea, the work of our hands, establish thou it'

Richard Blizzard's approach to life and work epitomises this prescription from the psalmist. As a designer and maker of wooden models and as a very able expositor, he has in the space of a few years developed and presented a range of products which stir the imagination and appeal to the aesthetic sense of young and old. I have no doubt that this, his latest series, will be every bit as popular and successful as his earlier ones.

Blizzard brings to his work a combination of thorough attention to detail and a keen sense of what will appeal. When he designs and makes toys his starting point is that the toy to a child is a friend, and a friend does not let you down. His toys therefore have a quality of strength and robustness, so that they will not, like so many toys, fall to pieces after a few hours of rugged play.

It is an honour to introduce this book.

Sir Alex Smith
November 1982

To me the saddest words to hear from anyone are 'I'm bored'. One of the great challenges of our age is how to use our increased leisure time purposefully. It is here that craftsmen, educationalists and the media have a great work to do – to encourage, inspire and help so that the idle hours can be filled with useful and satisfying activities. I hope that this book of wooden toys and models will be a source of inspiration and new ideas.

I have covered a large range of interests and skills. Some of you will get as much fun making the sand pit as your children do playing in it! Some youngsters will be a little more sophisticated and will appreciate the working parts of the mobile crane and go-cart.

For the skilled woodworker there is the challenge and appeal of the Rolls Royce 1907 Silver Ghost. For those who are interested in trucks, a Scania capable of hauling a tremendous load of building blocks and a Hyster fork lift truck to lift them on and off.

If you have young children and don't feel too confident about woodworking, start with something simple like the rope ladder and, dare I say it, climb to higher things. Basic tools are, of course, required – a tenon saw, hammer, hand-drill and screwdriver. You may well have many of the tools but if not once you have them you will always find further use for them around the house.

Although full line drawings have been prepared don't worry if your toy or model turns out looking a little different! It is probably better and at the worst it is unique! So often wood takes on the character of the person who is fashioning it.

Parents are sometimes a little diffident about how their wooden creations will be received. In my experience I find that a toy made at home, however humble in its construction and painting, is always a more treasured possession than the shop bought variety. I think this is due to the fact that the father, mother, grandparents and even aunts and uncles have made their contribution and it therefore has a far greater value.

There are good toys and bad toys. I believe the definition is really quite simple – a good toy is one that is strong and does not break, while a bad toy breaks easily and therefore causes great distress.

I hope that as you start to make these toys you will come to understand the words of my motto 'I too will something make, and joy in the making'.

Richard E Blizzard
1982

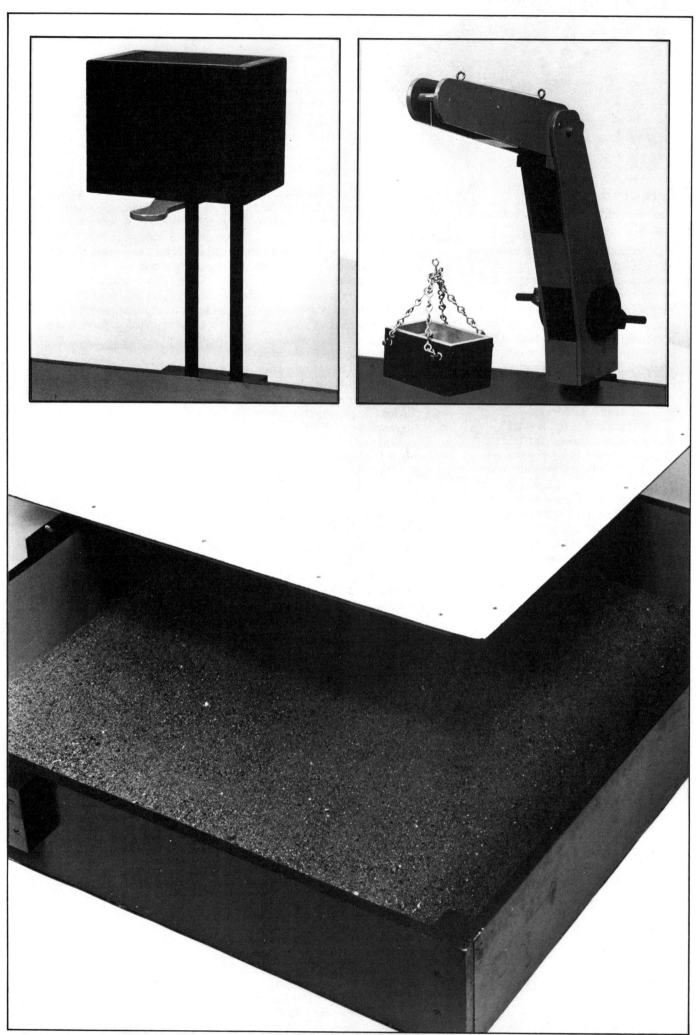

Sand and water play are among the most popular pursuits of all for young children. Digging, tunnelling, mining and building are all industriously carried on in the sand pit.

The crane, scoop, plough, dumper truck and hopper are all accessories and will add a great deal of pleasure to the busy sand pit.

The pit is designed to be used in the garden as a free standing unit or set into the lawn. The lid is an essential part to prevent cats and dogs fouling the sand.

The hopper provides tremendous fun for children, who never tire of filling it with sand, pulling the lever and watching the silver sand spilling out into their buckets.

The crane and skip make an ideal working combination in the sand pit. The crane makes it possible to refill the hopper or the dumper truck. The addition of twin winding handles makes it far more fun as two children are able to operate the crane simultaneously.

Before starting to build the crane you will find reference to the exploded parts drawing a great help as you familiarise yourself with all the pieces.

Painting

All the toys that are used in the sand pit will need painting. You will discover that it is far easier in many cases to paint some of the parts before final assembly takes place, eg the dump truck is far easier to paint if the wheels are not on. Good quality exterior paint is necessary.

Warning   Check that all paint used is non-toxic.

Sand pit and cover

1   Prepare the four side panels which are held together by four substantial corner blocks.

2   The corner blocks are screwed securely onto the side panels. Once one block has been secured, the other side panel is screwed onto it. Repeat this operation until all four sides are secure.

3   The base is made from oil tempered hardboard and secured to the bottom by galvanised clout nails. The clout nail has a large head and will help to hold the hardboard to the pit walls.

4   It is essential to make a lid to keep out cats and dogs. Five strips of wood are screwed onto a sheet of oil tempered hardboard. The strips of wood fit inside the walls of the sand pit and act as location points when covering down the pit. Handles are useful and if these are fitted the screws holding them must locate in the strips of wood beneath.

5   All the accessories are mounted onto the sand pit walls. The mounting blocks have large diameter holes drilled in them to accept either the crane or the hopper. You can position the mounting blocks anywhere on the pit sides.

Hopper

1   The hopper is virtually a box supported by two dowel rods which locate into blocks on the side of the sand pit.

2   The hopper box is glued and screwed together. Before fixing the floor drill all the necessary holes. Screw the floor onto the bottom.

3   Cut the discharge control lever to shape. The lever is fixed to the bottom of the hopper by a small nut and bolt. The lever's 'travel' is regulated by two small dowel rods that act as stops. These are glued into the bottom of the hopper.

4   Prepare a mounting block for the back of the hopper. Glue the two dowels into the block and screw the block onto the back of the hopper.

Crane

1   Mark and cut out a pair of crane tower sides. Keeping the sides together drill all the holes as shown on the plan.

2   Cut a block for the base of the crane tower. Drill a hole in the underside of the block to take the large dowel rod that provides a mounting place for the crane on the sand pit.

3   The sides of the crane are held together by blocks of wood. These are glued and screwed in position.

4   The hoist handle discs are made from plywood, and the handles from dowel rod. The handles are glued into the discs, but as plywood is relatively thin it gives very little 'glueing area' so it is essential to make the square blocks and glue these onto the disc and handle.

5   Cut out a pair of crane jib sides and drill the necessary holes while the pair are fixed together.

6   The jib sides are held together by blocks of wood glued and screwed into position.

7   Assemble the jib onto the crane tower by passing a dowel rod through the ready prepared holes. Now screw the sides of the tower to the jib.

8   Screw eyes are used to guide the nylon cord along the crane.

9   The nylon cord passes through a hole in the end of the crane jib. Wear can take place here unless a nylon tube is fitted. Any small length of plastic tube will do. Drill the hole large enough to take the tube. The nylon cord passes through the tube and thus stops the cord cutting the dowel rod away.

Skip

1   Glue a small box together. Holes should be drilled through the sides to take the dowel rods before glueing the box together.

2   Small chain can be bought from the ironmongers. Push the dowel rods through the box and attach the chain to the rods.

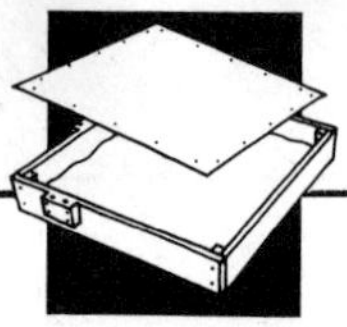

Cutting list

Sand pit and cover

Cover and base	2 off	1220 × 1220 × 3mm (48 × 48 × ⅛in)	Oil tempered hardboard
Cover support frame	2 off	1170 × 44 × 22mm (46 × 1¾ × ⅞in)	Timber
	3 off	1126 × 44 × 22mm (44¼ × 1¾ × ⅞in)	Timber
Side panels	2 off	1220 × 197 × 22mm (48 × 7¾ × ⅞in)	Timber
	2 off	1176 × 197 × 22mm (46¼ × 7¾ × ⅞in)	Timber
Corner blocks	4 off	152 × 44 × 44mm (6 × 1¾ × 1¾in)	Timber
Hopper mounting block	2 off	191 × 73 × 44mm (7½ × 2⅞ × 1¾in)	Timber
Crane mounting block	2 off	102 × 73 × 44mm (4 × 2⅞ × 1¾in)	Timber

Ancillaries

	2 off	Lifting handles

Hopper

Sides	2 off	229 × 197 × 22mm (9 × 7¾ × ⅞in)	Timber
	2 off	197 × 197 × 22mm (7¾ × 7¾ × ⅞in)	Timber
Floor	1 off	273 × 197 × 9mm (10¾ × 7¾ × ⅜in)	Plywood
Discharge control handle	1 off	279 × 102 × 9mm (11 × 4 × ⅜in)	Plywood
Mounting column	1 off	184 × 70 × 44mm (7¼ × 2¾ × 1¾in)	Timber
	2 off	560mm(22in) long × 22mm(⅞in) diameter dowels	
Control handle stops	2 off	25mm(1in) long × 6mm(¼in) diameter dowels	

Ancillaries

	1 off	25mm(1in) long × 6mm(¼in) diameter bolt, plain washer and lock nut

Crane

Tower assembly	2 off	569 × 292 × 9mm (22⅜ × 11½ × ⅜in)	Plywood
	1 off	178 × 89 × 70mm (7 × 3½ × 2¾in)	Timber
	1 off	191mm(7½in) long × 22mm(⅞in) diameter dowel	
	1 off	117 × 70 × 22mm (4⅝ × 2¾ × ⅞in)	Timber
	2 off	89 × 70 × 22mm (3½ × 2¾ × ⅞in)	Timber
	1 off	219 × 70 × 22mm (8⅝ × 2¾ × ⅞in)	Timber
Jib assembly	2 off	502 × 108 × 9mm (19¾ × 4¼ × ⅜in)	Plywood
	2 off	102 × 47 × 20mm (4 × 1⅞ × ¾in)	Timber
	1 off	127 × 47 × 20mm (5 × 1⅞ × ¾in)	Timber
	1 off	67mm(2⅝in) long × 16mm(⅝in) diameter dowel	
	1 off	114mm(4½in) long × 16mm(⅝in) diameter dowel	
Hoist handle assembly	1 off	146mm(5¾in) long × 16mm(⅝in) diameter dowel	
	2 off	76mm(3in) long × 16mm(⅝in) diameter dowel	
Discs	Make from	213 × 105 × 9mm (8⅜ × 4⅛ × ⅜in)	Plywood
	4 off	32 × 32 × 20mm (1¼ × 1¼ × ¾in)	Timber

Ancillaries

	4 off	20mm (¾in) diameter screwed eyes
	1 off	Length of strong cord

Skip

Sides	2 off	146 × 92 × 12mm (5¾ × 3⅝ × ½in)	Plywood
Ends	2 off	114 × 92 × 9mm (4½ × 3⅝ × ⅜in)	Plywood
Floor	1 off	146 × 89 × 9mm (5¾ × 3½ × ⅜in)	Plywood
Lifting bars	2 off	165mm(6½in) long × 9mm(⅜in) diameter dowels	

Ancillaries

	1 off	Approx. 762mm (30in) long length of chain

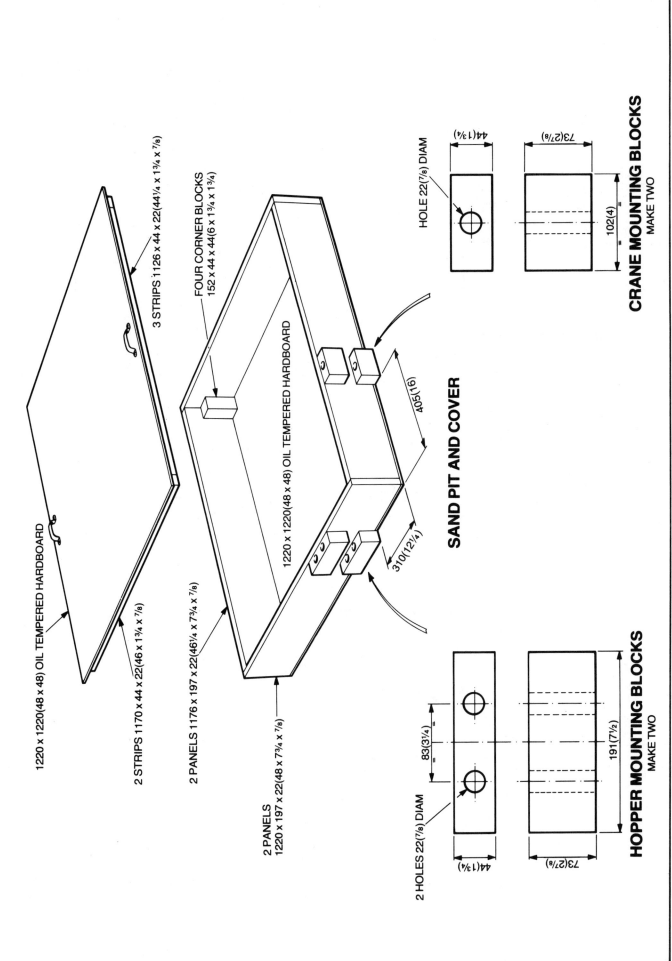

1220 x 1220(48 x 48) OIL TEMPERED HARDBOARD

3 STRIPS 1126 x 44 x 22(44¼ x 1¾ x ⅞)

FOUR CORNER BLOCKS
152 x 44 x 44(6 x 1¾ x 1¾)

2 STRIPS 1170 x 44 x 22(46 x 1¾ x ⅞)

2 PANELS 1176 x 197 x 22(46¼ x 7¾ x ⅞)

1220 x 1220(48 x 48) OIL TEMPERED HARDBOARD

2 PANELS
1220 x 197 x 22(48 x 7¾ x ⅞)

405(16)

310(12¼)

SAND PIT AND COVER

HOLE 22(⅞) DIAM

44(1¾)

73(2⅞)

102(4)

CRANE MOUNTING BLOCKS
MAKE TWO

2 HOLES 22(⅞) DIAM

44(1¾)

73(2⅞)

83(3¼)

191(7½)

HOPPER MOUNTING BLOCKS
MAKE TWO

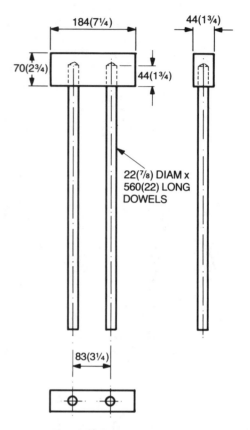

184(7¼) **44(1¾)**

70(2¾) **44(1¾)**

22(⅞) DIAM x
560(22) LONG
DOWELS

83(3¼)

HOPPER ASSEMBLY

MOUNTING COLUMN

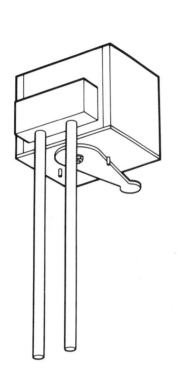

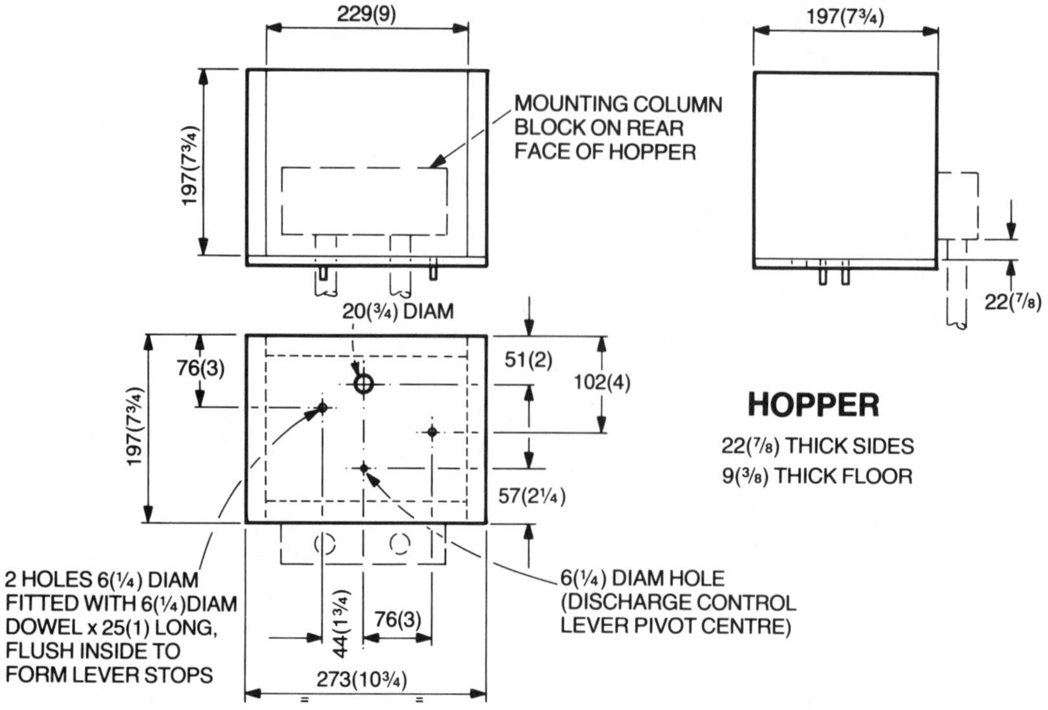

229(9)

197(7¾)

MOUNTING COLUMN
BLOCK ON REAR
FACE OF HOPPER

20(¾) DIAM

197(7¾)

76(3)

51(2)

102(4)

57(2¼)

44(1¾)

76(3)

273(10¾)

2 HOLES 6(¼) DIAM
FITTED WITH 6(¼)DIAM
DOWEL x 25(1) LONG,
FLUSH INSIDE TO
FORM LEVER STOPS

6(¼) DIAM HOLE
(DISCHARGE CONTROL
LEVER PIVOT CENTRE)

197(7¾)

22(⅞)

HOPPER

22(⅞) THICK SIDES
9(⅜) THICK FLOOR

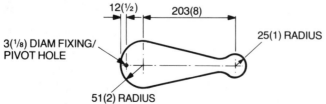

12(½) **203(8)**

3(⅛) DIAM FIXING/
PIVOT HOLE

25(1) RADIUS

51(2) RADIUS

DISCHARGE CONTROL LEVER
9(⅜) THICK

SECURED TO HOPPER WITH
6(¼) DIAM x 25(1) LONG BOLT
COMPLETE WITH PLAIN
WASHERS AND LOCKNUT

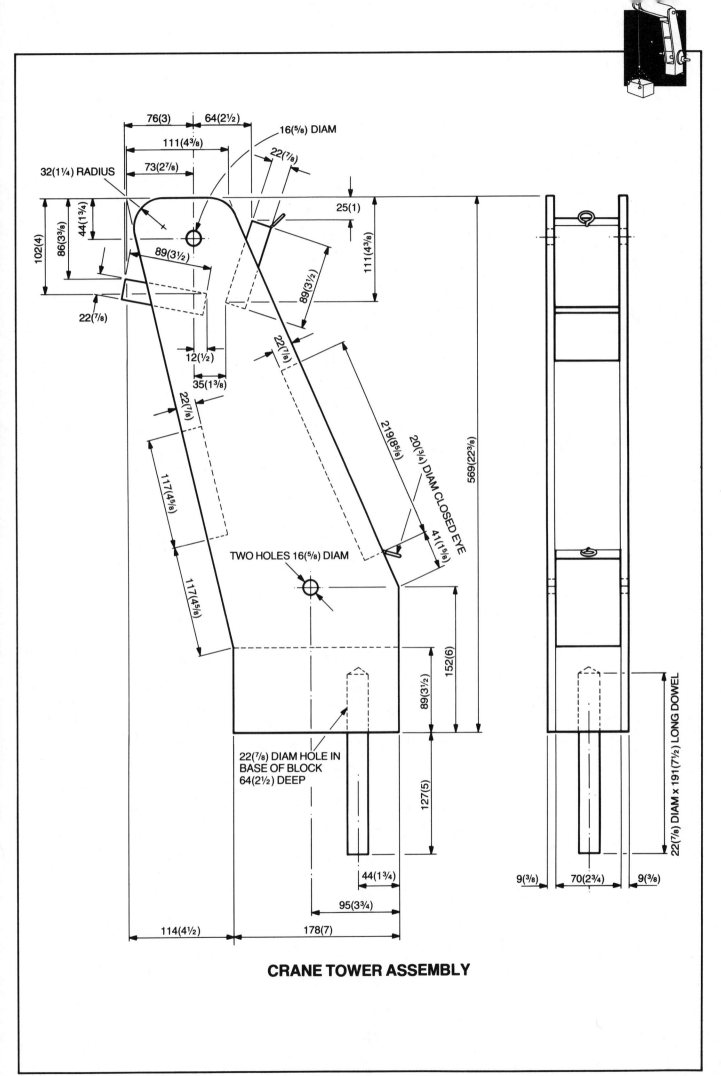

CRANE TOWER ASSEMBLY

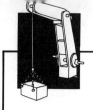

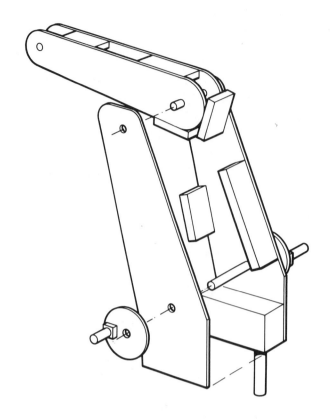

CRANE ASSEMBLY

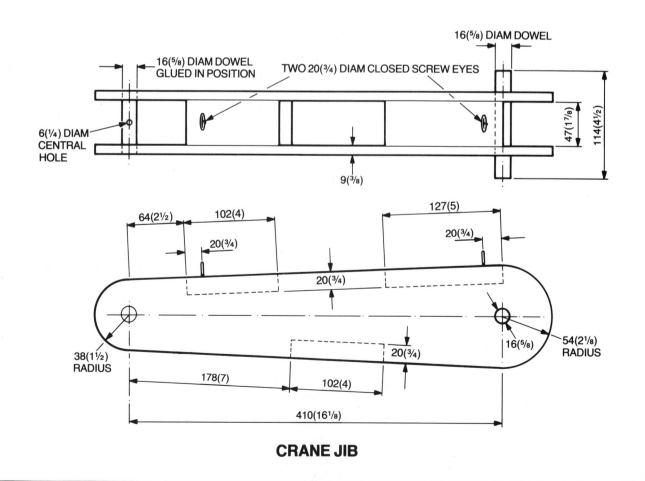

16(⅝) DIAM DOWEL

16(⅝) DIAM DOWEL
GLUED IN POSITION

TWO 20(¾) DIAM CLOSED SCREW EYES

6(¼) DIAM
CENTRAL
HOLE

47(1⅞)

114(4½)

9(⅜)

64(2½)

102(4)

127(5)

20(¾)

20(¾)

20(¾)

20(¾)

20(¾)

38(1½)
RADIUS

16(⅝)

54(2⅛)
RADIUS

178(7)

102(4)

410(16⅛)

CRANE JIB

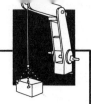

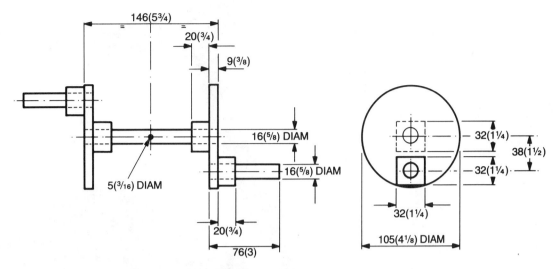

HOIST HANDLE ASSEMBLY
SYMMETRICAL ABOUT CENTRE LINE

SECURE SECOND END ONCE SPINDLE HAS BEEN PASSED THROUGH
CRANE TOWER SUCH THAT ASSEMBLY IS FREE TO ROTATE

146(5¾)
20(¾)
9(⅜)
16(⅝) DIAM
16(⅝) DIAM
5(³⁄₁₆) DIAM
20(¾)
76(3)

32(1¼)
38(1½)
32(1¼)
32(1¼)
105(4⅛) DIAM

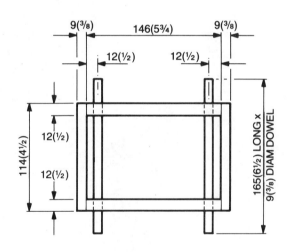

9(⅜)   146(5¾)   9(⅜)
12(½)   12(½)
114(4½)
12(½)
12(½)
165(6½) LONG x
9(⅜) DIAM DOWEL

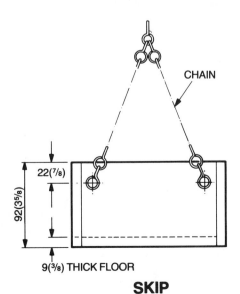

CHAIN

22(⅞)
92(3⅝)
9(⅜) THICK FLOOR

SKIP

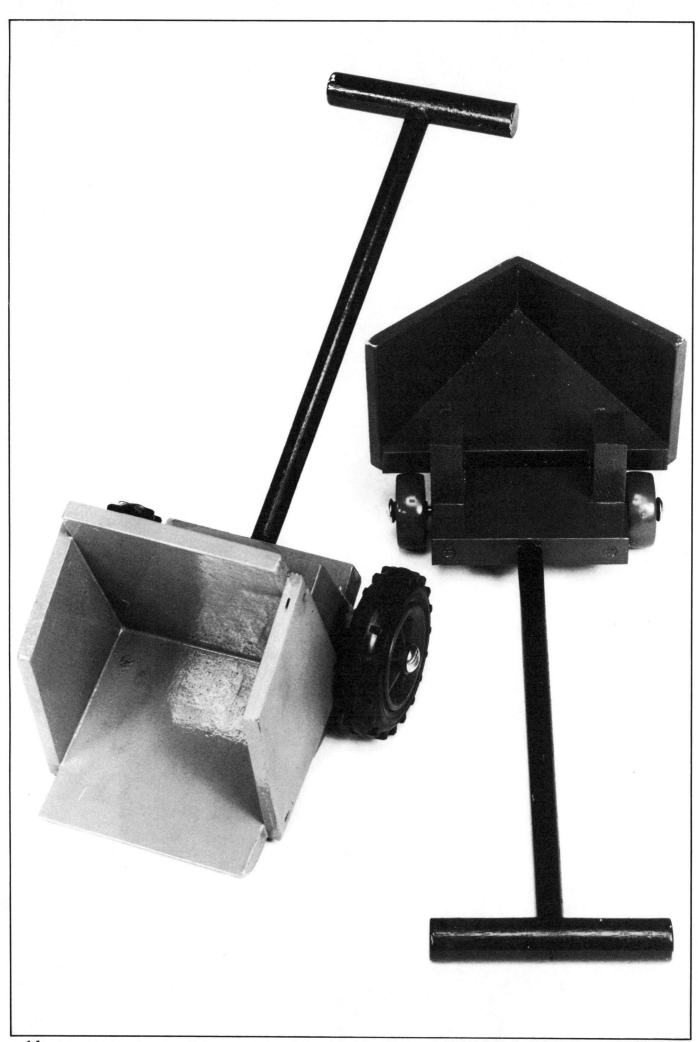

PLOUGH AND SCOOPER

The scoop allows a child to transport small quantities of sand around the sand pit. The flat blade on the front allows for a good scraping action, while the large wheels allow the load to be easily transported along the roads the sand plough has made.

This powerful little plough with its V-shaped blade is capable of making roadways for other vehicles in the sand. The wheels have been deliberately kept to a minimum to allow a good ploughing action through the sand.

Scooper

1   The scooper is very similar in construction to the plough.

2   Cut out the support frames and cross member, glue and screw together.

3   Make a pair of side walls and a rear wall. Glue and screw the walls to the floor. Now the scoop is attached to the support frame.

4   The handle is made in the same way as for the plough.

Plough

1   Cut the cross member and drill the centre hole to take the dowel rod handle.

2   Mark out a pair of support frames. Secure both frames together and drill the axle holes. Glue and screw the support frames onto the cross member.

3   Shape up the base plate and fix to the support frames.

4   Cut out the plough plates **A** and **B**. Fix together (masking tape is ideal) and plane up the edges. At the front edge plate **A** forms the leading edge and plate **B** is glued onto the side. Chamfer the edges as shown.

5   The side plates are now glued and screwed onto the plough base.

6   The handle is formed by drilling into a short length of dowel rod. The top part of the handle is of larger diameter than the shaft. The handle and shaft are glued together.

7   Fit the axle rod and slip the wheels on to it.

Cutting list

Scooper

Scoop	1 off	140 × 137 × 12mm (5½ × 5⅜ × ½in)	Plywood
	1 off	137 × 127 × 12mm (5⅜ × 5 × ½in)	Plywood
	2 off	121 × 108 × 9mm (4¾ × 4¼ × ⅜in)	Plywood
Support frame	2 off	111 × 102 × 22mm (4⅜ × 4 × ⅞in)	Timber
Cross member	1 off	137 × 47 × 22mm (5⅜ × 1⅞ × ⅞in)	Timber
Handle	1 off	127mm (5in) long × 22mm (⅞in) diameter dowel	
	1 off	356mm (14in) long × 16mm (⅝in) diameter dowel	

Ancillaries

	2 off	102mm (4in) diameter road wheels
	1 off	222mm (8¾in) long × 6mm (¼in) diameter steel axle
	2 off	11mm (⁷⁄₁₆in) long × 16mm (⅝in) o/d × 6mm (¼in) i/d spacers
	2 off	Spring dome caps to suit 6mm (¼in) diameter axle

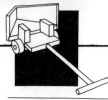

Plough

Base plate	1 off	194 × 127 × 22mm (7⅝ × 5 × ⅞in)	Timber
Side plate	1 off	170 × 117 × 9mm (6¹¹⁄₁₆ × 4⅝ × ⅜in)	Plywood
	1 off	160 × 117 × 9mm (6⁵⁄₁₆ × 4⅝ × ⅜in)	Plywood
Support frame	2 off	102 × 92 × 22mm (4 × 3⅝ × ⅞in)	Timber
Cross member	1 off	127 × 67 × 22mm (5 × 2⅝ × ⅞in)	Timber
Handle	1 off	127mm(5in) long × 22mm(⅞in) diameter dowel	
	1 off	356mm(14in) long × 16mm(⅝in) diameter dowel	

Ancillaries

	2 off	51mm (2in) diameter road wheels	
	1 off	184mm(7¼in) long × 6mm(¼in) diameter steel axle	
	2 off	3mm(⅛in) long × 16mm(⅝in) o/d × 6mm(¼in) i/d spacers	
	2 off	Spring dome caps to suit 6mm (¼in) diameter axle	

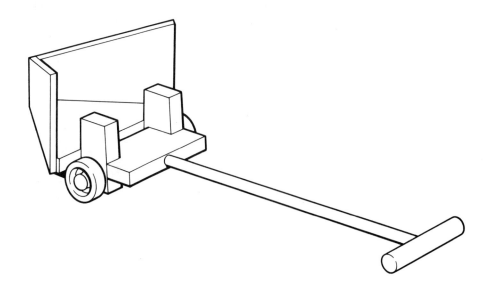

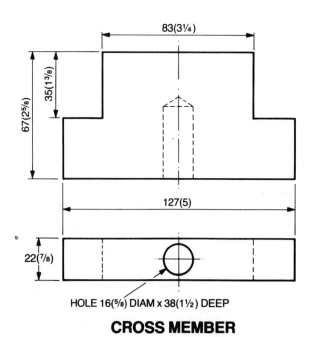

HOLE 16(⅝) DIAM x 38(1½) DEEP

CROSS MEMBER

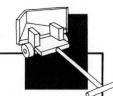

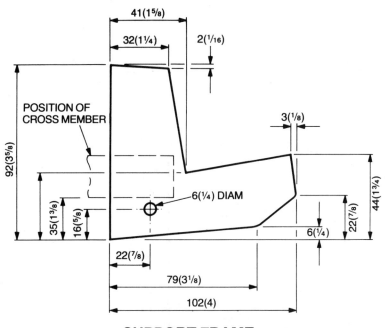

SUPPORT FRAME
MAKE TWO   22(⁷⁄₈) THICK

- 41(1⁵⁄₈)
- 32(1¼)
- 2(¹⁄₁₆)
- POSITION OF CROSS MEMBER
- 92(3⁵⁄₈)
- 3(¹⁄₈)
- 6(¼) DIAM
- 35(1³⁄₈)
- 16(⁵⁄₈)
- 44(1³⁄₄)
- 22(⁷⁄₈)
- 6(¼)
- 22(⁷⁄₈)
- 79(3¹⁄₈)
- 102(4)

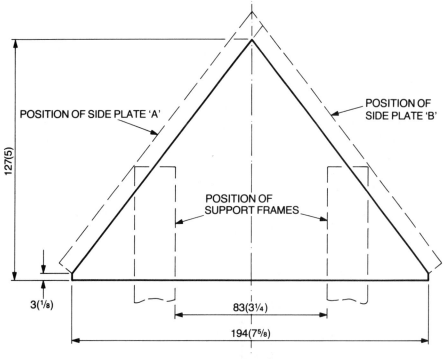

PLOUGH BASE PLATE
22(⁷⁄₈) THICK

- 127(5)
- POSITION OF SIDE PLATE 'A'
- POSITION OF SIDE PLATE 'B'
- POSITION OF SUPPORT FRAMES
- 3(¹⁄₈)
- 83(3¼)
- 194(7⁵⁄₈)

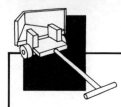

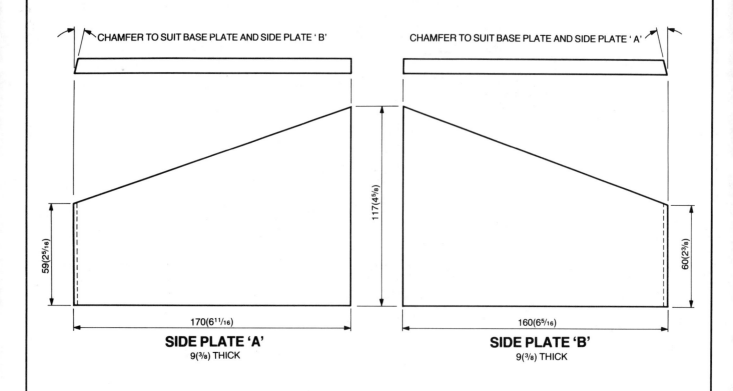

CHAMFER TO SUIT BASE PLATE AND SIDE PLATE 'B'

CHAMFER TO SUIT BASE PLATE AND SIDE PLATE 'A'

117(4⁵/₈)

59(2⁵/₁₆)

60(2³/₈)

170(6¹¹/₁₆)

160(6⁵/₁₆)

SIDE PLATE 'A'
9(³/₈) THICK

SIDE PLATE 'B'
9(³/₈) THICK

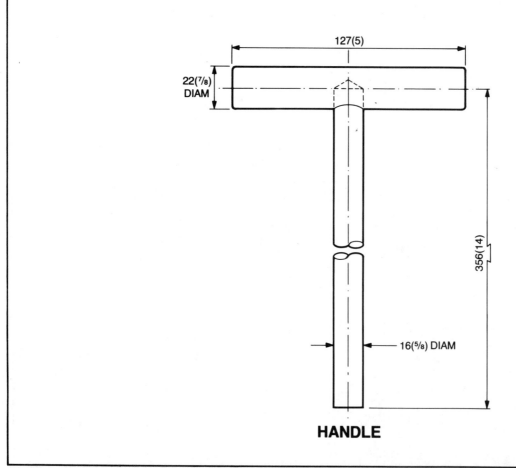

127(5)

22(⁷/₈) DIAM

356(14)

16(⁵/₈) DIAM

HANDLE

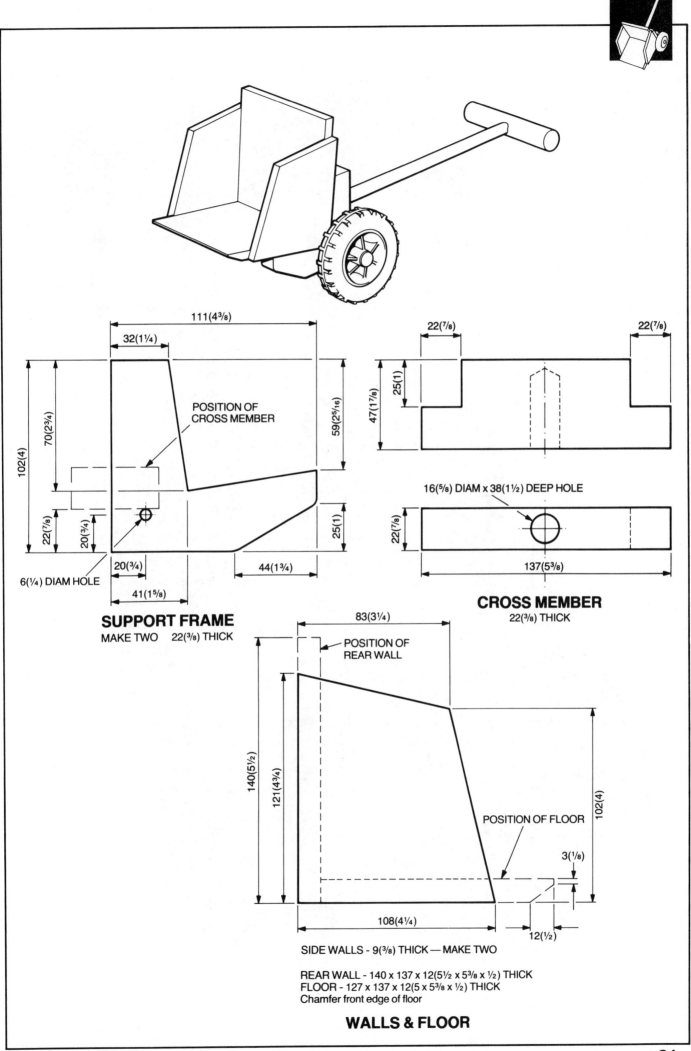

111(4³/₈)

32(1¹/₄)

POSITION OF
CROSS MEMBER

59(2⁵/₁₆)

70(2³/₄)

102(4)

22(⁷/₈)

20(³/₄)

25(1)

6(¹/₄) DIAM HOLE

20(³/₄)

44(1³/₄)

41(1⁵/₈)

SUPPORT FRAME
MAKE TWO   22(³/₈) THICK

22(⁷/₈)

22(⁷/₈)

25(1)

47(1⁷/₈)

16(⁵/₈) DIAM x 38(1¹/₂) DEEP HOLE

22(⁷/₈)

137(5³/₈)

CROSS MEMBER
22(³/₈) THICK

83(3¹/₄)

POSITION OF
REAR WALL

140(5¹/₂)

121(4³/₄)

102(4)

POSITION OF FLOOR

3(¹/₈)

108(4¹/₄)

12(¹/₂)

SIDE WALLS - 9(³/₈) THICK — MAKE TWO

REAR WALL - 140 x 137 x 12(5¹/₂ x 5³/₈ x ¹/₂) THICK
FLOOR - 127 x 137 x 12(5 x 5³/₈ x ¹/₂) THICK
Chamfer front edge of floor

WALLS & FLOOR

DUMPER TRUCK

These little 'dumpers' are to be found on all building sites and provide a great deal of enjoyment in the sand pit.

1 Cut the chassis base to size and also the two strips that screw on beneath it. These two strips hold the axles. To be certain the axles line up fix the two strips together and drill as a pair.

2 Screw onto the chassis the two blocks that act as mounts for the bumper body.

3 Cut a pair of sides for the dumper body. Glue and screw the back and front on. Drill a hole to take the dowel rod that acts as the closing mechanism for the body locking clip. Glue the dowel into the back.

4 Screw a length of piano hinge onto the underside of the dumper body and then screw the hinge onto the front mounting block of the chassis.

5 The engine block is shaped from a solid block. Mark in pencil the portion to be removed which will allow the driver foot room. This piece can be cut off using a tenon saw.

6 Cut a driver's seat from a piece of waste wood and glue onto the engine block.

7 The steering wheel is made from plywood and a short length of dowel rod acts as the steering column.

8 Making a realistic radiator grill is easily achieved by using a small piece of wire mesh (the grade used in car body repairs). Small strips of wood are glued around the front of the engine block and the wire mesh is fixed inside using four small panel pins.

9 The body locking clip must be made from plywood. It is screwed onto the front face of the engine and must be positioned before the engine block is screwed in place.

10 Shape up a pair of mudguards and glue onto the side of the engine block.

11 Fit the axles and wheels.

Cutting list

Main chassis	1 off	289 × 121 × 22mm (11⅜ × 4¾ × ⅞in)	Timber
	2 off	289 × 22 × 22mm (11⅜ × ⅞ × ⅞in)	Timber
	1 off	121 × 22 × 20mm (4¾ × ⅞ × ¾in)	Timber
	1 off	191 × 22 × 20mm (7½ × ⅞ × ¾in)	Timber
	1 off	121 × 41 × 22mm (4¾ × 1⅝ × ⅞in)	Timber
Engine block	1 off	137 × 92 × 22mm (5⅜ × 3⅝ × ⅞in)	Timber
	1 off	124 × 92 × 70mm (4⅞ × 3⅝ × 2¾in)	Timber
	1 off	92 × 20 × 12mm (3⅝ × ¾ × ½in)	Timber
	1 off	79 × 12 × 6mm (3⅛ × ½ × ¼in)	Timber
	2 off	51 × 12 × 6mm (2 × ½ × ¼in)	Timber
Mudguard	2 off	137 × 38 × 22mm (5⅜ × 1½ × ⅞in)	Timber
Seat	1 off	44 × 44 × 38mm (1¾ × 1¾ × 1½in)	Timber
Steering Wheel	1 off	89mm (3½in) long × 6mm (¼in) diameter dowel	
	1 off	6mm (¼in) long × 22mm (⅞in) diameter dowel	
Body locking clip	1 off	146 × 57 × 9mm (5¾ × 2¼ × ⅜in)	Plywood
Tipping body assembly	2 off	200 × 102 × 22mm (7⅞ × 4 × ⅞in)	Timber
	1 off	191 × 102 × 12mm (7½ × 4 × ½in)	Plywood
	1 off	191 × 114 × 22mm (7½ × 4½ × ⅞in)	Timber
	1 off	171 × 146 × 22mm (6¾ × 5¾ × ⅞in)	Timber
	1 off	32mm (1¼in) long × 6mm (¼in) diameter dowel	

Ancillaries

1 off	121mm (4¾in) long piano hinge
1 off	83 × 51mm (3¼ × 2in) wire mesh
4 off	102mm (4in) diameter road wheels
2 off	203mm (8in) long × 6mm (¼in) diameter steel axles
4 off	6mm (¼in) long × 16mm (⅝in) o/d × 6mm (¼in) i/d spacers
4 off	Spring dome caps to suit 6mm (¼in) diameter axles
2 off	9mm (⅜in) diameter dome headed drawing pins

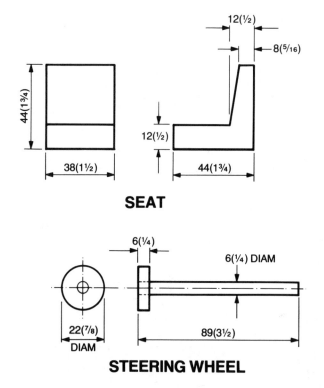

SEAT

STEERING WHEEL

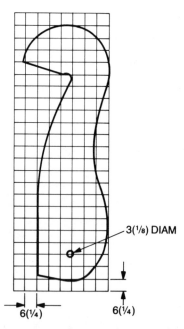

BODY LOCKING CLIP

9(⅜) THICK

MAIN CHASSIS ASSEMBLY

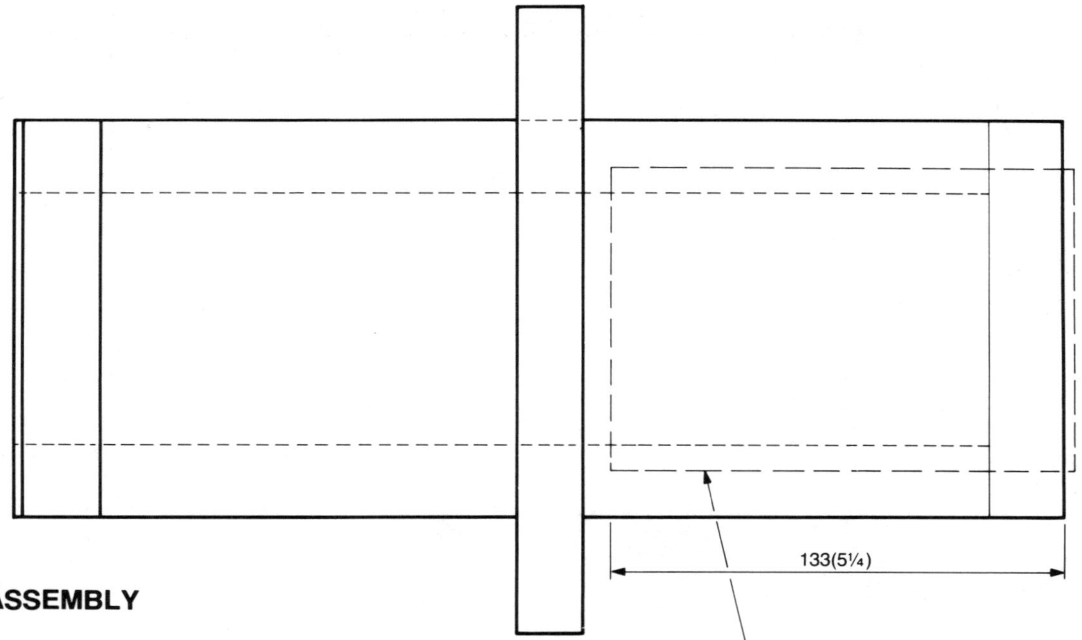
133(5¼)
POSITION OF ENGINE BLOCK

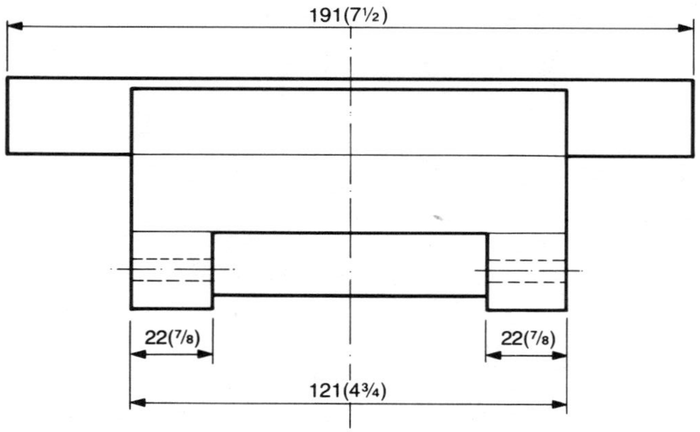
191(7½)
22(⅞)
22(⅞)
121(4¾)

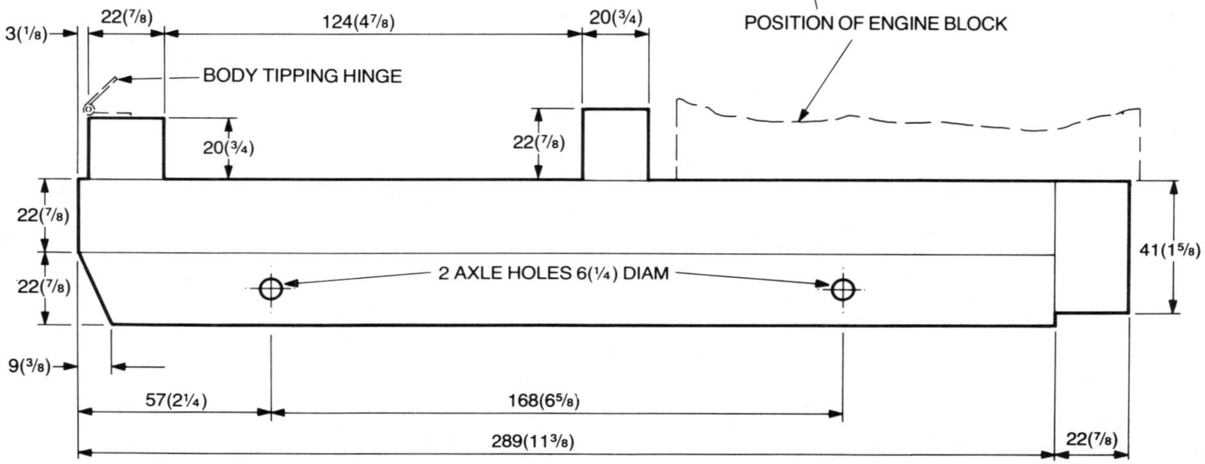
3(⅛)
22(⅞)
124(4⅞)
20(¾)
BODY TIPPING HINGE
20(¾)
22(⅞)
22(⅞)
22(⅞)
2 AXLE HOLES 6(¼) DIAM
41(1⅝)
9(⅜)
57(2¼)
168(6⅝)
289(11⅜)
22(⅞)

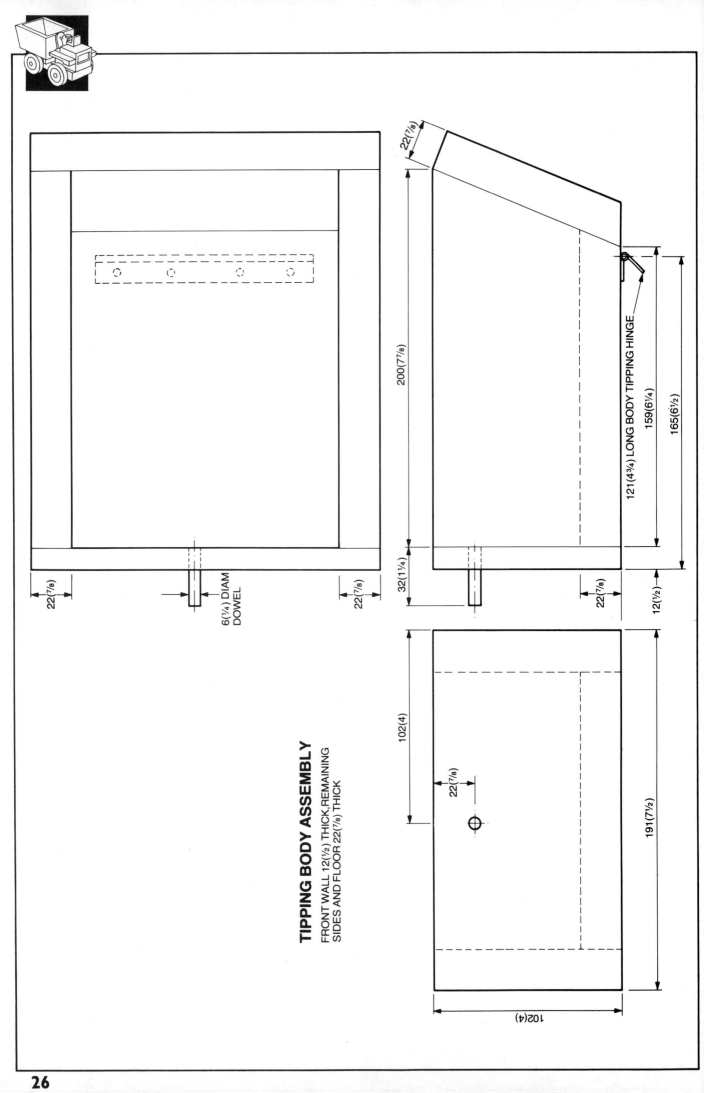

TIPPING BODY ASSEMBLY

FRONT WALL 12(½) THICK, REMAINING
SIDES AND FLOOR 22(⅞) THICK

22(⅞)

6(¼) DIAM
DOWEL

22(⅞)

200(7⅞)

32(1¼)

22(⅞)

22(⅞)

121(4¾) LONG BODY TIPPING HINGE

159(6¼)

165(6½)

12(½)

102(4)

22(⅞)

191(7½)

102(4)

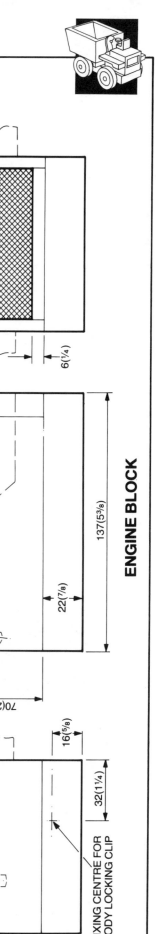

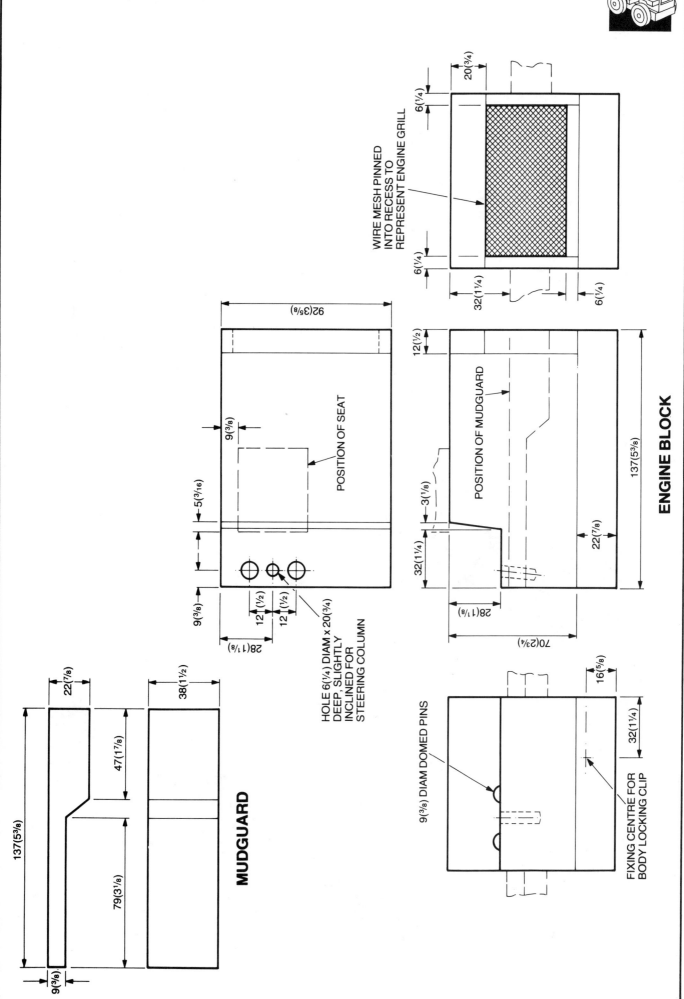

ENGINE BLOCK

WIRE MESH PINNED INTO RECESS TO REPRESENT ENGINE GRILL

20(3/4)

6(1/4)

6(1/4)

32(1 1/4)

6(1/4)

12(1/2)

137(5 3/8)

POSITION OF MUDGUARD

3(1/8)

32(1 1/4)

22(7/8)

28(1 1/8)

70(2 3/4)

9(3/8) DIAM DOMED PINS

16(5/8)

32(1 1/4)

FIXING CENTRE FOR BODY LOCKING CLIP

92(3 5/8)

POSITION OF SEAT

9(3/8)

5(3/16)

9(3/8)

12 (1/2)

12 (1/2)

28(1 1/8)

HOLE 6(1/4) DIAM x 20(3/4) DEEP, SLIGHTLY INCLINED FOR STEERING COLUMN

MUDGUARD

22(7/8)

38(1 1/2)

137(5 3/8)

47(1 7/8)

79(3 1/8)

9(3/8)

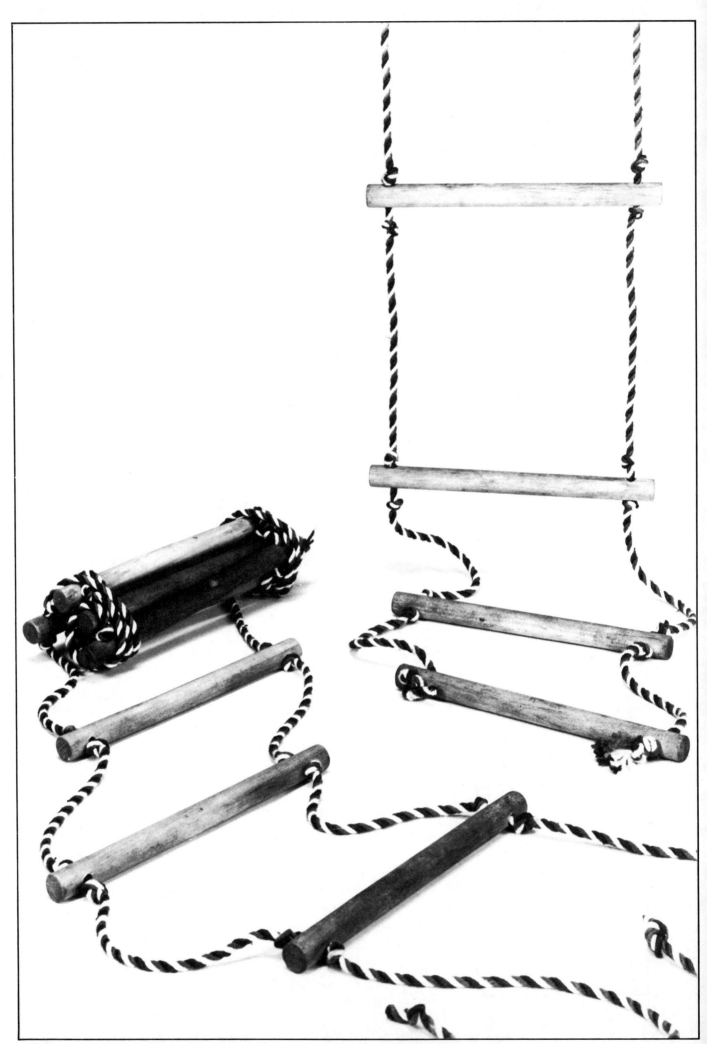

ROPE LADDER

Tree climbing is as natural to children as breathing! This rope ladder can be used for climbing or swinging. The rope or cord can be easily bought from hardware shops. Modern rope, which is extremely strong, will have the breaking strain clearly displayed on the box.

Caution Make sure that an adult ties the rope ladder on to the tree and that he or she is 'on duty' to supervise the first 'climbs' as rope ladders swing and twist about.

1 Tie a knot in one end of each of the two pieces of rope.

2 The rungs are made from very large dowel rod. Mark the position of the holes in each end. Drilling has to be done carefully. With a flat bit in an electric drill bore a hole half way through, turn over and the point of the flat bit will give you the location point to finish off the hole. Unless the hole is bored from both sides the rod will splinter.

3 Thread the rope through the dowel rod. Knot the rung in place on each side. Now take another rung and use it as a measuring stick to tie the next knot. Do this on both sides. Repeat the procedure for the next step until the ladder is finished.

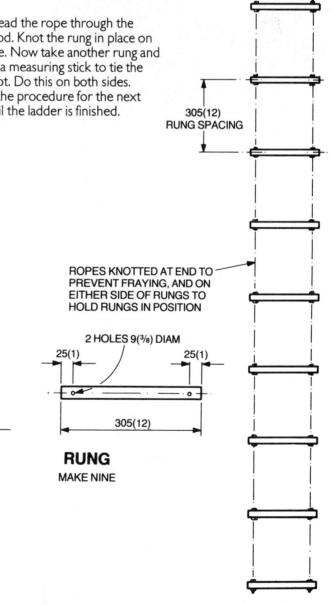

305(12)
RUNG SPACING

ROPES KNOTTED AT END TO PREVENT FRAYING, AND ON EITHER SIDE OF RUNGS TO HOLD RUNGS IN POSITION

2 HOLES 9(³⁄₈) DIAM

25(1)   25(1)

305(12)

RUNG
MAKE NINE

25(1)
DIAM

Cutting list

Rung	9 off	305mm (12in) long x 25mm (1in) diameter dowel
	2 off	3660mm (144in) long lengths of strong rope

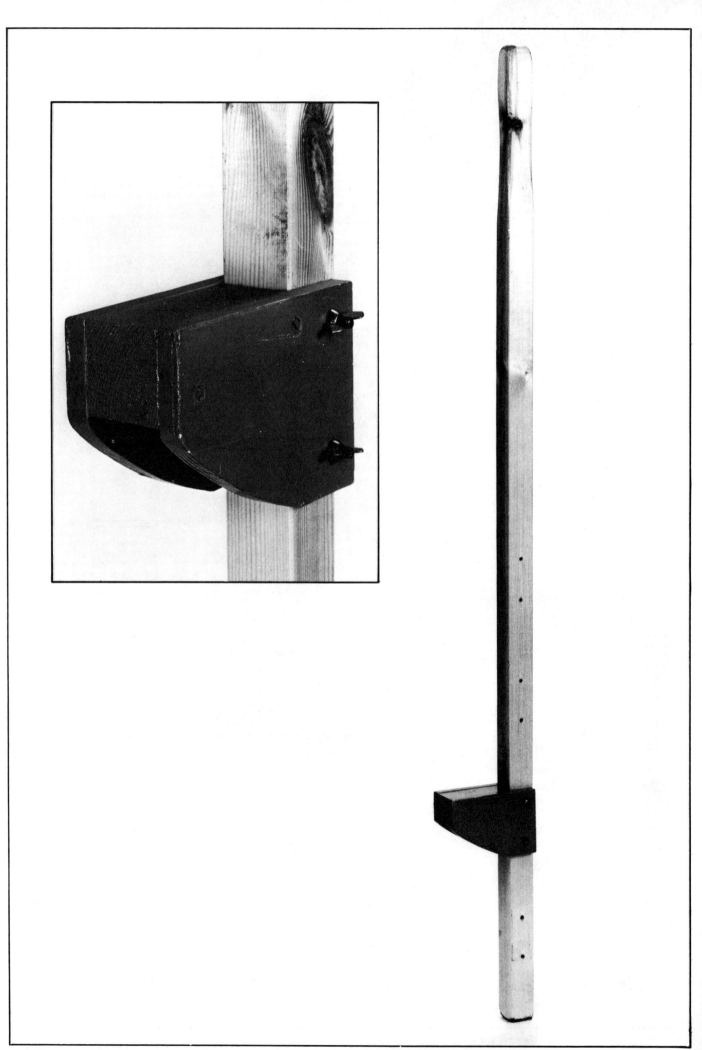

STILTS

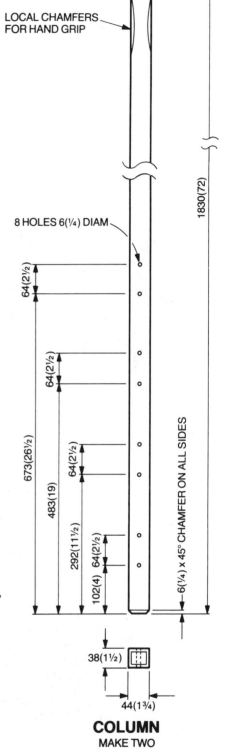

LOCAL CHAMFERS FOR HAND GRIP

1830(72)

8 HOLES 6(¼) DIAM

64(2½)

64(2½)

673(26½)

64(2½)

483(19)

64(2½)

292(11½)

102(4)

6(¼) x 45° CHAMFER ON ALL SIDES

38(1½)

44(1¾)

COLUMN
MAKE TWO

Stilts are great fun for all ages to stagger around the garden on! These are designed with teenagers in mind and are therefore very strong. If you have young children then the columns could well be thinner in section, as a young child will have difficulty holding the hand grip with the dimensions given.

It is best to start with the foot rests set at the bottom of the columns until confidence is built up.

1 Tape both columns together and mark in the positions of the bolt holes. It is critical that the holes are drilled at 90° to the sides. An assistant is helpful to watch the drilling process. A vertical drill stand will of course make this task quite simple. Buy the coach bolts before you drill the holes.

2 The foot of the column must be chamfered on all four sides. This prevents 'splitting out' of the ends.

3 Hand grips are chamfered and the best tool for this job is the spokeshave.

4 Foot rests are of a 'sandwich' construction, plywood, block, plywood. The block of wood in the middle has to be of the same thickness or fractionally larger than the width of the column. Plywood sides are cut as pairs and glued and screwed onto the centre block.

5 Very carefully mark the positions of the holes that go through the foot rests, as these have to 'line up' with the holes in the column.

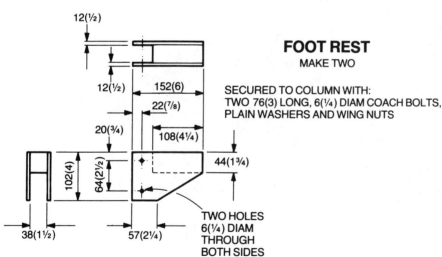

12(½)

12(½) 152(6)

22(⅞)

20(¾) 108(4¼)

102(4) 64(2½) 44(1¾)

38(1½) 57(2¼)

TWO HOLES 6(¼) DIAM THROUGH BOTH SIDES

FOOT REST
MAKE TWO

SECURED TO COLUMN WITH:
TWO 76(3) LONG, 6(¼) DIAM COACH BOLTS, PLAIN WASHERS AND WING NUTS

Cutting list

Column	2 off	1830 x 44 x 38mm (72 x 1¾ x 1½in)	Timber
Foot rest	4 off	152 x 102 x 12mm (6 x 4 x ½in)	Plywood
	2 off	108 x 44 x 38mm (4¼ x 1¾ x 1½in)	Timber
Ancillaries			
	4 off	76mm(3in) long x 6mm(¼in) diameter coach bolts	
	4 off	Plain washers	
	4 off	Wing nuts	

SEE-SAW

The see-saw is perhaps one of the oldest outdoor playthings and one that never loses its popularity. The only joints are halving joints, the other parts are assembled with screws.

The stand

1   Make a pair of pivot side plates. Drill the hole for the pivot dowel rod before shaping off the top. This is done by using a flat bit in an electric drill. Keep both sides together throughout the drilling process.

2   After the hole has been bored in the side plates, radius the ends and taper off the sides with a plane. A spokeshave will be of great help for 'rounding off' the top.

3   Cut two lengths to make the feet. To stabilise the see-saw it is necessary to make two foot-tie members. The foot-tie members are fitted to the foot with halving joints. Mark out the halving joints carefully on the timber. The sides of the joint are cut with a tenon saw, the bottom portion being removed with a chisel or a coping saw. The bottom of the halving joint must be 'levelled off' using a chisel.

4   Now drill holes in the foot to take the screws that hold the pivot side plates. Countersink the screw holes.

5   Assemble the feet and pivot side plates with screws. Now glue the foot-tie members into the feet. This completes the see-saw stand.

See-saw plank (main beam)

6   The main beam plank would obviously break unless it was stiffened by supports screwed underneath it. Cut out a pair of plank supports and with both pieces fastened together drill the pivot dowel rod hole. Using a plane shape up the supports.

7   The plank supports are screwed on from the top side. Firstly drill the screw pilot holes, not forgetting to countersink the holes. Now screw the plank supports onto the see-saw plank. I recommend screws at regular intervals to prevent the top plank flexing when in use. It is also necessary to use a fairly long screw to get a good fixing into the plank supports.

8   The shock absorbers are made from blocks of wood screwed into place at the ends of the plank. The underside of the wood block is covered with a strip of rubber.

9   Cut out four hand grip assemblies. Take a pair and drill the hole for the dowel rod. Radius off the ends.

10   The dowels are glued into the hand grip assemblies which are in turn screwed on to the main beam. As this toy will get a great deal of use it is advisable to drill pilot holes through the sides of the hand grips and then screw the handles into place.

11   This is an outside plaything so it is also advisable to paint it. Check that paint used is non-toxic.

Cutting list

Main beam		1 off	2440 x 197 x 20mm (96 x 7¾ x ¾in)	Timber
		2 off	1730 x 98 x 20mm (68 x 3⅞ x ¾in)	Timber
Hand grip	sideplates	4 off	381 x 70 x 20mm (15 x 2¾ x ¾in)	Timber
	rail	2 off	235mm(9¼in) long x 20mm(¾in) diameter dowel	
Shock absorber		Make from 206 x 70 x 51mm (8⅛ x 2¾ x 2in)		Timber
Foot		2 off	760 x 197 x 22mm (30 x 7¾ x ⅞in)	Timber
Tie member		2 off	825 x 70 x 22mm (32½ x 2¾ x ⅞in)	Timber
Pivot side plate		2 off	600 x 191 x 20mm (23½ x 7½ x ¾in)	Timber
Pivot pin		1 off	280mm(11in) long x 22mm(⅞in) diamater dowel	
		2 off	25mm (1in) long x 6mm (¼in) diameter dowel	
Ancillaries				
		25mm (1in) thick rubber for extra cushioning under shock absorbers		

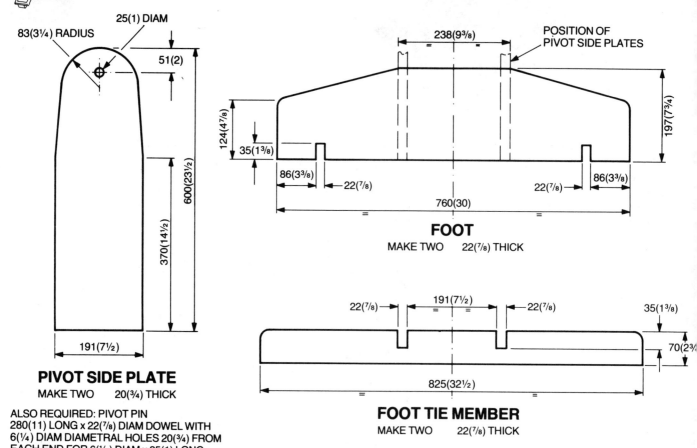

83(3¼) RADIUS
25(1) DIAM
51(2)
600(23½)
370(14½)
191(7½)

PIVOT SIDE PLATE
MAKE TWO   20(¾) THICK

ALSO REQUIRED: PIVOT PIN
280(11) LONG x 22(⅞) DIAM DOWEL WITH
6(¼) DIAM DIAMETRAL HOLES 20(¾) FROM
EACH END FOR 6(¼) DIAM x 25(1) LONG
DOWEL TO KEEP PIVOT PIN IN POSITION

238(9⅜)
POSITION OF
PIVOT SIDE PLATES
124(4⅞)
35(1⅜)
197(7¾)
86(3⅜)
22(⅞)
22(⅞)
86(3⅜)
760(30)

FOOT
MAKE TWO   22(⅞) THICK

22(⅞)
191(7½)
22(⅞)
35(1⅜)
70(2¾)
825(32½)

FOOT TIE MEMBER
MAKE TWO   22(⅞) THICK

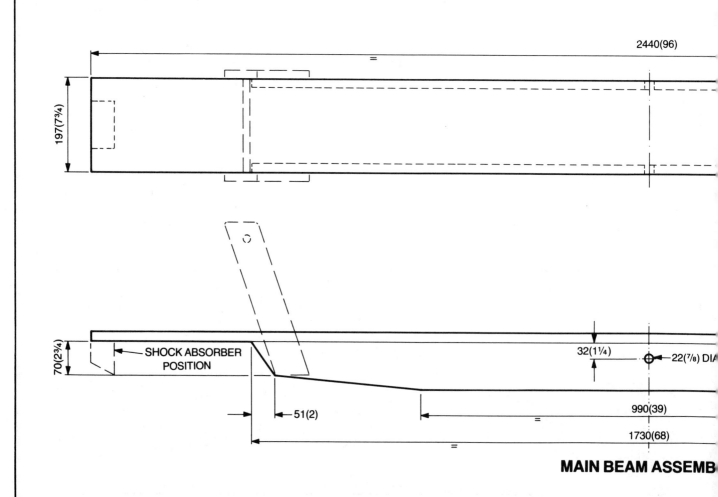

2440(96)
197(7¾)
32(1¼)
22(⅞) DIA
SHOCK ABSORBER
POSITION
70(2¾)
51(2)
990(39)
1730(68)

MAIN BEAM ASSEMB

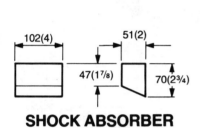

SHOCK ABSORBER
MAKE TWO

SECURE 25(1) THICK RUBBER STRIP TO
INCLINED FACE FOR EXTRA CUSHIONING

102(4) 51(2) 47(1⅞) 70(2¾)

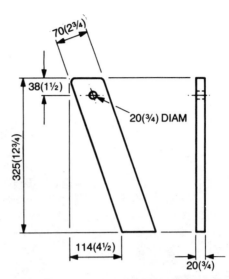

70(2¾) 38(1½) 20(¾) DIAM 325(12¾) 114(4½) 20(¾)

HAND GRIP SIDE PLATES
MAKE FOUR

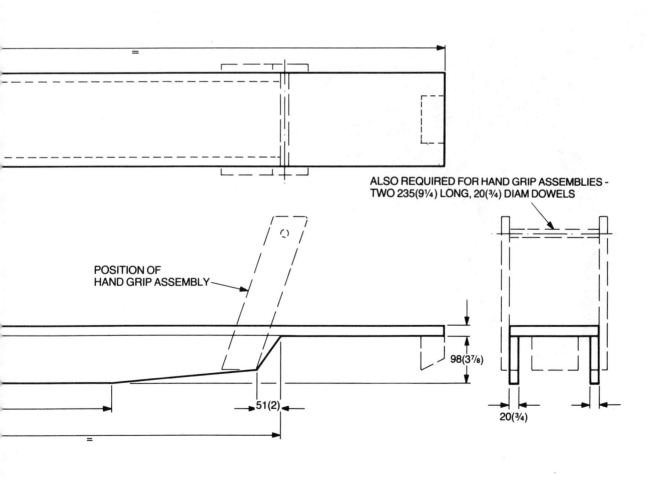

ALSO REQUIRED FOR HAND GRIP ASSEMBLIES -
TWO 235(9¼) LONG, 20(¾) DIAM DOWELS

POSITION OF
HAND GRIP ASSEMBLY

98(3⅞) 51(2) 20(¾)

WHEEL BARROWS

Children love to help wheel loads of sand, earth, potatoes, stone and groceries around even if they occasionally 'dump' them in the wrong places!

I have built two barrows, one with a single wheel and the modern equivalent with two wheels. The single wheel barrow is more difficult to use than the twin wheel. The twin wheel is really for the younger child as there is no 'balancing' of the barrow to be done, simply push or pull the load along.

The two barrow bodies are identical, only the underframes are different. It is slightly more difficult to build the single wheel barrow as there is a hole to be drilled at an angle for the axle. Therefore in the text I shall concentrate on the single wheel barrow.

1   Make two handles. The shaping for the handgrip is done first with a coping saw which 'roughs out' the basic shape and then finished off with a spokeshave. This should now form a good hand grip.

2   The most difficult task is to drill a hole at an angle through the end of the chassis to take the axle. On the twin wheel model this is not necessary as the handles are parallel. You will find that all axle holes are far more accurately drilled if you have a vertical drill stand for your electric drill. Drilling a hole at an angle presents altogether another problem but the important factor is to have either the drill or workpiece fastened firmly to a worktop. Assuming that you just have a drill, cramp the handle to the worktop and make a cardboard template in the shape of a set square. One side of the template should be cut at the angle you are drilling the hole. With an assistant to watch the angle of the drill and template make the hole. Drill handles individually, not taped together as a pair. You will find that the angle is not too critical as when it comes to assembly the soft pine will allow sufficient give for the axle and handles to be aligned.

3   With the axle fixed, cut and screw the front and back cross pieces into place. The barrow legs are now cut and screwed onto the sides. It is advisable to cut a small chamfer all around the bottom of the barrow legs. This will prevent the end grain splitting out when the barrow is put down fully loaded.

4   The barrow chassis is now ready for the barrow body.

5   The whole barrow body is made from plywood. Plywood is particularly suitable for this job as it is both light and very strong.

6   When cutting plywood always use a fine toothed saw. If you use a jigsaw fit it with a metal cutting blade and this will help to prevent 'spilches'.

7   Cut out and shape a pair of barrow sides. For the final shaping it is always best to fix them together then you will be assured of an accurate pair of sides.

8   Prepare the front and back wall of the barrow and radius the top corners before screwing the barrow together.

9   It is advisable to use the new type of wood screw that has been especially developed for fixing 'man-made' boards. This type of screw has a different pattern thread from the traditional wood screw and I have found them superior for fastening ply and chipboard. Drill 'pilot holes' for all fixing screws.

10   Besides the screw I recommend you also use 'screw cups', these act as washers and pull the sides together tighter. The cup also looks very smart and gives the barrow a distinctive look. It is advisable to glue as well as screw the sides together.

11   Screw and glue the bottom on.

12   The barrow is screwed onto the chassis at four points. Two screws are positioned at the back, just forward of the legs. The front fixing is taken through the base of the barrow near the bottom of the front wall. These four fixing points have been found sufficient for normal loads.

13   As the barrow will spend quite a considerable part of its life 'out of doors' varnish or paint will be necessary for protection. Check that the varnish or paint used is non-toxic.

Cutting list

Twin wheel version

Barrow body					
Barrow body	sides	2 off	581 × 238 × 12mm (22⅞ × 9⅜ × ½in)		Plywood
	front	1 off	305 × 286 × 12mm (12 × 11¼ × ½in)		Plywood
	rear	1 off	305 × 130 × 12mm (12 × 5⅛ × ½in)		Plywood
	bottom	1 off	419 × 330 × 9mm (16½ × 13 × ⅜in)		Plywood
Handle		2 off	727 × 41 × 22mm (28⅝ × 1⅝ × ⅞in)		Timber
Cross member		2 off	330 × 41 × 22mm (13 × 1⅝ × ⅞in)		Timber
Leg		2 off	280 × 41 × 22mm (11 × 1⅝ × ⅞in)		Timber

Ancillaries

2 off	210mm (8¼in) diameter wheels
1 off	425mm (16¾in) long × 9mm (⅜in) diameter steel axle
2 off	Spring dome caps to suit 9mm (⅜in) diameter axles

Single wheel version

Barrow body		As per twin wheel version		
Handle		2 off	914 × 41 × 22mm (36 × 1⅝ × ⅞in)	Timber
Cross piece	front	1 off	143 × 41 × 22mm (5⅝ × 1⅝ × ⅞in)	Timber
	rear	1 off	254 × 41 × 22mm (10 × 1⅝ × ⅞in)	Timber
Leg		2 off	280 × 41 × 22mm (11 × 1⅝ × ⅞in)	Timber

Ancillaries

1 off	210mm (8¼in) diameter wheel
1 off	108mm (4¼in) long × 9mm (⅜in) diameter steel axle
2 off	Spring dome caps to suit 9mm (⅜in) diameter axles

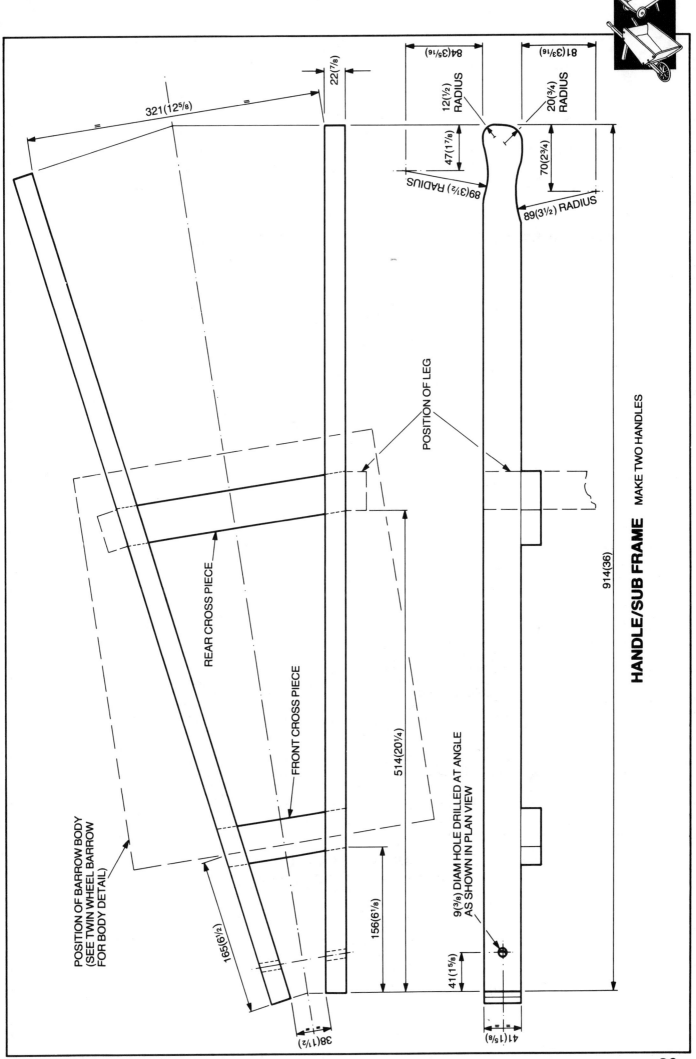

POSITION OF BARROW BODY
(SEE TWIN WHEEL BARROW
FOR BODY DETAIL)

REAR CROSS PIECE

FRONT CROSS PIECE

POSITION OF LEG

9(³/₈) DIAM HOLE DRILLED AT ANGLE
AS SHOWN IN PLAN VIEW

321(12⁵/₈)

22(⁷/₈)

84(3⁵/₁₆)

81(3³/₁₆)

12(¹/₂)
RADIUS

20(³/₄)
RADIUS

47(1⁷/₈)

70(2³/₄)

89(3¹/₂) RADIUS

89(3¹/₂) RADIUS

165(6¹/₂)

156(6¹/₈)

514(20¹/₄)

38(1¹/₂)

41(1⁵/₈)

41(1⁵/₈)

914(36)

HANDLE/SUB FRAME MAKE TWO HANDLES

39

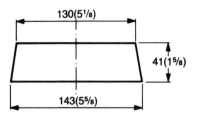

FRONT CROSS PIECE
130(5⅛)
143(5⅝)
41(1⅝)
22(⅞) THICK

REAR CROSS PIECE
241(9½)
254(10)
41(1⅝)
22(⅞) THICK

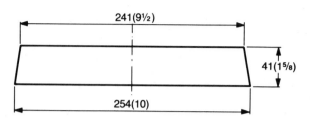

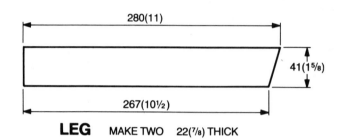

LEG MAKE TWO 22(⅞) THICK
280(11)
267(10½)
41(1⅝)

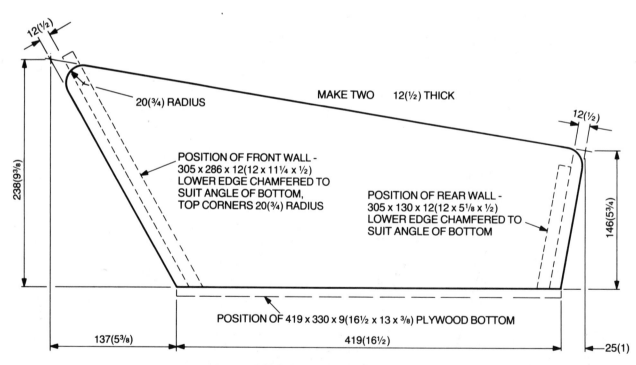

12(½)
20(¾) RADIUS
MAKE TWO 12(½) THICK
12(½)

POSITION OF FRONT WALL -
305 x 286 x 12(12 x 11¼ x ½)
LOWER EDGE CHAMFERED TO
SUIT ANGLE OF BOTTOM,
TOP CORNERS 20(¾) RADIUS

POSITION OF REAR WALL -
305 x 130 x 12(12 x 5⅛ x ½)
LOWER EDGE CHAMFERED TO
SUIT ANGLE OF BOTTOM

238(9⅜)

146(5¾)

POSITION OF 419 x 330 x 9(16½ x 13 x ⅜) PLYWOOD BOTTOM

137(5⅜)
419(16½)
25(1)

SIDE WALL DETAIL
(showing barrow body position)

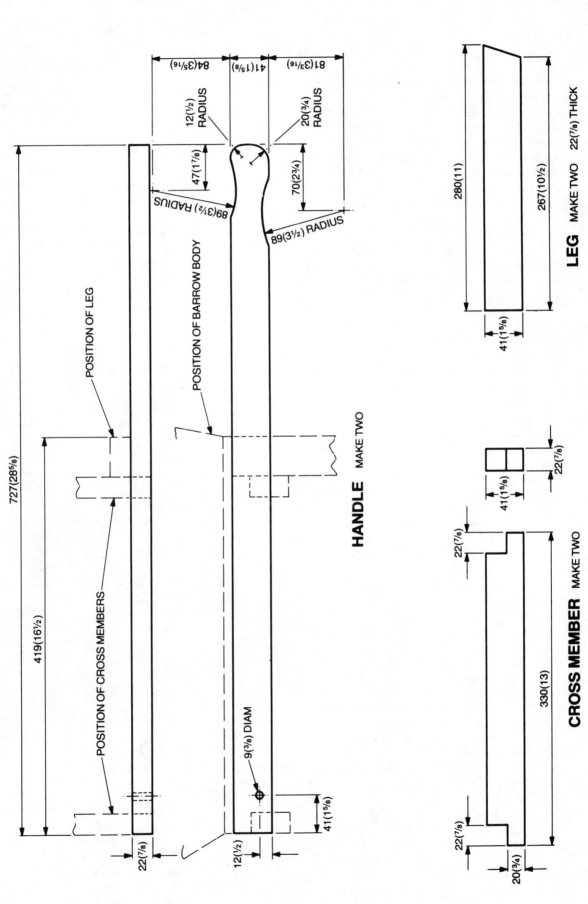

HANDLE MAKE TWO

POSITION OF LEG

POSITION OF BARROW BODY

POSITION OF CROSS MEMBERS

727(28⁵/₈)

419(16¹/₂)

22(⁷/₈)

12(¹/₂)

41(1⁵/₈)

9(³/₈) DIAM

84(3⁵/₁₆)

41(1⁵/₈)

81(3³/₁₆)

12(¹/₂) RADIUS

20(³/₄) RADIUS

47(1⁷/₈)

70(2³/₄)

89(3¹/₂) RADIUS

89(3¹/₂) RADIUS

LEG MAKE TWO   22(⁷/₈) THICK

280(11)

267(10¹/₂)

41(1⁵/₈)

CROSS MEMBER MAKE TWO

22(⁷/₈)

41(1⁵/₈)

22(⁷/₈)

22(⁷/₈)

330(13)

22(⁷/₈)

20(³/₄)

ROCKING DOG AND LLAMA

Rocking animals are always popular with children. The secret of animal making is to make sure that the 'beasty' has a friendly face.

The dog is a lovable hound while the llama has a majestic face with ears that give him a jaunty look. Both creatures have identical bodies and rockers, the only difference being the necks and heads.

1 Start by cutting out the ends of the body or seat supports. The body is barrel shaped and extremely strong. Cutting the rounded shapes of the two ends can be done with a bow or coping saw.

2 The ends are held together by slats. The slats are held onto the ends by glueing and screwing. In order to give the barrel shape an all wood finish I counterbored the slats to allow the screw heads to go well below the surface. A short length of dowel rod is then cut off and glued into the slat over the screw head. This gives the body of the animal a much better look.

3 The first slat to attach to the two ends is the top one. It is helpful to have a pencil mark in the middle of both curved pieces. This helps tremendously when attaching the first slat.

4 At this stage of construction it is essential to have someone to hold the two ends while the first seven or eight battens are attached.

5 Work from the middle of the top down both sides simultaneously until all battens are fixed. Now glue short lengths of dowel rod into the counterbored holes.

6 When the glue is dry, chisel off the odd lengths of dowel and round off the slat ends. Work over the body with glasspaper making sure that all rough edges have been removed.

7 Following the diagrams mark out the rockers on a sheet of paper or card. The shaping of the rocker itself is fairly critical; too much rock and the animal will turn over, too little and it's not much fun. The best tool to finish off the rocker is a spokeshave. Fix both rockers together in a vice and shape them up as a pair.

8 Drill and counterbore the sides of the rockers and then screw them onto the animal's sides.

9 Up to this point making a dog or a llama is the same, 'woodworkingly' speaking! If you wish to make a llama then a long neck is necessary. If on the other hand you wish to make a 'Baskerville' a shorter piece of wood is

needed. Necks and heads have the same cutting and shaping techniques, so I will describe this part in general terms.

10 Draw a cardboard template and from this mark out the neck shape on the wood. Cut it out using a coping or bow saw. Remove the saw cuts with a spokeshave or glasspaper.

11 Using a large flat bit the same diameter as the dowel rod handle, drill a hole in the neck. Push (or tap with a hammer) the dowel rod into the neck. Just before the dowel rod is half way in, apply some glue to the rod, then continue tapping it into the neck. A screw fixed from the back of the neck will hold the (rod) handle very firmly in place.

12 Shaping the head is not quite such a daunting task as it may look at first sight. If possible, get a piece of pine without knots or splits. Using a coping saw cut off the snout portion and around the mouth. Now cut down either side of the mouth, removing thinner pieces of wood. Obviously you will need to keep moving the head around in the vice as you cut.

Once all the rough shaping has been completed, fine shaping can start. A spokeshave is the best tool for this task or alternatively, a Stanley surform tool can be used. Finish off with glasspaper.

13 The eyes and nose can be purchased from shops that sell soft toy making materials. Drill holes in the block to take the eyes and nose. It is extremely important that they are fixed using epoxy resin glue otherwise eyes and nose could become detached and swallowed by a child. Epoxy resin glue is very strong, but a check should be kept on these parts just to make sure that after several months of use they are still firmly attached.

14 In the top of the dog's head bore a large hole and glue a short length of broom handle (if you can cut six inches off the kitchen brush it won't be noticed!) into the head. The mop attachment is then secured to the handle. Do check that there are no

metal parts that can scratch or damage hands or faces. Some mop heads have plastic fixtures and these are obviously the ones to choose.

15 All that is necessary to complete the dog is a length of rope knotted through a hole in the back upright for the tail.

16 The llama head is cut in much the same way as the dog head. The only difference is that two ears are cut,

shaped and screwed onto the llama's head.

17 The dog and llama heads are secured to the necks by glueing and screwing. It is best to use very long screws as the wooden heads are quite heavy. Use three screws, two through the back and one through the neck. On the llama it is possible to get one screw up under the chin through the underside of the neck.

18 The llama has a wooden tail glued onto the back end piece.

19 Once all the woodworking is finished, run your hands over the toy and check for splinters, sharp edges etc. If your hands don't find the rough pieces, be sure a child's little fingers will!

20 Several coats of matt varnish will finish off these toys rather well and give them a good protective coating.

Cutting list

Seat support	2 off	330 × 200 × 22mm (13 × 8 × ⅞in)	Timber
Seat battens	13 off	360 × 25 × 20mm (14 × 1 × ¾in)	Timber
Rockers	2 off	1000 × 140 × 22mm (39⅜ × 5½ × ⅞in)	Timber
Llama's head	1 off	210 × 150 × 70mm (8¼ × 6 × 2¾in)	Timber
Llama's neck	1 off	780 × 120 × 22mm (30¾ × 4¾ × ⅞in)	Timber
Llama's ears	2 off	200 × 80 × 22mm (8 × 3⅛ × ⅞in)	Timber
Llama's tail	1 off	180 × 70 × 22mm (7 × 2¾ × ⅞in)	Timber
Handle	1 off	230mm(9in) long × 16mm(⅝in) diameter dowel	
Reinforcing blocks	2 off	32mm (1¼in) o/d × 16mm (⅝in) i/d × 16mm (⅝in) thick	
Dog's head	1 off	270 × 150 × 70mm (10⅝ × 6 × 2¾in)	Timber
	1 off	76mm(3in) long × 22mm(⅞in) diameter dowel	
Dog's neck	1 off	343 × 127 × 22mm (13½ × 5 × ⅞in)	Timber
Handle	1 off	230mm (9in) long × 16mm (⅝in) diameter dowel	
Reinforcing blocks	2 off	32mm (1¼in) o/d × 16mm (⅝in) i/d × 16mm (⅝in) thick	
Ancillaries			
	1 off	Mop head for dog	

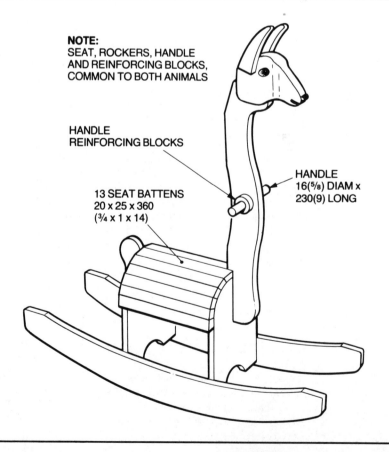

NOTE:
SEAT, ROCKERS, HANDLE AND REINFORCING BLOCKS, COMMON TO BOTH ANIMALS

HANDLE
REINFORCING BLOCKS

13 SEAT BATTENS
20 × 25 × 360
(¾ × 1 × 14)

HANDLE
16(⅝) DIAM x
230(9) LONG

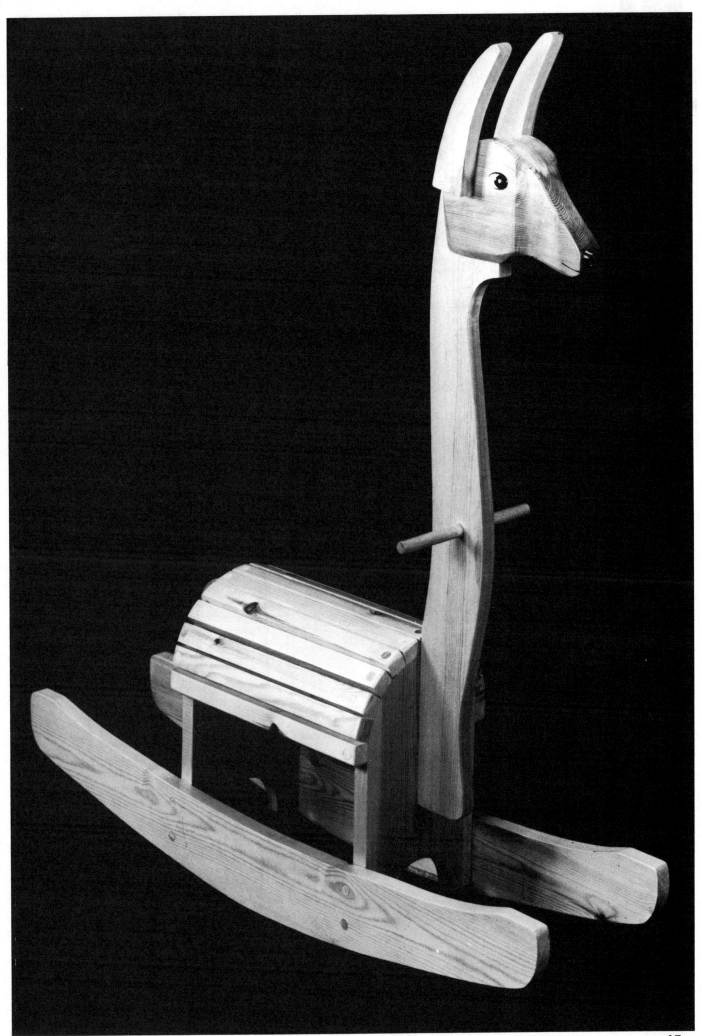

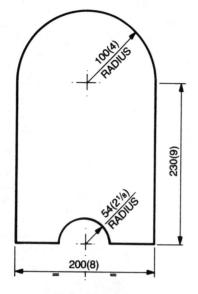

SEAT SUPPORT

22(⁷⁄₈) THICK   MAKE TWO

- 100(4) RADIUS
- 230(9)
- 54(2¹⁄₈) RADIUS
- 200(8)

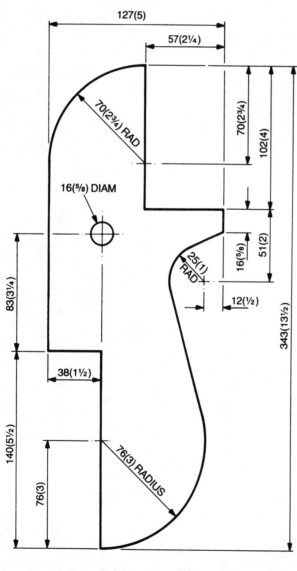

- 127(5)
- 57(2¹⁄₄)
- 70(2³⁄₄) RAD
- 70(2³⁄₄)
- 102(4)
- 16(⁵⁄₈) DIAM
- 51(2)
- 16(⁵⁄₈)
- 25(1) RAD
- 12(¹⁄₂)
- 83(3¹⁄₄)
- 343(13¹⁄₂)
- 38(1¹⁄₂)
- 140(5¹⁄₂)
- 76(3)
- 76(3) RADIUS

DOG'S NECK

22(⁷⁄₈) THICK

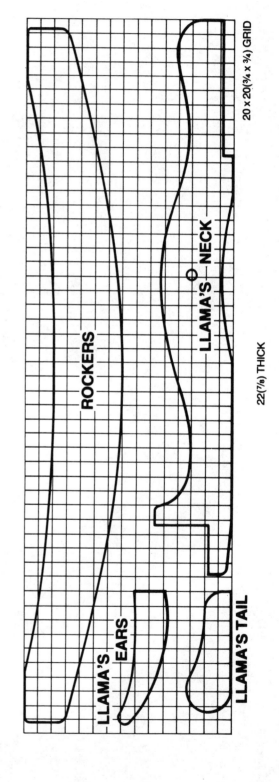

20 x 20(³⁄₄ x ³⁄₄) GRID

ROCKERS

LLAMA'S NECK

22(⁷⁄₈) THICK

LLAMA'S EARS

LLAMA'S TAIL

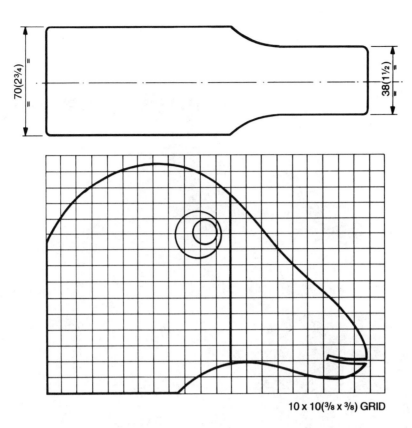

10 x 10(³⁄₈ x ³⁄₈) GRID

LLAMA'S HEAD

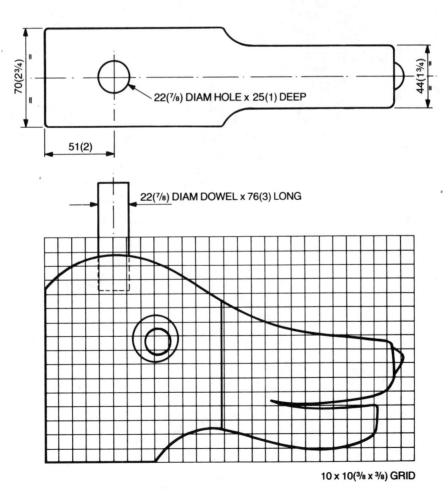

22(⁷⁄₈) DIAM HOLE x 25(1) DEEP

51(2)

22(⁷⁄₈) DIAM DOWEL x 76(3) LONG

10 x 10(³⁄₈ x ³⁄₈) GRID

DOG'S HEAD

GO-CART

There is no other feeling quite so exhilarating as racing down a grass track in an unsprung go-cart. From other go-carts I have designed I have now combined all the best features, and the result will give many years trouble free motoring!

Caution This vehicle should not be used on public roads.

1 First cut the main chassis, measure and drill all the screw holes and the large diameter hole to take the coach bolt which holds the front axle.

2 Now cut out the rear lower frame. Before screwing together, fix both sides together and drill the holes that take the back axle. Use both glue and screws when assembling the frame.

3 Screw the frame onto the chassis. Cut two side panels, drilling the axle hole in both sides. Before fixing the sides onto the chassis drill and screw the two strips of wood that hold the slatted seat.
Line up the axle holes with those in the rear lower frame and screw into place.

4 Shape the seat back and screw into place. Glue the strengthening strips into the corners.

5 Cut the slats for the seat. All the seat slats are screwed into place.

6 Make two mudguards, one for each hand, and screw them onto the sides. The mudguards will prevent fingers or arms getting entangled with the wheels.

7 Prepare the cab fascia, being careful to radius the corners.

8 The engine compartment bulkheads should be cut out as a pair. After cutting out, tape the bulkheads together and, using glasspaper, carefully smooth the edges.

9 Now glue and screw the bonnet lower tie member into the bulkheads. Prepare the bonnet hinge ridge and glue it onto the bulkheads. Using panel pins secure the bonnet hinge ridge.

10 To give the barrel shape to the top of the bonnet it is necessary to cut sixteen strips of wood which are glued and panel pinned onto the bulkheads. You may well find that a helping hand is of great assistance at this stage. After pinning all the strips in place glue the bonnet side panels in place. Don't forget to drill the hole for the headlamp bar.

11 The radiator cap can be made in a variety of ways, eg two different diameters of dowel rod glued together, or if you have an electric drill, 'turn up' a suitable cap.

12 Forming the radiator grill is done by glueing and panel-pinning strips of wood onto the front bulkhead.

13 The fascia is screwed onto the rear bulkhead, and the coach bolt is fitted through the lower tie member and chassis.

14 A very strong front axle is essential for such a vehicle. Make two crossmembers and four spacer blocks. Drill the axle holes in the two outer and two inner spacer blocks. The blocks are now glued and screwed into place. Before glueing and screwing the blocks check that the axle holes align.

15 Shape up the front mudguards and screw onto the front axle.

16 The steering rope is fixed by passing it through two holes drilled in the top of the axle cross member.

17 It is necessary to fit some form of brake. The one detailed here is very simple but reasonably effective. Tip the end with a piece of rubber tyre, as it helps to stop rapid wear on the brake lever. A large hefty screw is necessary to fix it to the side of the chassis. Use a washer under the screw head.

18 A coping saw is ideal for cutting the circular headlamps. A dowel rod passes right through the bonnet side panels, the headlamps being glued on each end.

19 Attach the number plate to the front axle.

20 Painting is of your own choice, but I suggest that the radiator is painted in matt black.

Cutting list

Main chassis	1 off	832 x 200 x 25mm (32¾ x 7⅞ x 1in)	Timber
	1 off	356 x 79 x 22mm (14 x 3⅛ x ⅞in)	Timber
Rear lower frame	2 off	356 x 73 x 22mm (14 x 2⅞ x ⅞in)	Timber
	2 off	330 x 73 x 22mm (13 x 2⅞ x ⅞in)	Timber
Seat	2 off	330 x 28 x 22mm (13 x 1⅛ x ⅞in)	Timber
	6 off	356 x 28 x 22mm (14 x 1⅛ x ⅞in)	Timber
Brake lever	1 off	438 x 41 x 22mm (17¼ x 1⅝ x ⅞in)	Timber
Side panel	2 off	346 x 330 x 12mm (13⅝ x 13 x ½in)	Plywood
Mudguard	2 off	330 x 67 x 25mm (13 x 2⅝ x 1in)	Timber
Seat back	1 off	419 x 235 x 9mm (16½ x 9¼ x ⅜in)	Plywood
	2 off	184 x 25 x 22mm (7¼ x 1 x ⅞in)	Timber
Engine bulkhead	2 off	260 x 222 x 12mm (10¼ x 8¾ x ½in)	Plywood
Grill	Make from	12 x 8 x 2280mm (½ x 5/16 x 90in)	Timber
Bonnet side panel	2 off	276 x 130 x 6mm (10⅞ x 5⅛ x ¼in)	Plywood
Bonnet lower tie	1 off	276 x 41 x 22mm (10⅞ x 1⅝ x ⅞in)	Timber
Curved section of bonnet	Make from	22 x 9 x 4470mm (⅞ x ⅜ x 176in)	Timber
Bonnet hinge ridge	1 off	276 x 38 x 20mm (10⅞ x 1½ x ¾in)	Timber
Radiator cap	1 off	102mm (4in) long x 41mm (1⅝in) diameter timber	
Head lamps	2 off	32mm (1¼in) long x 89mm (3½in) diameter timber	
	1 off	476mm (18¾in) long x 16mm (⅝in) diameter dowel	
Cab fascia	1 off	356 x 305 x 12mm (14 x 12 x ½in)	Plywood
Front axle beams	2 off	622 x 70 x 22mm (24½ x 2¾ x ⅞in)	Timber
spacers	Make from	41 x 32 x 356mm (1⅝ x 1¼ x 14in)	Timber
Front mudguard	2 off	270 x 194 x 6mm (10⅝ x 7⅝ x ¼in)	Plywood
Front number plate	1 off	343 x 86 x 9mm (13½ x 3⅜ x ⅜in)	Plywood
Ancillaries			
	4 off	203mm (8in) diameter road wheels	
	2 off	222mm (8¾in) long x 9mm (⅜in) diameter steel axles	
	1 off	483mm (19in) long x 9mm (⅜in) diameter steel axles	
	6 off	Spring dome caps to suit 9mm (⅜in) diameter axles	
	1 off	152mm (6in) long x 20mm (¾in) diameter coach bolt, washer and nut	
	1 off	1830mm (72in) length of thick cord for steering	

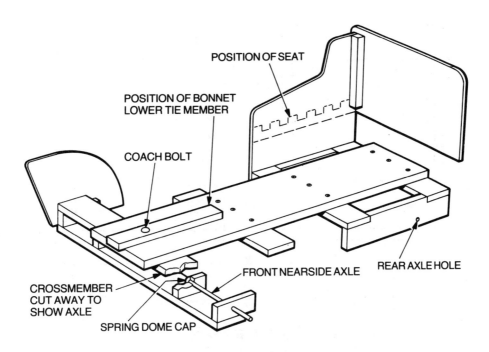

POSITION OF SEAT

POSITION OF BONNET
LOWER TIE MEMBER

COACH BOLT

CROSSMEMBER
CUT AWAY TO
SHOW AXLE

SPRING DOME CAP

FRONT NEARSIDE AXLE

REAR AXLE HOLE

PARTIALLY ASSEMBLED CHASSIS

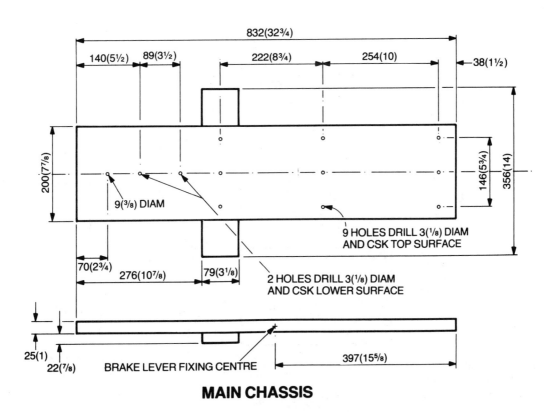

832(32¾)

140(5½)   89(3½)   222(8¾)   254(10)   38(1½)

200(7⅞)

9(³⁄₈) DIAM

146(5¾)   356(14)

9 HOLES DRILL 3(⅛) DIAM
AND CSK TOP SURFACE

70(2¾)   276(10⁷⁄₈)   79(3⅛)

2 HOLES DRILL 3(⅛) DIAM
AND CSK LOWER SURFACE

25(1)

22(⁷⁄₈)

BRAKE LEVER FIXING CENTRE

397(15⅝)

MAIN CHASSIS

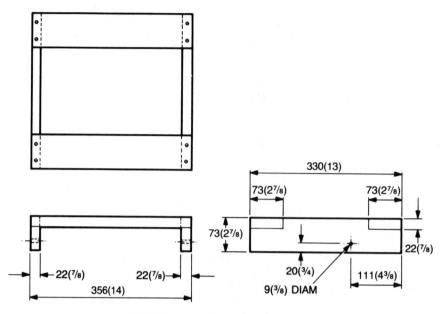

REAR LOWER FRAME

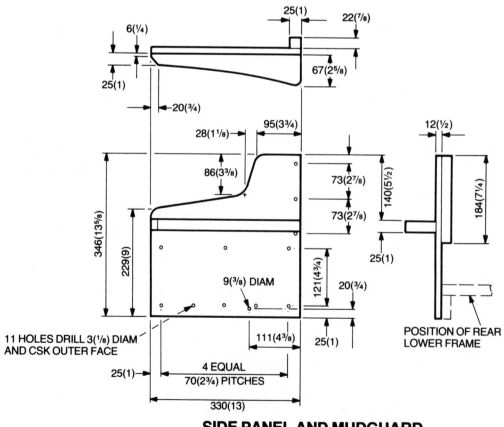

SIDE PANEL AND MUDGUARD
MAKE ONE OF EACH HAND

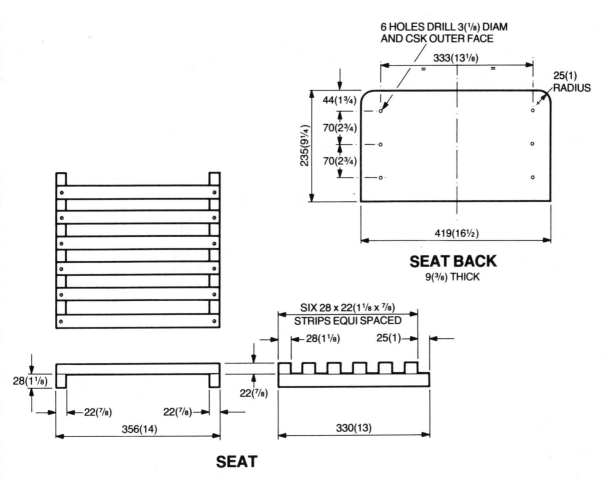

6 HOLES DRILL 3(⅛) DIAM
AND CSK OUTER FACE

333(13⅛)

25(1)
RADIUS

44(1¾)

235(9¼)

70(2¾)

70(2¾)

419(16½)

SEAT BACK
9(⅜) THICK

SIX 28 x 22(1⅛ x ⅞)
STRIPS EQUI SPACED

28(1⅛)   25(1)

28(1⅛)

22(⅞)

22(⅞)   22(⅞)

356(14)

330(13)

SEAT

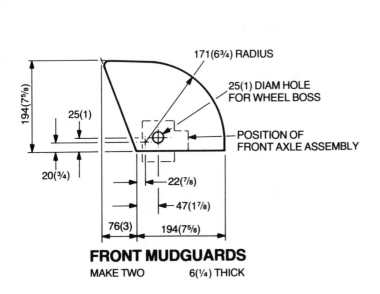

194(7⅝)

25(1)

20(¾)

171(6¾) RADIUS

25(1) DIAM HOLE
FOR WHEEL BOSS

POSITION OF
FRONT AXLE ASSEMBLY

22(⅞)

47(1⅞)

76(3)   194(7⅝)

FRONT MUDGUARDS
MAKE TWO   6(¼) THICK

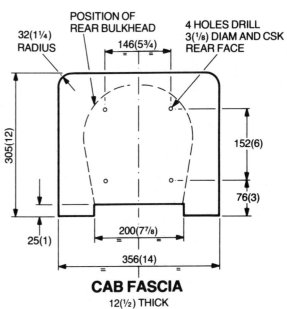

32(1¼)
RADIUS

POSITION OF
REAR BULKHEAD

146(5¾)

4 HOLES DRILL
3(⅛) DIAM AND CSK
REAR FACE

305(12)

152(6)

76(3)

25(1)

200(7⅞)

356(14)

CAB FASCIA
12(½) THICK

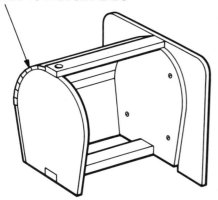

16 STRIPS 22 x 9 x 276($\frac{7}{8}$ x $\frac{3}{8}$ x 10$\frac{7}{8}$)
PINNED TO THE BULKHEADS

PARTIALLY ASSEMBLED BONNET

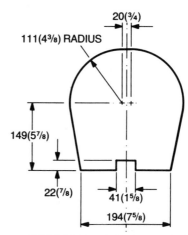

20($\frac{3}{4}$)

111(4$\frac{3}{8}$) RADIUS

149(5$\frac{7}{8}$)

22($\frac{7}{8}$)

41(1$\frac{5}{8}$)

194(7$\frac{5}{8}$)

ENGINE COMPARTMENT
FRONT AND REAR BULKHEADS

MAKE TWO   12($\frac{1}{2}$) THICK

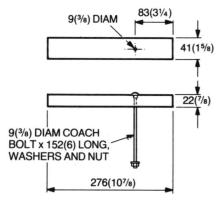

9($\frac{3}{8}$) DIAM   83(3$\frac{1}{4}$)

41(1$\frac{5}{8}$)

22($\frac{7}{8}$)

9($\frac{3}{8}$) DIAM COACH
BOLT x 152(6) LONG,
WASHERS AND NUT

276(10$\frac{7}{8}$)

BONNET LOWER TIE MEMBER

25(1) DIAM

38(1$\frac{1}{2}$)   60(2$\frac{3}{8}$)   41(1$\frac{5}{8}$)
DIAM

RADIATOR CAP

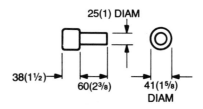

25(1) DIAM   22($\frac{7}{8}$)

38(1$\frac{1}{2}$)

276(10$\frac{7}{8}$)   20($\frac{3}{4}$)

BONNET HINGE RIDGE

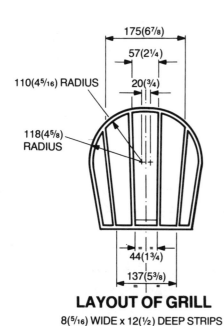

175(6$\frac{7}{8}$)

57(2$\frac{1}{4}$)

110(4$\frac{5}{16}$) RADIUS

20($\frac{3}{4}$)

118(4$\frac{5}{8}$)
RADIUS

44(1$\frac{3}{4}$)

137(5$\frac{3}{8}$)

LAYOUT OF GRILL

8($\frac{5}{16}$) WIDE x 12($\frac{1}{2}$) DEEP STRIPS
PINNED TO FRONT FACE OF
FRONT BULKHEAD

16($\frac{5}{8}$) DIAM HOLE   22($\frac{7}{8}$)
FOR HEADLAMP
SUPPORT BAR

12($\frac{1}{2}$)

130(5$\frac{1}{8}$)

276(10$\frac{7}{8}$)

BONNET SIDE PANEL

MAKE TWO   6($\frac{1}{4}$) THICK

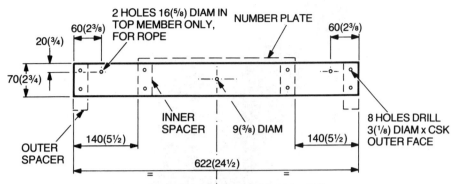

2 HOLES 16(5/8) DIAM IN TOP MEMBER ONLY, FOR ROPE

NUMBER PLATE

60(2³/₈)

20(³/₄)

70(2³/₄)

60(2³/₈)

INNER SPACER

9(³/₈) DIAM

8 HOLES DRILL 3(¹/₈) DIAM x CSK OUTER FACE

OUTER SPACER

140(5¹/₂)

140(5¹/₂)

622(24¹/₂)

FRONT AXLE CROSSMEMBER   MAKE TWO   22(⁷/₈) THICK
(showing position of outer and inner spacers, and number plate)

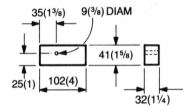

35(1³/₈)   9(³/₈) DIAM

41(1⁵/₈)

25(1)   102(4)

32(1¹/₄)

FRONT AXLE OUTER SPACER   MAKE TWO

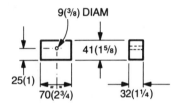

9(³/₈) DIAM

41(1⁵/₈)

25(1)   70(2³/₄)   32(1¹/₄)

FRONT AXLE INNER SPACER   MAKE TWO

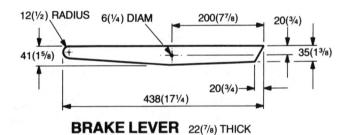

12(¹/₂) RADIUS   6(¹/₄) DIAM   200(7⁷/₈)   20(³/₄)

41(1⁵/₈)

35(1³/₈)

20(³/₄)

438(17¹/₄)

BRAKE LEVER   22(⁷/₈) THICK

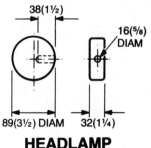

38(1¹/₂)

16(⁵/₈) DIAM

89(3¹/₂) DIAM   32(1¹/₄)

HEADLAMP
MAKE TWO

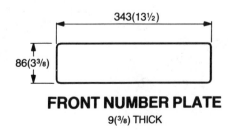

343(13¹/₂)

86(3³/₈)

FRONT NUMBER PLATE
9(³/₈) THICK

This large machine fills the minds of youngsters with so many possibilities. 'Why don't we empty the fish pond?', or 'We could pull some logs up the garden for the fire', or 'I wonder if it's strong enough to lift my tricycle', or 'With the bucket tied on I could empty the sand pit'.

Being mobile, the crane can be moved to different locations in the garden, that is if you can get big brother or sister to help push it along!

The control console has three winding handles and it takes most children a few minutes to find out just how to operate them. The bottom handle controls the raising and lowering of the crane jib. The middle handle raises and lowers the block and tackle. Both these handles are fitted with ratchets for holding the jib or block and tackle in a fixed position. The top lever is only used when operating the sand bucket and allows the bucket to be opened and closed. There is no need to fit a ratchet on this handle.

A strong good quality nylon cord is recommended for 'rigging' this machine but make sure that children understand that winding cord around arms, legs and necks etc, is a very dangerous game.

The stabiliser should always be fully extended when the crane is lifting loads.

The crane can be conveniently broken down into three parts for construction – chassis, cab and crane jib. The crane should be either varnished or painted. You will find that painting or varnishing is easier if some of the parts are not bolted on, for example cab, console and jib. Make sure that the paints or varnish used are non-toxic.

The chassis

1   Study the three-dimensional drawing of the chassis and familiarise yourself with the parts. The construction consists of a plywood decking onto which are screwed chassis members. The central chassis member runs the full length of the plywood decking and it is through this that the front axle is secured with a coach bolt. Before positioning the cross members drill the holes to take the stabiliser bar. Glue the dowel rods into the stabiliser bar and push them through the holes in the cross members. They are prevented from coming out by blocks of wood glued onto the other ends.

2   A block of wood is screwed to the side of the chassis to act as a step for the driver. The screws do need to be of a fairly large size, remember children will be stepping on it all the time!

3   The front axle is like a 'wooden sandwich'. The four centre blocks holding the axles are held together by two strips of wood. The centre axle blocks should be drilled in pairs to make alignment of the axles easy. The front axle rod is in two halves, both ends being secured by spring clips in the centre blocks. Glue and screw the front axle block together.

4   Drill holes in the top section of the axle to take the rope with which to pull the crane along.

5   Position the axle on the chassis and clamp in place. Now drill the hole to take the coach bolt. Bolt the axle on with washers under the nut.

The cab

6   The cab sides are the same external shape but that is where the similarity ends. On one side there is a window, and on the other side is the door which allows easy access. Cutting out such large shapes really requires a jigsaw. The cab sides are formed of plywood and then a framework of pine is glued and screwed onto the inside of the cab sides.

7   The top of the cab comprises two roof cross members and a roof panel. Two bulkhead cross members hold the frame at the front and bulkheads at the back. The cab is therefore very well 'braced' at all points and is extremely strong.

8   The bulkhead at the back of the cab has three holes drilled through it to take the 'rigging'. The holes that take the cord are 'bushed' with plastic tubing. Cut suitable lengths of plastic tube and insert these into the holes. This will prevent the cords fraying and cut down the friction when the cords are moving.

9   Screwed on to this bulkhead is a further cross member. There are two holes drilled in this to take the coach bolts that fasten the cab to the chassis.

10   The cab is held to the chassis at the front by the cab floor plate. The floor plate fits on top of the chassis framing. The plate is bolted to the chassis. Use coach bolts with wing nuts which makes dismantling a far easier job. Always check the floor bolts for tightness.

11   The seat is made from slats that are screwed to the framework. On the door side of the cab the seat support block is glued and screwed through the frame. On the window side of the cab the seat supports are simply screwed on to the plywood.

Before screwing the slats in place, plane off any sharp corners and glasspaper to be sure no sharp edges are left.

12   In order to get the brake lever clear of the chassis it is necessary to fix a block of wood on to the window side of the cab. This block is glued and screwed in place.

13   Cut and screw the windscreen frames into position. While working at the front of the cab screw in the three 'eye hooks' on to the bottom cab bulkhead. The purpose of the hooks is to guide the nylon cords directly into the control console.

14   Prepare and cut out two jib guide plates. With both sides fixed together

drill the pivot hole, for the crane jib. The guide plates are screwed on to the roof cross members from the under-side. Cut four support blocks and glue these to the guide plates and cross members.

15   Cut out a pair of console frame sides. Fix these firmly together with tape. Now mark on both sides the various positions of axles and bridging pieces. Do all the cutting and drilling while the sides are fixed together.

16   The console sides are held together by the bridging pieces which should now be glued and screwed in place. While fixing the sides it does help to have temporary dowel rods in the axle holes, this keeps the whole framework in line.

17   Study the winding handle assembly and make three identical units. You will only need two star wheels as the top winding handle does not need a ratchet holding device.

18   The winding handle is cut from plywood and square blocks are glued on to the back and axle unit. The reason being that there is very little glueing area for the plywood disc and axle unless the block is added.

19   Before final assembly of winding handles lubricate the axle holes with candle wax.

20   The locking lever and star wheels provide a positive locking device when loads are being lifted. The levers are bolted on to the sides of the console. Two screw eye hooks are fixed into the bottom bridging piece. These guide the cords onto the spindles.

The jib

21   Prepare two lengths of timber for the jib. Fix both pieces together and carefully mark out all the recesses that have to be cut. With both sides firmly together cut out the recesses for the seven cross members. Use a tenon saw to cut down the sides, the 'waste wood' is removed using a chisel and mallet. Don't attempt to remove all the waste wood from one side all at once otherwise it will lead to ugly splits. Work from both sides, turning the jib around in the vice.

22   Cut out the central cross member and the front cross member. These cross members carry the nylon cords. Holes are drilled in them and 'bushed' with plastic tube.

23   Now fix the whole jib together before any glue is applied. This is always a good step whatever you are making just to see that all the pieces fit well. If they don't adjustments can be made before the glue is applied.

Assembly

24   Now we can assemble chassis, cab and jib. Using four coach bolts fix the chassis to the cab. Make sure that the bolt heads are in the floor plate and not the wing nuts as a child could be hurt by these. To do this you will have to lay the cab and chassis on their sides. Do the wing nuts up tightly making sure that washers are placed under the wing nuts.

25   The jib is fixed to the crane by a large dowel rod. Lubricate the dowel rod with candle wax, position the jib in the guide plates and tap the dowel rod into place. On the prototype it was found that the dowel rod required no further securing as it moves only very slightly when the jib is being elevated.

Rigging

26   It is necessary to use a fairly substantial nylon cord for the winding and winching mechanisms on this crane. All the 'rigging' follows the same route through the crane cab- from the console to the bottom of the cab and through the screw eyes, under the floor plate and through the back cross member and up on to the jib.

Various operations are carried out by different handles, starting from the bottom of the console.

a   The bottom handle controls the raising and lowering of the jib. It is important that the cord for this handle goes through all the middle holes. It is tied off on the back cross member of the jib. When the handles are turned the jib is either raised or lowered.

b   The middle handle moves the block and tackle. It is this handle that will probably get the most use. The cord goes through the cab as previously described and then through the bushed hole in the back of the jib. From here it passes through the centre cross member and through the front cross member to be attached to the block and tackle.

c   The top handle is designed for the sand bucket or for extra winching power. It does not have a ratchet locking device. The cord follows the same route as the other rigging right

through the front cross member where it is tied until wanted. When it is being used this 'spare line' is attached to the bucket opening cord. The block and tackle is removed and the line attached to the bucket support frame. When the middle handles are moved the bucket can be raised or lowered. When the bucket is required to empty its contents the top handles are moved and the bucket opens.

Lifting tackle and chains (block and tackle)

27   This is made from an offcut of wood and allows children to attach all sorts of objects to the crane.

Two large diameter screwed eyes are attached to the top of the block. A chain is fastened to both eyes and joined with a metal ring at the top. This is then tied on to the nylon cord from the crane.

In the bottom of the block is set one screw eye on to which a length of chain is attached. The fourth screw eye is fixed into the side of the block and with round nosed pliers the 'eye' is opened out to form a hook. The chain is secured on this side hook. When a load is going to be lifted the chain is put around the article and the chain link dropped over the hook. In this way all different sizes of object can be handled using only one chain.

Bucket (for sand)

28   The bucket is made from plywood. It is easiest to glue and panel pin the sides together first, then with a hand saw cut the complete bucket in half, this sounds a bit drastic but if you mark a pencil line on the bucket first and cut carefully it works very well. Give the bucket sides as much support as possible throughout the cutting operation.

29   Following the plans, make the bucket support frame assembly. Dowel rods are pushed through the frame-work and into the bucket sides. A little work is necessary to get both buckets operating freely when the cord is pulled. The cord is knotted into either side of the bucket and threaded through the screw eyes, when the cord is pulled it opens the bucket halves.

The bucket frame central support has a hole bored in it so that it can be tied on to the crane.

Cutting list

Chassis assembly	1 off	864 × 451 × 9mm (34 × 17¾ × ⅜in)	Plywood
	1 off	864 × 67 × 44mm (34 × 2⅝ × 1¾in)	Timber
	2 off	521 × 67 × 44mm (20½ × 2⅝ × 1¾in)	Timber
	4 off	159 × 67 × 44mm (6¼ × 2⅝ × 1¾in)	Timber
	1 off	229 × 70 × 44mm (9 × 2¾ × 1¾in)	Timber
Front axle cross member	2 off	457 × 95 × 22mm (18 × 3¾ × ⅞in)	Timber
spacers	Make from	315 × 95 × 22mm (12⅜ × 3¾ × ⅞in)	Timber
Stabiliser	2 off	635mm (25in) long × 22mm (⅞in) diameter dowel	
	1 off	356 × 67 × 44mm (14¼ × 2⅝ × 1¾in)	Timber
	2 off	51 × 51 × 22mm (2 × 2 × ⅞in)	Timber
Cab wall panel	2 off	762 × 610 × 9mm (30 × 24 × ⅜in)	Plywood
frame	Make from	5185 × 35 × 25mm (204 × 1⅜ × 1in)	Timber
seat support	Make from	292 × 35 × 25mm (11½ × 1⅜ × 1in)	Timber
brake block	1 off	95 × 67 × 44mm (3¾ × 2⅝ × 1¾in)	Timber
seat block	1 off	225 × 102 × 25mm (8⅞ × 4 × 1in)	Timber
seat bars	6 off	381 × 44 × 25mm (15 × 1¾ × 1in)	Timber
Roof panel	1 off	400 × 178 × 9mm (15¾ × 7 × ⅜in)	Plywood
Roof cross members	2 off	400 × 102 × 22mm (15¾ × 4 × ⅞in)	Timber
Jib guide plates	2 off	508 × 203 × 22mm (20 × 8 × ⅞in)	Timber
Support blocks	Make from	495 × 89 × 28mm (19½ × 3½ × 1⅛in)	Timber
Lower rear cross member	1 off	400 × 102 × 22mm (15¾ × 4 × ⅞in)	Timber
	1 off	356 × 32 × 22mm (14 × 1¼ × ⅞in)	Timber
Brake lever	1 off	530 × 44 × 20mm (20⅞ × 1¾ × ¾in)	Timber
Floor plate	1 off	381 × 178 × 9mm (15 × 7 × ⅜in)	Plywood
Windscreen frame	2 off	400 × 89 × 9mm (15¾ × 3½ × ⅜in)	Plywood
Bulkhead cross members	2 off	400 × 102 × 22mm (15¾ × 4 × ⅞in)	Timber
Bulkhead panel	1 off	400 × 121 × 9mm (15¾ × 4¾ × ⅜in)	Plywood
Console frame	2 off	381 × 175 × 9mm (15 × 6⅞ × ⅜in)	Plywood
	1 off	102 × 76 × 22mm (4 × 3 × ⅞in)	Timber
	1 off	76 × 76 × 22mm (3 × 3 × ⅞in)	Timber
	1 off	64 × 76 × 22mm (2½ × 3 × ⅞in)	Timber
	1 off	57 × 76 × 22mm (2¼ × 3 × ⅞in)	Timber
Winding handle discs	Make from	298 × 197 × 9mm (11¾ × 7¾ × ⅜in)	Plywood
spindles	Make from	991mm (39in) long × 16mm (⅝in) diameter dowel	
blocks	Make from	286 × 44 × 22mm (11¼ × 1¾ × ⅞in)	Timber
Starwheel	Make from	96 × 44 × 12mm (3¾ × 1¾ × ½in)	Plywood
Locking lever	2 off	178 × 70 × 9mm (7 × 2¾ × ⅜in)	Plywood
Jib arm side plates	2 off	1670 × 111 × 22mm (65¾ × 4⅜ × ⅞in)	Timber
pivot pin	1 off	254mm (10in) long × 16mm (⅝in) diameter dowel	
cross members	7 off	102 × 35 × 25mm (4 × 1⅜ × 1in)	Timber
	1 off	165 × 35 × 25mm (6½ × 1⅜ × 1in)	Timber
Central jib cross member	1 off	305 × 102 × 25mm (12 × 4 × 1in)	Timber
Front jib cross member	1 off	127 × 102 × 25mm (5 × 4 × 1in)	Timber
Bucket support frame	1 off	235 × 35 × 22mm (9¼ × 1⅜ × ⅞in)	Timber
	2 off	260 × 25 × 22mm (10¼ × 1 × ⅞in)	Timber
	2 off	197 × 35 × 25mm (7¾ × 1⅜ × 1in)	Timber
	4 off	44mm (1¾in) long × 9mm (⅜in) diameter dowel	
Bucket	4 off	229 × 140 × 9mm (9 × 5½ × ⅜in)	Plywood
	2 off	241 × 203 × 6mm (9½ × 8 × ¼in)	Plywood
	2 off	86 × 203 × 6mm (3⅜ × 8 × ¼in)	Plywood

| Lifting block | 1 off | 140 × 70 × 70mm (5½ × 2¾ × 2¾in) | Timber |

Ancillaries

	4 off	203mm (8in) diameter road wheels
	2 off	178mm (7in) long × 12mm (½in) diameter steel front axles
	1 off	546mm (21½in) long × 12mm (½in) diameter steel rear axle
	4 off	Plain washers to suit 12mm (½in) diameter axles
	6 off	Spring dome caps to suit 12mm (½in) diameter axles
	1 off	140mm (5½in) long × 9mm (⅜in) diameter coach bolt
	1 off	Lock washer and nut to suit
	4 off	64mm (2½in) long × 6mm (¼in) diameter coach bolts
	4 off	Lock washers and nuts to suit
	1 off	4500mm (180in) length of strong rope
	9 off	51mm (2in) long × 9mm (⅜in) o/d × 6mm (¼in) i/d plastic tubes
	1 off	191 × 20mm (7½ × ¾in) wide webbing
	3 off	Brass upholstery pins
	10 off	20mm (¾in) screwed eyes
	2 off	54mm (2⅛in) long × 6mm (¼in) diameter coach bolts
	2 off	Lock washers and nuts to suit
	2 off	32mm (1¼in) long × 6mm (¼in) diameter round headed bolts
	4 off	Plain washers to suit
	2 off	Lock washers and nuts to suit
	3 off	Staples to secure cables to winding handles
	1 off	635mm (25in) length of chain for lifting block

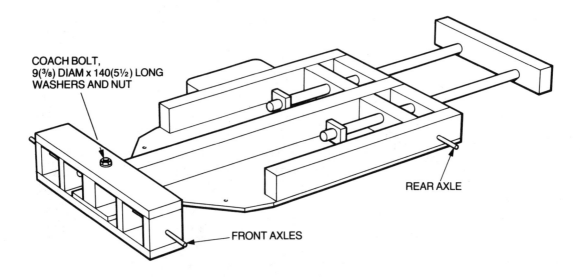

COACH BOLT,
9(⅜) DIAM x 140(5½) LONG
WASHERS AND NUT

REAR AXLE

FRONT AXLES

**VIEW ON UNDERSIDE OF CHASSIS, FRONT
AXLE AND STABILIZER ASSEMBLY**

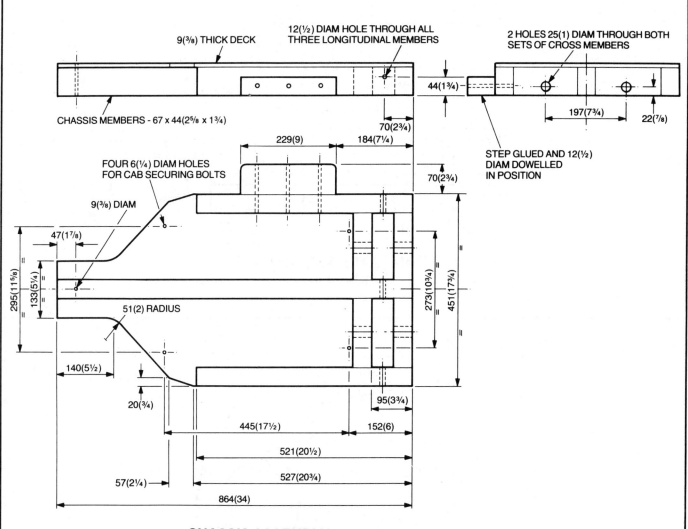

9(3/8) THICK DECK

12(1/2) DIAM HOLE THROUGH ALL THREE LONGITUDINAL MEMBERS

2 HOLES 25(1) DIAM THROUGH BOTH SETS OF CROSS MEMBERS

CHASSIS MEMBERS - 67 x 44(2⁵/₈ x 1³/₄)

44(1³/₄)

197(7³/₄)

22(⁷/₈)

70(2³/₄)

STEP GLUED AND 12(1/2) DIAM DOWELLED IN POSITION

FOUR 6(1/4) DIAM HOLES FOR CAB SECURING BOLTS

9(3/8) DIAM

229(9)

184(7¹/₄)

70(2³/₄)

47(1⁷/₈)

295(11⁵/₈)

133(5¹/₄)

273(10³/₄)

451(17³/₄)

51(2) RADIUS

140(5¹/₂)

20(³/₄)

95(3³/₄)

445(17¹/₂)

152(6)

521(20¹/₂)

527(20³/₄)

57(2¹/₄)

864(34)

CHASSIS ASSEMBLY

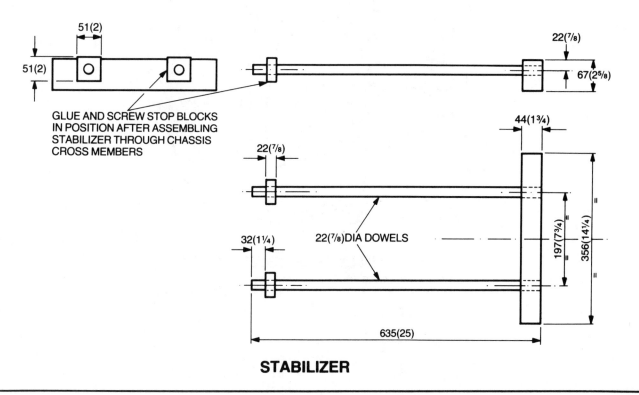

51(2)

51(2)

22(⁷/₈)

67(2⁵/₈)

GLUE AND SCREW STOP BLOCKS IN POSITION AFTER ASSEMBLING STABILIZER THROUGH CHASSIS CROSS MEMBERS

44(1³/₄)

22(⁷/₈)

22(⁷/₈) DIA DOWELS

32(1¹/₄)

197(7³/₄)

356(14¹/₄)

635(25)

STABILIZER

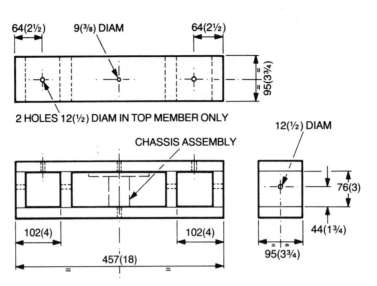

64(2½)   9(⅜) DIAM   64(2½)

2 HOLES 12(½) DIAM IN TOP MEMBER ONLY

95(3¾)

CHASSIS ASSEMBLY

12(½) DIAM

76(3)

102(4)   102(4)

44(1¾)

457(18)

95(3¾)

FRONT AXLE ASSEMBLY
22(⅞) THICK

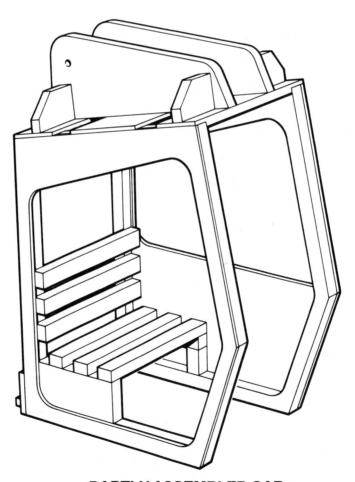

PARTLY ASSEMBLED CAB
CAB ASSEMBLY SECURED TO CHASSIS WITH FOUR
6(¼) DIAM x 64(2½) LONG COACH BOLTS, WASHERS AND NUTS

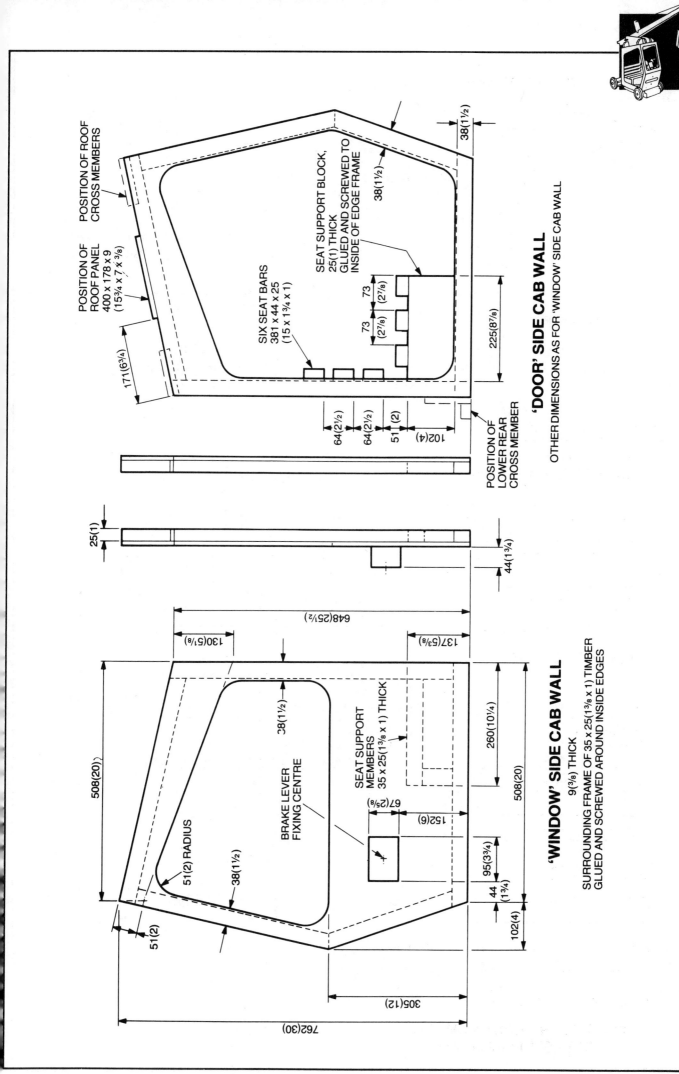

'DOOR' SIDE CAB WALL

OTHER DIMENSIONS AS FOR 'WINDOW' SIDE CAB WALL

POSITION OF ROOF CROSS MEMBERS

POSITION OF ROOF PANEL 400 x 178 x 9 (15¾ x 7 x ⅜)

171 (6¾)

38 (1½)

38 (1½)

SEAT SUPPORT BLOCK, 25(1) THICK GLUED AND SCREWED TO INSIDE OF EDGE FRAME

SIX SEAT BARS 381 x 44 x 25 (15 x 1¾ x 1)

73 (2⅞) 73 (2⅞)

225 (8⅞)

64 (2½) 64 (2½) 51 (2)

102 (4)

POSITION OF LOWER REAR CROSS MEMBER

25 (1)

44 (1¾)

'WINDOW' SIDE CAB WALL

9 (⅜) THICK

SURROUNDING FRAME OF 35 x 25 (1⅜ x 1) TIMBER GLUED AND SCREWED AROUND INSIDE EDGES

648 (25½)

130 (5⅝)

137 (5⅜)

38 (1½)

508 (20)

51 (2) RADIUS

BRAKE LEVER FIXING CENTRE

38 (1½)

51 (2)

51 (2)

SEAT SUPPORT MEMBERS 35 x 25 (1⅜ x 1) THICK

260 (10¼)

508 (20)

67 (2⅝)

152 (6)

95 (3¾)

44 (1¾)

102 (4)

305 (12)

762 (30)

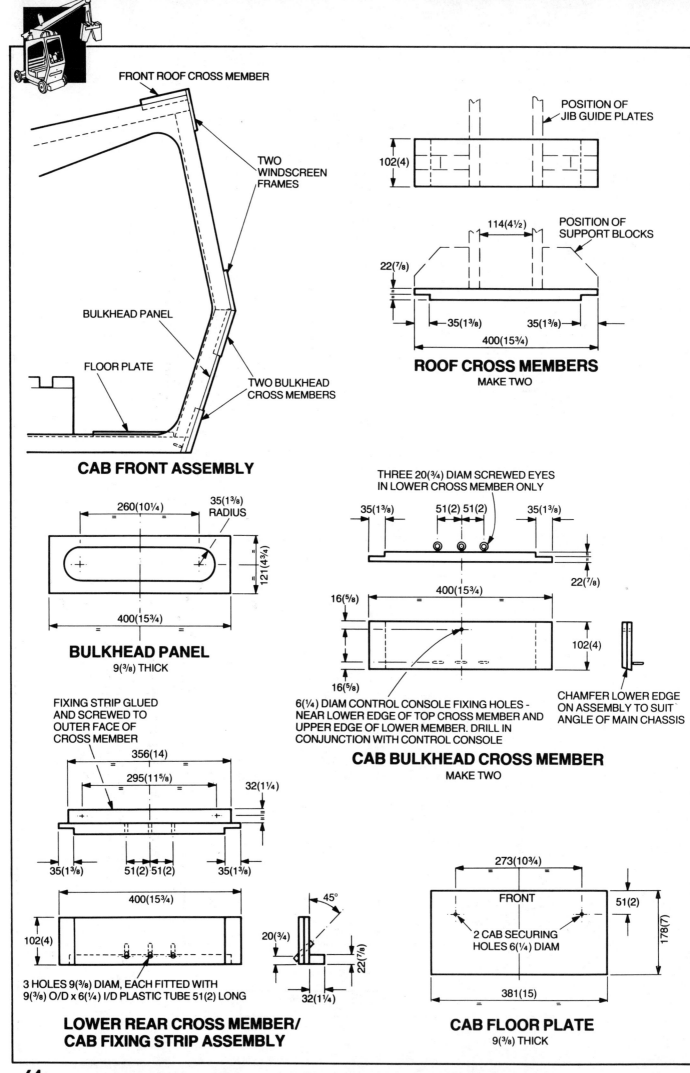

FRONT ROOF CROSS MEMBER

TWO WINDSCREEN FRAMES

BULKHEAD PANEL

FLOOR PLATE

TWO BULKHEAD CROSS MEMBERS

CAB FRONT ASSEMBLY

POSITION OF JIB GUIDE PLATES

102(4)

POSITION OF SUPPORT BLOCKS

114(4½)

22(⅞)

35(1⅜) 35(1⅜)

400(15¾)

ROOF CROSS MEMBERS
MAKE TWO

260(10¼)

35(1⅜) RADIUS

121(4¾)

400(15¾)

BULKHEAD PANEL
9(⅜) THICK

THREE 20(¾) DIAM SCREWED EYES IN LOWER CROSS MEMBER ONLY

35(1⅜)   51(2) 51(2)   35(1⅜)

22(⅞)

16(⅝)

400(15¾)

102(4)

16(⅝)

6(¼) DIAM CONTROL CONSOLE FIXING HOLES - NEAR LOWER EDGE OF TOP CROSS MEMBER AND UPPER EDGE OF LOWER MEMBER. DRILL IN CONJUNCTION WITH CONTROL CONSOLE

CHAMFER LOWER EDGE ON ASSEMBLY TO SUIT ANGLE OF MAIN CHASSIS

CAB BULKHEAD CROSS MEMBER
MAKE TWO

FIXING STRIP GLUED AND SCREWED TO OUTER FACE OF CROSS MEMBER

356(14)

295(11⅝)

32(1¼)

35(1⅜)   51(2) 51(2)   35(1⅜)

400(15¾)

102(4)

45°

20(¾)

22(⅞)

32(1¼)

3 HOLES 9(⅜) DIAM, EACH FITTED WITH 9(⅜) O/D x 6(¼) I/D PLASTIC TUBE 51(2) LONG

LOWER REAR CROSS MEMBER/ CAB FIXING STRIP ASSEMBLY

273(10¾)

FRONT

51(2)

178(7)

2 CAB SECURING HOLES 6(¼) DIAM

381(15)

CAB FLOOR PLATE
9(⅜) THICK

·OUTDOOR TOYS·

Instructions and plans for these toys can be found on pages 29 to 41

REB 1

BRAKE LEVER
20(¾) THICK

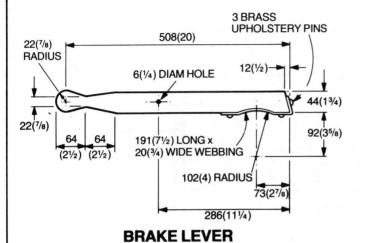

3 BRASS
UPHOLSTERY PINS

508(20)

22(⅞)
RADIUS

6(¼) DIAM HOLE

12(½)

44(1¾)

92(3⅝)

22(⅞)

64
(2½)

64
(2½)

191(7½) LONG x
20(¾) WIDE WEBBING

102(4) RADIUS

73(2⅞)

286(11¼)

WINDSCREEN FRAME
MAKE TWO   9(⅜) THICK
LOWER EDGE OF BOTTOM FRAME TO
BE CHAMFERED ON ASSEMBLY

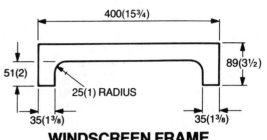

400(15¾)

51(2)

89(3½)

25(1) RADIUS

35(1⅜)

35(1⅜)

JIB GUIDE PLATES
MAKE TWO   22(⅞) THICK

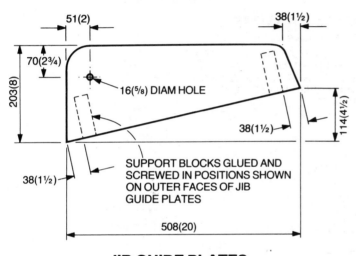

51(2)

38(1½)

70(2¾)

203(8)

16(⅝) DIAM HOLE

114(4½)

38(1½)

38(1½)

SUPPORT BLOCKS GLUED AND
SCREWED IN POSITIONS SHOWN
ON OUTER FACES OF JIB
GUIDE PLATES

508(20)

SUPPORT BLOCKS
MAKE FOUR   28(1⅛) THICK

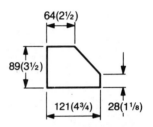

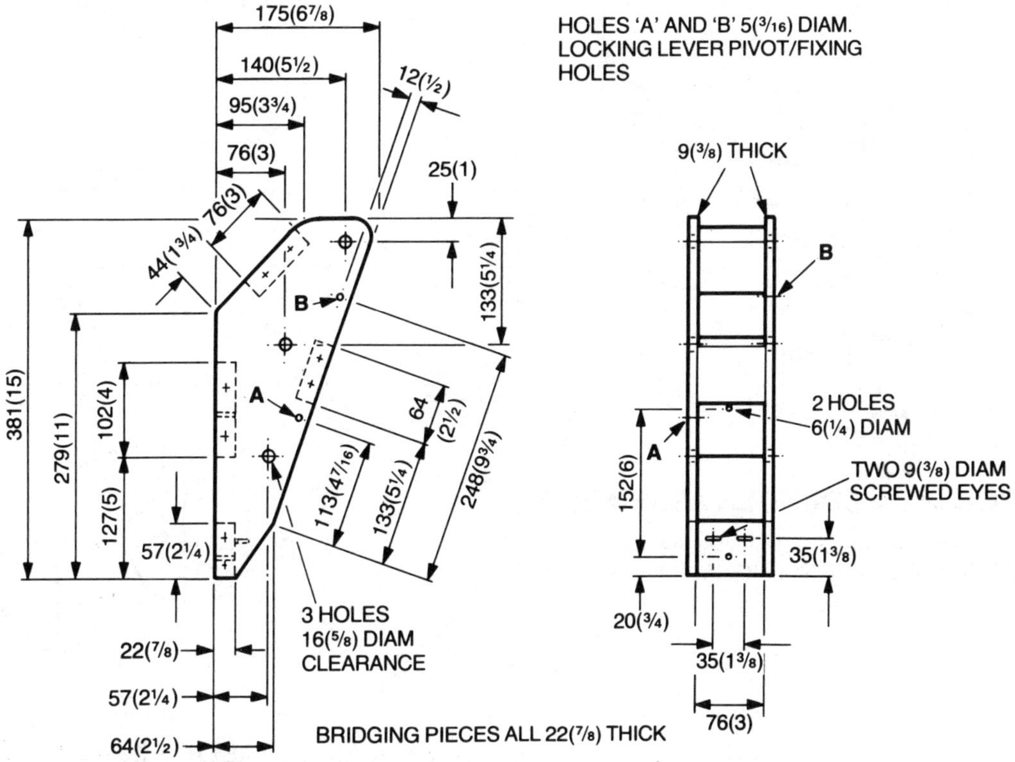

64(2½)

89(3½)

121(4¾)

28(1⅛)

CONTROL CONSOLE FRAME ASSEMBLY

175(6⅞)

140(5½)

95(3¾)

76(3)

12(½)

25(1)

76(3)

44(1¾)

133(5¼)

B

381(15)

279(11)

102(4)

127(5)

A

64
(2½)

248(9¾)

57(2¼)

113(4⁷/₁₆)

133(5¼)

22(⅞)

57(2¼)

3 HOLES
16(⅝) DIAM
CLEARANCE

64(2½)

BRIDGING PIECES ALL 22(⅞) THICK

HOLES 'A' AND 'B' 5(³/₁₆) DIAM.
LOCKING LEVER PIVOT/FIXING
HOLES

9(⅜) THICK

B

2 HOLES
6(¼) DIAM

TWO 9(⅜) DIAM
SCREWED EYES

152(6)

A

35(1⅜)

20(¾)

35(1⅜)

76(3)

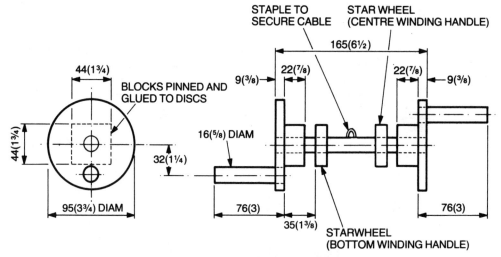

STAPLE TO
SECURE CABLE

STAR WHEEL
(CENTRE WINDING HANDLE)

44(1¾)

BLOCKS PINNED AND
GLUED TO DISCS

44(1¾)

32(1¼)

95(3¾) DIAM

165(6½)

9(³⁄₈) 22(⁷⁄₈) 22(⁷⁄₈) 9(³⁄₈)

16(⁵⁄₈) DIAM

76(3)

35(1³⁄₈)

STARWHEEL
(BOTTOM WINDING HANDLE)

76(3)

WINDING HANDLE ASSEMBLY

MAKE THREE (ONLY 2 WITH STARWHEELS)

STARWHEEL PINNED TO SPINDLE AND SECOND HANDLE DISC
SECURED IN POSITION AS CONSOLE FRAME IS ASSEMBLED.
WATCH CONFIGURATION OF STARWHEEL WITH DIRECTION OF
ROTATION OF HANDLE, LOCKING LEVER TO ENGAGE IN STARWHEEL
CUTOUT TO HOLD 'LOAD' IN PLACE

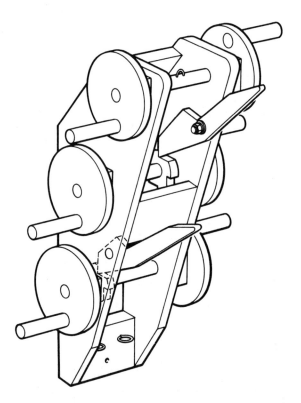

CONTROL CONSOLE ASSEMBLY

SECURED TO CAB BULKHEAD CROSS MEMBERS WITH TWO
6(¼) DIAM x 54(2⅛) LONG COACH BOLTS, WASHERS AND NUTS

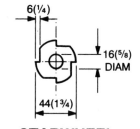

6(¼)

16(⁵⁄₈)
DIAM

44(1¾)

STARWHEEL

MAKE TWO   12(½) THICK

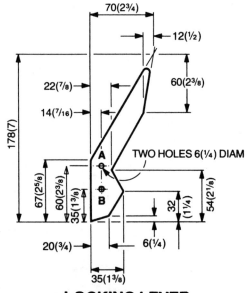

70(2¾)

12(½)

60(2³⁄₈)

22(⁷⁄₈)

14(⁷⁄₁₆)

178(7)

TWO HOLES 6(¼) DIAM

A

B

67(2⅝)

60(2³⁄₈)

35(1³⁄₈)

35

32
(1¼)

54(2⅛)

20(¾)

6(¼)

35(1³⁄₈)

LOCKING LEVER

MAKE TWO   9(³⁄₈) THICK

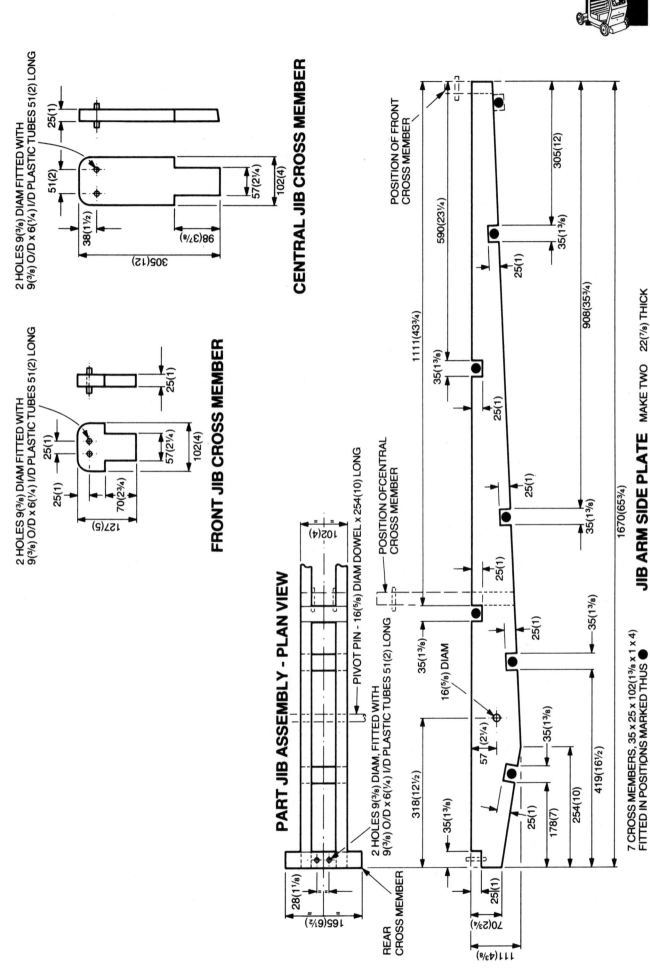

CENTRAL JIB CROSS MEMBER

2 HOLES 9(³⁄₈) DIAM FITTED WITH
9(³⁄₈) O/D x 6(¹⁄₄) I/D PLASTIC TUBES 51(2) LONG

25(1)

51(2)

38(1½)

102(4)

57(2¼)

98(3⁷⁄₈)

305(12)

FRONT JIB CROSS MEMBER

2 HOLES 9(³⁄₈) DIAM FITTED WITH
9(³⁄₈) O/D x 6(¹⁄₄) I/D PLASTIC TUBES 51(2) LONG

25(1)

25(1)

25(1)

102(4)

57(2¼)

70(2¾)

127(5)

PART JIB ASSEMBLY - PLAN VIEW

102(4)

PIVOT PIN - 16(⁵⁄₈) DIAM DOWEL x 254(10) LONG

POSITION OF CENTRAL
CROSS MEMBER

2 HOLES 9(³⁄₈) DIAM, FITTED WITH
9(³⁄₈) O/D x 6(¹⁄₄) I/D PLASTIC TUBES 51(2) LONG

28(1⅛)

165(6½)

REAR
CROSS MEMBER

JIB ARM SIDE PLATE   MAKE TWO   22(⁷⁄₈) THICK

POSITION OF FRONT
CROSS MEMBER

305(12)

590(23¾)

35(1³⁄₈)

25(1)

908(35¾)

1111(43¾)

35(1³⁄₈)

25(1)

25(1)

35(1³⁄₈)

25(1)

35(1³⁄₈)

1670(65¾)

318(12½)

35(1³⁄₈)

35(1³⁄₈)

16(⁵⁄₈) DIAM

57

25(1)

178(7)

254(10)

419(16½)

35(1³⁄₈)

25(1)

70(2¾)

111(4³⁄₈)

7 CROSS MEMBERS, 35 x 25 x 102(1³⁄₈ x 1 x 4)
FITTED IN POSITIONS MARKED THUS ●

67

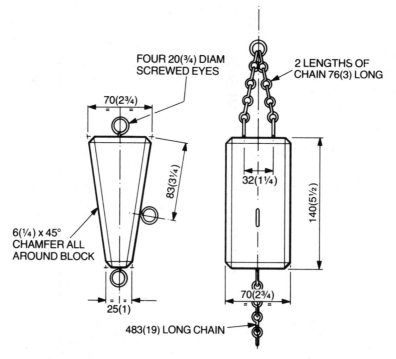

FOUR 20(¾) DIAM SCREWED EYES

2 LENGTHS OF CHAIN 76(3) LONG

70(2¾)

83(3¼)

32(1¼)

140(5½)

6(¼) x 45° CHAMFER ALL AROUND BLOCK

25(1)

70(2¾)

483(19) LONG CHAIN

LIFTING TACKLE AND CHAINS

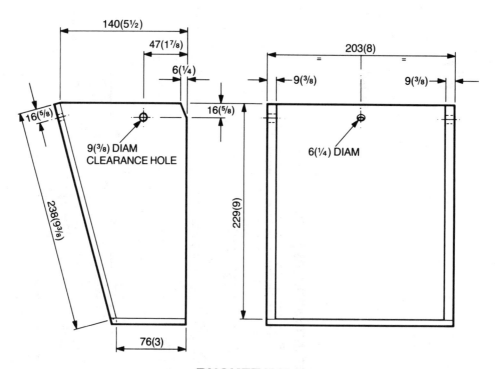

140(5½)

47(1⅞)

6(¼)

16(⅝)

203(8)

9(⅜)

9(⅜)

16(⅝)

9(⅜) DIAM CLEARANCE HOLE

6(¼) DIAM

238(9⅜)

229(9)

76(3)

BUCKET HALF
MAKE TWO

SIDE WALLS - 9(⅜) THICK
INCLINED WALL AND FLOOR 6(¼) THICK

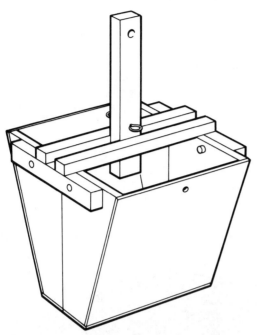

BUCKET AND SUPPORT FRAME ASSEMBLY

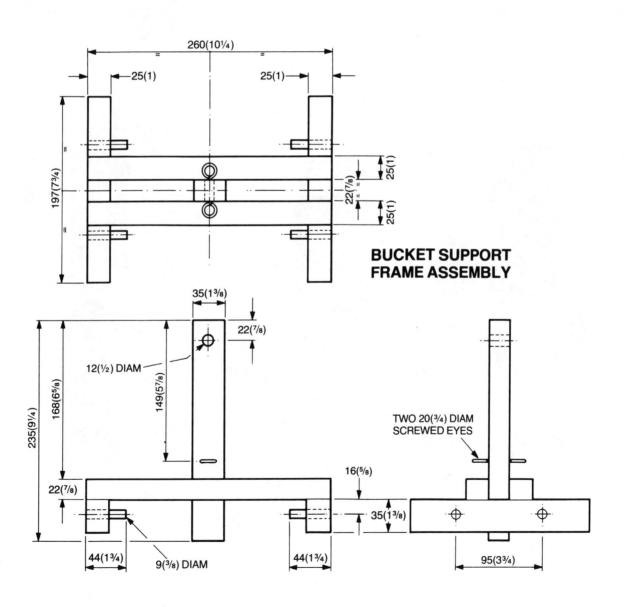

BUCKET SUPPORT FRAME ASSEMBLY

260(10¼)

25(1) 25(1)

197(7¾)

25(1)
22(⁷⁄₈)
25(1)

35(1³⁄₈)

22(⁷⁄₈)

12(½) DIAM

149(5⁷⁄₈)

168(6⁵⁄₈)

235(9¼)

TWO 20(¾) DIAM
SCREWED EYES

16(⁵⁄₈)

22(⁷⁄₈)

35(1³⁄₈)

44(1¾)

9(³⁄₈) DIAM

44(1¾)

95(3¾)

PLAY HOUSE

Young children have wonderfully refreshing imaginations. Just listen to any group of youngsters playing and you will discover that the tricycle is a star ship, a large cardboard box is a jungle in darkest Peru and the sand pit is a desert with forts and the Foreign Legion!

Now build a playhouse and you will suddenly discover that the garden is full of wolves and dozens of little pigs all trying to get through the door to safety at the same time. Alternatively, Little Red Riding Hood is walking through the forest (cabbage garden) pursued by a hungry looking wolf in wellington boots, cowboy hat and quite naturally on his or her trusty steed the tricycle.

This play house has room for tables, chairs, cooker etc. and four young children. If you intend to leave the house erected in summer months it is necessary to screw the roof into place otherwise an occasional gust of wind may blow the roof off.

Basic construction

Four equal sides of plywood are joined together at the corners. The ends fit into 'slots' and are then held in place by coach bolts. Two roof beams hold the apex ends in place and a ridge board secures them at the top. The roof covering is made from two sheets of melamine faced hardboard. The two sheets are laced together at the top with a length of nylon cord.

1   Plywood is available in sheet form measuring 8′ x 4′. Two sheets cut in half form the basic house.

2   The corners are joined together by wood strip guides. These slots are formed by screwing strips of timber onto the two end walls of the house. First screw one strip onto the outside edge of the wall. Now position pieces of scrap 9mm (⅜in) plywood against the first strip and position the second strip against these. A push fit is ideal – remember that after painting or varnishing the wood will be fractionally thicker and the fit tighter. Very tight joints make it very difficult to assemble and dismantle the house.

3   When a push fit has been achieved, drill holes at top and bottom right through the strips and the wall. The diameter of the hole will depend on the coach bolts available. It is advisable to buy 'wing' nuts for the bolts then you will be able to assemble and dismantle without a spanner.

4   Coach bolts are available in a variety of lengths. When buying bolts for this house I found the bolt end projecting some way beyond the wing nut. It is very important that this extra length is cut off with a hacksaw, otherwise some very nasty scratches will result.

5   The four wood strip guides are screwed onto all the end walls. The screws need to be put in on the plywood side of the wall, screwing into the wood strip. Make sure to countersink all screw heads.

6   Mark out the door and window with a good bold pencil line. All internal cuts have a common problem

and that is all conventional saws have a back or frame which cannot be used on this sort of cut. The hand saw for this task is a keyhole saw, but frequently the size of the teeth tend to tear the layers of plywood and leave ugly 'spilches'.

It is therefore well worth considering the purchase of a jigsaw or attachment for the electric drill. This tool is easy to operate and if you fit a metal cutting blade its fine teeth will help prevent the 'spilches' when cutting the plywood.

7   Drill several small holes in a line along the window line. Enlarge the holes just enough to get the jigsaw blade in. By using this method all the windows and the door can be cut out.

8   After cutting out, work around the edges with glasspaper to remove any small splinters and roughness.

9   The door will get a great deal of use so it must be fixed very securely. Two battens are screwed, one onto the door, the other onto the wall. The hinges are then screwed onto the battens. This method of fixing is far better than attaching the hinges direct onto the plywood

10   Assemble the four walls and bolt them together. Position the roof beams and mark where the notches need to be cut in the roof beams and side walls.

11   Now notch the top of the roof beams to take the two triangular 'A' frames.

12   As the notches in the roof beams are near the ends there is a tendency for the pieces to break off, due to the direction of the grain. To prevent this happening, laminate (stick on) small pieces of plywood and notch these in exactly the same way as the roof beams.

13   Mark and cut out a pair of roof 'A' frames (triangles) cutting notches to take the roof beams.

14   The roof panels are stiffened with four wood strips along the edges. Holes are drilled in the panels to take nylon cord which forms the hinge at the top. It is advisable to use an oil tempered hardboard which is resistant to rain.

15 The door catch can be fixed either on the outside or inside. I favour the catch fitted on the inside. The advantage here is that a young child can never get shut in by being unable to reach the latch. Don't forget that the hinges will need to be sited on the opposite side from the catch.

16 The door catch and latch bar are cut from pine. The latch is fixed on with a small nut and bolt.

17 If the house is to be left outside it is recommended that it is painted, and four temporary screws fitted at the four corners of the roof.

Cutting list

Front and rear walls	2 off	1220 × 1220 × 9mm (48 × 48 × ³⁄₈in)	Plywood
	2 off	610 × 25 × 16mm (24 × 1 × ⁵⁄₈in)	Timber
Door catch	1 off	102 × 28 × 25mm (4 × 1⅛ × 1in)	Timber
Door catch latch	1 off	165 × 25 × 16mm (6½ × 1 × ⁵⁄₈in)	Timber
End walls	2 off	1220 × 1220 × 9mm (48 × 48 × ³⁄₈in)	Plywood
	8 off	1220 × 25 × 22mm (48 × 1 × ⅞in)	Timber
Roof beams	2 off	1366 × 70 × 22mm (53¾ × 2¾ × ⅞in)	Timber
Roof 'A' frames	2 off	1170 × 305 × 9mm (46 × 12 × ³⁄₈in)	Plywood
Ridge board	1 off	1366 × 70 × 22mm (53¾ × 2¾ × ⅞in)	Timber
Roof panels	2 off	1220 × 762 × 3mm (48 × 30 × ⅛in)	Hardboard
	4 off	762 × 98 × 22mm (30 × 3⅞ × ⅞in)	Timber

Ancillaries

	2 off	51mm (2in) long brass hinges and screws	
	Strong cord to lace the roof		

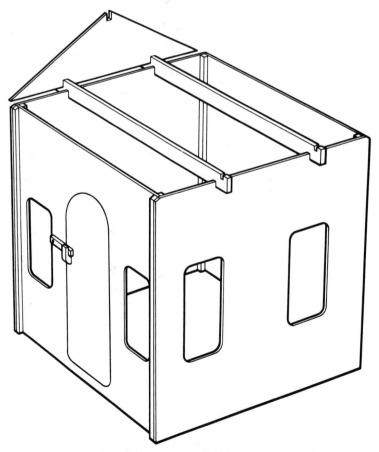

**PARTIALLY ASSEMBLED HOUSE
(showing position of ROOF BEAMS and slot in
ROOF 'A' FRAME for the ROOF RIDGE BOARD)**

CHAMFER TO SUIT SLOPE OF ROOF

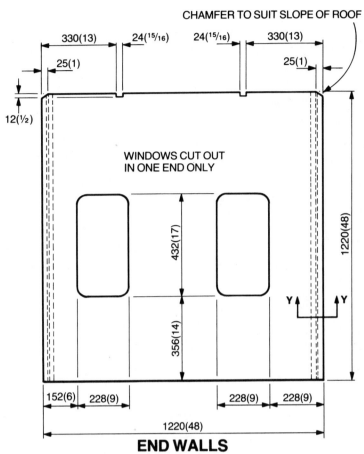

330(13) 24(¹⁵/₁₆)   24(¹⁵/₁₆) 330(13)

25(1)   25(1)

12(½)

WINDOWS CUT OUT
IN ONE END ONLY

432(17)

356(14)

1220(48)

Y   Y

152(6) 228(9)   228(9) 228(9)

1220(48)

END WALLS

9(³/₈) THICK   MAKE TWO

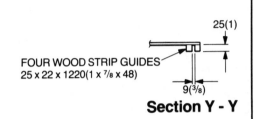

25(1)

FOUR WOOD STRIP GUIDES
25 x 22 x 1220(1 x ⁷/₈ x 48)

9(³/₈)

Section Y - Y

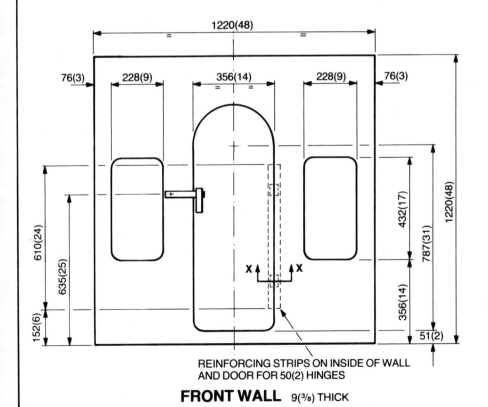

1220(48)

76(3) 228(9)   356(14)   228(9) 76(3)

610(24)

635(25)

152(6)

432(17)

787(31)

1220(48)

356(14)

51(2)

X   X

REINFORCING STRIPS ON INSIDE OF WALL
AND DOOR FOR 50(2) HINGES

FRONT WALL   9(³/₈) THICK

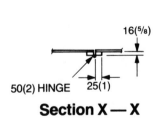

16(⁵/₈)

50(2) HINGE   25(1)

Section X — X

NOTE: All walls viewed from outside the building

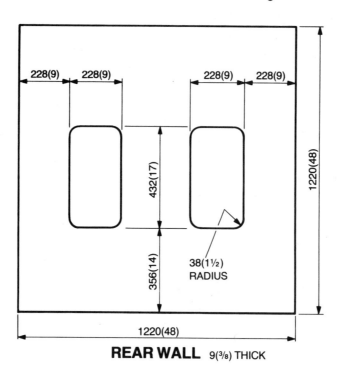

228(9) 228(9)   228(9) 228(9)

432(17)

356(14)

38(1½)
RADIUS

1220(48)

1220(48)

REAR WALL 9(³/₈) THICK

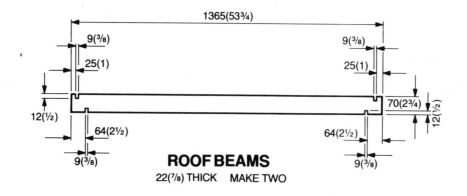

1365(53¾)

9(³/₈)   9(³/₈)

25(1)   25(1)

12(½)   70(2¾)   12(½)

64(2½)   64(2½)

9(³/₈)   9(³/₈)

ROOF BEAMS
22(⁷/₈) THICK   MAKE TWO

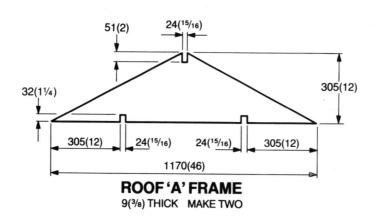

51(2)   24(¹⁵/₁₆)

32(1¼)   305(12)

305(12)   24(¹⁵/₁₆)   24(¹⁵/₁₆)   305(12)

1170(46)

ROOF 'A' FRAME
9(³/₈) THICK   MAKE TWO

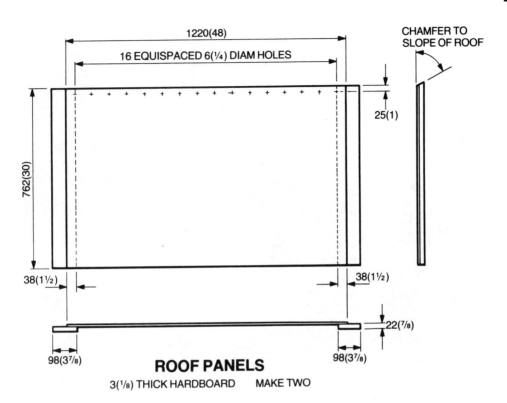

1220(48)

16 EQUISPACED 6(¼) DIAM HOLES

762(30)

CHAMFER TO
SLOPE OF ROOF

25(1)

38(1½)   38(1½)

22(⅞)

98(3⅞)   98(3⅞)

ROOF PANELS

3(⅛) THICK HARDBOARD   MAKE TWO

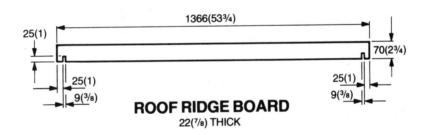

1366(53¾)

25(1)

70(2¾)

25(1)   25(1)

9(⅜)   9(⅜)

ROOF RIDGE BOARD

22(⅞) THICK

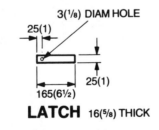

3(⅛) DIAM HOLE

25(1)

25(1)

165(6½)

LATCH 16(⅝) THICK

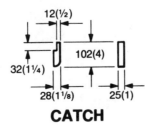

12(½)

32(1¼)

102(4)

28(1⅛)   25(1)

CATCH

TABLE AND BENCHES

To keep construction methods as simple as possible, I have designed both table and benches to be made in the same way, the only difference being the relative sizes of legs, rails, etc.

1 The three-dimensional drawing showing the underside of the table illustrates very clearly the construction.

2 The only two joints used are the halving joint and mortice and tenon.

3 The mortice and tenon is perhaps the only specialist joint that requires a marking gauge which some do-it-yourself carpenters may not possess.

4 Table and benches all have a foot, top support and leg.

5 The top and foot are jointed to the leg by halving joints. As the name suggests half of the leg is cut away and half the foot support, thus allowing both pieces to be assembled together.

6 From the drawings mark off the positions of the joints. When you are sure that all is right (check twice cut once) start cutting the halving joint on the leg. Cleaner cuts are always made if, before cutting with the saw, you use a marking knife to go over the pencil lines.

7 The secret of good joints is always clear precise marking cut.

8 The other joint is the mortice and tenon. A mortice is a hole and a tenon the piece of wood that goes into it. You will need a mortice or firmer chisel to cut the hole. The position of the mortice is marked by using a mortice gauge. This gauge has two sharp points on it that gouge out two parallel 'tracks' in the wood showing where to cut the mortice hole.

The mortice hole is cut in the legs and the tenon on the ends of the rail.

9 On the outside edge of the leg the mortice hole is elongated, this is done to take a wooden wedge that will be hammered and glued in when final assembly takes place.

10 Only after all the joints have been cut is any shaping done. Besides the use of bow or coping saw to get the curves on the legs you will find a spokeshave useful.

11 Holes are drilled in the top supports to take the screws that hold the table and bench tops on.

12 The tops are formed by strips of batton screwed on to the underside of the plywood top.

13 You will need a cramp to hold the joints firmly together while the glue is setting. The procedure is:

   i Glue the top and foot to the leg.

   ii Glue the leg tie bar in to the legs. Hold in place with a cramp while little wooden wedges are glued in. A small hammer is needed to tap the wedges in place.

   iii Clean off any surplus glue.

   iv Screw the top on.

Cutting list

Bench			
Top	1 off	610 x 279 x 9mm (24 x 11 x ⅜in)	Plywood
	2 off	610 x 22 x 16mm (24 x ⅞ x ⁵⁄₁₆in)	Timber
	2 off	235 x 22 x 16mm (9¼ x ⅞ x ⅝in)	Timber
Top support	2 off	229 x 41 x 22mm (9 x 1⅝ x ⅞in)	Timber
Leg	2 off	229 x 95 x 22mm (9 x 3¾ x ⅞in)	Timber
Foot	2 off	305 x 73 x 22mm (12 x 2⅞ x ⅞in)	Timber
Tie bar	1 off	521 x 57 x 22mm (20½ x 2¼ x ⅞in)	Timber
Table			
Table top	1 off	762 x 349 x 9mm (30 x 13¾ x ⅜in)	Plywood
	2 off	762 x 22 x 16mm (30 x ⅞ x ⅝in)	Timber
	2 off	305 x 22 x 16mm (12 x ⅞ x ⅝in)	Timber
Top support	2 off	298 x 41 x 22mm (11¾ x 1⅝ x ⅞in)	Timber
Leg	2 off	406 x 95 x 22mm (16 x 3¾ x ⅞in)	Timber
Foot	2 off	381 x 73 x 22mm (15 x 2⅞ x ⅞in)	Timber
Tie bar	1 off	584 x 83 x 22mm (23 x 3¼ x ⅞in)	Timber

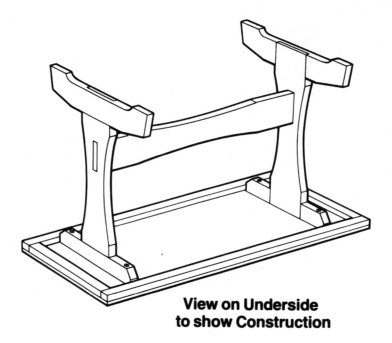

**View on Underside
to show Construction**

BENCH TOP - 610 x 279 x 9(24 x 11 x ³/₈)

610(24)

16 FIXING SCREWS AND CUP WASHERS

279(11)

POSITION OF SUPPORT LEGS

22 x 16(⁷/₈ x ⁵/₈) REINFORCING FRAME

521(20½)

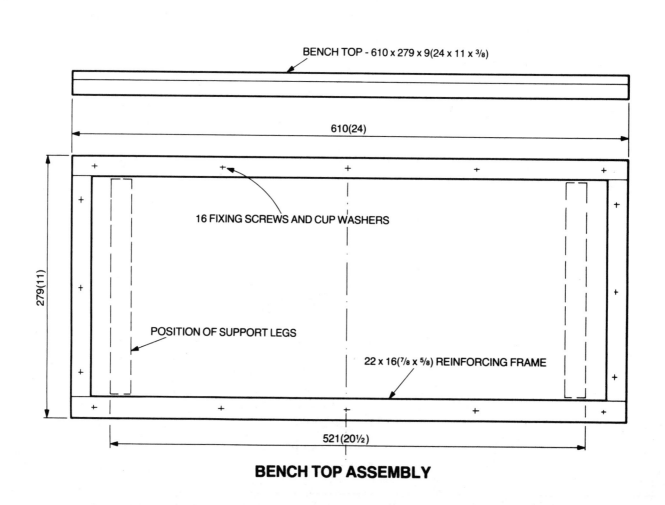

BENCH TOP ASSEMBLY

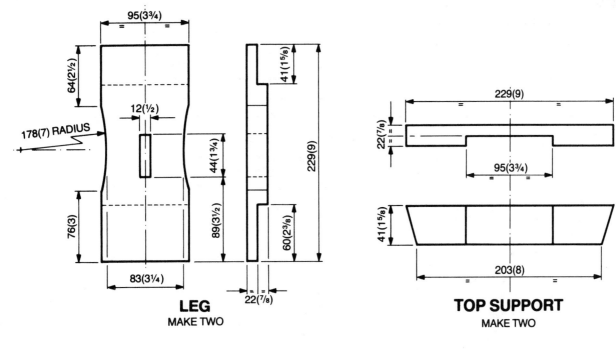

LEG
MAKE TWO

TOP SUPPORT
MAKE TWO

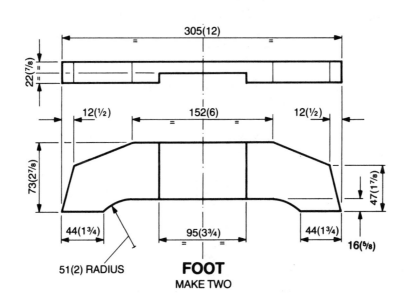

FOOT
MAKE TWO

51(2) RADIUS

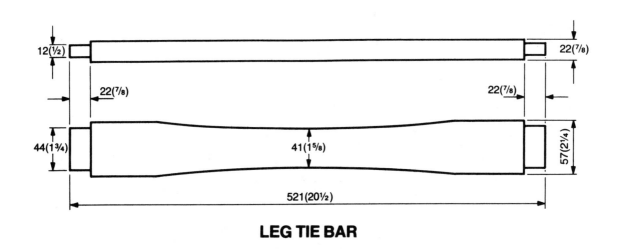

LEG TIE BAR

TABLE TOP - 762 x 349 x 9(30 x 13¾ x ⅜)

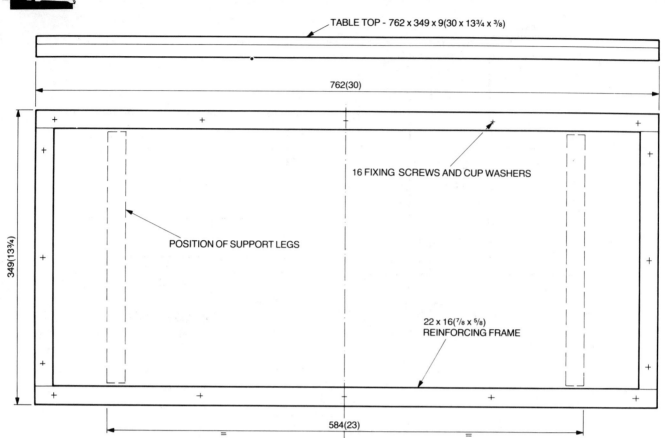

762(30)

349(13¾)

16 FIXING SCREWS AND CUP WASHERS

POSITION OF SUPPORT LEGS

22 x 16(⅞ x ⅝)
REINFORCING FRAME

584(23)

TABLE TOP ASSEMBLY

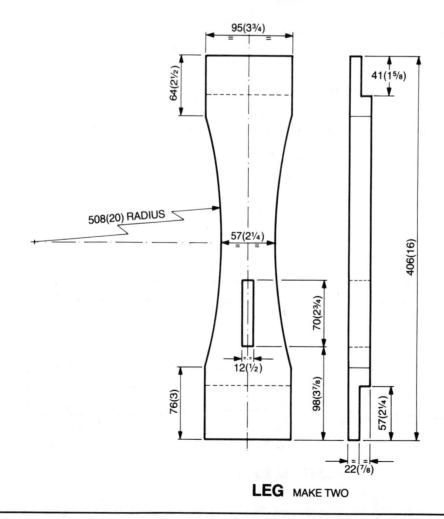

95(3¾)

64(2½)

41(1⅝)

508(20) RADIUS

57(2¼)

406(16)

70(2¾)

12(½)

98(3⅞)

76(3)

57(2¼)

22(⅞)

LEG MAKE TWO

TOP SUPPORT
MAKE TWO

298(11¾)

22(⅞)

95(3¾)

41(1⅝)

16(⅝)

16(⅝)

16(⅝)

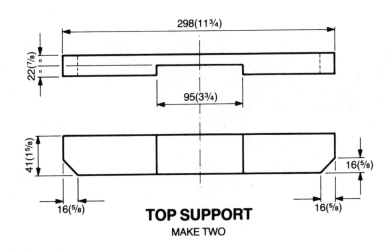

FOOT
MAKE TWO

381(15)

22(⅞)

12(½)

203(8)

12(½)

73(2⅞)

54(2⅛)

16(⅝)

51(2)

51(2)
RADIUS

95(3¾)

51(2)

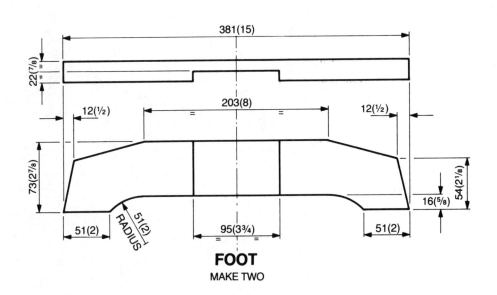

LEG TIE BAR

12(½)

22(⅞)

48(1⅞)

48(1⅞)

22(⅞)

22(⅞)

22(⅞)

70(2¾)

60(2⅜)

83(3¼)

584(23)

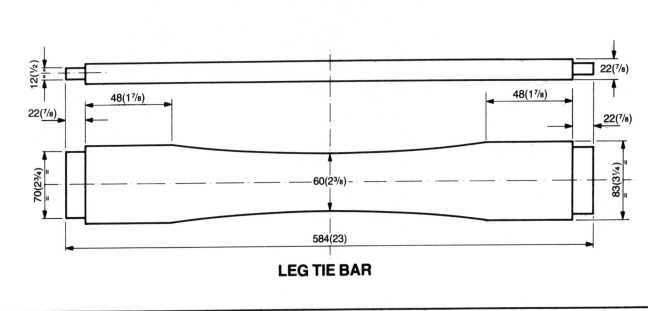

COOKER

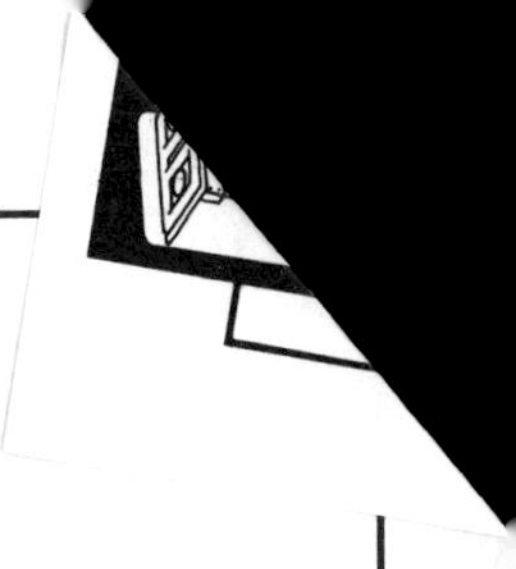

Many children thoroughly enjoy helping in the kitchen and therefore a small cooker is a real bonus. The little perspex window in the door will help to keep an eye on the pastries. To simulate nobs on the cooker I used three black wheels. The cooker burners were painted with silver paint.

1 Mark out and cut to size two side panels.

2 Cut out the back panel and radius the top corners.

3 The back is screwed in place and the front of the cooker held together by the two cross members.

4 To simulate control knobs I used small black wheels and spring caps. Any knob is suitable for this purpose.

5 The top is glued and panel pinned in place. The burners I made using a coping saw. The saucepan support frame is made from small strips of wood glued on to the top.

6 The door has a cut-out window which is covered with a perspex panel. This is not essential but makes a good feature.

7 Battens are screwed on to the top and bottom of the door. The top batten functions as the handle and the bottom one as a fixing point for the hinges.

8 Inside the cooker two small shelf supports are screwed on to the cooker sides. The shelf and supports are set back from the front of the cooker to allow the door to close.

9 Fit a small block of wood to act as a door stop. A small plastic door catch can be fitted in the top of the cross member.

10 To prevent accidental damage to cooker door when opening, screw eyes and nylon cord are attached inside.

Cutting list

Side panels	2 off	533 x 194 x 22mm (21 x 7⅝ x ⅞in)	Timber
Shelf supports	2 off	152 x 32 x 22mm (6 x 1¼ x ⅞in)	Timber
Shelf	1 off	305 x 159 x 9mm (12 x 6¼ x ⅜in)	Plywood
Base	1 off	349 x 191 x 22mm (13¾ x 7½ x ⅞in)	Timber
Back	1 off	584 x 349 x 9mm (23 x 13¾ x ⅜in)	Plywood
Top	1 off	349 x 200 x 6mm (13¾ x 7⅞ x ¼in)	Plywood
	2 off	311 x 20 x 9mm (12¼ x ¾ x ⅜in)	Plywood
	4 off	142 x 20 x 9mm (5⅝ x ¾ x ⅜in)	Plywood
	2 off	60mm (2⅜in) diameter x 9mm (⅜in) thick	Plywood
Cross members	2 off	349 x 54 x 22mm (13¾ x 2⅛ x ⅞in)	Timber
Door	1 off	422 x 302 x 9mm (16⅝ x 11⅞ x ⅜in)	Plywood
	1 off	302 x 38 x 22mm (11⅞ x 1½ x ⅞in)	Timber
	1 off	302 x 22 x 16mm (11⅞ x ⅞ x ⅝in)	Timber
Ancillaries			
	3 off	38mm (1½in) diameter wheels	
	3 off	57mm(2¼in) long x 6mm(¼in) diameter steel rods	
	6 off	Dome spring caps to suit 6mm (¼in) diameter rods	
	2 off	51mm (2in) chromed hinges and screws	
	2 off	Screwed eyes	
	1 off	305mm (12in) long length of nylon cord	
	1 off	254 x 127 x 2mm (10 x 5 x 1/16in) transparent plastic	

DOOR
STOP/CATCH

SHELF - 159 x 305 x 9
(6¼ x 12 x ⅜)
PINNED TO
SUPPORTS

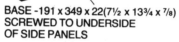

BASE -191 x 349 x 22(7½ x 13¾ x ⅞)
SCREWED TO UNDERSIDE
OF SIDE PANELS

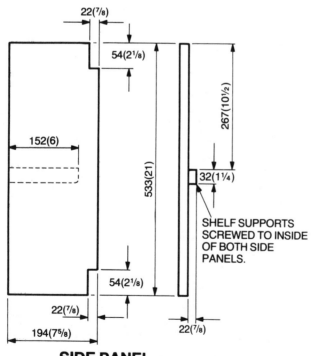

22(⅞)

54(2⅛)

152(6)

267(10½)

533(21)

32(1¼)

SHELF SUPPORTS
SCREWED TO INSIDE
OF BOTH SIDE
PANELS.

54(2⅛)

22(⅞)

194(7⅝)

22(⅞)

SIDE PANEL
22(⅞) THICK   MAKE TWO

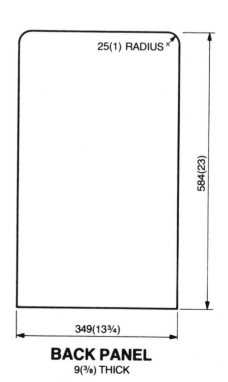

25(1) RADIUS

584(23)

349(13¾)

BACK PANEL
9(⅜) THICK

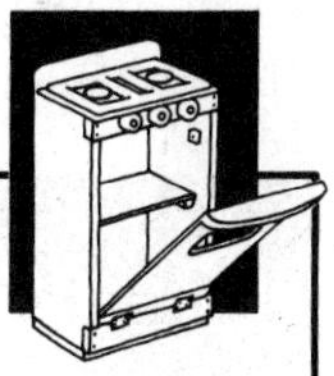

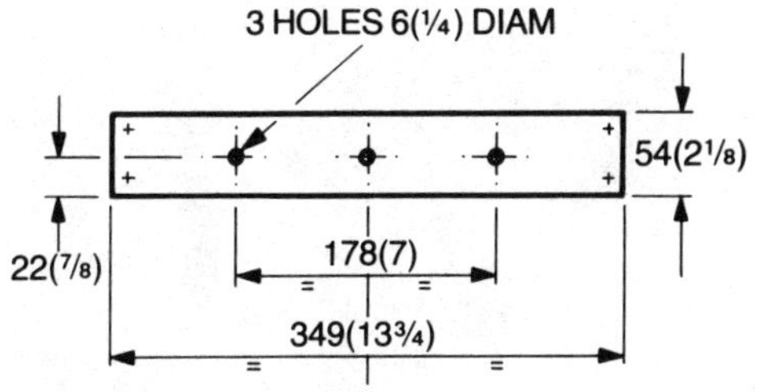
3 HOLES 6(1/4) DIAM
54(2 1/8)
22(7/8)
178(7)
349(13 3/4)

Control Knob Assembly
THREE 38(1 1/2) DIAM WHEELS
THREE 6(1/4) DIAM STEEL RODS x 57(2 1/4) LONG
SIX DOME SPRING CAPS TO SUIT 6(1/4) DIAM ROD

UPPER FRONT CROSS MEMBER WITH CONTROLS

22(7/8) THICK

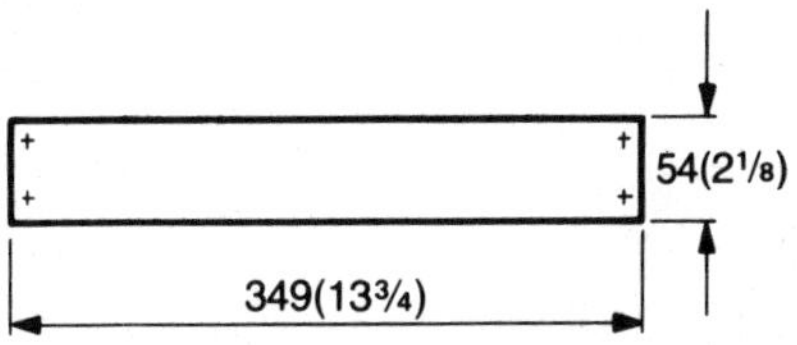
54(2 1/8)
349(13 3/4)

LOWER FRONT CROSS MEMBER

22(7/8) THICK

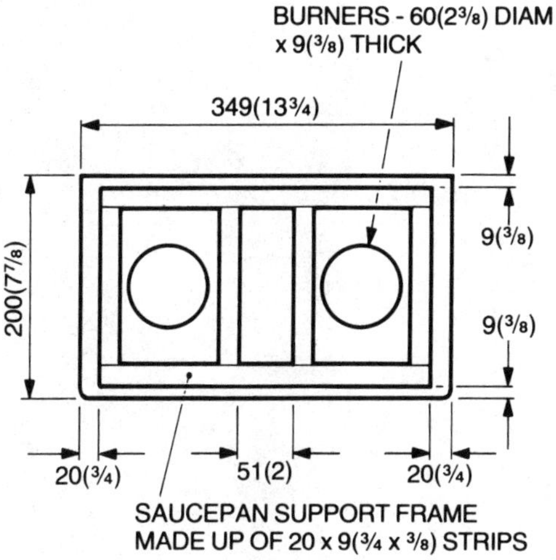
BURNERS - 60(2 3/8) DIAM
x 9(3/8) THICK
349(13 3/4)
200(7 7/8)
9(3/8)
9(3/8)
20(3/4)
51(2)
20(3/4)
SAUCEPAN SUPPORT FRAME
MADE UP OF 20 x 9(3/4 x 3/8) STRIPS

TOP 6(1/4) THICK

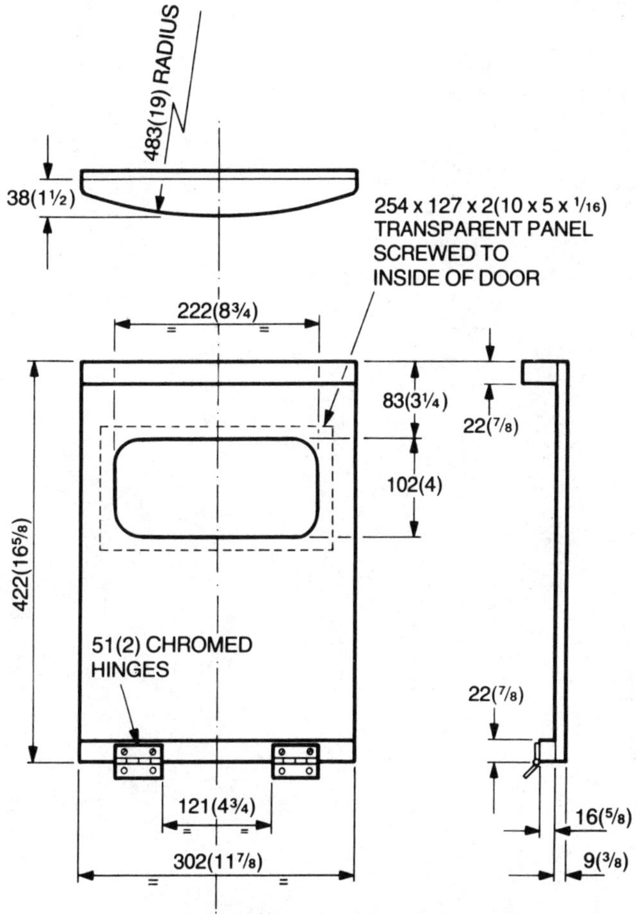
483(19) RADIUS
38(1 1/2)
254 x 127 x 2(10 x 5 x 1/16)
TRANSPARENT PANEL
SCREWED TO
INSIDE OF DOOR
222(8 3/4)
83(3 1/4)
22(7/8)
102(4)
422(16 5/8)
51(2) CHROMED
HINGES
22(7/8)
121(4 3/4)
16(5/8)
302(11 7/8)
9(3/8)

DOOR PANEL WITH WINDOW

ROCKING CRADLE

All young children have a special friend (old teddy or blanket) who needs to be put to bed at night. This rocking cradle is a perfect place for all tired bears to get a peaceful night.

This cradle has been designed for use only as a play item and should not be used for babies.

1 The frame of the rocking cradle is constructed in the same way as the table and benches ie using mortice tenon and halving joints.

2 The cradle supports have large diameter holes at the top. These are best drilled using a 'flat bit' in an electric drill. You will find a drill stand of tremendous help, but not essential.

3 The cradle sides are secured using a simple lap joint. A tenon saw and chisel are necessary for this process. Mark out clearly with a marking knife and cut away the waste wood.

4 Shaping of the sides and ends is only done after the joints have been cut but before the cradle is glued together.

5 The shaping of cradle sides, legs, rail etc will be far easier if you have a spokeshave. Obviously these can be glasspapered smooth but it takes a great deal of time and glasspaper.

6 The cradle is held in the frame by dowel rods. The dowels are pushed through the cradle supports and glued in. The cradle has to be held in the frame while this is being done. A little candle wax rubbed on to the ends of the rods will make the cradle swing smoothly.

Cutting list

Cradle supports	2 off	514 x 95 x 22mm (20¼ x 3¾ x ⅞in)	Timber
Feet	2 off	381 x 73 x 22mm (15 x 2⅞ x ⅞in)	Timber
Tie bar	1 off	584 x 76 x 22mm (23 x 3 x ⅞in)	Timber
Cradle head and foot	2 off	267 x 197 x 22mm (10½ x 7¾ x ⅞in)	Timber
Cradle sides	2 off	527 x 197 x 22mm (20¾ x 7¾ x ⅞in)	Timber
Cradle bottom	1 off	527 x 222 x 9mm (20¾ x 8¾ x ⅜in)	Plywood
Rocking pins	2 off	51mm(2in) long x 16mm(⅝in) diameter dowel	

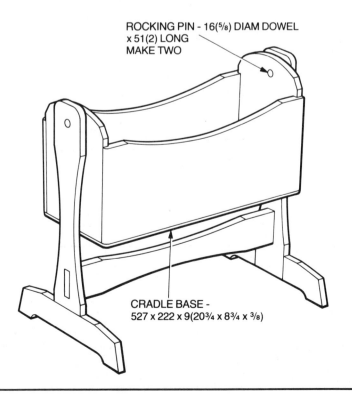

ROCKING PIN - 16(⅝) DIAM DOWEL
x 51(2) LONG
MAKE TWO

CRADLE BASE -
527 x 222 x 9(20¾ x 8¾ x ⅜)

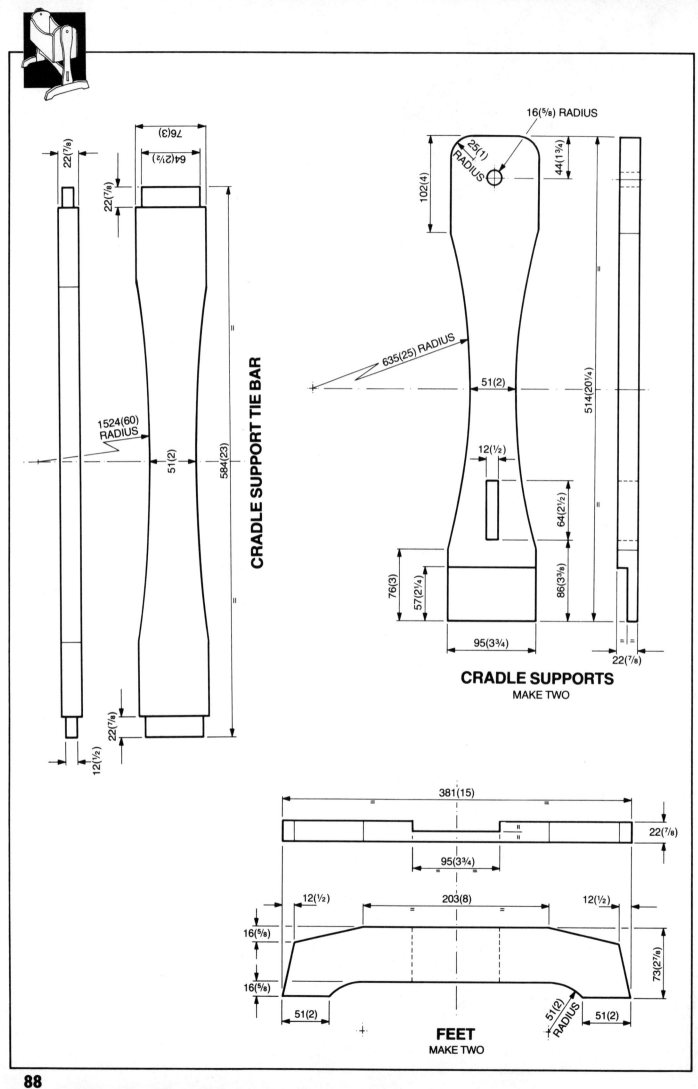

CRADLE SUPPORT TIE BAR

76(3)

64(2½)

22(⅞)

22(⅞)

22(⅞)

1524(60)
RADIUS

51(2)

584(23)

22(⅞)

12(½)

16(⅝) RADIUS

25(1)
RADIUS

102(4)

44(1¾)

635(25) RADIUS

51(2)

514(20¼)

12(½)

64(2½)

76(3)

57(2¼)

86(3⅜)

95(3¾)

22(⅞)

CRADLE SUPPORTS
MAKE TWO

381(15)

22(⅞)

95(3¾)

12(½)

203(8)

12(½)

16(⅝)

16(⅝)

73(2⅞)

51(2)

51(2)
RADIUS

51(2)

FEET
MAKE TWO

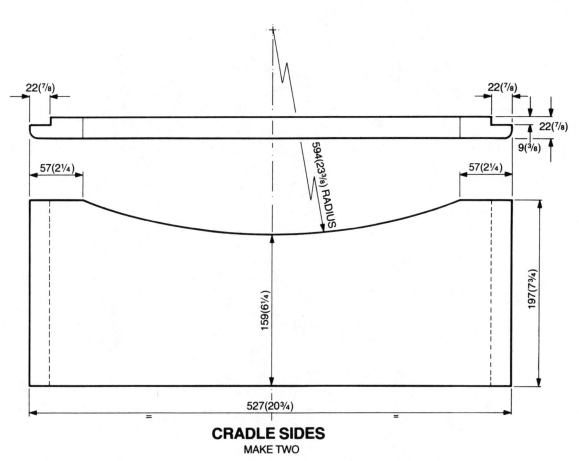

CRADLE SIDES
MAKE TWO

22(⁷⁄₈) 22(⁷⁄₈) 22(⁷⁄₈) 9(³⁄₈)

57(2¼) 57(2¼)

594(23³⁄₈) RADIUS

159(6¼) 197(7³⁄₄)

527(20³⁄₄)

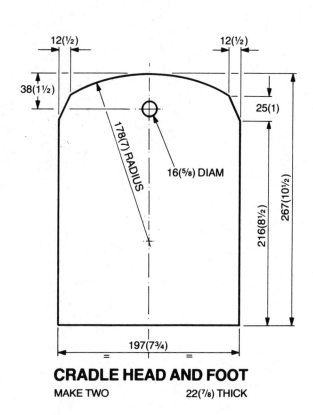

CRADLE HEAD AND FOOT
MAKE TWO   22(⁷⁄₈) THICK

12(½) 12(½)

38(1½)

178(7) RADIUS

16(⁵⁄₈) DIAM

25(1)

216(8½) 267(10½)

197(7³⁄₄)

GARAGE

All model cars, lorries, tractors and motorbikes will at some time need fuel. This garage is well equipped with a car wash and a ramp. To add a little realism to the plywood I have used a miniature brick wall paper, although this is not essential.

1   Cut the base and radius the corners.

2   Mark in pencil the positions of the pump islands and mark garage building.

3   Mark and cut out a pair of side walls. Cut out front, rear and roof.

4   Glue sides, front and back together. Sandpaper any rough edges.

5   The roof is glued on in two separate pieces. Where the two pieces meet make a chamfered joint, not essential but far more satisfying and neater.

6   Place the finished main building on to the base and mark around it with a pencil. Remove the building and you will now have the position to drill four small holes for the fixing screws. It is

best to glue and screw the main building on to the base. Make sure you countersink the screw holes on the base side. Care is necessary when screwing the base to the main building.

7   Shape up three petrol pump islands. These like the main buildings are glued and screwed on to the base.

8   The petrol pumps, car wash and ramp are glued on to the garage with epoxy-resin glue. This is very strong but it must be emphasised not suitable for children to use.

9   All the various accessories were bought at a large model shop. To give protection to the miniature brick paper I varnished over this, using matt finish varnish.

Cutting list

Base board	1 off	521 × 457 × 9mm (20½ × 18 × ⅜in)	Plywood
Side walls	2 off	244 × 152 × 9mm (9⅝ × 6 × ⅜in)	Plywood
Front and rear walls	2 off	235 × 127 × 9mm (9¼ × 5 × ⅜in)	Plywood
Rear roof panel	1 off	343 × 178 × 5mm (13½ × 7 × 3⁄16in)	Plywood
Front roof panel	1 off	343 × 105 × 5mm (13½ × 4⅛ × 3⁄16in)	Plywood
Pump islands	3 off	168 × 22 × 12mm (6⅝ × ⅞ × ½in)	Timber

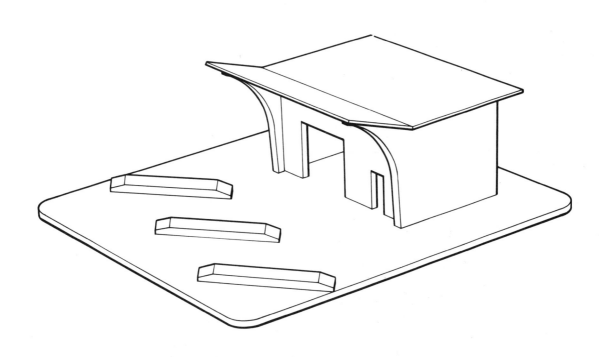

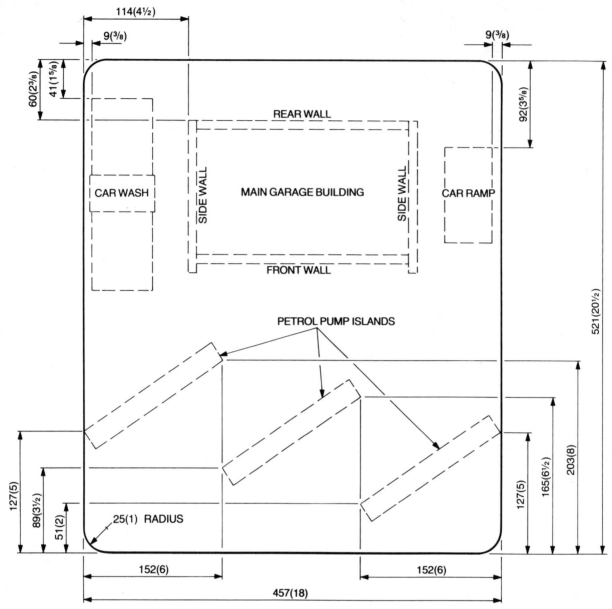

114(4½)

9(³⁄₈)

9(³⁄₈)

60(2³⁄₈)

41(1⁵⁄₈)

92(3⁵⁄₈)

REAR WALL

SIDE WALL

MAIN GARAGE BUILDING

SIDE WALL

CAR WASH

CAR RAMP

FRONT WALL

521(20½)

PETROL PUMP ISLANDS

127(5)

89(3½)

51(2)

25(1) RADIUS

127(5)

165(6½)

203(8)

152(6)

152(6)

457(18)

BASE BOARD 9(³⁄₈) THICK PLYWOOD
SHOWING POSITION OF BUILDING
AND OTHER FIXTURES

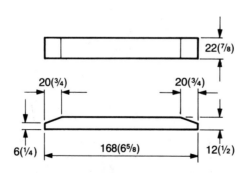

22(⁷⁄₈)

20(³⁄₄)

20(³⁄₄)

6(¼)

168(6⁵⁄₈)

12(½)

PETROL PUMP ISLANDS
MAKE THREE

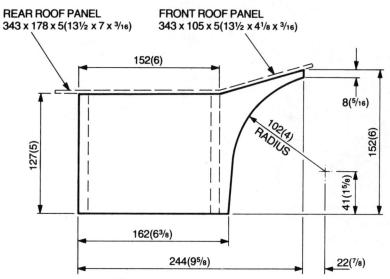

REAR ROOF PANEL
343 x 178 x 5(13½ x 7 x ³/₁₆)

FRONT ROOF PANEL
343 x 105 x 5(13½ x 4¹/₈ x ³/₁₆)

152(6)

127(5)

8(⁵/₁₆)

102(4)
RADIUS

152(6)

41(1⁵/₈)

162(6³/₈)

244(9⁵/₈)

22(⁷/₈)

SIDE WALLS 9(³/₈) THICK   MAKE TWO
SHOWING POSITION OF FRONT AND REAR WALLS,
AND DETAILS OF ROOF PANELS

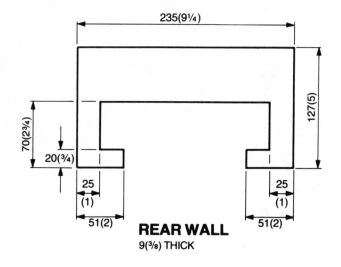

235(9¼)

127(5)

70(2³/₄)

20(³/₄)

25
(1)

25
(1)

51(2)

51(2)

REAR WALL
9(³/₈) THICK

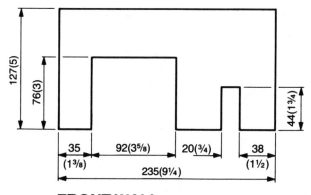

127(5)

76(3)

44(1³/₄)

35
(1³/₈)

92(3⁵/₈)

20(³/₄)

38
(1½)

235(9¼)

FRONT WALL 9(³/₈) THICK

93

FARM BUILDINGS

All children love playing with farms. There are so many possibilities with the variety of animals and machines now available.

The multi-purpose stock building is sufficiently large to take tractors and combines.

The method of construction for the multi-purpose stock building and the other two stock buildings is identical. I shall therefore describe the construction generally.

1 The buildings are built from plywood. The only parts that are not are the pine 'ties' that hold the back and front together, gutters and ridge pieces.

2 Mark out in pencil the ends. Fix them together with tape and cut them out as a pair. The ties that hold the building together fit into 'notches'.

3 The 'notches' that take the ties are cut out with a tenon and coping saw. Using a fine toothed saw cut down both sides of the notch. Now using a coping saw with the blade turned at 90° to the 'back' cut out the bottom of the notch. Tidy up all the notches with a very sharp chisel.

4 Cut the ties to the same length and glue into the notches (see drawing showing roof and side walls removed).

5 Prepare the roof panels. These are held in place by glueing and panel pinning. The panel pins are fixed through the plywood roof panel onto the ties. Use a panel pin punch to push the heads below the surface. You will have to support the ties while hammering the panel pins in.

6 To simulate corrugated sheet use a black pencil and draw lines the full length of the roof. This looks most effective especially on birch plywood which has a creamy colour.

7 Glue and panel pin the ridge pieces and gutters in place. Drainpipes are made from coax cable which is available at motor accessory shops. The clips holding the drainpipes to the walls are found in most electrical shops and are sold as cable clips.

Cutting list

Multi-purpose stock building

Front and rear walls	2 off	711 x 229 x 9mm (28 x 9 x ⅜in)	Plywood
Side walls	1 off	318 x 133 x 5mm (12½ x 5¼ x ³⁄₁₆in)	Plywood
	1 off	318 x 175 x 5mm (12½ x 6⅞ x ³⁄₁₆in)	Plywood
Roof panels	1 off	560 x 337 x 5mm (22 x 13¼ x ³⁄₁₆in)	Plywood
	1 off	222 x 337 x 5mm (8¾ x 13¼ x ³⁄₁₆in)	Plywood
Roof and wall ties	11 off	318 x 16 x 8mm (12½ x ⅝ x ⁵⁄₁₆in)	Timber
Guttering and roof ridge	4 off	337 x 16 x 8mm (13¼ x ⅝ x ⁵⁄₁₆in)	Timber

Single span stock building

Front and rear walls	2 off	403 x 197 x 9mm (15⅞ x 7¾ x ⅜in)	Plywood
Side walls	2 off	229 x 130 x 5mm (9 x 5⅛ x ³⁄₁₆in)	Plywood
Roof panels	2 off	248 x 235 x 5mm (9¾ x 9¼ x ³⁄₁₆in)	Plywood
Roof and wall ties	9 off	229 x 16 x 8mm (9 x ⅝ x ⁵⁄₁₆in)	Timber
Roof ridge	2 off	248 x 16 x 8mm (9¾ x ⅝ x ⁵⁄₁₆in)	Timber

Stock building

Front and rear walls	2 off	311 x 197 x 9mm (12¼ x 7¾ x ⅜in)	Plywood
Side walls	2 off	343 x 149 x 5mm (13½ x 5⅞ x ³⁄₁₆in)	Plywood
Roof panels	2 off	368 x 191 x 5mm (14½ x 7½ x ³⁄₁₆in)	Plywood
Roof and wall ties	9 off	343 x 16 x 8mm (13½ x ⅝ x ⁵⁄₁₆in)	Timber
Guttering and roof ridge	4 off	368 x 16 x 8mm (14½ x ⅝ x ⁵⁄₁₆in)	Timber

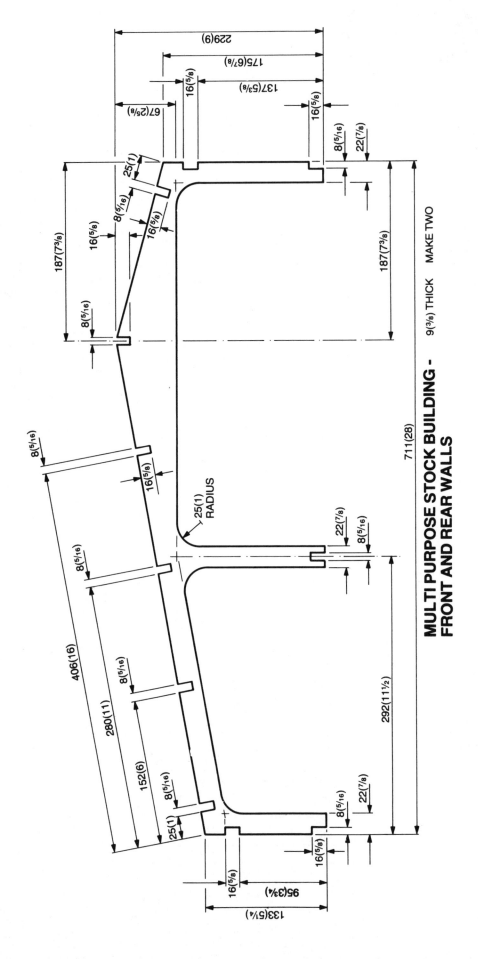

**MULTI PURPOSE STOCK BUILDING –
FRONT AND REAR WALLS** 9(³/₈) THICK MAKE TWO

229(9)

175(6⁷/₈)

137(5³/₈)

16(⁵/₈)

67(2⁵/₈)

25(1)

8(⁵/₁₆)

16(⁵/₈)

16(⁵/₈)

187(7³/₈)

8(⁵/₁₆)

8(⁵/₁₆)

22(⁷/₈)

187(7³/₈)

16(⁵/₈)

711(28)

8(⁵/₁₆)

16(⁵/₈)

25(1)
RADIUS

22(⁷/₈)

8(⁵/₁₆)

8(⁵/₁₆)

406(16)

8(⁵/₁₆)

292(11½)

280(11)

152(6)

8(⁵/₁₆)

22(⁷/₈)

25(1)

8(⁵/₁₆)

16(⁵/₈)

16(⁵/₈)

95(3¾)

133(5¼)

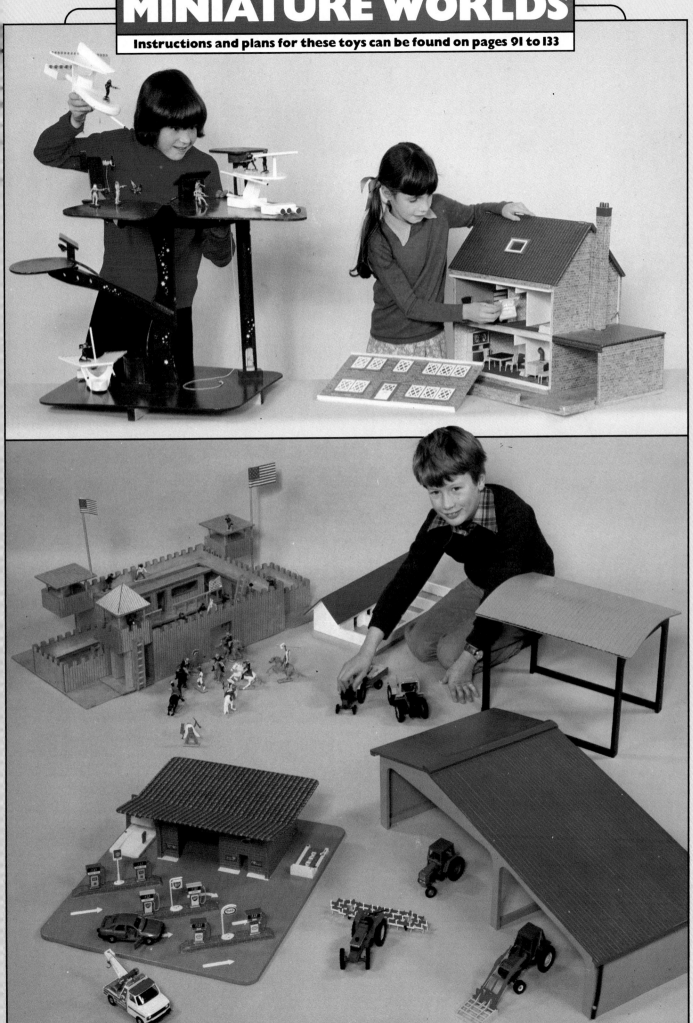

MINIATURE WORLDS

Instructions and plans for these toys can be found on pages 91 to 133

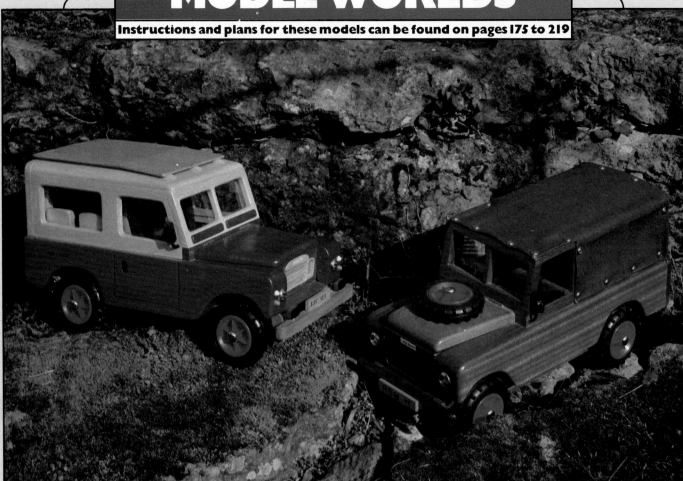

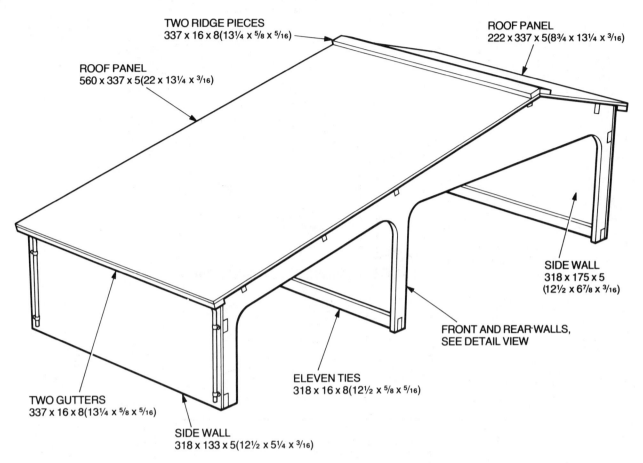

TWO RIDGE PIECES
337 x 16 x 8(13¼ x ⅝ x ⁵/₁₆)

ROOF PANEL
222 x 337 x 5(8¾ x 13¼ x ³/₁₆)

ROOF PANEL
560 x 337 x 5(22 x 13¼ x ³/₁₆)

SIDE WALL
318 x 175 x 5
(12½ x 6⅞ x ³/₁₆)

FRONT AND REAR WALLS,
SEE DETAIL VIEW

ELEVEN TIES
318 x 16 x 8(12½ x ⅝ x ⁵/₁₆)

TWO GUTTERS
337 x 16 x 8(13¼ x ⅝ x ⁵/₁₆)

SIDE WALL
318 x 133 x 5(12½ x 5¼ x ³/₁₆)

MULTI PURPOSE STOCK BUILDING

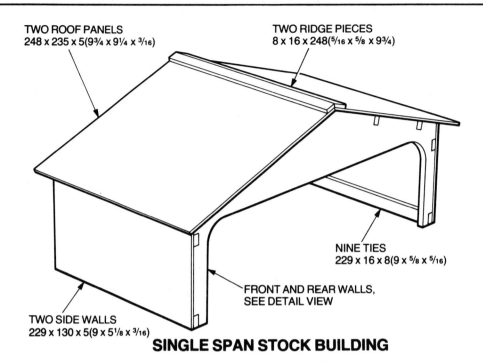

TWO ROOF PANELS
248 x 235 x 5(9¾ x 9¼ x ³/₁₆)

TWO RIDGE PIECES
8 x 16 x 248(⁵/₁₆ x ⁵/₈ x 9¾)

NINE TIES
229 x 16 x 8(9 x ⁵/₈ x ⁵/₁₆)

FRONT AND REAR WALLS,
SEE DETAIL VIEW

TWO SIDE WALLS
229 x 130 x 5(9 x 5⅛ x ³/₁₆)

SINGLE SPAN STOCK BUILDING

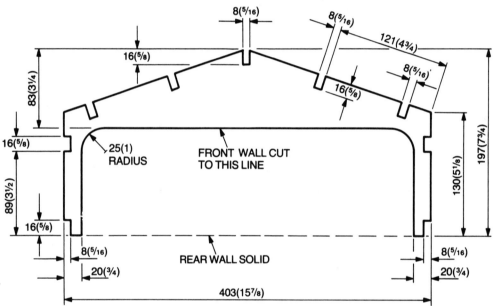

8(⁵/₁₆)

8(⁵/₁₆)

121(4¾)

16(⁵/₈)

8(⁵/₁₆)

83(3¼)

16(⁵/₈)

197(7¾)

16(⁵/₈)

25(1)
RADIUS

FRONT WALL CUT
TO THIS LINE

130(5⅛)

89(3½)

16(⁵/₈)

8(⁵/₁₆)

REAR WALL SOLID

8(⁵/₁₆)

20(¾)

20(¾)

403(15⅞)

SINGLE SPAN STOCK BUILDING – FRONT AND REAR WALLS

9(³/₈) THICK   MAKE TWO

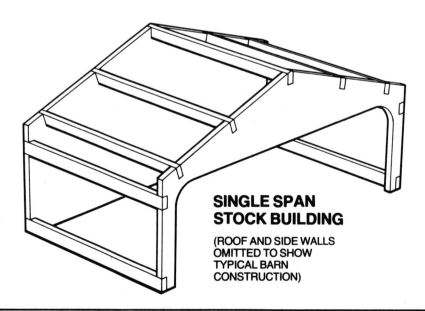

SINGLE SPAN
STOCK BUILDING

(ROOF AND SIDE WALLS
OMITTED TO SHOW
TYPICAL BARN
CONSTRUCTION)

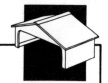

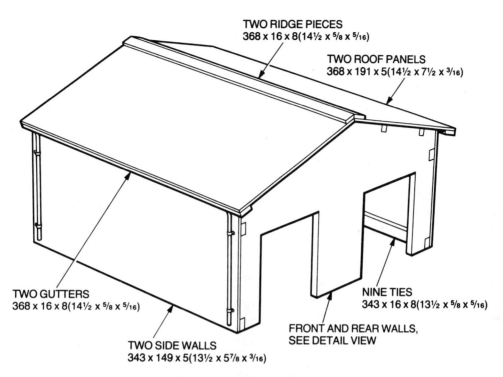

TWO RIDGE PIECES
368 x 16 x 8(14½ x ⅝ x ⁵⁄₁₆)

TWO ROOF PANELS
368 x 191 x 5(14½ x 7½ x ³⁄₁₆)

TWO GUTTERS
368 x 16 x 8(14½ x ⅝ x ⁵⁄₁₆)

NINE TIES
343 x 16 x 8(13½ x ⅝ x ⁵⁄₁₆)

FRONT AND REAR WALLS,
SEE DETAIL VIEW

TWO SIDE WALLS
343 x 149 x 5(13½ x 5⅞ x ³⁄₁₆)

STOCK BUILDING

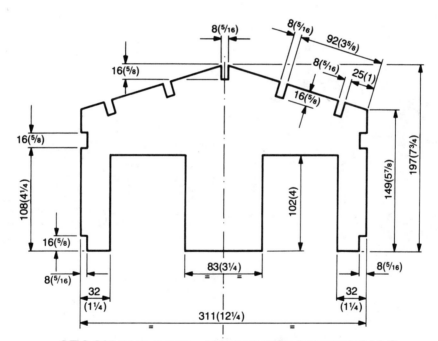

8(⁵⁄₁₆)

8(⁵⁄₁₆)

92(3⅝)

16(⅝)

8(⁵⁄₁₆)

25(1)

16(⅝)

16(⅝)

197(7¾)

108(4¼)

149(5⅞)

102(4)

16(⅝)

8(⁵⁄₁₆)

83(3¼)

8(⁵⁄₁₆)

32
(1¼)

32
(1¼)

311(12¼)

STOCK BUILDING - FRONT AND REAR WALLS
9(⅜) THICK   MAKE TWO

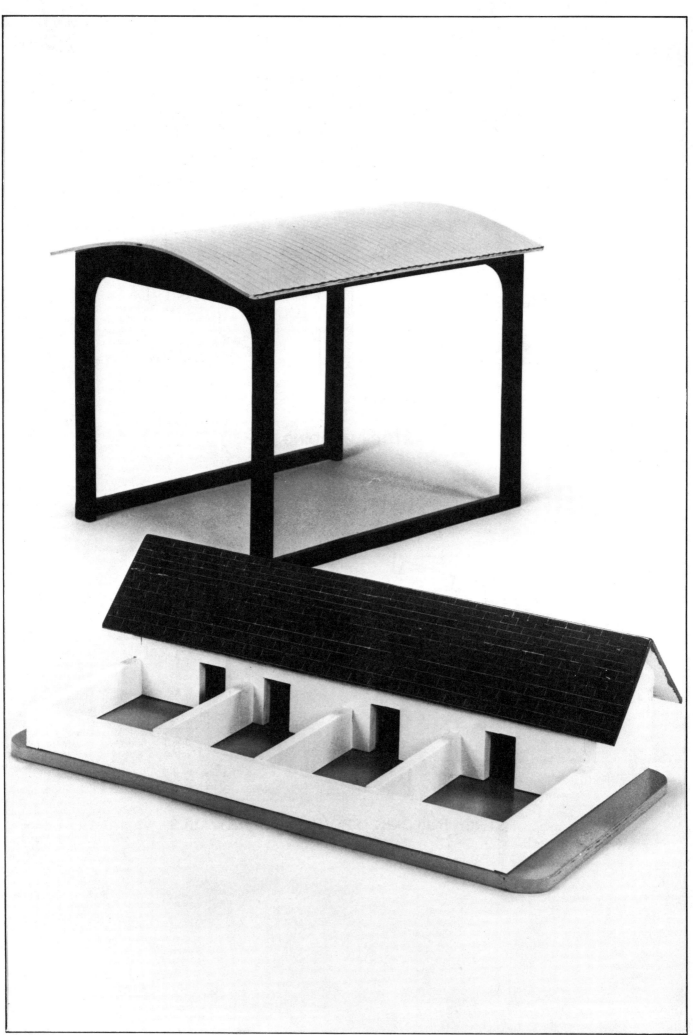

What 'pretend' farm would be complete without the pigsty. In order to prevent pigs getting 'stuck' inside the sty the roof lifts off allowing the child to arrange the pigs inside.

Dutch barn

1 The dutch barn front and rear frames will have to be cut out with a keyhole saw or jigsaw since there is not sufficient clearance between the saw and the saw frame to allow for cutting the bottom of the curve with a coping saw.

2 Once the frames have been cut out the ties are glued into the slots.

3 The roof as you can see is curved and therefore fixing the plywood can be a little difficult unless you follow this method:
    i Panel pin the roof into place on the middle tie.
    ii Gently bend the roof to the next tie and panel pin in place.
    iii Now go back to the other side of the centre tie and repeat the process.
    iv Bend the roof down to the last stretcher and panel pin in place.
You will find a second pair of hands very helpful as the barn is a 'leggy' construction and not easy to hold while working on.

Pigsty

1 Mark out and cut a pair of end walls.

2 Cut out the doorways in the front wall. The method is the same as the slots for the ties described in 'stock buildings'.

3 Now glue the front and back walls onto the end walls.

4 Cut out all the notches in the run wall and internal walls. Glue together.

5 Shape up a suitable baseboard and glue the sty onto this.

6 Glue all the internal walls into the pigsty which only leaves the roof to be made.

7 The roof is glued onto a batten running lengthways. The batten is cut to fit inside the end walls and holds the roof securely in place.

Cutting list

Dutch barn

Front and rear frames	2 off	289 x 279 x 9mm (11⅜ x 11 x ⅜in)	Plywood
Roof panel	1 off	425 x 305 x 5mm (16¾ x 12 x ³⁄₁₆in)	Plywood
Roof and wall ties	7 off	368 x 16 x 8mm (14½ x ⅝ x ⁵⁄₁₆in)	Timber

Pigsty

Base board	1 off	457 x 229 x 9mm (18 x 9 x ⅜in)	Plywood
End and internal walls	5 off	229 x 111 x 9mm (9 x 4⅜ x ⅜in)	Plywood
Front and rear walls	2 off	408 x 64 x 9mm (16 x 2½ x ⅜in)	Plywood
Front run wall	1 off	408 x 28 x 9mm (16 x 1⅛ x ⅜in)	Plywood
Roof panels front	1 off	445 x 84 x 5mm (17½ x 3⁵⁄₁₆ x ³⁄₁₆in)	Plywood
rear	1 off	445 x 79 x 5mm (17½ x 3⅛ x ³⁄₁₆in)	Plywood
Roof bracing	1 off	387 x 22 x 22mm (15¼ x ⅞ x ⅞in)	Timber

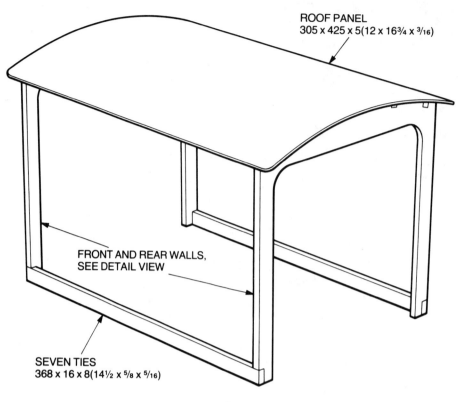

ROOF PANEL
305 x 425 x 5(12 x 16¾ x ³/₁₆)

FRONT AND REAR WALLS,
SEE DETAIL VIEW

SEVEN TIES
368 x 16 x 8(14½ x ⁵/₈ x ⁵/₁₆)

DUTCH BARN

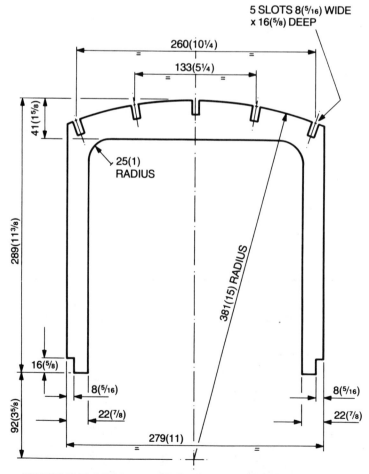

5 SLOTS 8(⁵/₁₆) WIDE
x 16(⁵/₈) DEEP

260(10¼)

133(5¼)

41(1⁵/₈)

25(1)
RADIUS

289(11³/₈)

381(15) RADIUS

16(⁵/₈)

8(⁵/₁₆)

8(⁵/₁₆)

22(⁷/₈)

22(⁷/₈)

92(3⁵/₈)

279(11)

DUTCH BARN - FRONT AND REAR FRAMES
9(³/₈) THICK   MAKE TWO

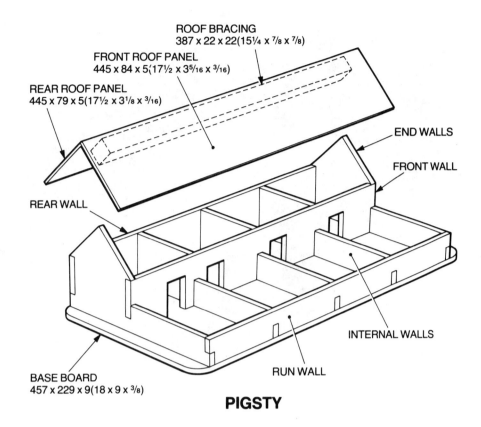

ROOF BRACING
387 x 22 x 22(15¼ x ⅞ x ⅞)

FRONT ROOF PANEL
445 x 84 x 5(17½ x 3⁵⁄₁₆ x ³⁄₁₆)

REAR ROOF PANEL
445 x 79 x 5(17½ x 3⅛ x ³⁄₁₆)

END WALLS

FRONT WALL

REAR WALL

INTERNAL WALLS

RUN WALL

BASE BOARD
457 x 229 x 9(18 x 9 x ⅜)

PIGSTY

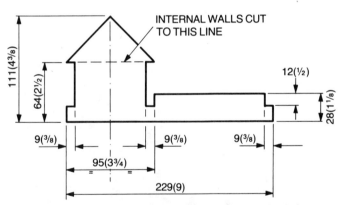

INTERNAL WALLS CUT
TO THIS LINE

111(4⅜)

64(2½)

12(½)

28(1⅛)

9(⅜)

9(⅜)

9(⅜)

95(3¾)

229(9)

PIGSTY - END AND INTERNAL WALLS

MAKE TWO END WALLS
MAKE THREE INTERNAL WALLS   9(⅜) THICK

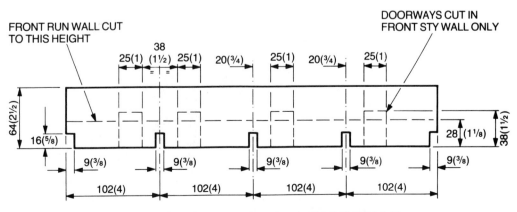

FRONT RUN WALL CUT
TO THIS HEIGHT

DOORWAYS CUT IN
FRONT STY WALL ONLY

25(1)   38
(1½)   25(1)   20(¾)   25(1)   20(¾)   25(1)

64(2½)

16(⅝)

28(1⅛)

38(1½)

9(⅜)   9(⅜)   9(⅜)   9(⅜)   9(⅜)

102(4)   102(4)   102(4)   102(4)

PIGSTY - FRONT, REAR AND RUN WALLS
9(⅜) THICK

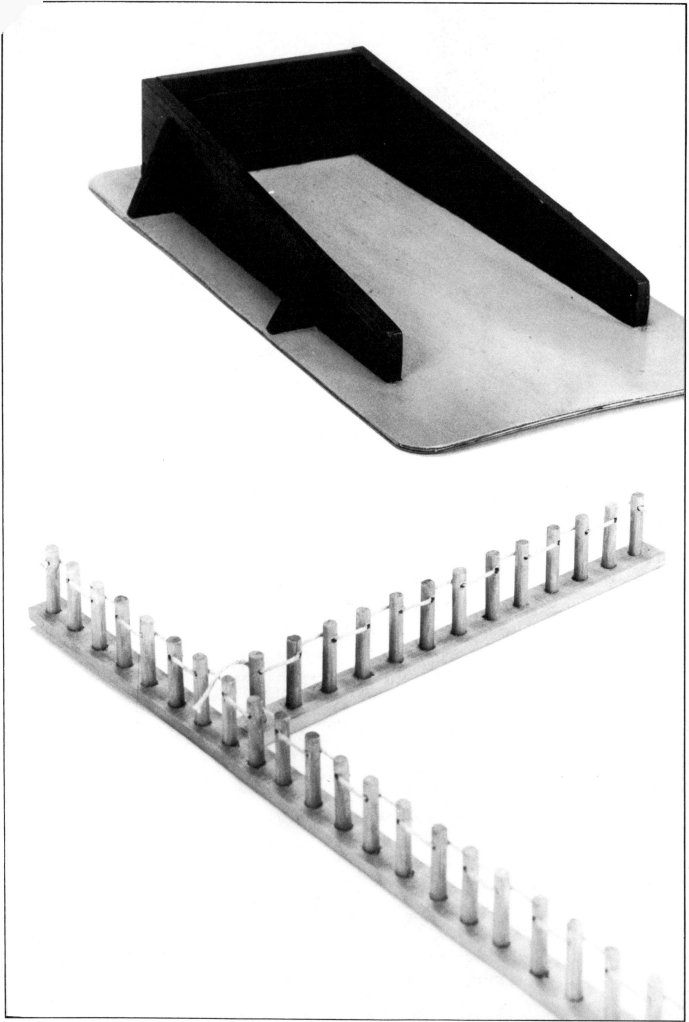

FENCES AND BUNKER

The fences are designed so that any length can be made. The fields can therefore be of any shape. The fences are tied together with string, thus allowing easy movement of animals from one field to another.

Bunker

The sides and wedge supports are shaped and then glued onto the base. If the silo is left until last you will probably have sufficient off-cuts of plywood to make two.

Fences

1   These are best made in long strips of timber. Fix two lengths of timber together with tape and mark the positions of the dowel holes. Drill holes for the dowels.

2   Make a small simple jig to speed the cutting of equal lengths of dowel rod. Drill a small hole in the top of each dowel rod. Care is needed here as there is a tendency for the drill to split the back of the dowel as the drill point comes through.

3   Put a spot of glue on the end of each dowel rod and tap them gently into the ready prepared holes in the base.

4   Check for rough edges and sandpaper off any splinters.

5   Thread the string through the holes leaving a good length at each end.

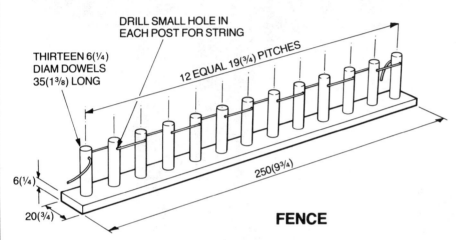

FENCE

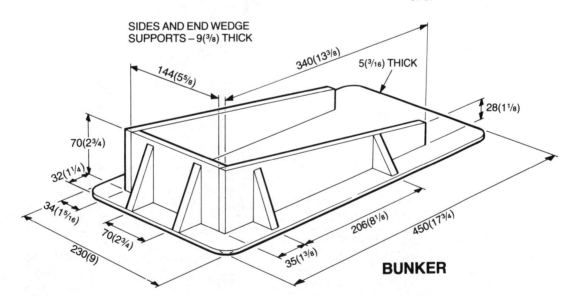

BUNKER

Cutting list

Bunker			
Base board	1 off	450 × 230 × 5mm (17¾ × 9 × ³⁄₁₆in)	Plywood
Side walls	2 off	340 × 70 × 9mm (13⅜ × 2¾ × ⅜in)	Plywood
End wall	1 off	144 × 70 × 9mm (5⅝ × 2¾ × ⅜in)	Plywood
Wedge supports	6 off	Make from 9mm (⅜in) plywood off-cuts	
Fencing			
Bases		Lengths and numbers as required from 20 × 6mm (¾ × ¼in) timber	
Posts		Numbers off as required 35mm (1⅜in) long × 6mm (¼in) diameter dowel	

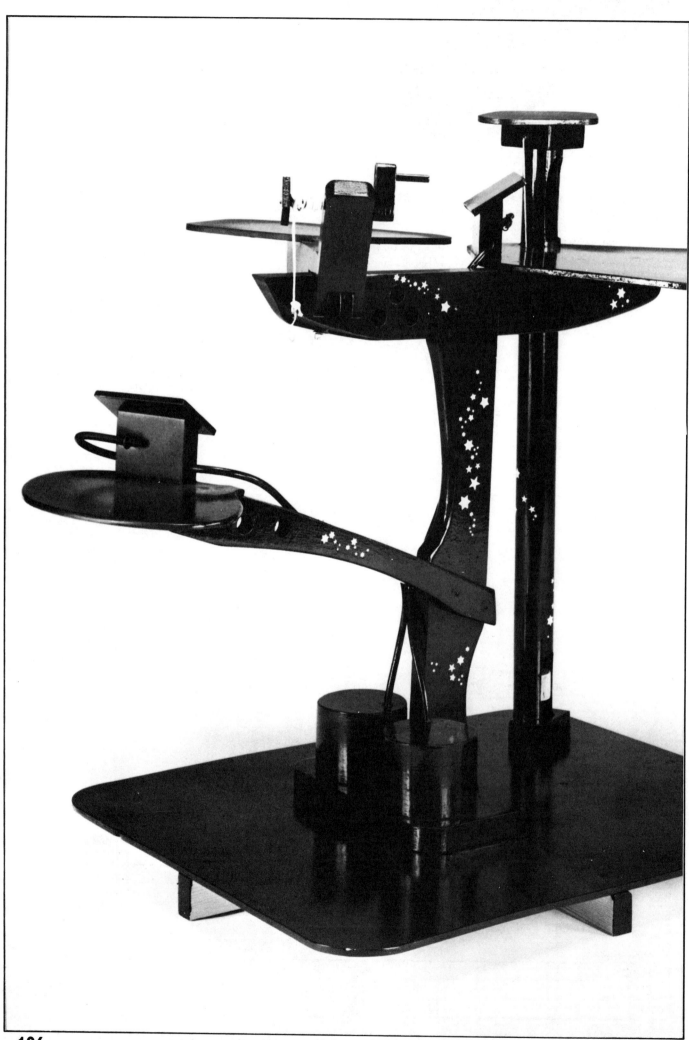

SPACE STATION

From this station star ships are able to refuel and refit for journeys into other galaxies. A small crane is fitted to raise damaged space ships as well as a lift to convey personnel to the upper level platform.

There is a temptation when building space stations to add lots of masts, aerials, radar scanners etc. However younger children can damage themselves if they fall on these. Realism will depend on the age of the child and if he has younger brothers or sisters!

1 To provide a fixing point for the central support column it is essential to make a base stiffening frame. This frame is held together in the middle by a halving joint.

2 Cut and shape the working platform central support column. The base of the column is cut out to fit over the stiffening frame. The column is then screwed and glued on to the frame. A good strong base and column are now ready to take all the landing platforms, fuel tanks etc.

3 Cut and shape the base board. Screw the base board on to the stiffening frame.

4 Make and screw the intermediate platform support arm in position on to the central support column.

5 Shape up the top level support structure. This is fitted on to the central support column by a housing joint. The holes that are drilled in this piece are just for effect.

6 Cut out and shape up the three landing platforms. If you cut these out first you will have offcuts that will be ideal for making the space craft.

7 The elevator shaft is made from a length of standard plastic drain pipe (available from builders merchants). It is quite an easy material to cut providing you use a fine toothed saw. I trimmed up the holes and slots with a Stanley knife. To get the slot started at the top of the elevator it is easiest to drill a hole – or several holes.

8 To make the elevator cage I cut and shaped up a circular block of wood. This must fit inside the elevator shaft tube. Glasspaper the block until it slides easily up and down inside the tube. This takes a little time and patience to get a good sliding fit.

9 Cut two slots in the sides of the cage and shape up a piece of wire. Both ends of the wire need a small

hook bent in them. A length of cord is then tied on to both hooks. Now check that the cage still slides easily in the shaft tube.

10 To get the cage to travel smoothly up and down in the shaft tube particular care is needed when making the roof assembly.

11 The elevator roof assembly has a small hole drilled in the side to take a small plastic tube. The tube by projecting into the centre of the elevator shaft ensures that the cord pulling up the cage is kept in the centre of the shaft.

12 Now cut out the circle in the upper level platform to take the elevator shaft. Glue and screw the upper level platform in position.

13 Cut and shape the elevator base block, fit it on to the tube and glue the base block on to the base board. Check with a set square that the elevator shaft is at 90° to the base.

14 Now cut and make the swinging platform arm. It fits over the top of the upper level support structure by cutting a halving joint. A coach bolt passes through the arm and superstructure and allows the platform to swing.

15 Shape up the crane jib and the handle and fit on to the end of the swinging platform arm.

16 Now glue and screw the platforms on to the swing platform and intermediate platform.

17 The two fuel storage tanks can be made from wood, or large diameter plastic pipe. The fuel supply pipes are made from 'coax' cable.

18 The refuelling stations are made from offcuts. A small hook holds the end of the pipe ready to refuel the space ships. The stations are glued and screwed on to the platforms.

Cutting list

Base board	1 off	610 x 508 x 6mm (24 x 20 x ¼in)	Plywood
Base stiffeners	1 off	610 x 38 x 22mm (24 x 1½ x ⅞in)	Timber
	1 off	508 x 38 x 22mm (20 x 1½ x ⅞in)	Timber

Central column	1 off	521 × 73 × 22mm (20½ × 2⅞ × ⅞in)	Timber
Upper level support	1 off	483 × 64 × 22mm (19 × 2½ × ⅞in)	Timber
Intermediate level support	1 off	432 × 64 × 22mm (17 × 2½ × ⅞in)	Timber
Swinging platform arm	1 off	413 × 47 × 22mm (16¼ × 1⅞ × ⅞in)	Timber
Upper level platform	1 off	483 × 420 × 6mm (19 × 16½ × ¼in)	Plywood
Intermediate platform	1 off	305 × 203 × 6mm (12 × 8 × ¼in)	Plywood
Swinging platform	1 off	330 × 305 × 6mm (13 × 12 × ¼in)	Plywood
Crane jib	1 off	140 × 41 × 22mm (5½ × 1⅝ × ⅞in)	Timber
	1 off	41mm(1⅝in) long × 6mm(¼in) diameter dowel	
Handle assembly	1 off	51 × 22 × 16mm (2 × ⅞ × ⅝in)	Timber
	1 off	32 × 32 × 6mm (1¼ × 1¼ × ¼in)	Plywood
	1 off	95mm(3¾in) long × 6mm(¼in) diameter dowel	
	1 off	44mm (1¾in) long × 6mm (¼in) diameter dowel	
Refuelling station	2 off	102 × 64 × 6mm (4 × 2½ × ¼in)	Plywood
	2 off	76 × 60 × 22mm (3 × 2⅜ × ⅞in)	Timber
Fuel storage tanks	1 off	241 × 108 × 22mm (9½ × 4¼ × ⅞in)	Timber
	2 off	70mm(2¾in) long × 89mm(3½in) diameter timber	
Shaft roof	1 off	222 × 140 × 6mm (8¾ × 5½ × ¼in)	Plywood
	1 off	64 × 64 × 25mm (2½ × 2½ × 1in)	Timber
Cage	1 off	57mm(2¼in) long × 38mm(1½in) diameter timber	
Base block	1 off	70 × 38 × 22mm (2¾ × 1½ × ⅞in)	Timber

Ancillaries

	1 off	89mm(3½in) long × 6mm(¼in) diameter coach bolt, plain washer and nut	
	1 off	1220mm (48in) long × 6mm (¼in) diameter coaxial cable	
	1 off	641mm (25¼in) long × 44mm (1¾in) o/d plastic water pipe	
	1 off	1220 (48in) long length of fine thread	
	1 off	38mm(1½in) long × 6mm(¼in) diameter plastic tube	
	1 off	203mm(8in) long length of 2mm(1⁄16in) diameter steel wire	

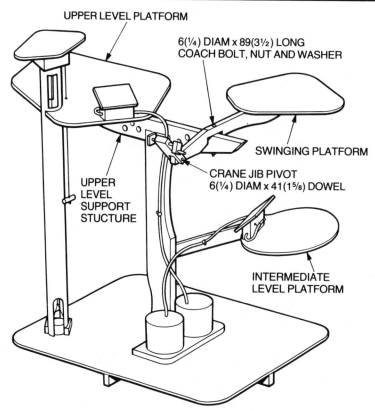

UPPER LEVEL PLATFORM

6(¼) DIAM x 89(3½) LONG
COACH BOLT, NUT AND WASHER

SWINGING PLATFORM

UPPER LEVEL SUPPORT STUCTURE

CRANE JIB PIVOT
6(¼) DIAM x 41(1⅝) DOWEL

INTERMEDIATE LEVEL PLATFORM

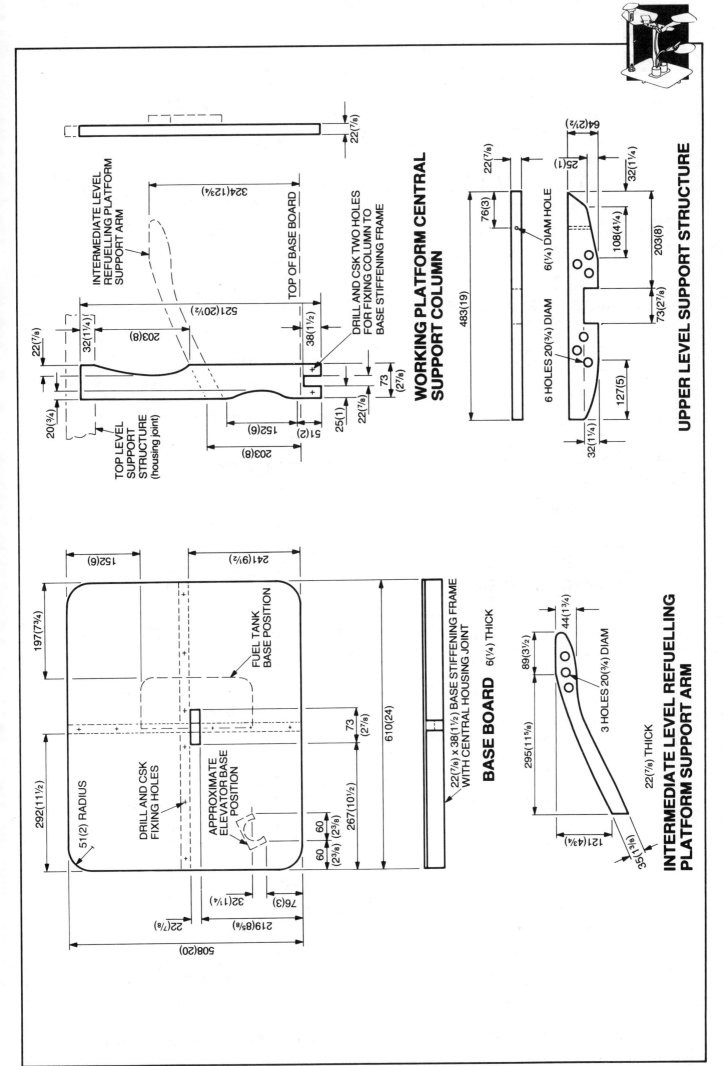

WORKING PLATFORM CENTRAL SUPPORT COLUMN

INTERMEDIATE LEVEL REFUELLING PLATFORM SUPPORT ARM

TOP OF BASE BOARD

324 (12¾)

52¹ (20½)

DRILL AND CSK TWO HOLES FOR FIXING COLUMN TO BASE STIFFENING FRAME

38 (1½)

22 (⅞)

32 (1¼)

203 (8)

73 (2⅞)

25 (1)

22 (⅞)

152 (6)

51 (2)

203 (8)

20 (¾)

TOP LEVEL SUPPORT STRUCTURE (housing joint)

22 (⅞)

UPPER LEVEL SUPPORT STRUCTURE

64 (2½)

25 (1)

32 (1¼)

108 (4¼)

203 (8)

73 (2⅞)

127 (5)

32 (1¼)

22 (⅞)

76 (3)

6 (¼) DIAM HOLE

6 HOLES 20 (¾) DIAM

483 (19)

BASE BOARD 6 (¼) THICK

FUEL TANK BASE POSITION

152 (6)

241 (9½)

197 (7¾)

73 (2⅞)

610 (24)

267 (10½)

292 (11½)

51 (2) RADIUS

DRILL AND CSK FIXING HOLES

APPROXIMATE ELEVATOR BASE POSITION

60   60

60 (2⅜)   (2⅜)

(2⅜)

32 (1¼)

76 (3)

22 (⅞)

219 (8⅝)

508 (20)

22 (⅞) x 38 (1½) BASE STIFFENING FRAME WITH CENTRAL HOUSING JOINT

INTERMEDIATE LEVEL REFUELLING PLATFORM SUPPORT ARM

44 (1¾)

89 (3½)

295 (11⅝)

3 HOLES 20 (¾) DIAM

22 (⅞) THICK

121 (4¾)

35 (1⅜)

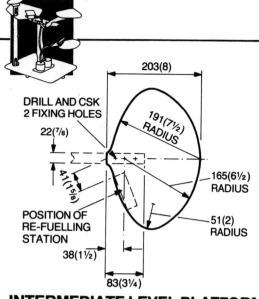

INTERMEDIATE LEVEL PLATFORM
6(¼) THICK

203(8)

DRILL AND CSK
2 FIXING HOLES

191(7½)
RADIUS

22(⅞)

41(1⅝)

165(6½)
RADIUS

51(2)
RADIUS

POSITION OF
RE-FUELLING
STATION

38(1½)

83(3¼)

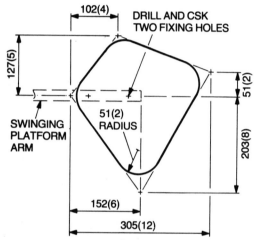

SWINGING PLATFORM
6(¼) THICK

102(4)

DRILL AND CSK
TWO FIXING HOLES

127(5)

51(2)

51(2)
RADIUS

203(8)

SWINGING
PLATFORM
ARM

152(6)

305(12)

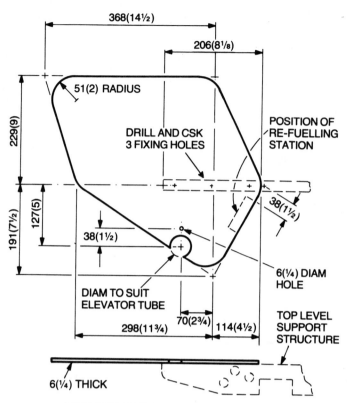

UPPER LEVEL PLATFORM

368(14½)

206(8⅛)

51(2) RADIUS

DRILL AND CSK
3 FIXING HOLES

POSITION OF
RE-FUELLING
STATION

229(9)

191(7½)

127(5)

38(1½)

38(1½)

DIAM TO SUIT
ELEVATOR TUBE

6(¼) DIAM
HOLE

70(2¾)

114(4½)

298(11¾)

TOP LEVEL
SUPPORT
STRUCTURE

6(¼) THICK

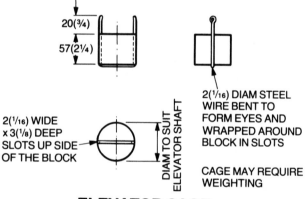

ELEVATOR CAGE

20(¾)

57(2¼)

2(¹⁄₁₆) WIDE
x 3(⅛) DEEP
SLOTS UP SIDE
OF THE BLOCK

DIAM TO SUIT
ELEVATOR SHAFT

2(¹⁄₁₆) DIAM STEEL
WIRE BENT TO
FORM EYES AND
WRAPPED AROUND
BLOCK IN SLOTS

CAGE MAY REQUIRE
WEIGHTING

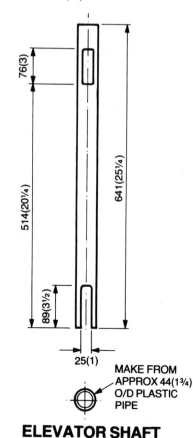

ELEVATOR SHAFT

76(3)

641(25¼)

514(20¼)

89(3½)

25(1)

MAKE FROM
APPROX 44(1¾)
O/D PLASTIC
PIPE

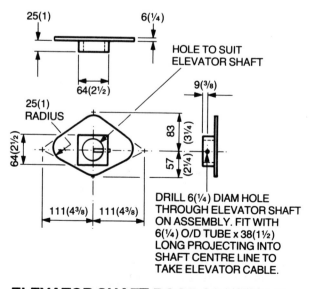

ELEVATOR SHAFT ROOF ASSEMBLY

25(1)

6(¼)

HOLE TO SUIT
ELEVATOR SHAFT

64(2½)

9(⅜)

25(1)
RADIUS

64(2½)

83
(3¼)

57
(2¼)

111(4⅜)

111(4⅜)

DRILL 6(¼) DIAM HOLE
THROUGH ELEVATOR SHAFT
ON ASSEMBLY. FIT WITH
6(¼) O/D TUBE x 38(1½)
LONG PROJECTING INTO
SHAFT CENTRE LINE TO
TAKE ELEVATOR CABLE.

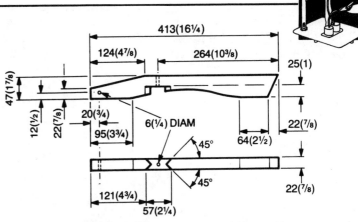

ELEVATOR BASE BLOCK

DIAM TO SUIT ELEVATOR SHAFT

38(1½)
28(1⅛)
70(2¾)
22(⅞)

POSITION AND SECURE ELEVATOR BASE BLOCK
ON MAIN SPACE STATION BASE BOARD AFTER
ASSEMBLY OF ELEVATOR SHAFT THROUGH
UPPER LEVEL PLATFORM

SWINGING PLATFORM ARM

413(16¼)
124(4⅞)
264(10⅜)
25(1)
47(1⅞)
12(½)
22(⅞)
20(¾)
6(¼) DIAM
64(2½)
22(⅞)
95(3¾)
45°
45°
121(4¾)
57(2¼)
22(⅞)

REFUELLING STATIONS
MAKE TWO

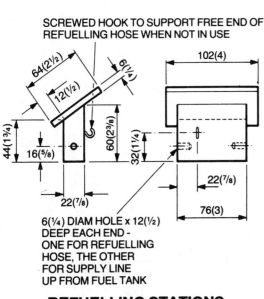

SCREWED HOOK TO SUPPORT FREE END OF
REFUELLING HOSE WHEN NOT IN USE

64(2½)
6(¼)
12(½)
102(4)
44(1¾)
16(⅝)
60(2⅜)
32(1¼)
22(⅞)
22(⅞)
76(3)

6(¼) DIAM HOLE x 12(½)
DEEP EACH END -
ONE FOR REFUELLING
HOSE, THE OTHER
FOR SUPPLY LINE
UP FROM FUEL TANK

FUEL STORAGE TANKS

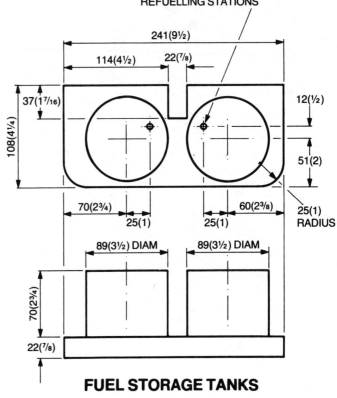

TWO HOLES 6(¼) DIAM x 12(½) DEEP
FOR FUEL SUPPLY LINES UP TO
REFUELLING STATIONS

241(9½)
114(4½)
22(⅞)
12(½)
37(1⁷⁄₁₆)
108(4¼)
51(2)
70(2¾)
60(2⅜)
25(1)
25(1)
25(1)
RADIUS

89(3½) DIAM
89(3½) DIAM
70(2¾)
22(⅞)

CRANE HANDLE ASSEMBLY

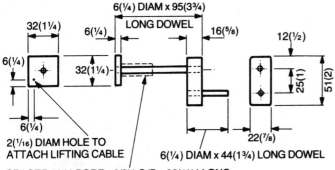

6(¼) DIAM x 95(3¾)
LONG DOWEL
32(1¼)
6(¼)
16(⅝)
12(½)
6(¼)
32(1¼)
25(1)
51(2)
6(¼)
22(⅞)

2(¹⁄₁₆) DIAM HOLE TO
ATTACH LIFTING CABLE

6(¼) DIAM x 44(1¾) LONG DOWEL

SPACER 6(¼) BORE x 9(⅜) O/D x 32(1¼) LONG
TO PREVENT ASSEMBLY SLIDING
TO AND FRO THROUGH JIB

HANDLE GLUED AND PINNED IN POSITION ONCE
SPINDLE IS ASSEMBLED THROUGH JIB

CRANE JIB

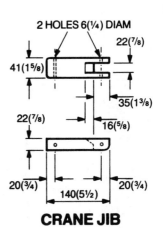

2 HOLES 6(¼) DIAM
22(⅞)
41(1⅝)
35(1⅜)
22(⅞)
16(⅝)
20(¾)
20(¾)
140(5½)

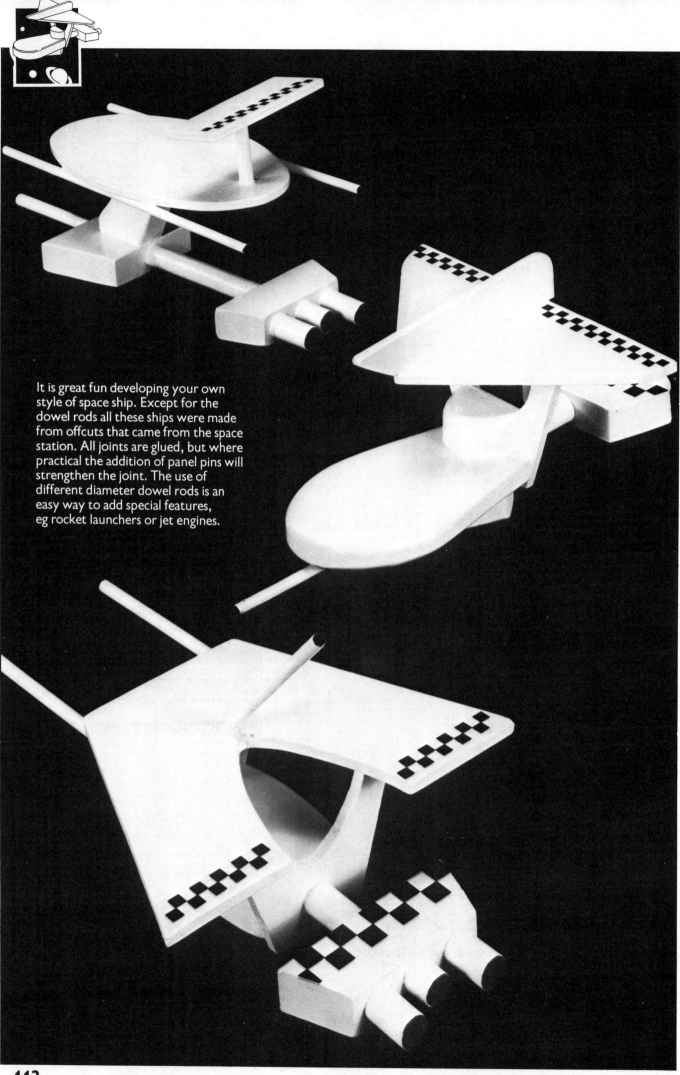

It is great fun developing your own style of space ship. Except for the dowel rods all these ships were made from offcuts that came from the space station. All joints are glued, but where practical the addition of panel pins will strengthen the joint. The use of different diameter dowel rods is an easy way to add special features, eg rocket launchers or jet engines.

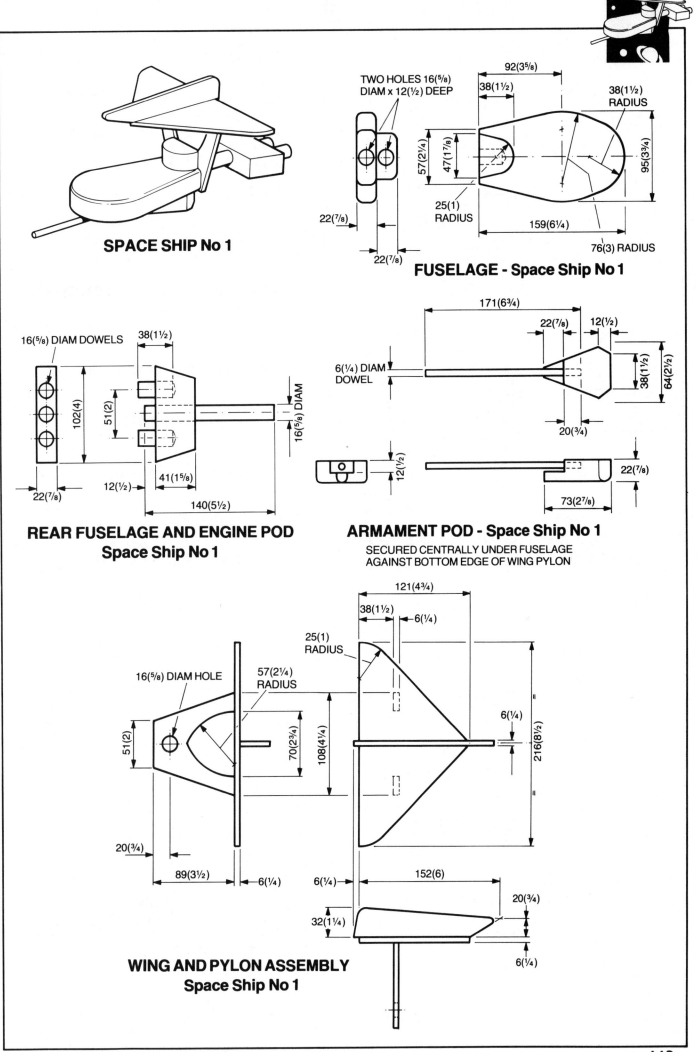

SPACE SHIP No 1

TWO HOLES 16(⁵⁄₈) DIAM x 12(½) DEEP

92(3⁵⁄₈)
38(1½)
38(1½) RADIUS
95(3¾)
57(2¼)
47(1⁷⁄₈)
25(1) RADIUS
159(6¼)
22(⁷⁄₈)
22(⁷⁄₈)
76(3) RADIUS

FUSELAGE - Space Ship No 1

16(⁵⁄₈) DIAM DOWELS
38(1½)
102(4)
51(2)
16(⁵⁄₈) DIAM
41(1⁵⁄₈)
12(½)
22(⁷⁄₈)
140(5½)

REAR FUSELAGE AND ENGINE POD
Space Ship No 1

171(6¾)
22(⁷⁄₈)
12(½)
6(¼) DIAM DOWEL
38(1½)
64(2½)
20(¾)
12(½)
73(2⁷⁄₈)
22(⁷⁄₈)

ARMAMENT POD - Space Ship No 1
SECURED CENTRALLY UNDER FUSELAGE
AGAINST BOTTOM EDGE OF WING PYLON

121(4¾)
38(1½)
6(¼)
25(1) RADIUS
16(⁵⁄₈) DIAM HOLE
57(2¼) RADIUS
51(2)
70(2¾)
108(4¼)
6(¼)
216(8½)
20(¾)
89(3½)
6(¼)
6(¼)
152(6)
20(¾)
32(1¼)
6(¼)

WING AND PYLON ASSEMBLY
Space Ship No 1

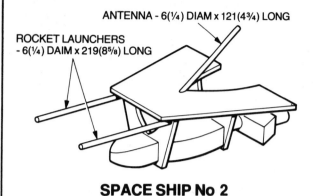

ANTENNA - 6(¼) DIAM x 121(4¾) LONG

ROCKET LAUNCHERS
- 6(¼) DAIM x 219(8⅝) LONG

SPACE SHIP No 2

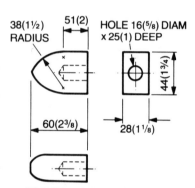

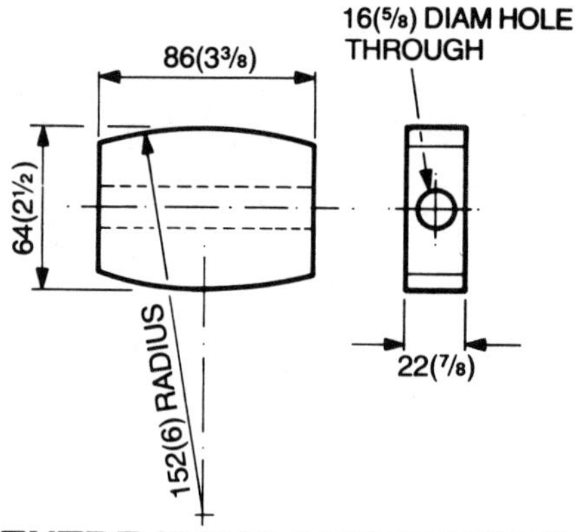

16(⅝) DIAM HOLE THROUGH

86(3⅜)

64(2½)

152(6) RADIUS

22(⅞)

CENTRE FUSELAGE SECTION - Space Ship No 2

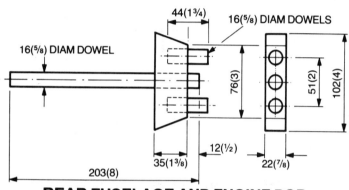

44(1¾)

16(⅝) DIAM DOWELS

16(⅝) DIAM DOWEL

76(3)

51(2)

102(4)

12(½)

35(1⅜)

22(⅞)

203(8)

REAR FUSELAGE AND ENGINE POD - Space Ship No 2

38(1½) RADIUS

51(2)

HOLE 16(⅝) DIAM x 25(1) DEEP

44(1¾)

60(2⅜)

28(1⅛)

NOSE SECTION - Space Ship No 2

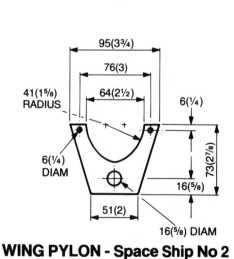

95(3¾)

76(3)

64(2½)

41(1⅝) RADIUS

6(¼)

6(¼) DIAM

73(2⅞)

16(⅝)

51(2)

16(⅝) DIAM

WING PYLON - Space Ship No 2

MAKE TWO   6(¼) THICK

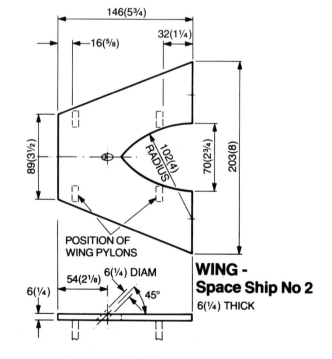

146(5¾)

16(⅝)

32(1¼)

89(3½)

102(4) RADIUS

70(2¾)

203(8)

POSITION OF WING PYLONS

54(2⅛)

6(¼) DIAM

45°

6(¼)

WING - Space Ship No 2

6(¼) THICK

114

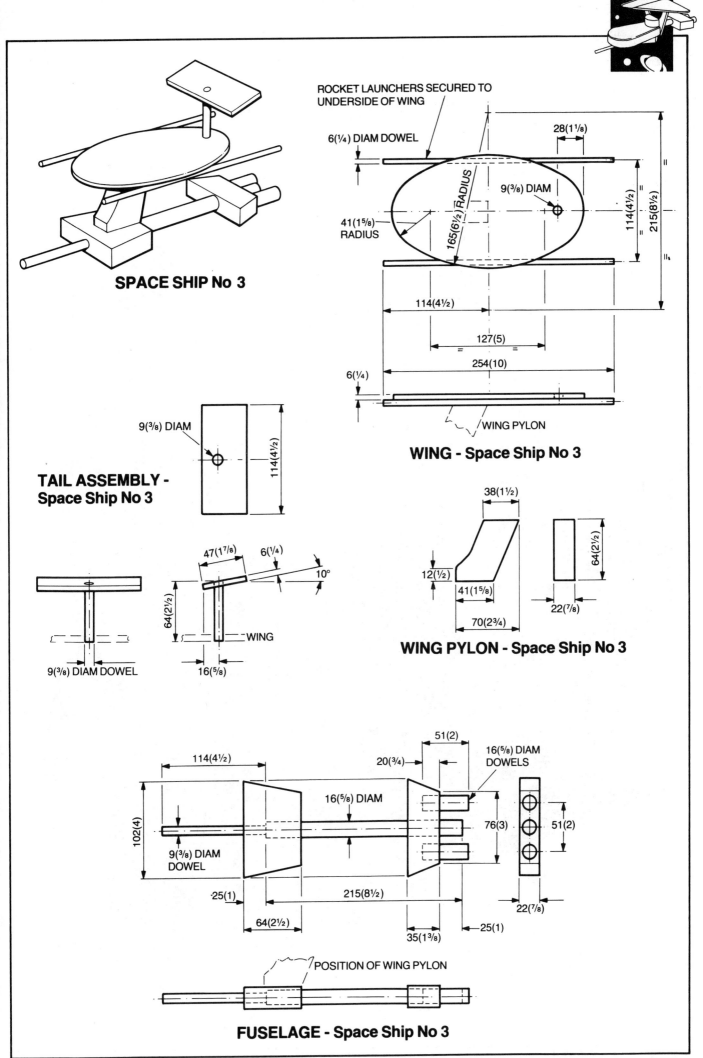

SPACE SHIP No 3

ROCKET LAUNCHERS SECURED TO UNDERSIDE OF WING

6(¼) DIAM DOWEL

28(1⅛)

9(⅜) DIAM

165(6½) RADIUS

41(1⅝) RADIUS

114(4½)

215(8½)

114(4½)

127(5)

254(10)

6(¼)

WING PYLON

WING - Space Ship No 3

9(⅜) DIAM

114(4½)

TAIL ASSEMBLY - Space Ship No 3

47(1⅞)

6(¼)

10°

64(2½)

WING

9(⅜) DIAM DOWEL

16(⅝)

38(1½)

12(½)

41(1⅝)

70(2¾)

64(2½)

22(⅞)

WING PYLON - Space Ship No 3

51(2)

20(¾)

16(⅝) DIAM DOWELS

114(4½)

16(⅝) DIAM

102(4)

9(⅜) DIAM DOWEL

76(3)

51(2)

25(1)

215(8½)

64(2½)

35(1⅜)

25(1)

22(⅞)

POSITION OF WING PYLON

FUSELAGE - Space Ship No 3

115

DOLL'S HOUSE

At some stage nearly all children will want a doll's house. This playing with the 'miniature world' allows the wonderful imagination of the child to develop. Perhaps the most rewarding experience to the 'house maker' is to sit and listen quietly while the children explore the house, arrange the carpet, find the bathroom, and put some boxes in the attic.

The interior of a doll's house can be as simple or as complex as you wish. Perhaps it is in this toy more than any other that parents and grandparents can share in making different parts of the house. And if you have an uncle who is good at electrics, he can install miniature lights.

1   Mark in pencil the two end walls and the positions of the wood strips that hold the walls together. Fix them together with tape and cut out as a pair. Tidy up the slots with a piece of glasspaper wrapped around a piece of waste wood.

2   Now glue the wood strips into the slots. When the glue is dry check that the strips do not stand 'proud' of the walls. The strips on the first floor will project over the garage space and will hold the garage roof.

3   Glue strips of wood inside the walls to carry the first floor and ceiling.

4   Cut the base board, position the house on it and mark its position in pencil. Remove the house and drill the necessary holes to screw the house to the base board.

5   Glue a strip of timber in the centre of the ground floor, running from the back wall to the front. Cover the ground floor with a piece of plywood.

6   With the house fixed to the base cut and fit the garage wall and roof.

7   Strips of wood are glued to both ground floor frame and first floor ceiling assembly to take the plastic door runner strip. The plastic runner is available from hardware and DIY shops and is used for sliding door units.

8   The front wall of the house slides on the plastic track and can be completely removed to allow children unhindered access. The plastic track on the front wall has to be modified, it being necessary to cut off the third 'web'.

9   Half the rear wall is hinged to allow access. The fixed section is glued and screwed into place after the window has been cut.

10   Cutting the windows out is perhaps the hardest part of building the house. Plywood is a very useful material but if it is not cut with a very fine toothed saw, huge jagged splinters will result. The method for cutting windows is as follows:
   i   Mark out all windows in pencil.
   ii   Drill two small holes in the

corner of the window, just large enough to get the saw blade in.
   iii   Using a keyhole saw with a fine blade, cut the window out.
   iv   Clean up the window hole with fine glasspaper.
If you have an electric jigsaw the method is exactly the same. You will find that the use of a metal cutting blade in the jigsaw will give a very fine cut and prevent any splinters.

11   There are many patterns of window available and if you intend to fit plastic ones it is a good idea to get them first and check the sizes to be cut in the walls.

12   Now cut and fit the first floor and ceiling. Before fitting cut the stair well hole and loft access hole.

13   Cut and glue into place the ground floor internal walls **A** and **B**.

14   The staircase is of the open tread pattern. Cut the staircase and then glue the stair treads on.

15   On the first floor cut and glue the internal walls **C**, **D** and **E** into position.

16   The little loft ladder is now made. This is done more easily if both sides of the ladder are taped together. In this way the holes drilled for the dowel rod rungs will align easily. Glasspaper the ends of each rung before glueing them into the ladder sides.

17   Glue strips of wood on the inside of the walls to take the roof.

18   Cut, glue and screw the rear roof in place. Note the overlaps on the end walls.

19   The front roof section is hinged. I could not find the right hinges for this job so I bought some long flap (blade) hinges and with a pair of pliers bent one flap on the ridge line and then screwed it into the fixed rear section of the roof. Bending mild steel hinges is quite easy, but it is necessary to get it right first time otherwise the hinge flap will just break off if you have to re-bend it.

20   Shape up the chimney, then glue and screw it in place.

21 Hinge the rear wall section and fix it in position. A small hook is used to keep the wall closed.

22 A small strip of wood glued onto the front of the base simulates the garden wall. It must not fit against the house or garage wall otherwise the front wall will not be able to slide freely.

The house illustrated is fitted with leaded light windows and miniature pattern wall papers. Brick and tile papers are used on the outside. The majority of furniture can be made, but for real detail I do like the miniature plastic bathroom fittings that are available. Fablon self-adhesive baize makes some very attractive carpets. There is really no limit to the amount of details you can add.

Cutting list

Base board	1 off	632 x 432 x 9mm (24⅞ x 17 x ⅜in)	Plywood
	1 off	280 x 16 x 16mm (11 x ⅝ x ⅝in)	Timber
Garden walls	Make from	22 x 16 x 675mm (⅞ x ⅝ x 26½in)	Timber
Ground floor assembly	1 off	413 x 280 x 5mm (16¼ x 11 x 3/16in)	Plywood
	2 off	432 x 22 x 16mm (17 x ⅞ x ⅝in)	Timber
	3 off	236 x 22 x 16mm (9¼ x ⅞ x ⅝in)	Timber
	1 off	432 x 20 x 16mm (17 x ¾ x ⅝in)	Timber
	1 off	Plastic 'door runner' strip 432mm (17in) long	
End walls	2 off	457 x 280 x 9mm (18 x 11 x ⅜in)	Plywood
	4 off	235 x 22 x 16mm (9¼ x ⅞ x ⅝in)	Timber
	2 off	171 x 22 x 16mm (6¾ x ⅞ x ⅝in)	Timber
	2 off	165 x 22 x 16mm (6½ x ⅞ x ⅝in)	Timber
Garage wall	1 off	280 x 165 x 9mm (11 x 6½ x ⅜in)	Plywood
Garage roof	1 off	280 x 197 x 5mm (11 x 7¾ x 3/16in)	Plywood
Ground floor internal walls	1 off	280 x 144 x 5mm (11 x 5 11/16 x 3/16in)	Plywood
	1 off	146 x 144 x 5mm (5¾ x 5 11/16 x 3/16in)	Plywood
Stairs support	1 off	190 x 22 x 16mm (7½ x ⅞ x ⅝in)	Timber
treads	Make from	178 x 32 x 5mm (7 x 1¼ x 3/16in)	Plywood
First floor assembly	1 off	413 x 280 x 5mm (16¼ x 11 x 3/16in)	Plywood
	2 off	619 x 22 x 16mm (24⅜ x ⅞ x ⅝in)	Timber
	1 off	64 x 16 x 6mm (2½ x ⅝ x ¼in)	Plywood
First floor internal walls	2 off	280 x 124 x 5mm (11 x 4⅞ x 3/16in)	Plywood
	1 off	146 x 124 x 5mm (5¾ x 4⅞ x 3/16in)	Plywood
First floor ceiling assembly	1 off	413 x 280 x 5mm (16¼ x 11 x 3/16in)	Plywood
	2 off	432 x 22 x 16mm (17 x ⅞ x ⅝in)	Timber
Loft ladder stringers	2 off	133 x 9 x 5mm (5¼ x ⅜ x 3/16in)	Timber
rungs	Make from	222mm (8¾in) long x 6mm (¼in) diameter dowel	
Hinged roof panel	1 off	457 x 210 x 9mm (18 x 8¼ x ⅜in)	Plywood
	2 off	20 wide x 32mm (¾ x 1¼in) long hinges	
Rear roof panel	1 off	457 x 228 x 9mm (18 x 9 x ⅜in)	Plywood
Ridge board	1 off	432 x 22 x 16mm (17 x ⅞ x ⅝in)	Timber
Front top runner assembly	1 off	432 x 20 x 16mm (17 x ¾ x ⅝in)	Timber
	1 off	Plastic 'door runner' strip 432mm (17in) long	
Chimney	1 off	330 x 47 x 22mm (13 x 1⅞ x ⅞in)	Timber
Front wall	1 off	432 x 260 x 9mm (17 x 10¼ x ⅜in)	Plywood
	2 off	Plastic 'door runner' strips 432mm (17in) long	
Rear wall (hinged)	1 off	302 x 267 x 9mm (11⅞ x 10½ x ⅜in)	Plywood
	1 off	302 x 22 x 16mm (11⅞ x ⅞ x ⅝in)	Timber
	2 off	51mm (2in) Brass hinges	
Rear wall fixed	1 off	302 x 165 x 9mm (11⅞ x 6½ x ⅜in)	Plywood
	1 off	302 x 22 x 16mm (11⅞ x ⅞ x ⅝in)	Timber

Ancillaries

	Various papers for covering internal and external walls and 'tiled' paper for roofs
	Various fabrics for internal carpeting, curtains and front garden 'lawn'
	Bathroom suite
	'Hobbies Ltd' doors and windows:
2 off	Doors
2 off	Three bay windows
5 off	Double bay windows
1 off	Single window for roof skylight
1 off	Single trellised window
	Chimney pot assembly

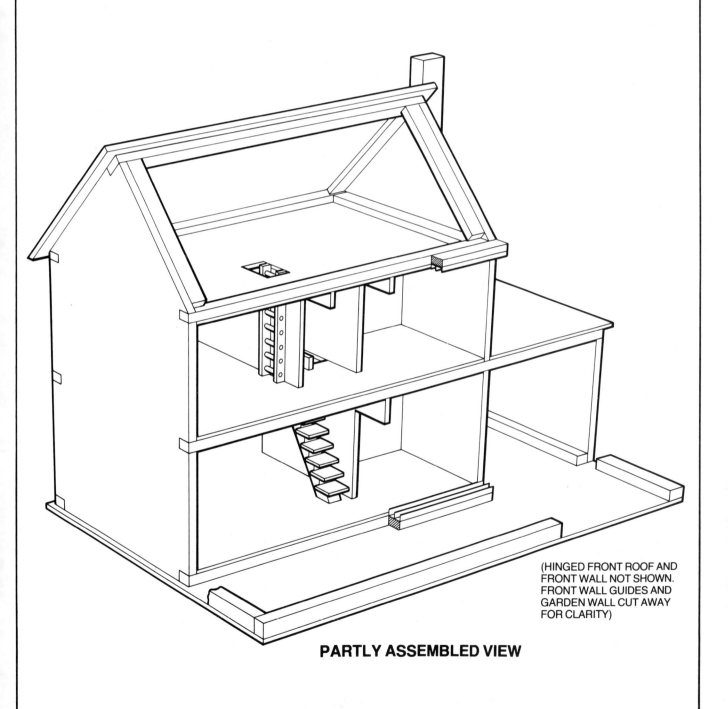

(HINGED FRONT ROOF AND
FRONT WALL NOT SHOWN.
FRONT WALL GUIDES AND
GARDEN WALL CUT AWAY
FOR CLARITY)

PARTLY ASSEMBLED VIEW

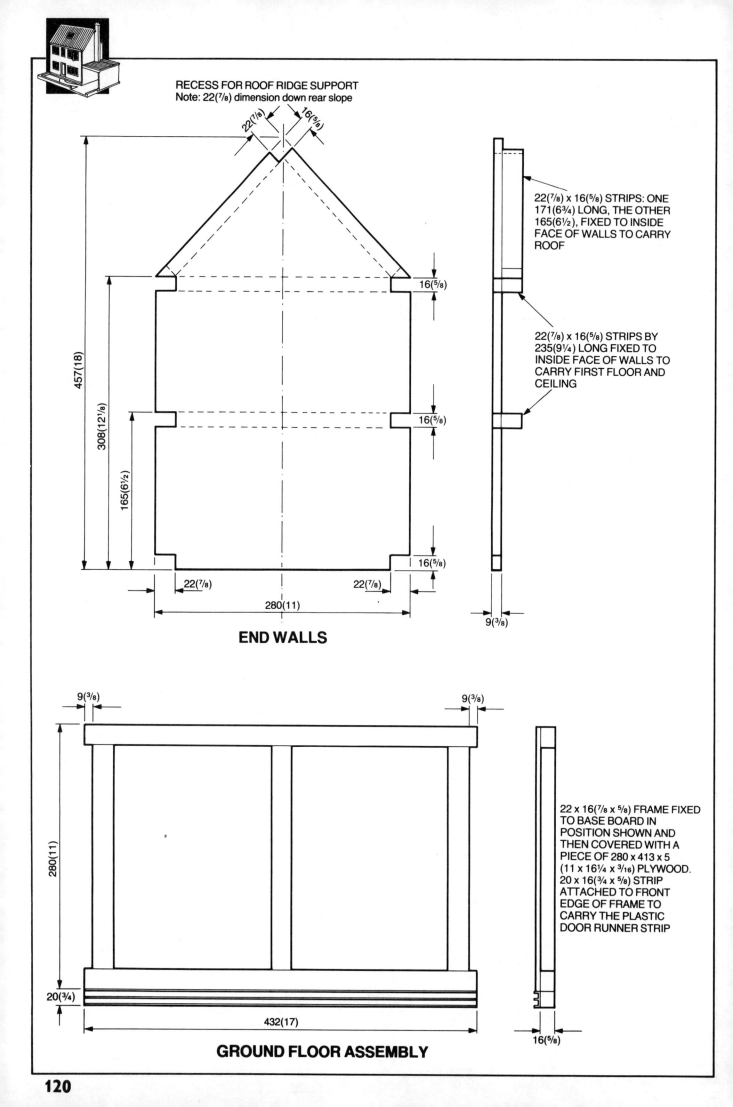

RECESS FOR ROOF RIDGE SUPPORT
Note: 22(⁷/₈) dimension down rear slope

22(⁷/₈) 16(⁵/₈)

16(⁵/₈)

22(⁷/₈) x 16(⁵/₈) STRIPS: ONE 171(6¾) LONG, THE OTHER 165(6½), FIXED TO INSIDE FACE OF WALLS TO CARRY ROOF

457(18)

308(12¹/₈)

165(6½)

16(⁵/₈)

22(⁷/₈) x 16(⁵/₈) STRIPS BY 235(9¼) LONG FIXED TO INSIDE FACE OF WALLS TO CARRY FIRST FLOOR AND CEILING

16(⁵/₈)

22(⁷/₈)   22(⁷/₈)

280(11)

9(³/₈)

END WALLS

9(³/₈)   9(³/₈)

280(11)

22 x 16(⁷/₈ x ⁵/₈) FRAME FIXED TO BASE BOARD IN POSITION SHOWN AND THEN COVERED WITH A PIECE OF 280 x 413 x 5 (11 x 16¼ x ³/₁₆) PLYWOOD. 20 x 16(¾ x ⁵/₈) STRIP ATTACHED TO FRONT EDGE OF FRAME TO CARRY THE PLASTIC DOOR RUNNER STRIP

20(¾)

432(17)

16(⁵/₈)

GROUND FLOOR ASSEMBLY

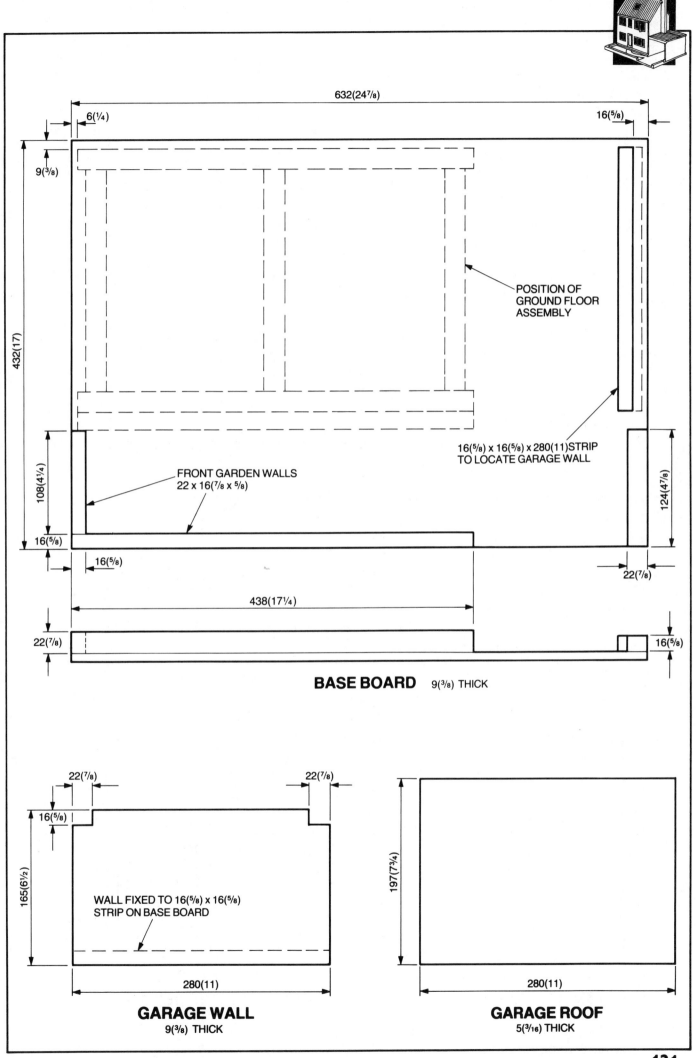

632(24⅞)

6(¼)

16(⅝)

9(⅜)

432(17)

POSITION OF
GROUND FLOOR
ASSEMBLY

16(⅝) x 16(⅝) x 280(11) STRIP
TO LOCATE GARAGE WALL

108(4¼)

FRONT GARDEN WALLS
22 x 16(⅞ x ⅝)

124(4⅞)

16(⅝)

16(⅝)

22(⅞)

438(17¼)

22(⅞)

16(⅝)

BASE BOARD   9(⅜) THICK

22(⅞)

22(⅞)

16(⅝)

165(6½)

WALL FIXED TO 16(⅝) x 16(⅝)
STRIP ON BASE BOARD

197(7¾)

280(11)

280(11)

GARAGE WALL
9(⅜) THICK

GARAGE ROOF
5(³⁄₁₆) THICK

PLASTIC DOOR RUNNER
STRIP, TOP AND BOTTOM,
WITH 3rd WEB CUT OFF

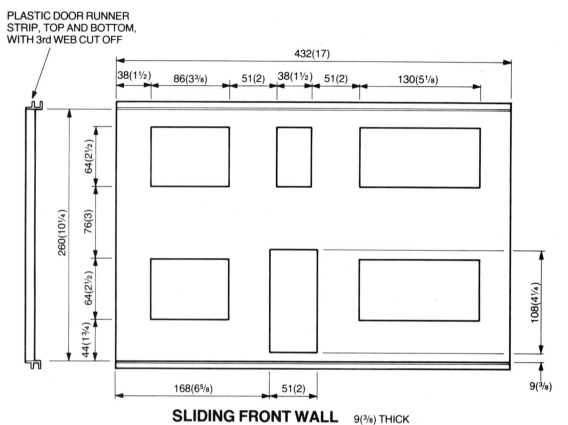

SLIDING FRONT WALL 9(³/₈) THICK

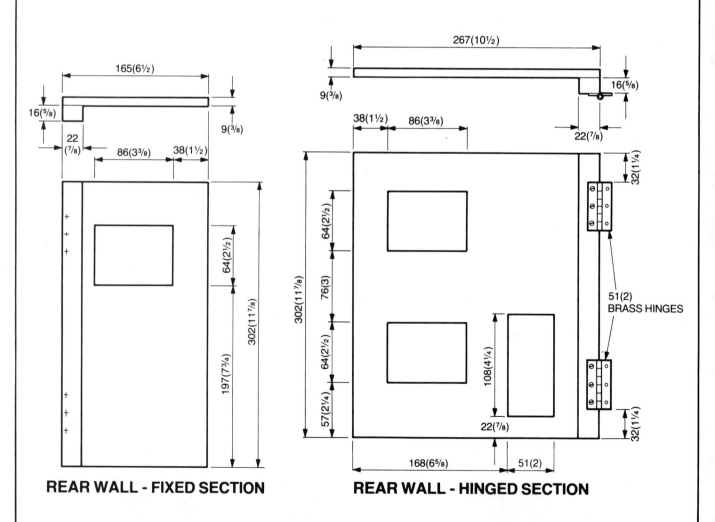

REAR WALL - FIXED SECTION

REAR WALL - HINGED SECTION

51(2)
BRASS HINGES

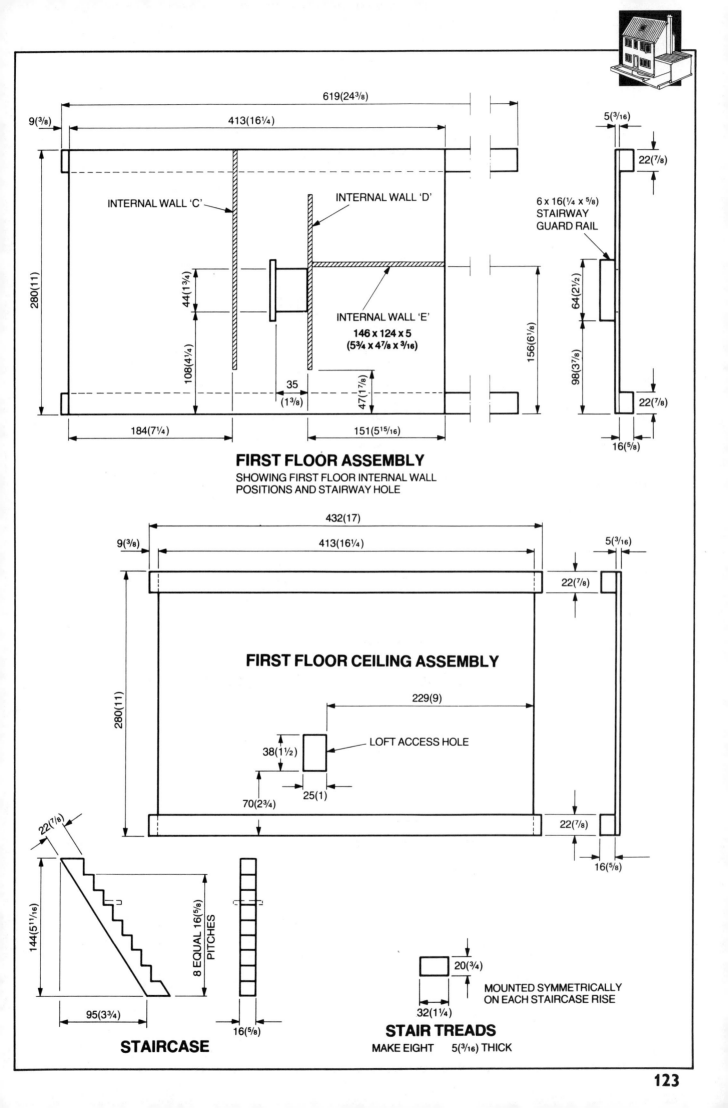

FIRST FLOOR ASSEMBLY

SHOWING FIRST FLOOR INTERNAL WALL
POSITIONS AND STAIRWAY HOLE

INTERNAL WALL 'C'

INTERNAL WALL 'D'

INTERNAL WALL 'E'

146 x 124 x 5
(5¾ x 4⅞ x 3⁄16)

6 x 16(¼ x ⅝)
STAIRWAY
GUARD RAIL

619(24⅜)

413(16¼)

9(⅜)

280(11)

44(1¾)

108(4¼)

35
(1⅜)

47(1⅞)

184(7¼)

151(5¹⁵⁄₁₆)

156(6⅛)

5(³⁄₁₆)

22(⅞)

64(2½)

98(3⅞)

22(⅞)

16(⅝)

FIRST FLOOR CEILING ASSEMBLY

432(17)

413(16¼)

9(⅜)

280(11)

229(9)

LOFT ACCESS HOLE

38(1½)

25(1)

70(2¾)

22(⅞)

5(³⁄₁₆)

22(⅞)

16(⅝)

STAIRCASE

22(⅞)

144(5¹¹⁄₁₆)

8 EQUAL 16(⅝)
PITCHES

95(3¾)

16(⅝)

STAIR TREADS

MAKE EIGHT   5(³⁄₁₆) THICK

20(¾)

32(1¼)

MOUNTED SYMMETRICALLY
ON EACH STAIRCASE RISE

123

413(16¼)

280(11)

INTERNAL WALL 'A'

INTERNAL WALL 'B'

STAIRCASE

137(5⅜)

57(2¼)

47(1⅞)

244(9⅝)

146(5¾)

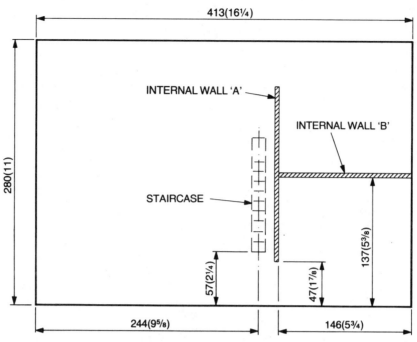

GROUND FLOOR PLAN

22(⅞)

22(⅞)

16(⅝)

144(5¹¹/₁₆)

102(4)

47(1⅞)

47(1⅞)

280(11)

INTERNAL WALL 'A'
5(³/₁₆) THICK

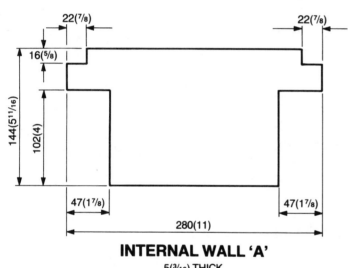

22(⅞)

16(⅝)

144(5¹¹/₁₆)

146(5¾)

INTERNAL WALL 'B'
5(³/₁₆) THICK

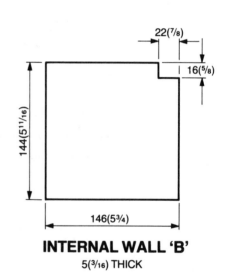

89(3½)

POSITION OF LOFT LADDER

124(4⅞)

102(4)

232(9⅛)

47(1⅞)

INTERNAL WALL 'C'
5(³/₁₆) THICK

280(11)

124(4⅞)

102(4)

47(1⅞)

47(1⅞)

INTERNAL WALL 'D'
5(³/₁₆) THICK

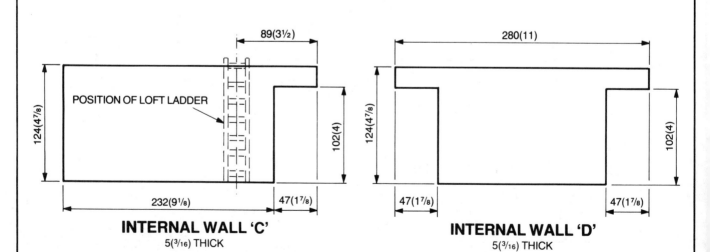

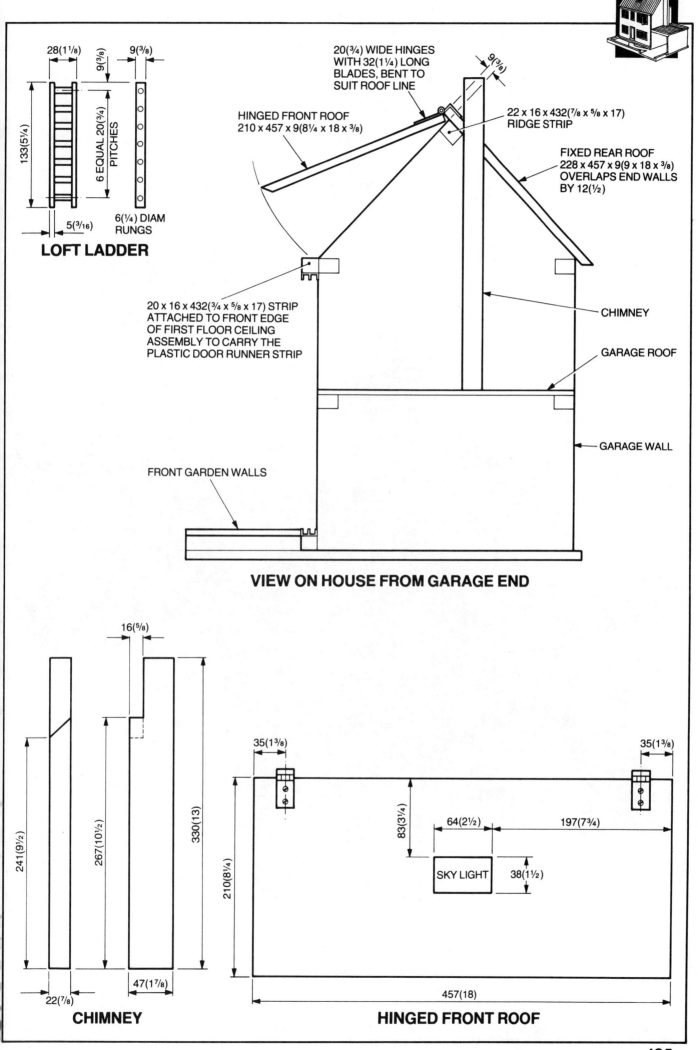

LOFT LADDER

28(1⅛)
9(⅜)
9(⅜)
133(5¼)
6 EQUAL 20(¾) PITCHES
5(³/₁₆)
6(¼) DIAM RUNGS

20(¾) WIDE HINGES WITH 32(1¼) LONG BLADES, BENT TO SUIT ROOF LINE

9(⅜)

HINGED FRONT ROOF 210 x 457 x 9(8¼ x 18 x ⅜)

22 x 16 x 432(⅞ x ⅝ x 17) RIDGE STRIP

FIXED REAR ROOF 228 x 457 x 9(9 x 18 x ⅜) OVERLAPS END WALLS BY 12(½)

20 x 16 x 432(¾ x ⅝ x 17) STRIP ATTACHED TO FRONT EDGE OF FIRST FLOOR CEILING ASSEMBLY TO CARRY THE PLASTIC DOOR RUNNER STRIP

CHIMNEY

GARAGE ROOF

GARAGE WALL

FRONT GARDEN WALLS

VIEW ON HOUSE FROM GARAGE END

16(⅝)

241(9½)
267(10½)
330(13)
22(⅞)
47(1⅞)

CHIMNEY

35(1⅜)
35(1⅜)
83(3¼)
64(2½)
197(7¾)
210(8¼)
SKY LIGHT
38(1½)
457(18)

HINGED FRONT ROOF

125

FORT

Watching my boys play with soldiers I have discovered that an essential part of such a defensive building is lots of castellations, look-out towers, walkways, ladders and some movable structures inside. Another essential is a door with a closing bar to keep the 'baddies' out.

The flag poles do represent a hazard for a young child and therefore these can be left off until he or she is older.

The fort consists of a main enclosure with smaller enclosures on right and left hand sides. The whole structure is mounted on a plywood base.

1 Start by cutting to width and length the plywood for the main enclosure.

2 Mark out in pencil on the walls all the pieces that have to be cut out.

3 Use the following method for cutting out all castellations:
  i Fix the plywood in the vice as near the castellations to be cut out as is practical.
  ii Cut down both sides with a tenon saw.
  iii Using a coping saw with the blade turned at 90° to the top of the frame it is possible to cut along the bottom of the castellation.
  All the remaining castellations are cut in this way including those for the enclosures and watchtower.

4 Cut out the doorways and screw the hinges on to the main gates. The catch and locking bar are then fixed in position.

5 Before fixing any side walls together carefully glasspaper all the castellations. This is easily done if the glasspaper is wrapped around a piece of waste wood.

6 The four walls of the main enclosure are glued together at the corners. As there is very little glueing area, the addition of four corner blocks is essential. However these do not run the full height of the wall but stop below the walkways.

7 The left and right hand enclosures are now glued together. Once again small blocks are glued into the corners.

8 Cut and glue all the walkways into place.

9 Mark the position of the walls and corner blocks on the base board. From the underside screw the base on to the walls. Screws must be countersunk and should be positioned so that they go into the corner blocks.

10 Although there are several ladders it is best to make them all in one long length, and then cut off shorter lengths.

11 To make the ladders prepare two equal stringers. Fix these together at the ends with tape. Mark the centres

of the rungs. Using a drill of the same diameter as the dowel rod, drill all the rung holes.

12 Now cut the rungs. These must all be the same length. 'Tidy up' the ends of each dowel rod with glasspaper, putting a slight chamfer on the end of each one.

13 Now check that the dowel rods fit the stringers before glueing them in the holes.

14 The simplest way to glue the rungs in place is to put a little glue on the end of each rung. When this has been done push all the rungs into one side only. Now put a spot of glue on all the other rung ends. Position the rungs in the holes. This may take a little care. Now when all the ends are in the holes place the ladder in a vice and squeeze both sides together, working carefully from each end.

15 Now cut suitable lengths of ladder for the watchtower, main enclosure etc.

16 The two look-out boxes are constructed from plywood and all corners are glued together. The roof is held by the four dowel rods which are glued in to the corners.
  The look-out boxes are fixed on to the main enclosure by screws passing through the castellations from the inside.

17 The watchtower is movable and can therefore be used in any position within the main enclosure. Cut the base plate and pillars. The pillars are screwed on to the base plate.

18 The same method is used to cut the castellations on the watchtower walls as for the main enclosure walls.

19 The roof is made up of four sloping panels. The edges of the four panels should be chamfered to get a nice tight fit. A medium grit glasspaper is best for this job.

20 Holding the four sloping panels together while the glue sets can be difficult, therefore make up a small jig to hold the pieces. On a piece of scrap plywood mark in pencil the area the roof base will cover (see drawing). At

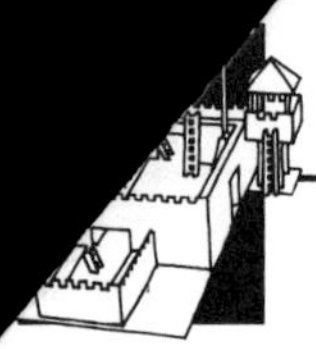

each corner and half way along the sides fix a small nail. Now when glue is applied to all corners, the nails will hold the panels upright as the glue sets.

21 Four dowel rods hold the roof platform in place above the walls. The dowel rods are glued in to the corners of the watchtower and the roof is fixed on.

22 The ladder is glued to the side.

23 The main building in the fort is also movable or can be left out.

24 Mark out the building platform and the centres of all the posts. Drill the post holes.

25 The posts project through the base to lift the building off the ground. In order that each post goes through the base exactly the right length, position a piece of waste wood of the correct thickness under the platform. Put a little glue on each post and with a light hammer tap the post in place.

26 All the walls and roof of the main building are glued together. It is a good practice to use panel pins as well as glue, but remember to use a panel pin punch to drive the head below the surface. This small hole should be filled before painting or varnishing.

27 The base of the main flag pole is made from an offcut and the pole from a dowel rod. Do put a brightly coloured flag on this otherwise it could be dangerous.

Cutting list

Base board		1 off	816 x 388 x 5mm (32 x 15¼ x 3/16in)	Plywood
Main enclosure	front and rear walls	2 off	445 x 140 x 9mm (17½ x 5½ x ⅜in)	Plywood
	end walls	2 off	370 x 140 x 9mm (14½ x 5½ x ⅜in)	Plywood
Right hand enclosure	front and rear walls	2 off	160 x 76 x 9mm (6¼ x 3 x ⅜in)	Plywood
	side wall	1 off	166 x 76 x 9mm (6½ x 3 x ⅜in)	Plywood
Left hand enclosure	front and rear walls	2 off	211 x 76 x 9mm (8¼ x 3 x ⅜in)	Plywood
	side wall	1 off	140 x 76 x 9mm (5½ x 3 x ⅜in)	Plywood
Look-out boxes	roof	2 off	127 x 114 x 5mm (5 x 4½ x 3/16in)	Plywood
	front and rear walls	4 off	102 x 51 x 9mm (4 x 2 x ⅜in)	Plywood
	sides	4 off	84 x 51 x 9mm (3¼ x 2 x ⅜in)	Plywood
	floor	2 off	83 x 83 x 5mm (3¼ x 3¼ x 3/16in)	Plywood
	corner posts	8 off	76 long x 6mm (3 x ¼in) diameter dowel	
	flag staff	2 off	216 long x 6mm (8½ x ¼in) diameter dowel	
Corner blocks		Make from 25 x 25 x 610mm (1 x 1 x 24in)		Timber
Wall walkways		Make from 28 x 9 x 2640mm (1⅛ x ⅜ x 104in		Timber
Ladders	stringers	Make from 16 x 16 x 1450mm (⅝ x ¼ x 57in		Timber
	rungs	Make from 864 long x 6mm (34 x ¼in) diameter dowel		
Door catch		1 off	51 long x 6mm (2 x ¼in) diameter dowel	
		1 off	41 x 16 x 9mm (1⅝ x ⅝ x ⅜in)	Plywood
Ancillaries				
		2 off	25mm (1in) long brass hinges and screws	
Watch tower				
Roof	flat	1 off	102 x 102 x 5mm (4 x 4 x 3/16in)	Plywood
	sloping	4 off	102 x 76 x 5mm (4 x 3 x 3/16in)	Plywood
Floor		1 off	83 x 83 x 5mm (3¼ x 3¼ x 3/16in)	Plywood
Walls		2 off	102 x 64 x 9mm (4 x 2½ x ⅜in)	Plywood
		2 off	83 x 64 x 9mm (3¼ x 2½ x ⅜in)	Plywood
Corner posts		4 off	84mm (3¼in) long x 6mm (¼in) diameter dowel	
Support pillars		2 off	127 x 44 x 20mm (5 x 1¾ x ¾in)	Timber
Base plate		1 off	121 x 95 x 5mm (4¾ x 3¾ x 3/16in)	Plywood
Ladder	stringers	Make from 16 x 6 x 275mm (⅝ x ¼ x 10¾in)		Timber
	rungs	Make from 190mm (7½in) long x 6mm (¼in) diameter dowel		
Outbuilding				
Base		1 off	375 x 114 x 9mm (14¾ x 4½ x ⅜in)	Plywood
Wall, front and rear		2 off	305 x 76 x 9mm (12 x 3 x ⅜in)	Plywood
		2 off	76 x 57 x 9mm (3 x 2¼ x ⅜in)	Plywood
Fencing		Make from 1220 long x 6mm (48 x ¼in) diameter dowel		

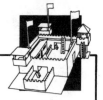

Flag pole

Base	1 off	76 × 44mm (3 × 1¾in)
Pole	1 off	368mm (14½in) long × 6mm (¼in) diameter dowel

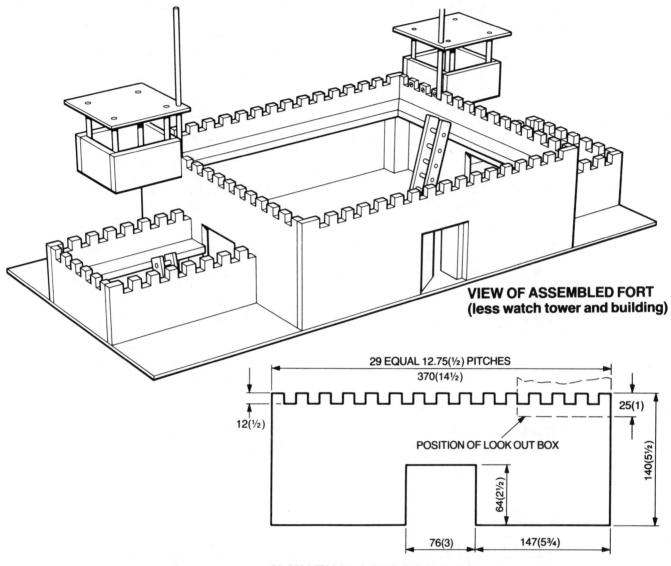

VIEW OF ASSEMBLED FORT
(less watch tower and building)

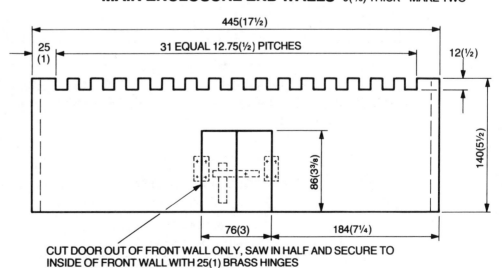

29 EQUAL 12.75(½) PITCHES

370(14½)

25(1)

12(½)

POSITION OF LOOK OUT BOX

140(5½)

64(2½)

76(3)   147(5¾)

MAIN ENCLOSURE END WALLS 9(⅜) THICK   MAKE TWO

445(17½)

25 (1)

31 EQUAL 12.75(½) PITCHES

12(½)

140(5½)

86(3⅜)

76(3)   184(7¼)

CUT DOOR OUT OF FRONT WALL ONLY, SAW IN HALF AND SECURE TO
INSIDE OF FRONT WALL WITH 25(1) BRASS HINGES

FRONT AND REAR WALLS OF MAIN ENCLOSURE

MAKE TWO   9(⅜) THICK

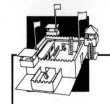

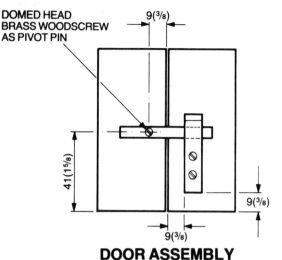

DOMED HEAD
BRASS WOODSCREW
AS PIVOT PIN

9($\frac{3}{8}$)

41(1$\frac{5}{8}$)

9($\frac{3}{8}$)

9($\frac{3}{8}$)

DOOR ASSEMBLY
AS VIEWED FROM INSIDE

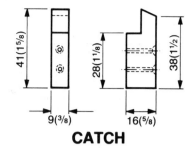

41(1$\frac{5}{8}$)   28(1$\frac{1}{8}$)   38(1$\frac{1}{2}$)

9($\frac{3}{8}$)   16($\frac{5}{8}$)

CATCH
COUNTERSINK FIXING HOLES

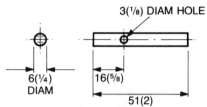

3($\frac{1}{8}$) DIAM HOLE

6($\frac{1}{4}$)
DIAM

16($\frac{5}{8}$)

51(2)

LOCKING BAR

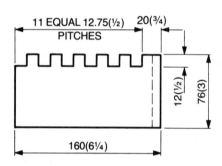

11 EQUAL 12.75($\frac{1}{2}$)   20($\frac{3}{4}$)
PITCHES

12($\frac{1}{2}$)   76(3)

160(6$\frac{1}{4}$)

RIGHT HAND ENCLOSURE
FRONT AND REAR WALLS
9($\frac{3}{8}$) THICK   MAKE TWO

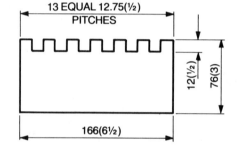

13 EQUAL 12.75($\frac{1}{2}$)
PITCHES

12($\frac{1}{2}$)   76(3)

166(6$\frac{1}{2}$)

RIGHT HAND ENCLOSURE
SIDE WALL   9($\frac{3}{8}$) THICK

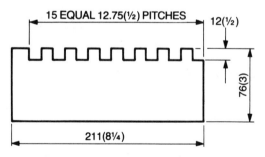

15 EQUAL 12.75($\frac{1}{2}$) PITCHES   12($\frac{1}{2}$)

76(3)

211(8$\frac{1}{4}$)

LEFT HAND ENCLOSURE
FRONT AND REAR WALLS
9($\frac{3}{8}$) THICK   MAKE TWO

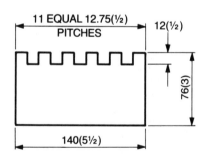

11 EQUAL 12.75($\frac{1}{2}$)   12($\frac{1}{2}$)
PITCHES

76(3)

140(5$\frac{1}{2}$)

LEFT HAND ENCLOSURE
SIDE WALL   9($\frac{3}{8}$) THICK

WALL WALKWAYS

28(1$\frac{1}{8}$) WIDE x 9($\frac{3}{8}$) THICK PLYWOOD
WITH MITRED ENDS RESTING ON
THE CORNER BLOCKS

OVERALL LENGTHS – 2 OFF AT 425(16$\frac{3}{4}$)
2 OFF AT 368(14$\frac{1}{2}$)
2 OFF AT 149(5$\frac{7}{8}$))
1 OFF AT 165(6$\frac{1}{2}$)
2 OFF AT 200(7$\frac{7}{8}$))
1 OFF AT 140(5$\frac{1}{2}$)

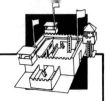

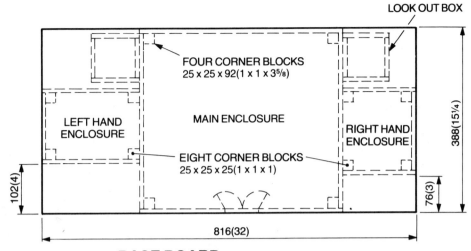

LOOK OUT BOX

FOUR CORNER BLOCKS
25 x 25 x 92(1 x 1 x 3⅝)

MAIN ENCLOSURE

LEFT HAND
ENCLOSURE

RIGHT HAND
ENCLOSURE

EIGHT CORNER BLOCKS
25 x 25 x 25(1 x 1 x 1)

388(15¼)

102(4)

76(3)

816(32)

BASE BOARD 5(³⁄₁₆) THICK

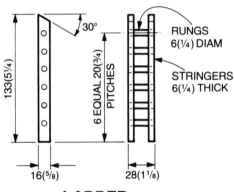

30°

133(5¼)

6 EQUAL 20(¾) PITCHES

RUNGS
6(¼) DIAM

STRINGERS
6(¼) THICK

16(⅝)

28(1⅛)

LADDER

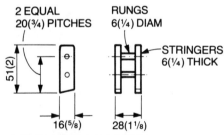

2 EQUAL
20(¾) PITCHES

RUNGS
6(¼) DIAM

STRINGERS
6(¼) THICK

51(2)

16(⅝)

28(1⅛)

**SIDE ENCLOSURE
LADDERS** MAKE SIX

BOTTOM EDGE CHAMFERED
TO SUIT INSTALLATION ANGLE

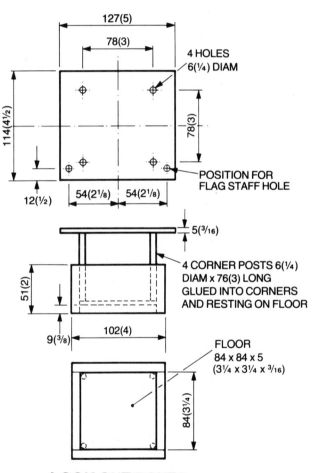

127(5)

78(3)

4 HOLES
6(¼) DIAM

114(4½)

78(3)

12(½)

54(2⅛)   54(2⅛)

POSITION FOR
FLAG STAFF HOLE

5(³⁄₁₆)

4 CORNER POSTS 6(¼)
DIAM x 76(3) LONG
GLUED INTO CORNERS
AND RESTING ON FLOOR

51(2)

102(4)

9(⅜)

FLOOR
84 x 84 x 5
(3¼ x 3¼ x ³⁄₁₆)

84(3¼)

LOOK OUT BOXES

WALLS – 9(⅜) PLYWOOD
MAKE TWO

FLAG STAFF – 1 EACH BOX
6(¼) DIAM BY 216(8½) LONG

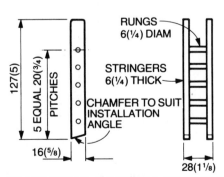

RUNGS
6(¼) DIAM

127(5)

5 EQUAL 20(¾) PITCHES

STRINGERS
6(¼) THICK

CHAMFER TO SUIT
INSTALLATION
ANGLE

16(⅝)

28(1⅛)

MAIN ENCLOSURE LADDERS

MAKE THREE

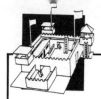

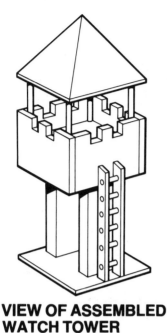

VIEW OF ASSEMBLED WATCH TOWER

76(3)

102(4)

SLOPING ROOF
PANELS MAKE FOUR
5(³/₁₆) THICK

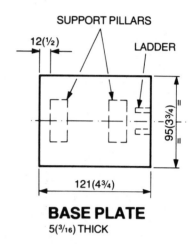

SUPPORT PILLARS

12(½)

LADDER

95(3¾)

121(4¾)

BASE PLATE
5(³/₁₆) THICK

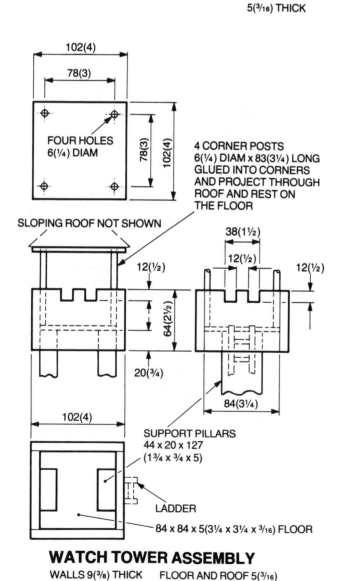

102(4)

78(3)

FOUR HOLES
6(¼) DIAM

78(3)

102(4)

4 CORNER POSTS
6(¼) DIAM x 83(3¼) LONG
GLUED INTO CORNERS
AND PROJECT THROUGH
ROOF AND REST ON
THE FLOOR

SLOPING ROOF NOT SHOWN

38(1½)

12(½)

12(½)

12(½)

64(2½)

20(¾)

84(3¼)

102(4)

SUPPORT PILLARS
44 x 20 x 127
(1¾ x ¾ x 5)

LADDER

84 x 84 x 5(3¼ x 3¼ x ³/₁₆) FLOOR

WATCH TOWER ASSEMBLY
WALLS 9(³/₈) THICK   FLOOR AND ROOF 5(³/₁₆)

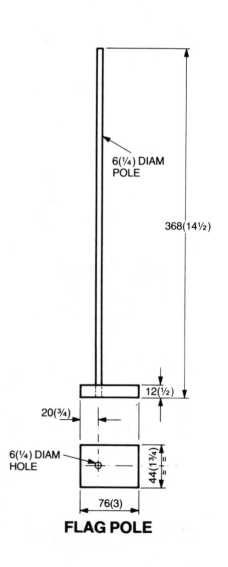

6(¼) DIAM
POLE

368(14½)

12(½)

20(¾)

6(¼) DIAM
HOLE

44(1¾)

76(3)

FLAG POLE

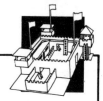

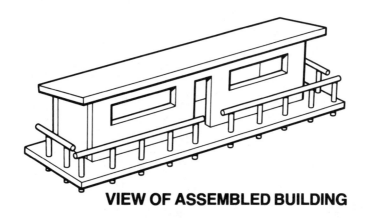

VIEW OF ASSEMBLED BUILDING

171(6¾)

9(⅜)

6(¼) DIAM RAIL AND POSTS

89(3½)

25(1)

44(1¾)

9(⅜)

9(⅜)

4 EQUAL 38(1½) PITCHES

4 EQUAL 38(1½) PITCHES

9(⅜)

2 EQUAL 38(1½) PITCHES

14 HOLES 6(¼) DIAM

114(4½)

POSITION OF BUILDING

35 (1⅜)

375(14¾)

BUILDING PLATFORM   9(⅜) THICK

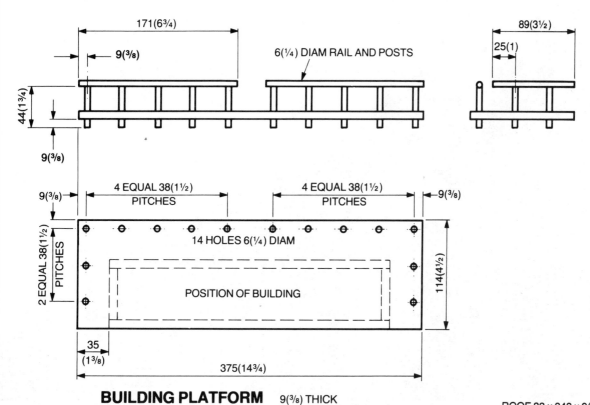

ROOF 83 x 343 x 9(3¼ x 13½ x ⅜) FRONT EDGE CHAMFERED TO GIVE VERTICAL FACE.

12(½)

305(12)

83(3¼)

CHAMFER TO SUIT ANGLE OF ROOF

76(3)

60(2⅜)

75(2¹⁵⁄₁₆)

38(1½)

64(2½)

25(1)

89(3½)

89(3½)

25(1)

57(2¼)

25(1)

140(5½)

REAR WALL 60 x 305 x 9(2⅜ x 12 x ⅜) CHAMFER TOP EDGE TO SUIT ROOF

BUILDING FRONT WALL   9(⅜) THICK

BUILDING END WALLS

MAKE TWO   9(⅜) THICK

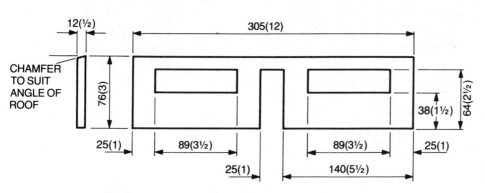

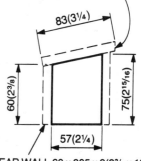

133

1902 SCANIA

The history of transport is a fascinating subject, as it clearly demonstrates man's genius when faced with either getting himself around the world or taking goods from one part of the globe to another.

This 1902 Scania truck is the first one ever produced by the company. The engine rating was 10-12 horsepower and the rear wheels were chain driven. It was capable of hauling 1.5 tons.

These early vehicle makers were intent on removing the limitations of the horse-drawn vehicle. It may seem incongruous to us now but it was a natural progression to use the existing four-wheel farm cart technology and put an engine in it. This is clearly demonstrated on this first Scania, particularly when one examines the brakes and springs.

However, the whole concept of design and high technology that now surrounds the truck industry can be gauged by looking at the magnificent 1980 range of vehicles.

It was the contrast between old and new that inspired me to tackle the task of building this beautiful old truck. I generally try to avoid specifying woods to build models in but do try to build this one in oak, it really is worth the effort and looks rather good when finished.

1   The first job is to cut out the lorry bed. Cut an elongated hole in the front end to take the brake handle. The handle is held in position by a steel pin that is inserted through the side of the bed, through the handle, and fixed onto the other side of lorry bed!

2   I imitated the springs in oak. These are cut out with a coping saw, and the sawmarks removed with a sharp chisel.

The main chassis members may now be glued and screwed in place.

3   Cut out the front and back axles and rebate the ends to allow a nice tight fit up against the springs. Drill holes to take the axles before you cut the 'bow' shape on the underside of the axle block.

4   Study the underside of chassis assembly drawing.

5   The front axle has a hole drilled through it to take the brake cord. The back brake is made from a short length of wood and dowel rod. A small spring is fitted to return the brake to the 'off' position.

6   The gear box and drive unit are shaped up from a block of oak. Drill a hole in the box to take a steel axle. The axle needs to be the same bore as the small wheel. A small chain is attached between the drive gear wheel and the back axle. A plastic or wooden disc fitted onto the axle behind the wheel gives the chain something to run around, and if a little tension is given to the chain it will turn around the drive gear wheel realistically when the truck is moved.

7   Cut to shape the under chassis block which fits between the front bulkhead and front axle.

8   The front bulkhead was a bit of a mystery. Was there a radiator fitted into the front? Or was it just a protection for the driver? In spite of all the help I received from Scania, no one was able to find a picture of the front. The only picture that exists is the side view. I have put a filler cap on the top but left the front blank. It is up to you to add or leave off a radiator grill. The bulkhead is shaped to fit between the main chassis members. The front of the chassis is finished by glueing in the main chassis front cross member. A hole is drilled in the bulkhead to take the starting handle.

9   Make the steering column and steering wheel. The column is glued onto the back of the bulkhead. The steering wheel is left to turn freely in the column.

10   I bought a pair of brass carriage lamps which I attached to the side of the bulkhead.

11   The driver's seat is the next piece to make. Small vent lines should be carved in the side. The handle or driver's support rail I bent from a piece of mild steel rod.

12   The truck back, side and front walls on the original were simply planks held together by uprights. To add realism I grooved the side pieces and panel pinned small uprights across the grooves. Small hooks and chains keep the sides securely fastened.

13   Along the plank sides of the walls the company had painted in black letters SCANIA. The work force were obviously as proud of their 1902 vehicle as they are of their 1982 models.

14   I suggest finishing the lorry in a good quality matt varnish.

Cutting list

Lorry bed	1 off	470 x 156 x 14mm (18½ x 6⅛ x 9/16in)	Timber
Main chassis member	2 off	505 x 20 x 12mm (19⅞ x ¾ x ½in)	Timber
Main chassis front cross member	1 off	111 x 20 x 9mm (4⅜ x ¾ x ⅜in)	Timber
Front bulkhead	1 off	165 x 111 x 32mm (6½ x 4⅜ x 1¼in)	Timber
Radiator cap	1 off	25mm (1in) long x 12mm (½in) diameter dowel	
Steering column	1 off	89 x 22 x 12mm (3½ x ⅞ x ½in)	Timber
Steering wheel	1 off	28mm (1⅛in) diameter x 12mm (½in) thick	Timber
	1 off	89mm (3½in) long x 6mm (¼in) diameter dowel	
Starting handle	Make from	102mm (4in) long x 6mm (¼in) diameter dowel	
	1 off	44 x 12 x 12mm (1¾ x ½ x ½in)	Timber
Under chassis block	1 off	65 x 32 x 22mm (2 9/16 x 1¼ x ⅞in)	Timber
Front spring assemby	2 off	152 x 32 x 12mm (6 x 1¼ x ½in)	Timber
Front axle block	1 off	111 x 73 x 35mm (4⅜ x 2⅞ x 1⅜in)	Timber
Rear spring assembly	2 off	191 x 32 x 12mm (7½ x 1¼ x ½in)	Timber
Rear axle block	1 off	111 x 57 x 35mm (4⅜ x 2¼ x 1⅜in)	Timber
Gear box/drive unit	1 off	102 x 70 x 51mm (4 x 2¾ x 2in)	Timber
	1 off	102mm (4in) long x 9mm (⅜in) diameter dowel	
Brake lever	1 off	51 x 20 x 12mm (2 x ¾ x ½in)	Timber
	1 off	57mm (2¼in) long x 6mm (¼in) diameter dowel	
Brake handle	1 off	108 x 12 x 9mm (4¼ x ½ x ⅜in)	Timber
Seat assembly	Make from	184 x 48 x 11mm (7¼ x 1⅞ x 7/16in)	Timber
	Make from	171 x 44 x 11mm (6¾ x 1¾ x 7/16in)	Timber
	1 off	117 x 73 x 11mm (4⅝ x 2⅞ x 7/16in)	Timber
Side wall	2 off	356 x 51 x 12mm (14 x 2 x ½in)	Timber
Side wall straps	Make from	216 x 16 x 3mm (8½ x ⅝ x ⅛in)	Timber
Front and rear walls	2 off	130 x 51 x 12mm (5⅛ x 2 x ½in)	Timber
Brake shoe	1 off	41 x 20 x 16mm (1⅝ x ¾ x ⅝in)	Timber
Ancillaries			
Lorry bed	1 off	51mm (2in) long x 5mm (3/16in) diameter steel brake lever pin	
Main chassis member	1 off	9mm (⅜in) screwed eye	
Front bulkhead	2 off	'Brass' coach lamps (Hobbies Limited)	
Front axle	1 off	178mm (7in) long x 6mm (¼in) diameter steel axle	
	2 off	76mm (3in) diameter 'Cart' wheels	
Rear axle	1 off	181mm (7⅛in) long x 6mm (¼in) diameter steel axle	
	2 off	114mm (4½in) diameter 'Cart' wheels	
	4 off	Spring dome caps to suit 6mm (¼in) diameter axles	
Gear box/drive unit	1 off	114mm (4½in) long x 5mm (3/16in) diameter steel rod	
	1 off	9mm (⅜in) o/d x 5mm (3/16in) i/d x 25mm (1in) long spacer	
	1 off	Spring dome cap to suit 5mm (3/16in) diameter rod	
	1 off	330mm (13in) length of 8mm (5/16in) pitch chain	
Driving gear wheel	Make from	22mm (⅞in) diameter disc x 16mm (⅝in) thick plastic	
Rear axle drive spacer	Make from	41mm (1⅝in) diameter disc x 6mm (¼in) thick plastic	
Brake lever/handle	3 off	9mm (⅜in) diameter screwed eyes	
	1 off	32mm (1¼in) long extension spring	
	1 off	460mm (18in) length of strong cord	
Seat assembly	Make from	178mm (7in) long x 5mm (3/16in) diameter steel arm rest	
Side walls	4 off	25mm (1in) long brass hinges	
	4 off	12mm (½in) screwed hooks	
Front and rear walls	4 off	9mm (⅜in) long wood screws with 114mm (4½in) lengths of chain	
Guide for brake cable through front axle	1 off	9 mm (⅜in) o/d x 6mm (¼in) i/d x 38mm (1½in) plastic tube	

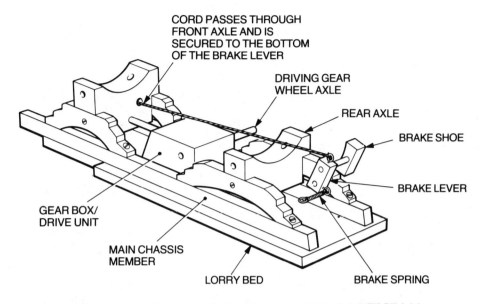

CORD PASSES THROUGH
FRONT AXLE AND IS
SECURED TO THE BOTTOM
OF THE BRAKE LEVER

DRIVING GEAR
WHEEL AXLE

REAR AXLE

BRAKE SHOE

BRAKE LEVER

BRAKE SPRING

GEAR BOX/
DRIVE UNIT

MAIN CHASSIS
MEMBER

LORRY BED

VIEW ON UNDERSIDE OF CHASSIS ASSEMBLY

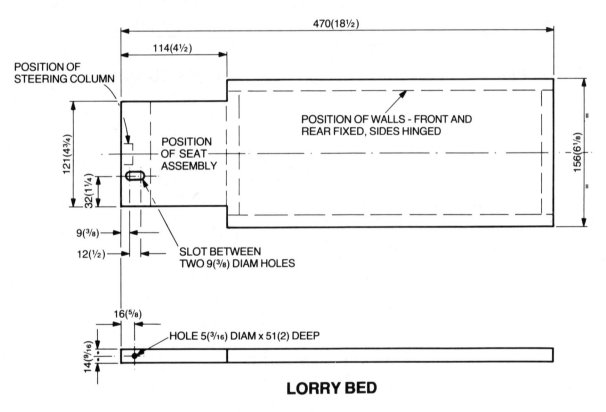

470(18½)

114(4½)

POSITION OF
STEERING COLUMN

121(4¾)

32(1¼)

POSITION
OF SEAT
ASSEMBLY

POSITION OF WALLS - FRONT AND
REAR FIXED, SIDES HINGED

156(6⅛)

9(³/₈)

12(½)

SLOT BETWEEN
TWO 9(³/₈) DIAM HOLES

16(⁵/₈)

14(⁹/₁₆)

HOLE 5(³/₁₆) DIAM x 51(2) DEEP

LORRY BED

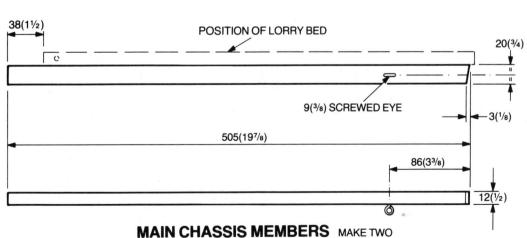

38(1½)

POSITION OF LORRY BED

20(³/₄)

9(³/₈) SCREWED EYE

3(⅛)

505(19⁷/₈)

86(3³/₈)

12(½)

MAIN CHASSIS MEMBERS MAKE TWO

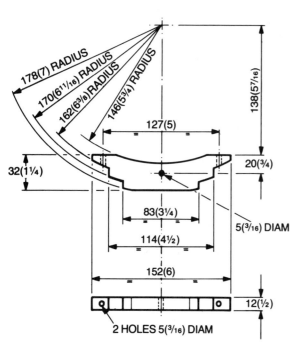

FRONT SPRING ASSEMBLY
MAKE TWO

178(7) RADIUS
170(6¹¹/₁₆) RADIUS
162(6⅜) RADIUS
146(5¾) RADIUS
138(5⁷/₁₆)
127(5)
32(1¼)
20(¾)
83(3¼)
114(4½)
152(6)
5(³/₁₆) DIAM
12(½)
2 HOLES 5(³/₁₆) DIAM

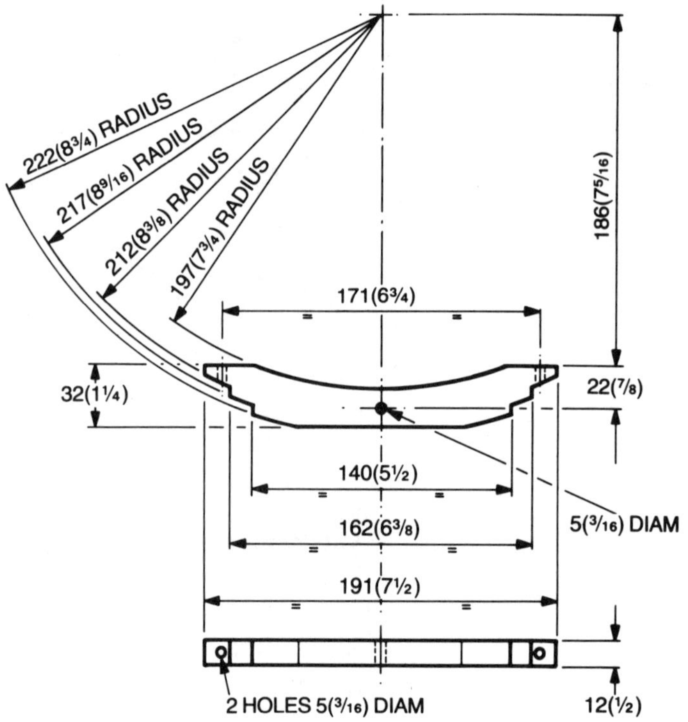

REAR SPRING ASSEMBLY
MAKE TWO

222(8¾) RADIUS
217(8⁹/₁₆) RADIUS
212(8⅜) RADIUS
197(7¾) RADIUS
186(7⁵/₁₆)
171(6¾)
32(1¼)
22(⅞)
140(5½)
162(6⅜)
191(7½)
5(³/₁₆) DIAM
12(½)
2 HOLES 5(³/₁₆) DIAM
12(½)

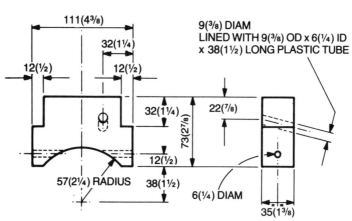

FRONT AXLE BLOCK

111(4⅜)
32(1¼)
12(½)
12(½)
9(⅜) DIAM
LINED WITH 9(⅜) OD x 6(¼) ID
x 38(1½) LONG PLASTIC TUBE
32(1¼)
22(⅞)
73(2⅞)
12(½)
57(2¼) RADIUS
38(1½)
6(¼) DIAM
35(1⅜)

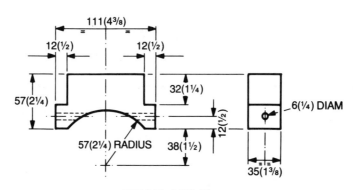

REAR AXLE

111(4⅜)
12(½)
12(½)
57(2¼)
32(1¼)
12(½)
6(¼) DIAM
57(2¼) RADIUS
38(1½)
35(1⅜)

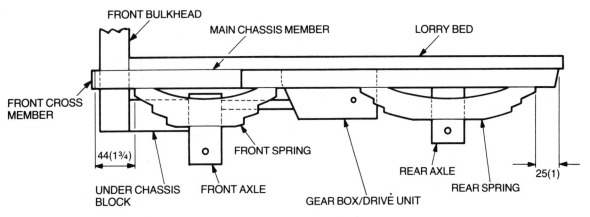

FRONT BULKHEAD

MAIN CHASSIS MEMBER

LORRY BED

FRONT CROSS MEMBER

44(1¾)

UNDER CHASSIS BLOCK

FRONT SPRING

FRONT AXLE

GEAR BOX/DRIVE UNIT

REAR AXLE

REAR SPRING

25(1)

CHASSIS BUILD UP

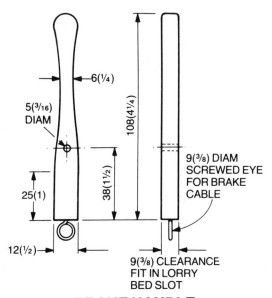

6(¼)

5(³/₁₆) DIAM

108(4¼)

38(1½)

25(1)

12(½)

9(³/₈) DIAM SCREWED EYE FOR BRAKE CABLE

9(³/₈) CLEARANCE FIT IN LORRY BED SLOT

BRAKE HANDLE

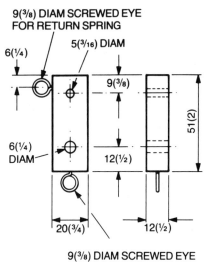

9(³/₈) DIAM SCREWED EYE FOR RETURN SPRING

5(³/₁₆) DIAM

6(¼)

9(³/₈)

6(¼) DIAM

12(½)

51(2)

20(¾)

12(½)

9(³/₈) DIAM SCREWED EYE FOR BRAKE CABLE

BRAKE LEVER

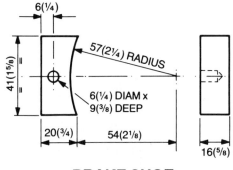

6(¼)

57(2¼) RADIUS

41(1⁵/₈)

6(¼) DIAM x 9(³/₈) DEEP

20(¾)

54(2⅛)

16(⁵/₈)

BRAKE SHOE

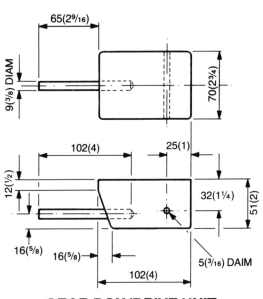

65(2⁹/₁₆)

9(³/₈) DIAM

70(2¾)

102(4)

25(1)

12(½)

32(1¼)

51(2)

16(⁵/₈)

16(⁵/₈)

102(4)

5(³/₁₆) DAIM

GEAR BOX/DRIVE UNIT

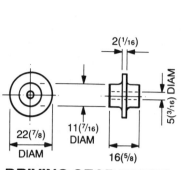

DRIVING GEAR WHEEL
PLASTIC

2(1/16)
22(7/8) DIAM
11(7/16) DIAM
5(3/16) DIAM
16(5/8)

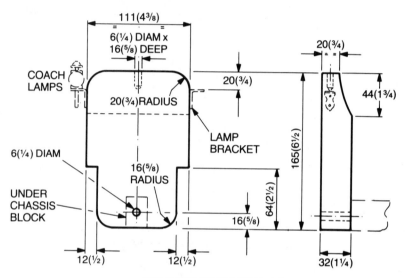

REAR AXLE DRIVE SPACER
PLASTIC

6(1/4)
6(1/4) DIAM
3(1/8)
30(1 3/16) DIAM
41(1 5/8) DIAM

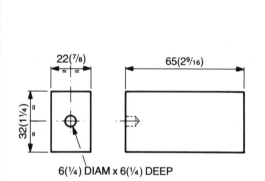

22(7/8)
65(2 9/16)
32(1 1/4)
6(1/4) DIAM x 6(1/4) DEEP

UNDER CHASSIS BLOCK

111(4 3/8)
6(1/4) DIAM x
16(5/8) DEEP
COACH LAMPS
20(3/4) RADIUS
20(3/4)
20(3/4)
44(1 3/4)
LAMP BRACKET
6(1/4) DIAM
165(6 1/2)
16(5/8) RADIUS
UNDER CHASSIS BLOCK
64(2 1/2)
16(5/8)
12(1/2)
12(1/2)
32(1 1/4)

FRONT BULKHEAD

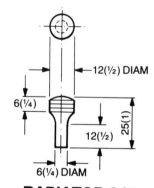

12(1/2) DIAM
6(1/4)
25(1)
12(1/2)
6(1/4) DIAM

RADIATOR CAP

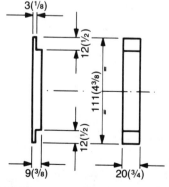

3(1/8)
12(1/2)
111(4 3/8)
12(1/2)
9(3/8)
20(3/4)

MAIN CHASSIS
FRONT CROSS MEMBER

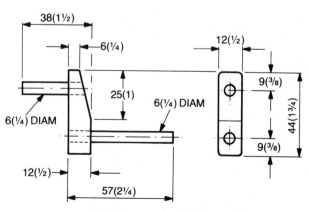

38(1 1/2)
6(1/4)
12(1/2)
25(1)
9(3/8)
6(1/4) DIAM
6(1/4) DIAM
44(1 3/4)
9(3/8)
12(1/2)
57(2 1/4)

STARTING HANDLE

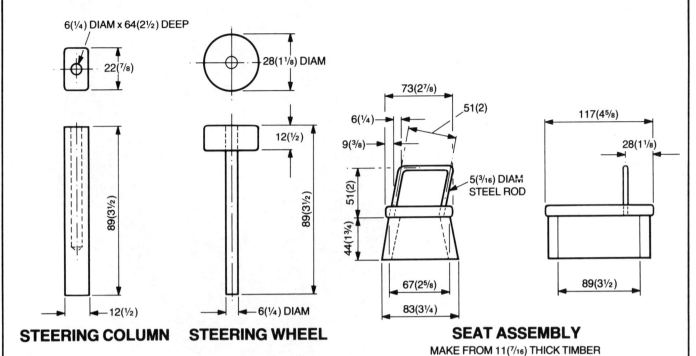

6(¼) DIAM x 64(2½) DEEP

22(⁷/₈)

28(1⅛) DIAM

89(3½)

12(½)

12(½)

89(3½)

6(¼) DIAM

STEERING COLUMN

STEERING WHEEL

73(2⁷/₈)

51(2)

6(¼)

9(³/₈)

51(2)

44(1¾)

5(³/₁₆) DIAM STEEL ROD

67(2⁵/₈)

83(3¼)

117(4⁵/₈)

28(1⅛)

89(3½)

SEAT ASSEMBLY
MAKE FROM 11(⁷/₁₆) THICK TIMBER

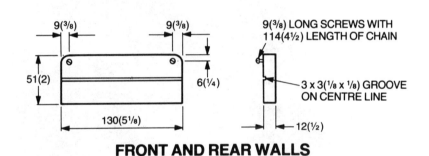

9(³/₈)

9(³/₈)

51(2)

6(¼)

130(5⅛)

9(³/₈) LONG SCREWS WITH
114(4½) LENGTH OF CHAIN

3 x 3(⅛ x ⅛) GROOVE
ON CENTRE LINE

12(½)

FRONT AND REAR WALLS

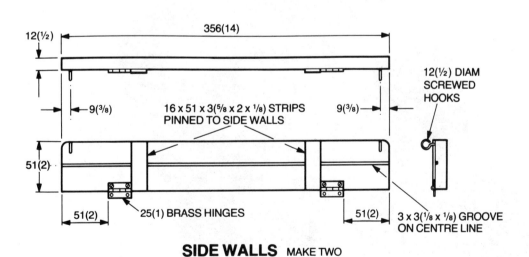

12(½)

356(14)

9(³/₈)

16 x 51 x 3(⁵/₈ x 2 x ⅛) STRIPS
PINNED TO SIDE WALLS

9(³/₈)

12(½) DIAM
SCREWED
HOOKS

51(2)

51(2)

25(1) BRASS HINGES

51(2)

3 x 3(⅛ x ⅛) GROOVE
ON CENTRE LINE

SIDE WALLS MAKE TWO

141

1982 SCANIA

Building this wooden model was something I thoroughly enjoyed. It is not a scale model, but does represent the Scania 142 E V8 and like its big brother will give many years of hard work.

After sitting in the cab and driving the real vehicle, I came to appreciate just how well it was made and how sumptuously fitted out. When I built the model I tried to capture the comfort of the cab fittings by including such details as curtains and upholstered beds.

1   Start by cutting two longitudinal chassis members one of each hand. The strength is given to the chassis by the use of traditional woodworking joints. The stub tenons are cut with a tenon saw and the mortice holes with a chisel. The mortices do not go right through the chassis but are 'stopped'.

The front bumper and tail boards are all jointed with mortice and tenons. The fourth cross member of the chassis is morticed and tenoned giving the chassis rigidity. The first and second cross members are just glued onto the chassis. The third cross member is glued onto the bottom of the chassis and takes the end of the prop shaft. The rear bogie is held onto the chassis by two strips of wood which are in turn screwed onto the longitudinal chassis members. It is through the hole in these two pieces of timber that the bogie is held onto the chassis with a steel bar. With a 'one fixing' point it allows the bogie to pivot and adds realism to the vehicle when crossing rough ground.

2   The fifth wheel (the technical term for the mounting block for trailer hitch) is screwed onto the top of the chassis. This method of securing the hitch is important as it provides the anchorage point for the trailer. To assist coupling of the trailer two ramps are glued onto the back. The first and second cross members are now glued into place.

3   Air cylinders, batteries, fuel tank and spare wheel are all mounted on an underframe. The underframe is screwed onto the chassis after all the accessories have been made.

The air cylinders are made from lengths of dowel rod. Round off the ends to give the appearance of a tank. These are glued into ready prepared holes drilled in a piece of beech which in turn is mounted onto the underframe. Fuel tank and battery boxes are shaped from beech blocks.

4   The chassis is not ready for this equipment until the two tapered lengths of wood are glued onto the side of the chassis.

Looking at a Scania chassis you find that it tapers off behind the cab. To give the appearance of this curve in the chassis I added two additional side pieces which taper off to a fine edge just behind the cat walk (bridge piece). With these two pieces glued in position cut out the recess for the front axle.

Now screw the underframe and accessories to the chassis.

5   The front axle assembly allows for steering. In spite of the small blocks having holes drilled in them, the axle is very strong due to the addition of a bearing plate.

Cut out the main axle beam and drill the holes for king pins. The steering blocks are now cut and shaped. It is best to fit the steering blocks into the main beam before drilling the king pin holes. Now make the holes in the steering blocks by drilling through the existing holes in the main axle beam. This will ensure that the holes will line up. Holes must now be drilled to take the stub axles and the steering tie bar.

Before fixing the king pins in with spring caps make sure that the steering blocks swivel freely in the front axle beam. The front axle bearing plate is now glued into place and the whole axle assembly fixed onto the chassis.

6   The engine block is not detailed but could very easily be made far more realistic. The only moving part is the cooling fan on the front. Once the engine, gearbox and prop shaft are fitted, the cat walk (chassis bridge piece) can be screwed down. This consists of two small strips of wood covered with a fine aluminium mesh.

7   The rear wheel bogie is held to the main chassis by a mild steel bar running right through the whole assembly. Shape up the two bogie frames drilling axle holes, main fixing pin hole and the holes to take the tie rods at the bottom. Drill the wheel axle holes fractionally oversize. The bogie frames are not attached to the chassis other than by the main fixing pin. The frames themselves are held together by the two tie bars situated directly beneath

the main fixing pin. Building the bogie by this method allows a certain flexibility in the frame, and allows only one of the wheels to be lifted leaving the other three on the road.

When fitting wheels it is necessary to use a very short length of rubber tube as a spacer between the bogie side frame and the wheel.

8　To add realism to the bogie, dummy springs are fitted onto the top. Cut varying lengths of spring steel. Cut small spring straps from waste material and using a pair of pliers, bend them onto and around the leaves to keep them together. Holes are drilled in the end of the springs, the springs are held onto the bogie frames with screws.

Apart from small details this completes the chassis.

The cab

9　Start by cutting out two side panels, one of each hand (left and right). Cut the windows out and 'round off' the edges. The rounding of edges completely changes the shape of the cab from a box shape to a nice aerodynamic shape, but remember shaping except for the windows is left until last.

The back of the cab side is rebated to take the cab rear wall. The cab floor, made from plywood, is rebated into the sides. Now cut out the recess at the front to take the radiator panel.

10　Cut out and shape the cab rear wall. At the base, three holes are drilled

to take the air lines. These are made from telephone cables which you can buy in different colours, or talk to a friendly post office engineer – they sometimes have offcuts of cable in their vans! Glue the cab together.

11　Fitted beneath the cab floor on either side are two panel sections which serve to hold the mudguards and steps. Glue and screw these onto the cab side panels.

12　The mudguards I cut from a solid block of wood. You can use a bow saw or coping saw for this job. Holding the block of wood in the vice, cut out the outside curve first and before going on use a spokeshave to remove all the saw marks. You will need a spokeshave with a convex sole to work on this shape. When all smoothing is complete you can then cut the outside shape of the mudguard. Round off all the edges of the mudguards then glue and screw them onto the side panel sections.

13　The radiator has to be carefully detailed otherwise the truck will not look right. Fix the radiator front firmly to the bench, and using a plough plane, groove out two trenches. The radiator itself is recessed below the two grooves. This has to be done with a large sharp chisel. Before 'chiselling out' the radiator, mark the edges very deeply with a Stanley knife. This will stop the fibres breaking out as you chisel down. A piece of aluminium mesh is cut and fitted into the radiator

recess. Narrow strips of wood are now glued onto the outside of the radiator. The headlamps are also glued onto the front. The finished radiator is now glued onto the front of the cab.

14　Now work can begin on the inside of the cab. The seats are shaped from blocks of pine. The bunk beds are made from plywood and covered with felt. The central console gear lever, steering wheel and dashboard are all shaped and fitted. I used felt throughout the cab interior. Small pieces of felt fitted into the corners of the windows act as curtains. Perspex has to be carefully cut and fitted for the windows.

The roof is now fitted. I used cup washers and screws to hold the roof on. Make the visor for the front screen which is then screwed onto the roof. A little more time is needed to shape the aerofoil for the roof. It is fixed onto the roof by two screws that pass up through the roof from the inside.

15　Using two small brass hinges, attach the cab onto the chassis. To prevent damage after the hinges are in place, I fitted two hook eyes and a length of nylon cord.

16　The steps are covered in aluminium mesh.

The wing mirrors and windscreen wiper arms are plastic covered curtain wire painted matt black.

17　Screw the air cleaner onto the cab back wall.

Cutting list

Longitudinal chassis member	2 off	660 x 38 x 12mm (26 x 1½ x ½in)	Timber
	2 off	305 x 38 x 12mm (12 x 1½ x ½in)	Timber
	2 off	98 x 25 x 20mm (3⅞ x 1 x 1in)	Timber
	2 off	124 x 22 x 12mm (4⅞ x ⅞ x ½in)	Timber
First and second cross member	2 off	89 x 22 x 16mm (3½ x ⅞ x ⅝in)	Timber
Third cross member	1 off	89 x 25 x 16mm (3½ x 1 x ⅝in)	Timber
Fourth cross member	1 off	79 x 38 x 16mm (3⅛ x 1½ x ⅝in)	Timber
Tail board	2 off	81 x 38 x 16mm (3 3/16 x 1½ x ⅝in)	Timber
Front bumper	1 off	235 x 25 x 20mm (9¼ x 1 x ¾in)	Timber
	1 off	194 x 25 x 12mm (7⅝ x 1 x ½in)	Timber
	1 off	133 x 16 x 3mm (5¼ x ⅝ x ⅛in)	Timber
Fifth wheel	1 off	127 x 89 x 22mm (5 x 3½ x ⅞in)	Timber
	2 off	124 x 36 x 22mm (4⅞ x 1⅜ x ⅞in)	Timber
Chassis bridge piece	2 off	95 x 9 x 8mm (3¾ x ⅜ x 5/16in)	Timber
Underframe cross member	2 off	171 x 20 x 6mm (6¾ x ¾ x ¼in)	Timber
Underframe tie member	1 off	133 x 20 x 6mm (5¼ x ¾ x ¼in)	Timber
Air bottle carrier	1 off	152 x 27 x 20mm (6 x 1 1/16 x ¾in)	Timber
Air bottles	Make from 178mm (7in) long x 22mm (⅞in) diameter dowel		
Battery pack	1 off	89 x 51 x 16mm (3½ x 2 x ⅝in)	Timber
Fuel tank	1 off	57 x 57 x 38mm (2¼ x 2¼ x 1½in)	Timber
Rear wheel bogie	1 off	171 x 47 x 16mm (6¾ x 1⅞ x ⅝in)	Timber
Front axle beam	1 off	178 x 51 x 20mm (7 x 2 x ¾in)	Timber
Front axle steering blocks	2 off	64 x 38 x 16mm (2½ x 1½ x ⅝in)	Timber
Front axle bearing plate	1 off	178 x 22 x 12mm (7 x ⅞ x ½in)	Timber
Steering tie bar	1 off	171 x 12 x 12mm (6¾ x ½ x ½in)	Timber
Engine block	1 off	171 x 67 x 41mm (6¾ x 2⅝ x 1⅝in)	Timber
Fan	1 off	51 x 51 x 3mm (2 x 2 x ⅛in)	Plywood
Gear box	1 off	89 x 32 x 20mm (3½ x 1¼ x ¾in)	Timber
	1 off	28mm (1⅛in) long x 9mm (⅜in) diameter dowel	
Prop shaft	1 off	270mm (10⅝in) long x 9mm (⅜in) diameter dowel	
Bottom step	2 off	70 x 22 x 20mm (2¾ x ⅞ x ¾in)	Timber
Side panel	2 off	205 x 156 x 16mm (8 1/16 x 6⅛ x ⅝in)	Timber
	2 off	171 x 95 x 12mm (6¾ x 3¾ x ½in)	Timber
Wing mirror	Make from	91 x 20 x 9mm (3¾ x ¾ x ⅜in)	Timber
Cab rear wall	1 off	203 x 184 x 16mm (8 x 7¼ x ⅝in)	Timber
	1 off	184 x 12 x 6mm (7¼ x ½ x ¼in)	Timber
Cab roof	1 off	222 x 168 x 16mm (8¾ x 6⅝ x ⅝in)	Timber
	1 off	60 x 60 x 6mm (2⅜ x 2⅜ x ¼in)	Timber
Air intake	1 off	263 x 28 x 20mm (10⅜ x 1⅛ x ¾in)	Timber
	1 off	41 x 28 x 20mm (1⅝ x 1⅛ x ¾in)	Timber
Visor	1 off	210 x 51 x 14mm (8¼ x 2 x 9/16in)	Timber
Aerofoil	1 off	210 x 76 x 47mm (8¼ x 3 x 1⅞in)	Timber
Mudguard	2 off	133 x 89 x 38mm (5¼ x 3½ x 1½in)	Timber
Side panel decorative strips	2 off	187 x 22 x 3mm (7⅜ x ⅞ x ⅛in)	Timber
	2 off	187 x 16 x 3mm (7⅜ x ⅝ x ⅛in)	Timber
Side panel upper step	2 off	57 x 16 x 6mm (2¼ x ⅝ x ¼in)	Timber
lower step	2 off	46 x 22 x 6mm (1 13/16 x ⅞ x ¼in)	Timber
Front cab bulkhead	1 off	222 x 113 x 16mm (8¾ x 4 7/16 x ⅝in)	Timber
Front cab grill	1 off	206 x 24 x 3mm (8⅛ x 15/16 x ⅛in)	Timber
	10 strips, make from 1980 x 3 x 3mm (78 x ⅛ x ⅛in)		Timber

	1 off	140 × 9 × 3mm (5½ × ⅜ × ⅛in)	Timber
	2 off	28 × 21 × 3mm (1⅛ × ¹³⁄₁₆ × ⅛in)	Timber
Wiper blade	2 off	60 × 6 × 1½mm (2⅜ × ¼ × ¹⁄₁₆in)	
Fascia	1 off	191 × 35 × 22mm (7½ × 1⅜ × ⅞in)	Timber
Shelf	1 off	140 × 28 × 3mm (5½ × 1⅛ × ⅛in)	Timber
Steering column	1 off	51 × 22 × 20mm (2 × ⅞ × ¾in)	Timber
Steering wheel	1 off	38mm (1½in) diameter × 9mm (⅜in) thick	Timber
	1 off	25mm (1in) long × 6mm (¼in) diameter dowel	
Central console	1 off	89 × 47 × 28mm (3½ × 1⅞ × 1⅛in)	Timber
Gear lever	1 off	44mm (1¾in) long × 6mm (¼in) diameter dowel	
Seats	2 off	76 × 57 × 64mm (3 × 2¼ × 2½in)	Timber
	2 strips, make from 51 × 9 × 6mm (2 × ⅜ × ¼in)		Timber
Bunks	2 off	187 × 57 × 3mm (7⅜ × 2¼ × ⅛in)	Plywood
	2 off	187 × 16 × 3mm (7⅜ × ⅝ × ⅛in)	Plywood
Cab floor	1 off	191 × 171 × 3mm (7½ × 6¾ × ⅛in)	Plywood
Ancillaries			
Axles, front and rear	11 off	102mm (4in) diameter road wheels	
	2 off	76mm (3in) long × 6mm (¼in) diameter steel front axles	
	2 off	12mm (½in) o/d × 6mm (¼in) i/d × 3mm (⅛in) thick spacers	
	4 off	Spring dome caps to suit 6mm (¼in) diameter axles	
	2 off	264mm (10⅜in) long × 6mm (¼in) diameter steel rear axles	
	4 off	12mm (½in) o/d × 6mm (¼in) i/d × 6mm (¼in) thick spacers	
	4 off	Spring dome caps to suit 6mm (¼in) diameter axles	
	1 off	133mm (5¼in) long × 9mm (⅜in) diameter steel bogie pivot pin	
	2 off	Spring dome caps to suit 9mm (⅜in) diameter pins	
	2 off	133mm (5¼in) long × 5mm (³⁄₁₆in) diameter steel bogie tie bars	
	4 off	Spring dome caps to suit 5mm (³⁄₁₆in) diameter bars	
Spare wheel	1 off	12mm (½in) o/d × 3mm (⅛in) i/d × 6mm (¼in) thick spacer	
Front axle beam	2 off	57mm (2¼in) long × 5mm (³⁄₁₆in) diameter steel pivot pins	
	4 off	Spring dome caps to suit 5mm (³⁄₁₆in) diameter pins	
	2 off	35mm (1⅜in) long × 3mm (⅛in) diameter bolts, washers and nuts	
Spring	Make from 3000 × 16mm × 1½mm (118 × ⅝ × ¹⁄₁₆in) spring steel		
Fan	1 off	6mm (¼in) o/d × 3mm (⅛in) i/d × 5mm (³⁄₁₆in) thick spacer	
	4 off	Screwed eyes for tilting cab retaining cord	
	1 off	450mm (18in) length of strong cab retaining cord	
	2 off	Swing hooks, screwed eyes, washers amd screws	
	2 off	25mm (1in) brass hinges – cab tilt	
	1 off	64 × 64mm (2½ × 2½in) wire mesh for bridge piece	
	1 off	51mm (2in) long × 5mm (³⁄₁₆in) diameter steel for towing pin	
	1 off	230 × 76mm (9 × 3in) wire mesh for steps and radiator	
	3 off	89mm (3½in) long coiled telephone cables	
Mirror arms	Make from 305 × 3mm (12 × ⅛in) diameter plastic covered curtain wire		
Windows	Make from 305 × 254 × 1½mm (12 × 10 × ¹⁄₁₆in) thick clear plastic		
Wiper arms	Make from 127mm (5in) long × 5mm (³⁄₁₆in) diameter steel wire		
Gear lever		9mm (⅜in) o/d × 6mm (¼in) i/d × 16mm (⅝in) long grip	
		305 × 305mm (12 × 12in) felt	

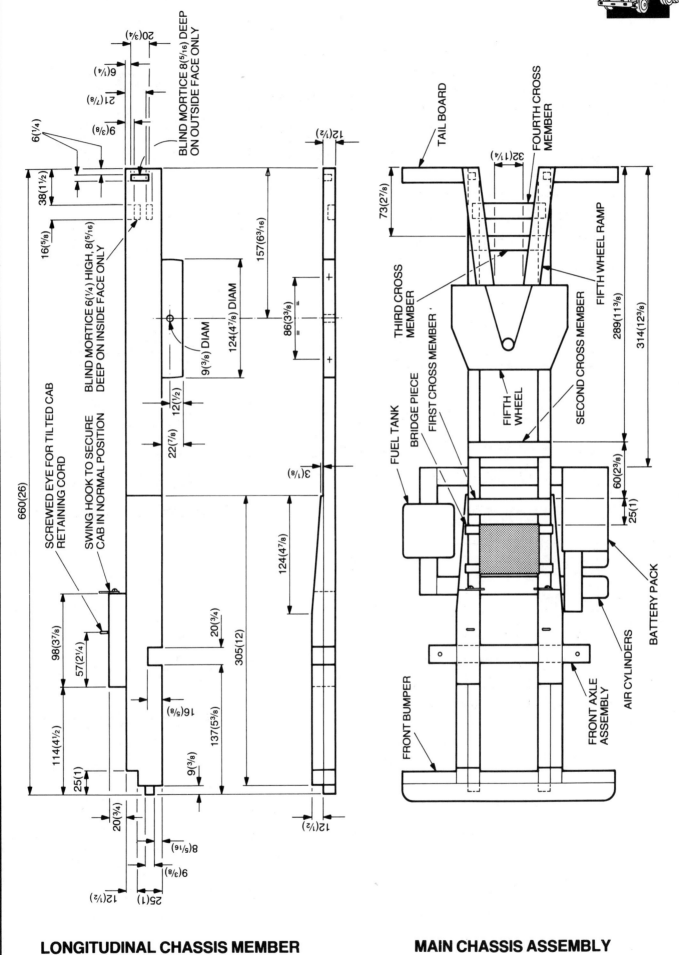

LONGITUDINAL CHASSIS MEMBER
MAKE ONE OF EACH HAND

MAIN CHASSIS ASSEMBLY

660(26)

SCREWED EYE FOR TILTED CAB
RETAINING CORD

SWING HOOK TO SECURE
CAB IN NORMAL POSITION

BLIND MORTICE 6(¼) HIGH, 8(⁵/₁₆)
DEEP ON INSIDE FACE ONLY

BLIND MORTICE 8(⁵/₁₆) DEEP
ON OUTSIDE FACE ONLY

20(¾)
6(¼)
21(⁷/₈)
9(³/₈)
6(¼)
38(1½)
16(⁵/₈)
157(6³/₁₆)
86(3³/₈)
124(4⁷/₈) DIAM
9(³/₈) DIAM
12(½)
22(⁷/₈)
3(⅛)
12(½)
124(4⁷/₈)
98(3⁷/₈)
57(2¼)
114(4½)
25(1)
20(¾)
305(12)
20(¾)
16(⁵/₈)
137(5³/₈)
9(³/₈)
20(¾)
8(⁵/₁₆)
9(³/₈)
25(1)
12(½)

TAIL BOARD
FOURTH CROSS MEMBER
THIRD CROSS MEMBER
FIFTH WHEEL RAMP
SECOND CROSS MEMBER
FIFTH WHEEL
FIRST CROSS MEMBER
BRIDGE PIECE
FUEL TANK
FRONT BUMPER
FRONT AXLE ASSEMBLY
AIR CYLINDERS
BATTERY PACK

73(2⁷/₈)
32(1¼)
289(11³/₈)
314(12³/₈)
60(2³/₈)
25(1)

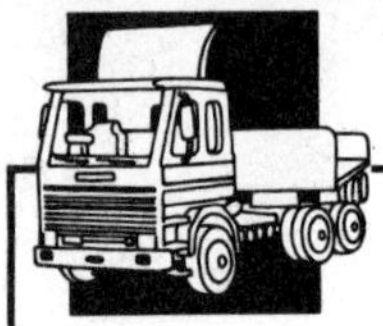

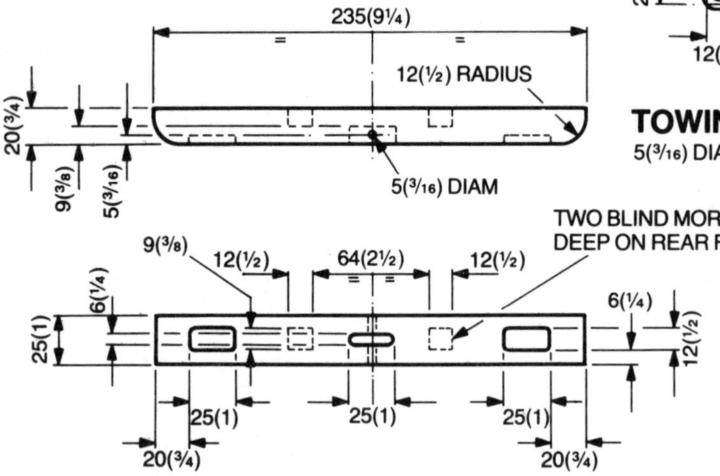

235(9 1/4)
12(1/2) RADIUS
20(3/4)
9(3/8)
5(3/16)
5(3/16) DIAM
TWO BLIND MORTICES 9(3/8) DEEP ON REAR FACE ONLY
9(3/8)
12(1/2)
64(2 1/2)
12(1/2)
6(1/4)
25(1)
6(1/4)
12(1/2)
25(1)
25(1)
25(1)
20(3/4)
20(3/4)

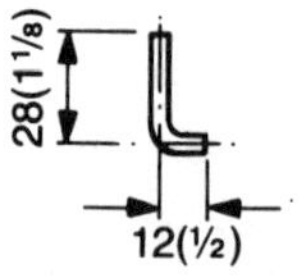

28(1 1/8)
12(1/2)

TOWING PIN

5(3/16) DIAM STEEL

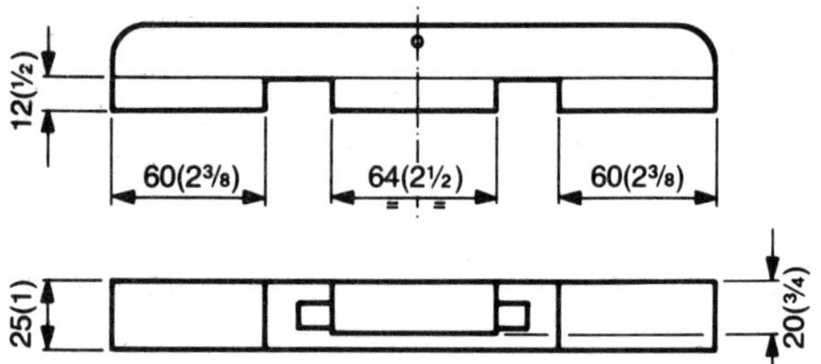

12(1/2)
60(2 3/8)
64(2 1/2)
60(2 3/8)
25(1)
20(3/4)

EXTENSION TO REAR FACE OF BUMPER

FRONT BUMPER

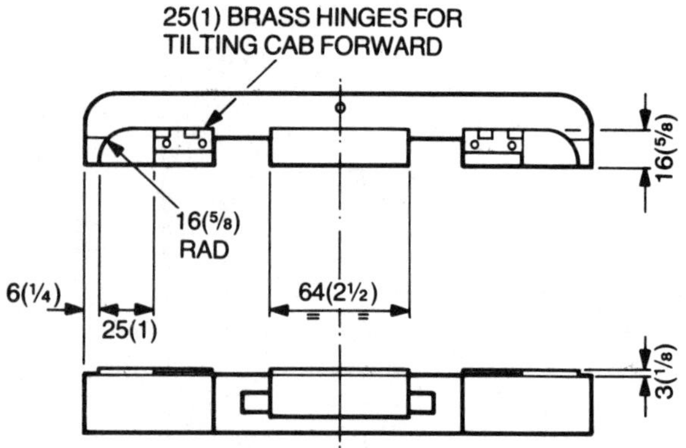

25(1) BRASS HINGES FOR TILTING CAB FORWARD
16(5/8)
16(5/8) RAD
6(1/4)
25(1)
64(2 1/2)
3(1/8)

BUILD UP ON TOP FACE OF BUMPER

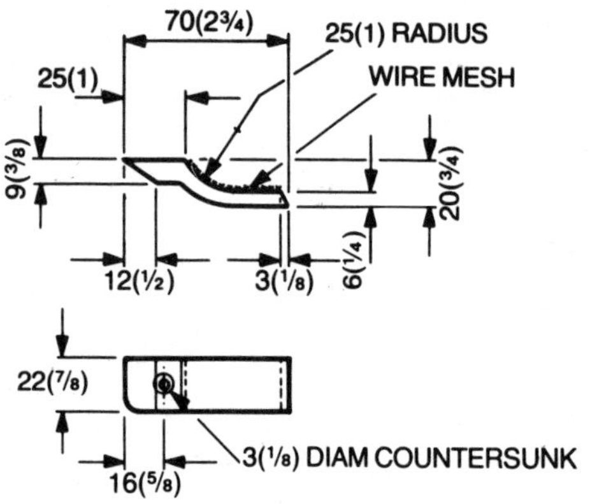

70(2 3/4)
25(1) RADIUS
WIRE MESH
25(1)
9(3/8)
20(3/4)
12(1/2)
3(1/8)
6(1/4)
22(7/8)
3(1/8) DIAM COUNTERSUNK
16(5/8)

BOTTOM STEP

MAKE ONE OF EACH HAND

FIXED BELOW EXTREME ENDS OF FRONT BUMPER

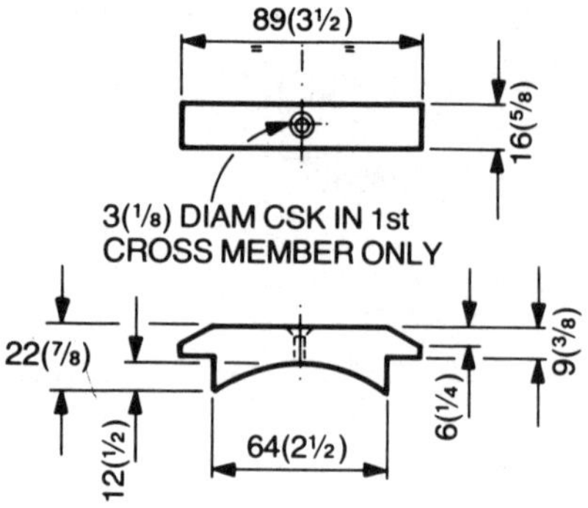

89(3 1/2)
16(5/8)
3(1/8) DIAM CSK IN 1st CROSS MEMBER ONLY
22(7/8)
9(3/8)
6(1/4)
12(1/2)
64(2 1/2)

FIRST AND SECOND CROSS MEMBERS

MAKE ONE OF EACH

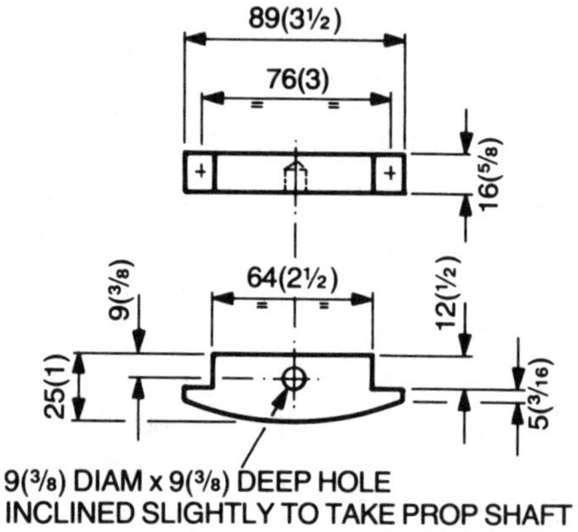

89(3 1/2)
76(3)
16(5/8)
9(3/8)
64(2 1/2)
12(1/2)
25(1)
5(3/16)
9(3/8) DIAM x 9(3/8) DEEP HOLE INCLINED SLIGHTLY TO TAKE PROP SHAFT

THIRD CROSS MEMBER

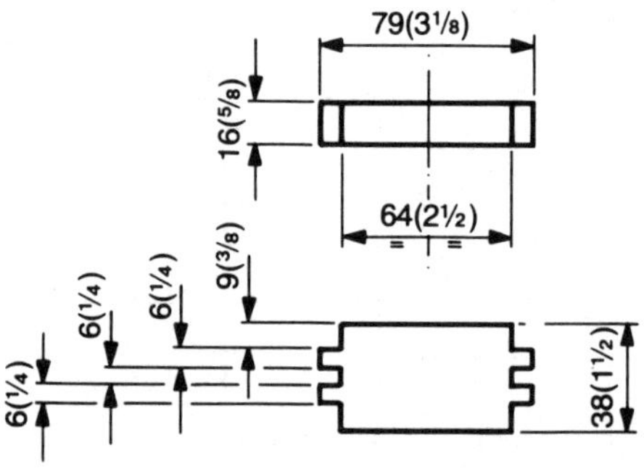

79(3 1/8)
16(5/8)
64(2 1/2)
9(3/8)
6(1/4)
6(1/4)
6(1/4)
38(1 1/2)

FOURTH CROSS MEMBER

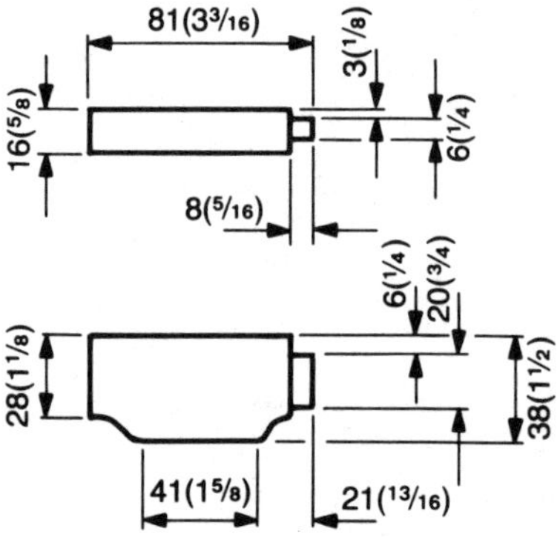

81(3 3/16)
3(1/8)
16(5/8)
6(1/4)
8(5/16)
6(1/4)
20(3/4)
28(1 1/8)
38(1 1/2)
41(1 5/8)
21(13/16)

TAIL BOARD

MAKE ONE OF EACH HAND

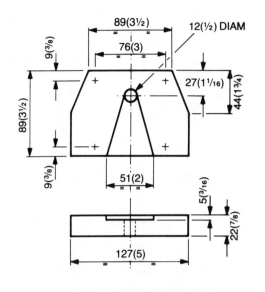

FIFTH WHEEL

22(⅞)   20(¾)

124(4⅞)   16(⅝)

FIFTH WHEEL RAMP

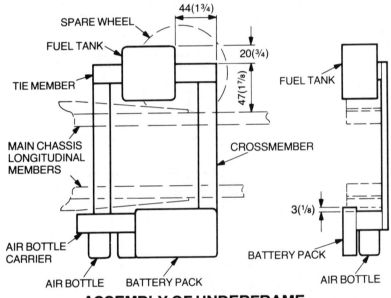

SPARE WHEEL
FUEL TANK
TIE MEMBER
MAIN CHASSIS
LONGITUDINAL
MEMBERS

44(1¾)
20(¾)
47(1⅞)

FUEL TANK

CROSSMEMBER

3(⅛)

AIR BOTTLE
CARRIER

AIR BOTTLE   BATTERY PACK

BATTERY PACK

AIR BOTTLE

ASSEMBLY OF UNDERFRAME

ALSO REQUIRED:
ONE 102(4) WHEEL
ONE 12(½) O/D x 3(⅛) I/D x 6(¼) THICK SPACER
ONE WOODSCREW AND CUP WASHER

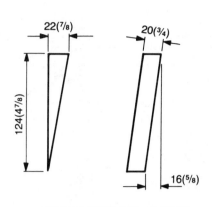

133(5¼)
9(⅜)   28(1⅛)   9(⅜)
20(¾)

2 HOLES 3(⅛) DIAM
CENTRE FOR SPARE
WHEEL FIXING

3(⅛)
20(¾)   6(¼) THICK   20(¾)

DRIVER'S SIDE UNDERFRAME
TIE MEMBER

171(6¾)
9(⅜)   32(1¼)   76(3)
20(¾)

3 HOLES 3(⅛) DIAM

UNDERFRAME CROSS MEMBER
MAKE TWO   6(¼) THICK

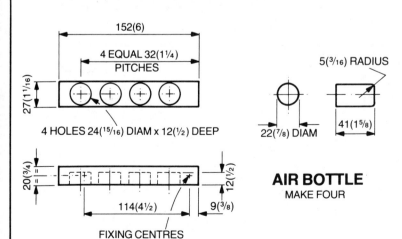

152(6)
4 EQUAL 32(1¼)
PITCHES
27(1¹⁄₁₆)

4 HOLES 24(¹⁵⁄₁₆) DIAM x 12(½) DEEP

20(¾)
12(½)
114(4½)   9(⅜)

FIXING CENTRES

AIR BOTTLE CARRIER

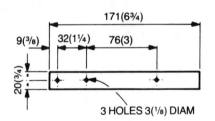

5(³⁄₁₆) RADIUS

22(⅞) DIAM   41(1⅝)

AIR BOTTLE
MAKE FOUR

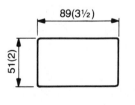

89(3½)   57(2¼)
51(2)   57(2¼)   6(¼)
RADIUS

BATTERY PACK   FUEL TANK
16(⅝) THICK   38(1½) THICK

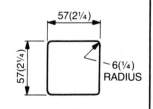
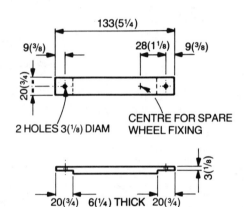

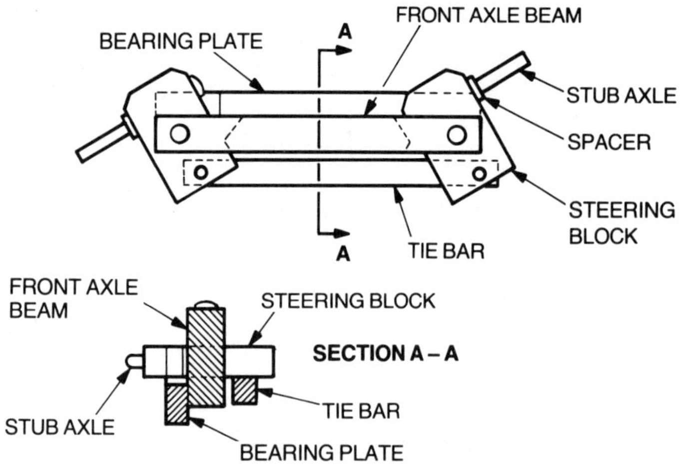

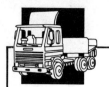

FRONT AXLE BEAM
BEARING PLATE
A
STUB AXLE
SPACER
STEERING BLOCK
TIE BAR
A
FRONT AXLE BEAM
STEERING BLOCK
SECTION A – A
STUB AXLE
TIE BAR
BEARING PLATE

FRONT AXLE ASSEMBLY

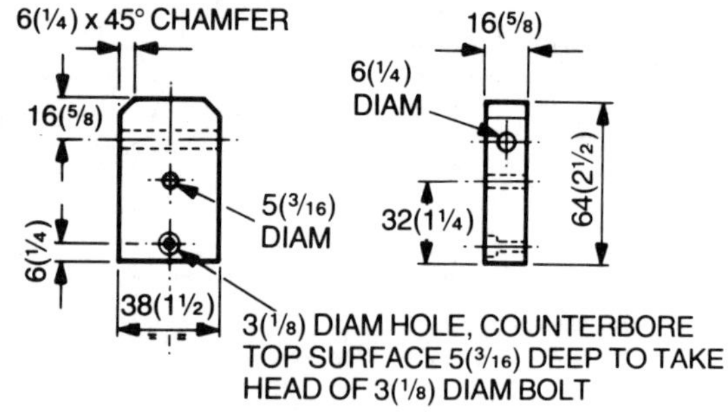

6(1/4) x 45° CHAMFER
16(5/8)
16(5/8)
6(1/4) DIAM
5(3/16) DIAM
6(1/4)
38(1 1/2)
32(1 1/4)
64(2 1/2)
3(1/8) DIAM HOLE, COUNTERBORE TOP SURFACE 5(3/16) DEEP TO TAKE HEAD OF 3(1/8) DIAM BOLT

STEERING BLOCKS

MAKE TWO

ALSO REQUIRED:
TWO 6(1/4) DIAM x 76(3) LONG STEEL STUB AXLES
TWO 12(1/2) O/D x 6(1/4) I/D x 3(1/8) THICK SPACERS
FOUR SPRING DOME CAPS TO SUIT 6(1/4) DIAM AXLES
TWO 102(4) WHEELS

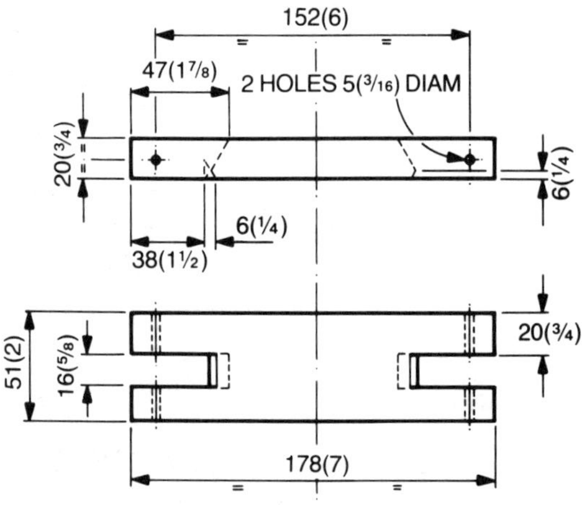

152(6)
47(1 7/8)
2 HOLES 5(3/16) DIAM
20(3/4)
6(1/4)
6(1/4)
38(1 1/2)
51(2)
16(5/8)
20(3/4)
178(7)

FRONT AXLE BEAM

ALSO REQUIRED:
TWO 5(3/16) DIAM x 57(2 1/4) STEEL PIVOT PINS
FOUR SPRING DOME CAPS TO SUIT 5(3/16) DIAM PINS

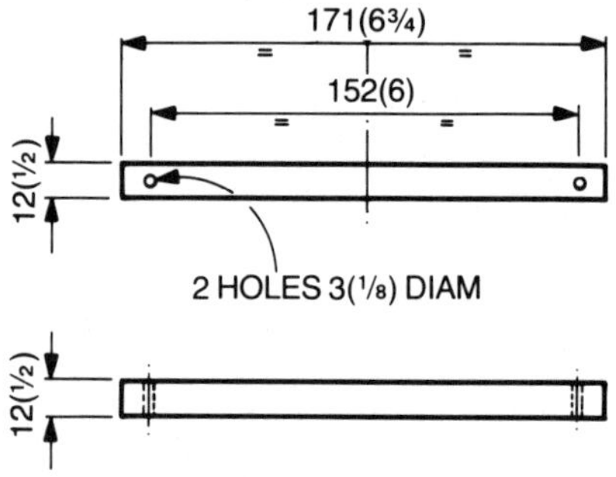

171(6 3/4)
152(6)
12(1/2)
2 HOLES 3(1/8) DIAM
12(1/2)

STEERING TIE BAR

ALSO REQUIRED:
TWO 3(1/8) DIAM BOLTS x 35(1 3/8) LONG, WASHERS AND LOCKNUTS

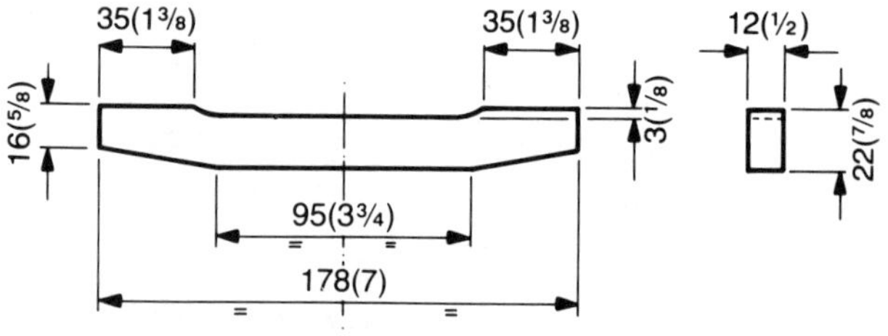

35(1 3/8)
35(1 3/8)
12(1/2)
16(5/8)
3(1/8)
22(7/8)
95(3 3/4)
178(7)

FRONT AXLE BEARING PLATE

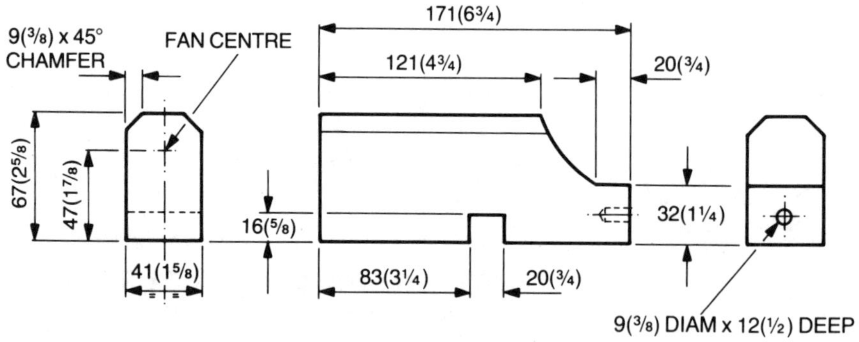

9(3/8) x 45° CHAMFER
FAN CENTRE
171(6 3/4)
121(4 3/4)
20(3/4)
67(2 5/8)
47(1 7/8)
16(5/8)
32(1 1/4)
41(1 5/8)
83(3 1/4)
20(3/4)
9(3/8) DIAM x 12(1/2) DEEP

ENGINE BLOCK

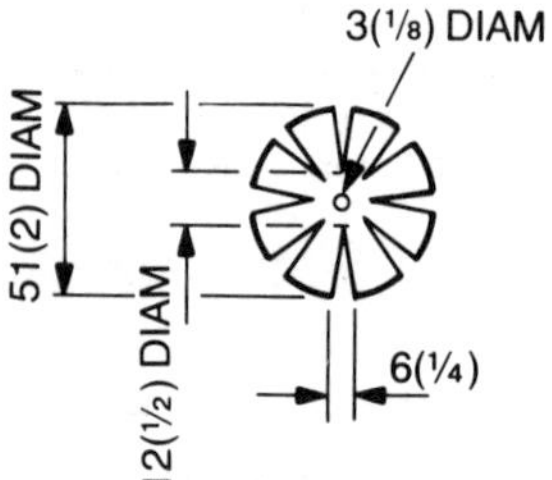

3(1/8) DIAM
51(2) DIAM
12(1/2) DIAM
6(1/4)

FAN

3(1/8) THICK PLYWOOD
ALSO REQUIRED:
6(1/4) O/D x 3(1/8) I/D x 5(3/16) LONG SPACER AND WOOD SCREW

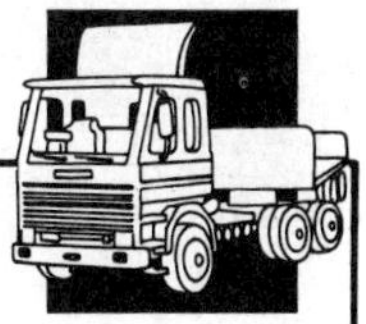

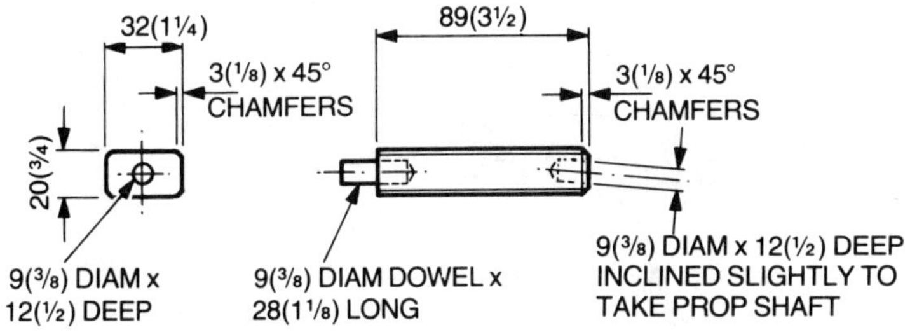
32(1¼)
89(3½)
3(1/8) x 45° CHAMFERS
3(1/8) x 45° CHAMFERS
20(¾)
9(3/8) DIAM x 12(½) DEEP
9(3/8) DIAM DOWEL x 28(1 1/8) LONG
9(3/8) DIAM x 12(½) DEEP INCLINED SLIGHTLY TO TAKE PROP SHAFT

GEAR BOX

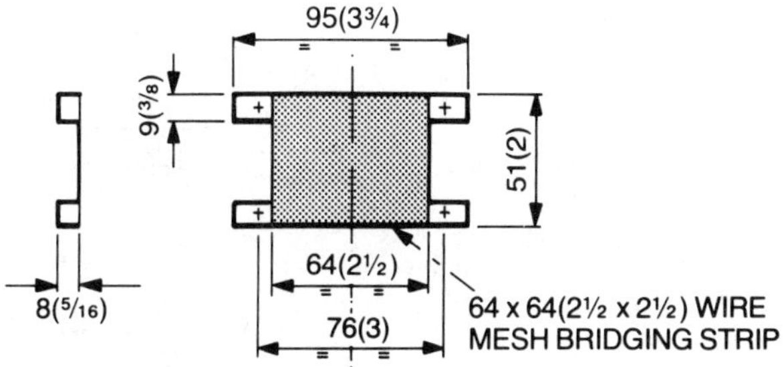
95(3¾)
9(3/8)
51(2)
64(2½)
8(5/16)
76(3)
64 x 64(2½ x 2½) WIRE MESH BRIDGING STRIP

CHASSIS BRIDGE PIECE

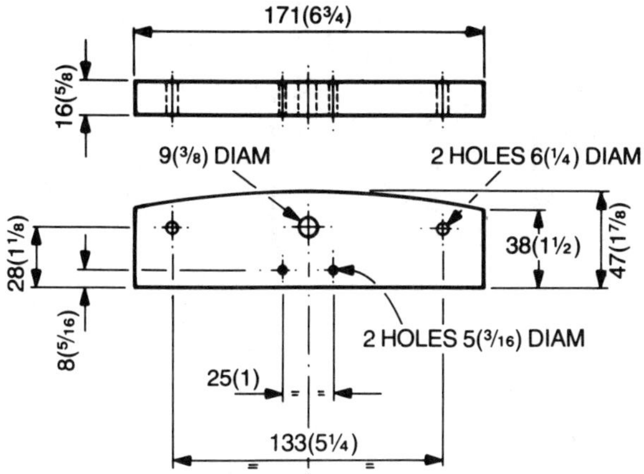
171(6¾)
16(5/8)
9(3/8) DIAM
2 HOLES 6(¼) DIAM
28(1 1/8)
38(1½)
47(1 7/8)
8(5/16)
2 HOLES 5(3/16) DIAM
25(1)
133(5¼)

REAR WHEEL BOGIE

MAKE TWO

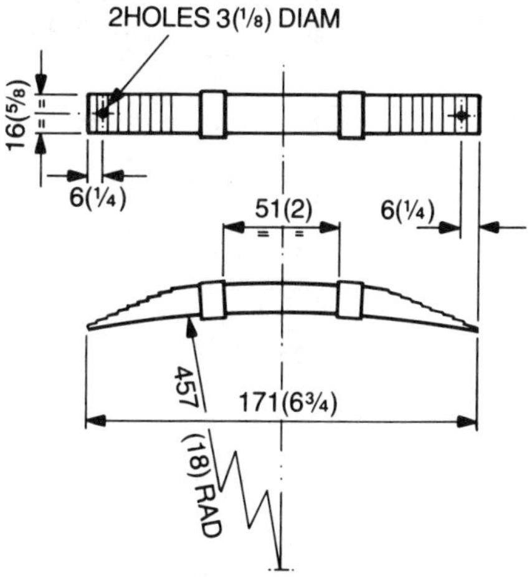
2HOLES 3(1/8) DIAM
16(5/8)
6(¼)
51(2)
6(¼)
457
171(6¾)
(18) RAD

DUMMY SPRING

MAKE TWO ASSEMBLIES

9 LEAVES 1.5(1/16) THICK SPRING STEEL REDUCING IN LENGTH BY 9(3/8)

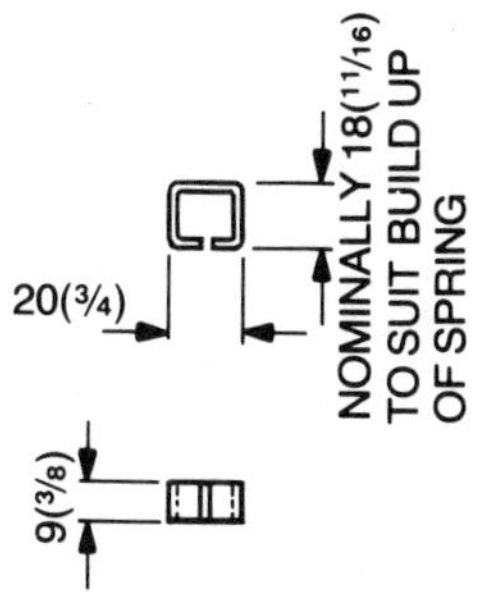
NOMINALLY 18(11/16) TO SUIT BUILD UP OF SPRING
20(¾)
9(3/8)

SPRING STRAP

MAKE FOUR

1.5(1/16) THICK SPRING STEEL

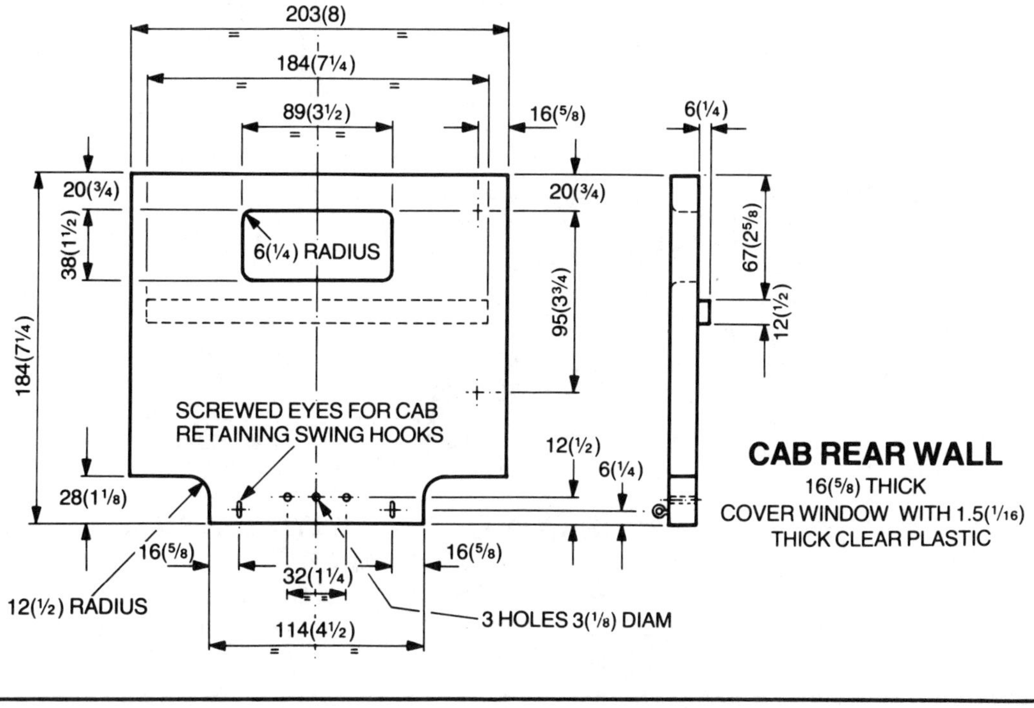
203(8)
184(7¼)
89(3½)
16(5/8)
6(¼)
20(¾)
20(¾)
38(1½)
6(¼) RADIUS
67(2 5/8)
95(3¾)
12(½)
184(7¼)
SCREWED EYES FOR CAB RETAINING SWING HOOKS
12(½)
6(¼)
28(1 1/8)
16(5/8)
16(5/8)
32(1¼)
12(½) RADIUS
3 HOLES 3(1/8) DIAM
114(4½)

CAB REAR WALL

16(5/8) THICK

COVER WINDOW WITH 1.5(1/16) THICK CLEAR PLASTIC

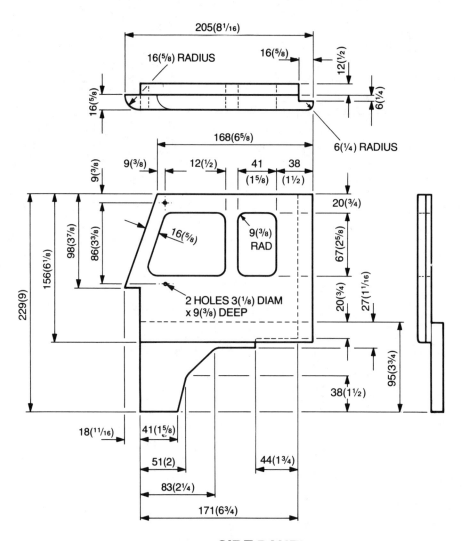

SIDE PANEL

MAKE ONE OF EACH HAND

COVER WINDOWS WITH 1.5(¹/₁₆) THICK CLEAR PLASTIC

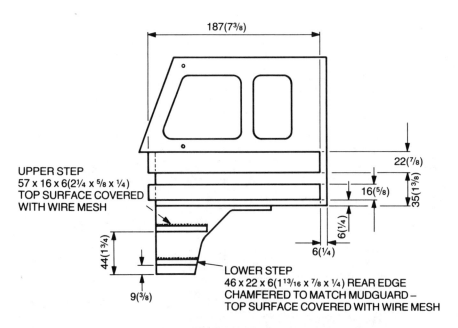

UPPER STEP
57 x 16 x 6(2¹/₄ x ⁵/₈ x ¹/₄)
TOP SURFACE COVERED
WITH WIRE MESH

LOWER STEP
46 x 22 x 6(1¹³/₁₆ x ⁷/₈ x ¹/₄) REAR EDGE
CHAMFERED TO MATCH MUDGUARD –
TOP SURFACE COVERED WITH WIRE MESH

POSITION OF DECORATIVE STRIPS
AND STEPS

MAKE TWO OF EACH

DECORATIVE STRIPS 3(¹/₈) THICK, FORWARD EDGE ROUNDED TO
SUIT CONTOUR OF CAB WHEN CAB IS FULLY ASSEMBLED

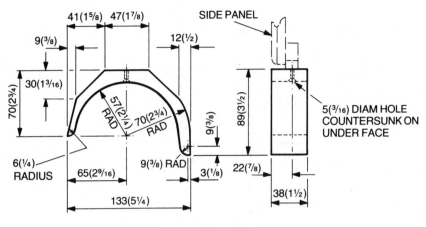

MUDGUARD
MAKE TWO

FRONT CAB BULKHEAD

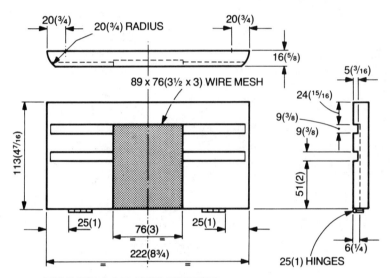

89 x 76(3½ x 3) WIRE MESH

25(1) HINGES

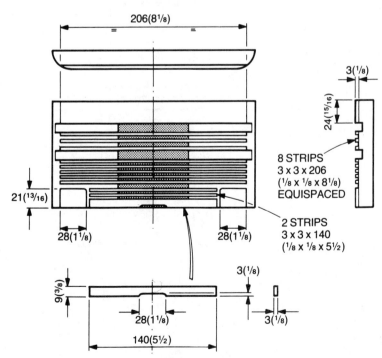

8 STRIPS
3 x 3 x 206
(⅛ x ⅛ x 8⅛)
EQUISPACED

2 STRIPS
3 x 3 x 140
(⅛ x ⅛ x 5½)

BUILD UP OF FRONT GRILL
ALL ENDS ROUNDED TO THE 20(¾) RADIUS

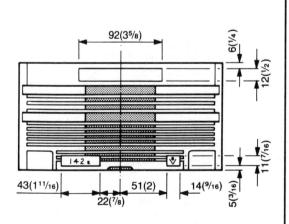

POSITIONING OF GRILL DECORS

153

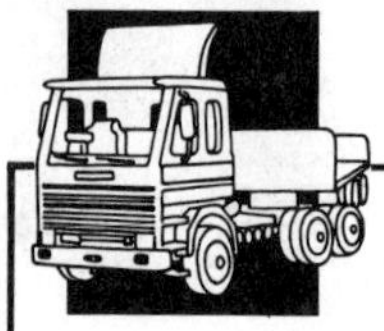

CAB SEATING AND SLEEPING ARRANGEMENT

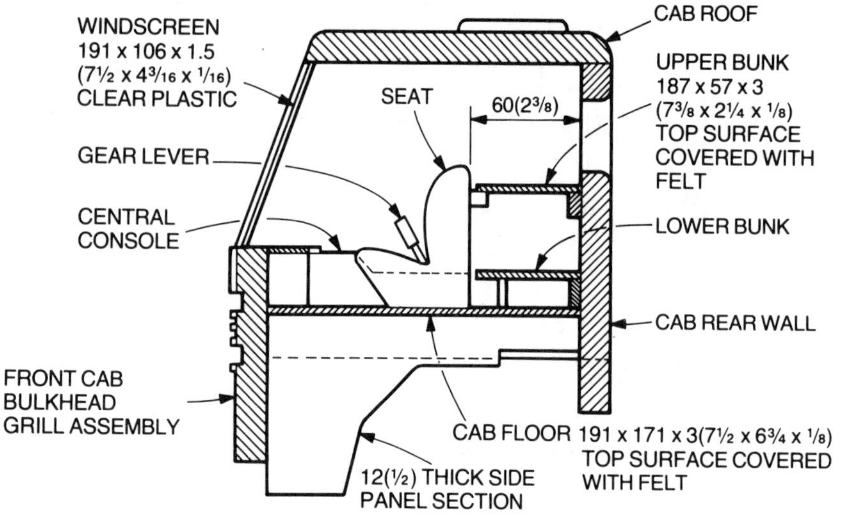
WINDSCREEN
191 x 106 x 1.5
(7 1/2 x 4 3/16 x 1/16)
CLEAR PLASTIC
GEAR LEVER
CENTRAL
CONSOLE
FRONT CAB
BULKHEAD
GRILL ASSEMBLY
SEAT
60(2 3/8)
CAB ROOF
UPPER BUNK
187 x 57 x 3
(7 3/8 x 2 1/4 x 1/8)
TOP SURFACE
COVERED WITH
FELT
LOWER BUNK
CAB REAR WALL
CAB FLOOR 191 x 171 x 3(7 1/2 x 6 3/4 x 1/8)
TOP SURFACE COVERED
WITH FELT
12(1/2) THICK SIDE
PANEL SECTION

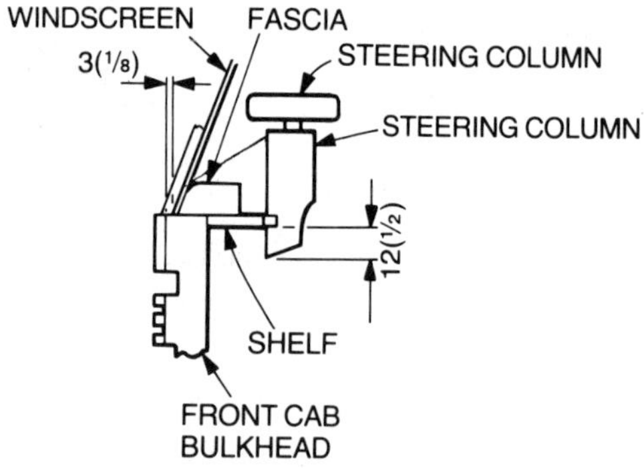
WINDSCREEN
FASCIA
3(1/8)
STEERING COLUMN
STEERING COLUMN
12(1/2)
SHELF
FRONT CAB
BULKHEAD

CAB DASH PANEL BUILD UP

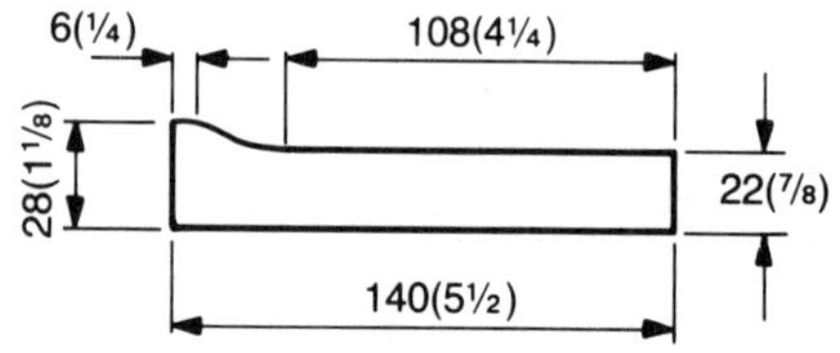
6(1/4)
108(4 1/4)
28(1 1/8)
22(7/8)
140(5 1/2)

SHELF

3(1/8) THICK

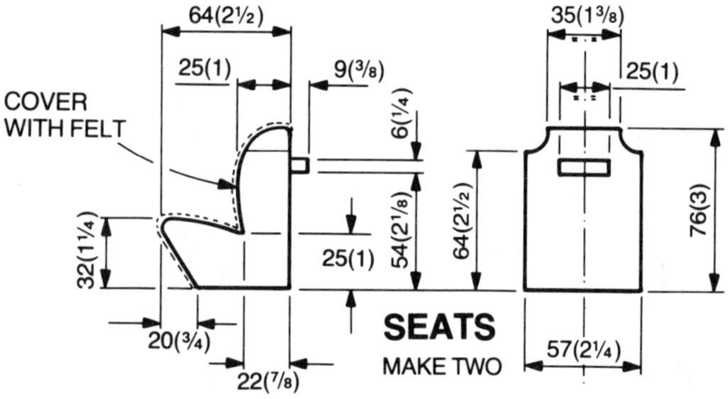
64(2 1/2)
25(1)
9(3/8)
COVER
WITH FELT
6(1/4)
54(2 1/8)
32(1 1/4)
25(1)
20(3/4)
22(7/8)
35(1 3/8)
25(1)
64(2 1/2)
76(3)
57(2 1/4)

SEATS

MAKE TWO

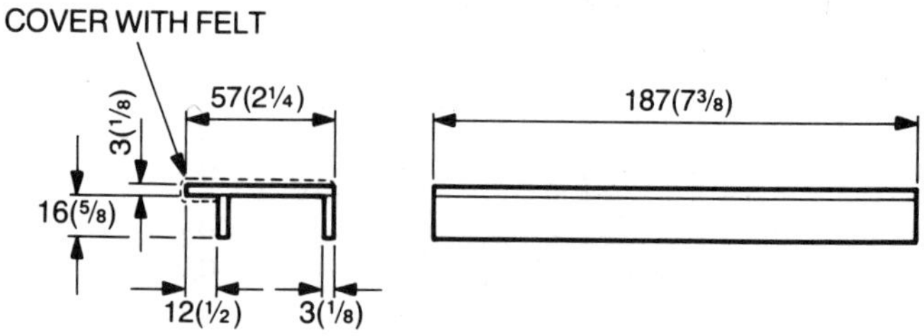
COVER WITH FELT
57(2 1/4)
3(1/8)
16(5/8)
12(1/2)
3(1/8)
187(7 3/8)

LOWER BUNK

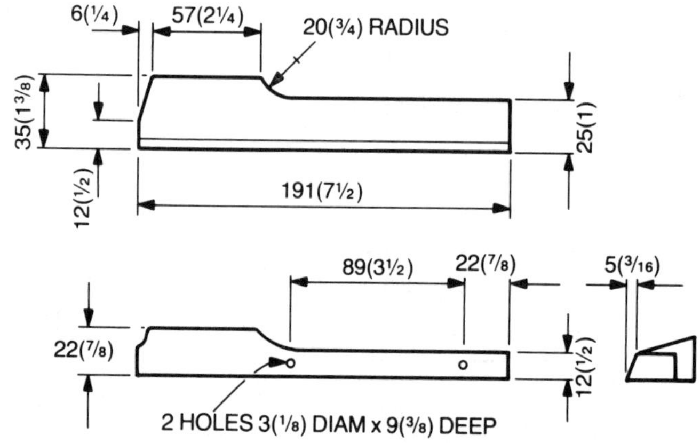
6(1/4)
57(2 1/4)
20(3/4) RADIUS
35(1 3/8)
25(1)
12(1/2)
191(7 1/2)
89(3 1/2)
22(7/8)
5(3/16)
22(7/8)
12(1/2)
2 HOLES 3(1/8) DIAM x 9(3/8) DEEP

FASCIA

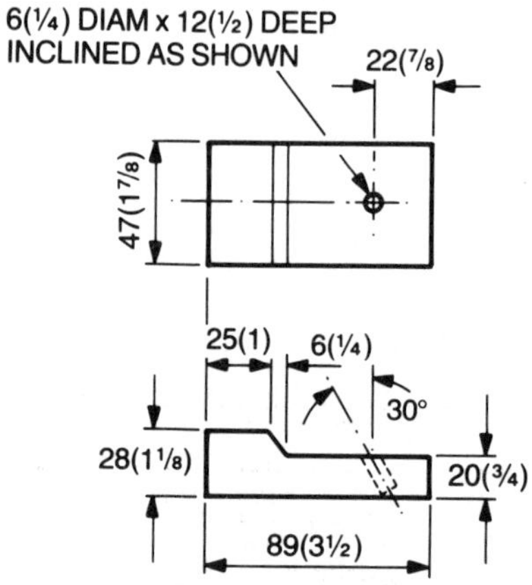
6(1/4) DIAM x 12(1/2) DEEP
INCLINED AS SHOWN
22(7/8)
47(1 7/8)
25(1)
6(1/4)
30°
28(1 1/8)
20(3/4)
89(3 1/2)

CENTRAL CONSOLE

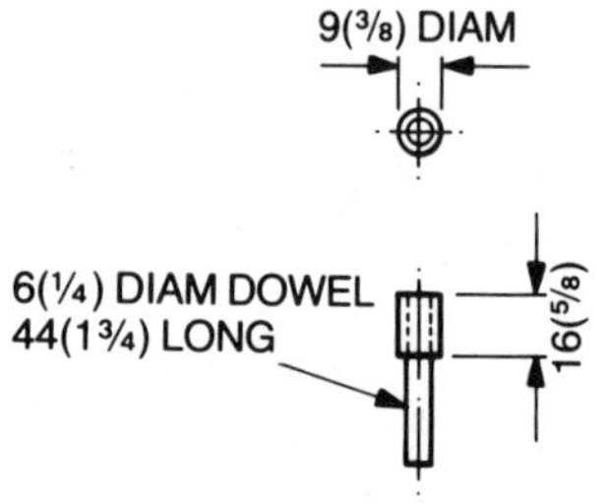
9(3/8) DIAM
6(1/4) DIAM DOWEL
44(1 3/4) LONG
16(5/8)

GEAR LEVER

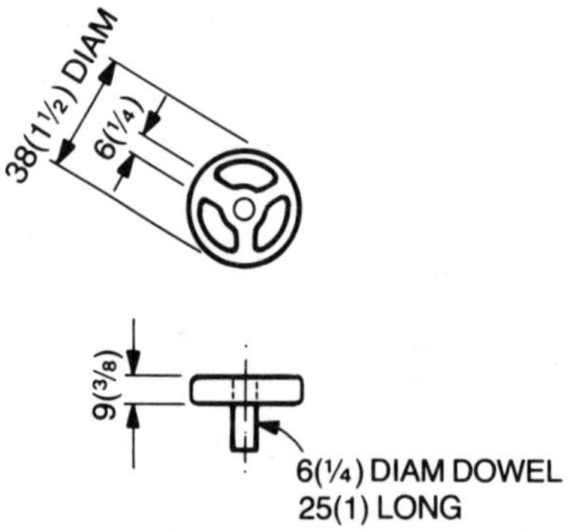
38(1 1/2) DIAM
6(1/4)
9(3/8)
6(1/4) DIAM DOWEL
25(1) LONG

STEERING WHEEL

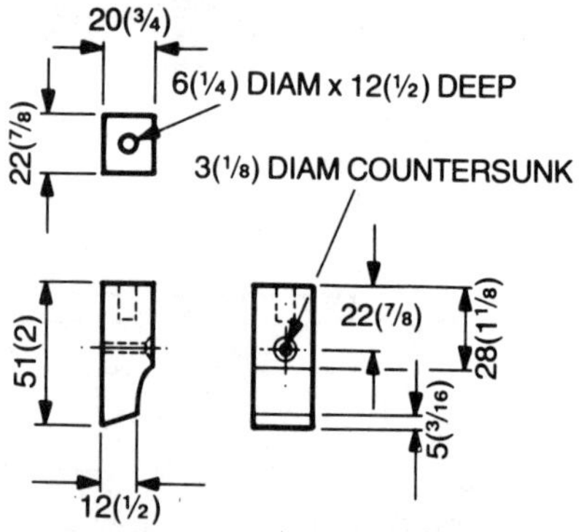
20(3/4)
6(1/4) DIAM x 12(1/2) DEEP
22(7/8)
3(1/8) DIAM COUNTERSUNK
51(2)
22(7/8)
28(1 1/8)
5(3/16)
12(1/2)

STEERING COLUMN

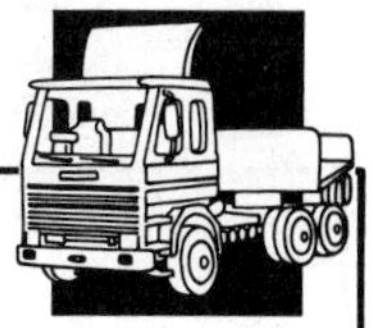

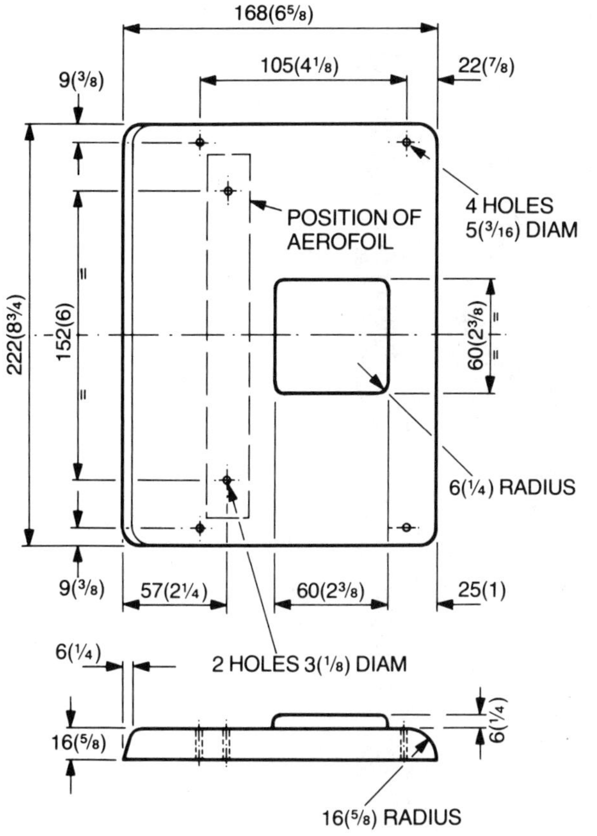

168(6 5/8)
105(4 1/8)
22(7/8)
9(3/8)
POSITION OF AEROFOIL
4 HOLES 5(3/16) DIAM
222(8 3/4)
152(6)
60(2 3/8)
6(1/4) RADIUS
9(3/8)
57(2 1/4)
60(2 3/8)
25(1)
6(1/4)
2 HOLES 3(1/8) DIAM
16(5/8)
6(1/4)
16(5/8) RADIUS

CAB ROOF

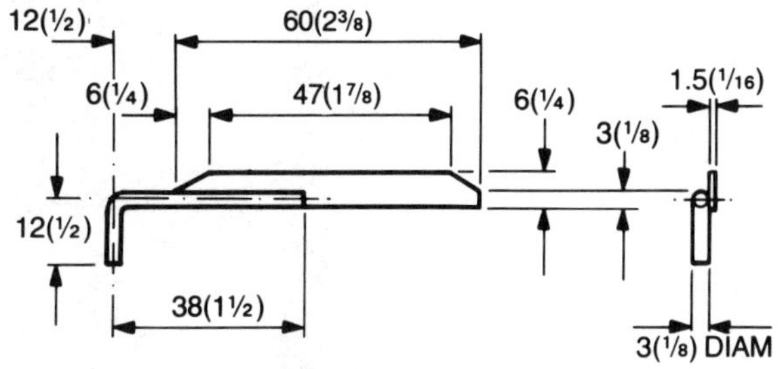

12(1/2)
60(2 3/8)
6(1/4)
47(1 7/8)
6(1/4)
1.5(1/16)
3(1/8)
12(1/2)
38(1 1/2)
3(1/8) DIAM

WINDSCREEN WIPER ASSEMBLY

MAKE TWO

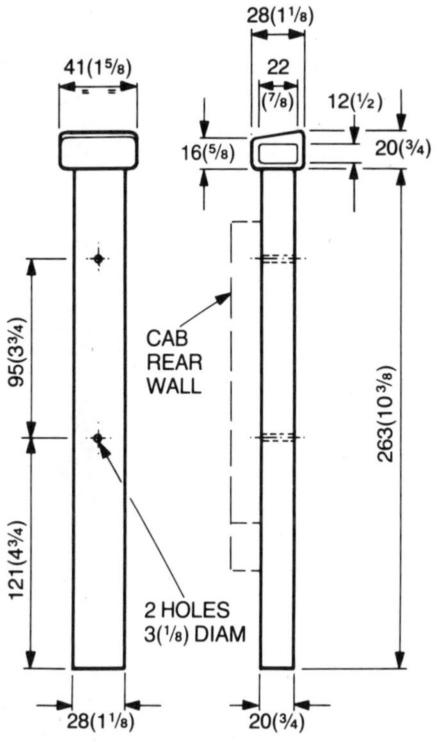

28(1 1/8)
41(1 5/8)
22
(7/8)
12(1/2)
16(5/8)
20(3/4)
95(3 3/4)
CAB REAR WALL
263(10 3/8)
121(4 3/4)
2 HOLES 3(1/8) DIAM
28(1 1/8)
20(3/4)

AIR INTAKE

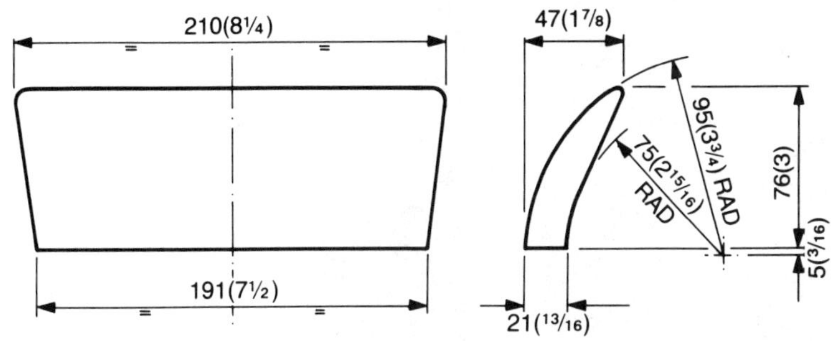

210(8 1/4)
191(7 1/2)
47(1 7/8)
95(3 3/4) RAD
75(2 15/16) RAD
76(3)
5(3/16)
21(13/16)

AEROFOIL

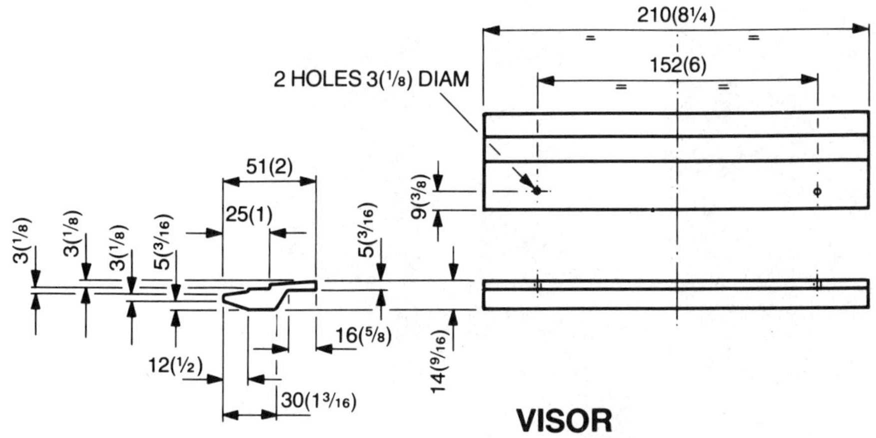

210(8 1/4)
152(6)
2 HOLES 3(1/8) DIAM
51(2)
25(1)
9(3/8)
3(1/8)
3(1/8)
3(1/8)
5(3/16)
5(3/16)
16(5/8)
12(1/2)
14(9/16)
30(1 3/16)

VISOR

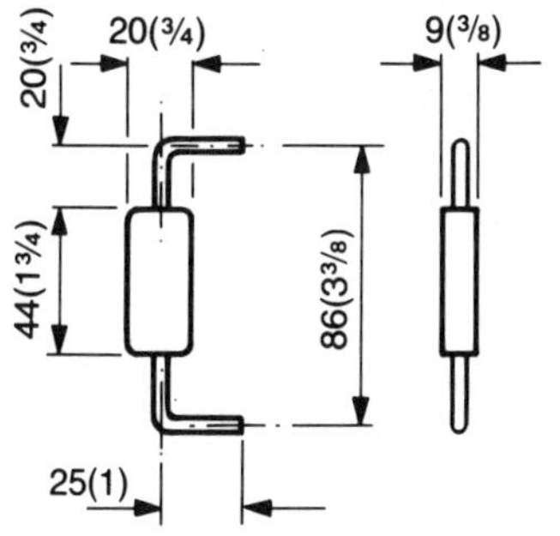

20(3/4)
20(3/4)
9(3/8)
44(1 3/4)
86(3 3/8)
25(1)

WING MIRROR

MAKE TWO

SUPPORT ARM FORMED FROM 3(1/8) DIAM PLASTIC COVERED CURTAIN WIRE

Building the chassis is rather like making a ladder. It is built of two main chassis members with cross members fixed at intervals along its length. Onto this framework is fixed a sheet of plywood which has edging strips. A head and tail board complete the trailer.

1 Cut the two main chassis members and mark in pencil the position of the cross members.

2 Cramp all the cross members together and mark out the pieces to be cut out. It is important to mark them all together otherwise great difficulty will be experienced when trying to fit them onto the chassis members.

3 After cutting out the cross members glue them all onto the main chassis.

4 Mark out a pair of axle supports. It is best to fix them together while drilling the axle holes. Axle holes are best drilled a fraction larger than the axle itself. Now cut and fit the rear axle support tie member. This whole unit is now fitted onto the main chassis members. Pilot holes are drilled through the chassis members for four hefty screws to pass through and hold the completed rear axle bogie unit.

5 The modern trailer unit has a large rear bumper unit fitted low down (to stop cars that crash into the back getting caught under the trailer). This bumper is fitted onto the rear chassis cross member.

6 A prominent feature of any trailer unit is the massive mudflaps. Cut two from black plastic sheet and attach them to the mudflap support bar.

7 The jockey wheel assembly is shaped up from a piece of beech. Drill a hole through the bottom to take the axle. The unit is held to the trailer by a hinge. It is important that when the jockey wheel is fitted it is at an angle to the bed. Otherwise, when the trailer is loaded without the truck attached, the jockey wheel will tend to fold underneath. A plastic ball catch is fitted to hold the unit in place when the trailer is on the move.

8 The hitch pin assembly is glued and screwed at the front between the main chassis cross members.

9 The bed of the trailer is made from plywood. Birch ply is ideal for this as it has a creamy colour. To add realism it is important to draw black lines along the length of the bed to simulate the planking. Edging strips are then screwed onto the sides of the trailer unit. The use of chrome plated cup washers under the screw heads adds a finishing touch.

10 Paint or varnish the trailer unit before fitting the wheels.

11 In order that the Hyster Fork Lift truck can load and off-load the wooden blocks it is necessary to make wooden pallets. These consist of plywood bases onto which two strips of wood are glued and screwed. The strips fitted to the plywood base allow the forks of the Hyster to get underneath the load.

12 When making wooden blocks it is best to use beech; however, other woods will do. A variety of shapes are necessary to allow young children scope to build towers, bridges etc. You will find that a few lengths of plywood offcuts will add greatly to the buildings that can be made. Children love wooden blocks; they give great scope for their imagination.

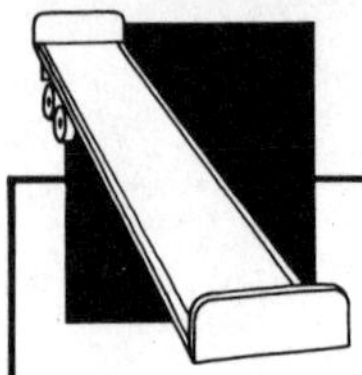

Scania trailer

Main chassis members	2 off	1086 x 38 x 22mm (42¾ x 1½ x ⅞in)	Timber
Trailer bed	1 off	1086 x 241 x 3mm (42¾ x 9½ x ⅛in)	Plywood
Edging strip	2 off	1086 x 25 x 9mm (42¾ x 1 x ⅜in)	Timber
Head board	1 off	260 x 95 x 20mm (10¼ x 3¾ x ¾in)	Timber
Tail board	1 off	260 x 86 x 20mm (10¼ x 3⅜ x ¾in)	Timber
Chassis cross members	5 off	241 x 64 x 20mm (9½ x 2½ x ¾in)	Timber
	2 off	241 x 54 x 20mm (9½ x 2⅛ x ¾in)	Timber
Hitch pin assembly	1 off	76 x 51 x 20mm (3 x 2 x ¾in)	Timber
	1 off	76mm(3in) long x 12mm(½in) diameter dowel	
Jockey wheel leg	1 off	152 x 51 x 20mm (6 x 2 x ¾in)	Timber
Rear axle support	2 off	286 x 86 x 22mm (11¼ x 3⅜ x ⅞in)	Timber
Rear axle support tie member	1 off	165 x 51 x 20mm (6½ x 2 x ¾in)	Timber
Rear mud flap support bar	1 off	241 x 32 x 16mm (9½ x 1¼ x ⅝in)	Timber
Rear bumper bar assembly	1 off	241 x 16 x 16mm (9½ x ⅝ x ⅝in)	Timber
	2 off	86 x 35 x 16mm (3⅜ x 1⅜ x ⅝in)	Timber
Ancillaries			
	8 off	102 mm (4in) diameter road wheels	
	2 off	254mm(10in) long x 6mm(¼in) diameter steel axles	
	4 off	12mm(½in) o/d x 6mm(¼in) i/d x 6mm(¼in) thick spacers	
	4 off	Spring dome caps to suit 6mm (¼in) diameter axles	
	1 off	25mm (1in) brass hinge	
	1 off	Spring loaded ball type door catch assembly	
	2 off	38mm (1½in) diameter wheels	
	1 off	95mm(3¾) long x 6mm(¼in) diameter steel axle	
	2 off	Spring dome caps to suit 6mm (¼in) diameter axle	
	1 off	51 x 20 x 1½mm (2 x ¾ x 1/16in) thick rubber	
Mud flaps	Make from 165 x 114 x 1½mm (6½ x 4½ x 1/16in) thick stiff plastic		

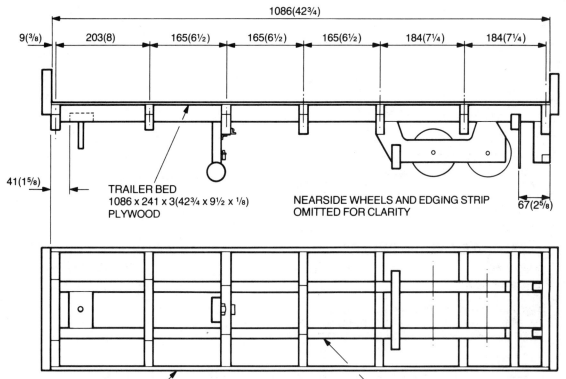

1086(42¾)

9(³⁄₈)   203(8)   165(6½)   165(6½)   165(6½)   184(7¼)   184(7¼)

41(1⁵⁄₈)

TRAILER BED
1086 x 241 x 3(42¾ x 9½ x ⅛)
PLYWOOD

NEARSIDE WHEELS AND EDGING STRIP
OMITTED FOR CLARITY

67(2⁵⁄₈)

EDGING STRIPS, MAKE TWO
1086 x 25 x 9(42¾ x 1 x ³⁄₈)

MAIN CHASSIS MEMBERS, MAKE TWO
1086 x 38 x 22(42¾ x 1½ x ⁷⁄₈)

VIEW ON UNDERSIDE OF TRAILER
WHEELS OMITTED FOR CLARITY

GENERAL ARRANGEMENT OF TRAILER

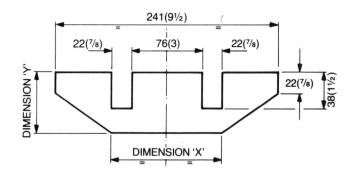

241(9½)

22(⁷⁄₈)   76(3)   22(⁷⁄₈)

22(⁷⁄₈)
38(1½)

DIMENSION 'Y'

DIMENSION 'X'

CHASSIS CROSS MEMBERS

MAKE SIX   20(¾) THICK

CROSS MEMBERS No 1 & 2:   DIM 'X' = 146(5¾), DIM 'Y' = 54(2⅛)
CROSS MEMBERS No 3, 4, 5 & 6: DIM 'X' = 121(4¾), DIM 'Y' = 64(2½)

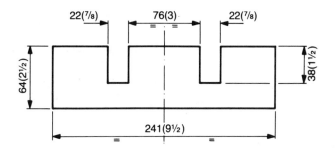

22(⁷⁄₈)   76(3)   22(⁷⁄₈)

64(2½)   38(1½)

241(9½)

REAR CHASSIS CROSS MEMBER
20(¾) THICK

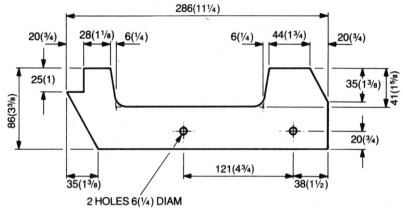

REAR AXLE SUPPORT

MAKE TWO   22(⅞) THICK

ALSO REQUIRED:
EIGHT 102(4) DIAM WHEELS
TWO 6(¼) DIAM x 254(10) LONG STEEL AXLES
FOUR 12(½) O/D x 6(¼) I/D x 6(¼) THICK SPACERS
FOUR SPRING DOME CAPS TO SUIT AXLE DIAM

2 HOLES 6(¼) DIAM

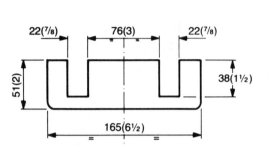

REAR AXLE SUPPORT
TIE MEMBER

20(¾) THICK

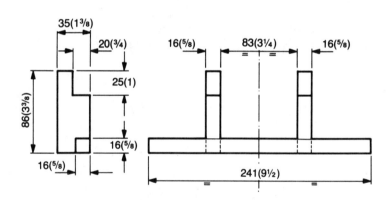

REAR BUMPER BAR ASSEMBLY

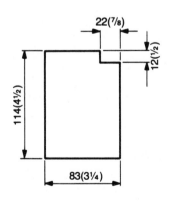

MUDFLAP

1.5(¹⁄₁₆) THICK STIFF PLASTIC
MAKE TWO

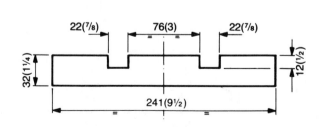

REAR MUDFLAP SUPPORT BAR

16(⅝) THICK

51 x 20 x 1.5(2 x ¾ x ¹⁄₁₆)
RUBBER FRICTION PAD
PINNED TO TOP OF LEG

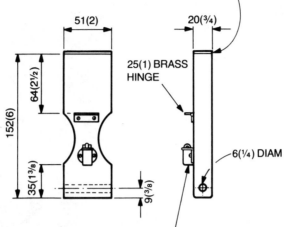

25(1) BRASS
HINGE

6(¼) DIAM

SPRING LOADED BALL TYPE DOOR CATCH,
BAR POSITIONED ON REAR FACE OF 3rd
CHASSIS CROSS MEMBER

JOCKEY WHEEL LEG ASSEMBLY

ALSO REQUIRED:
TWO 38(1½) DIAM WHEELS
ONE 6(¼) DIAM x 95(3¾) LONG STEEL AXLE
TWO SPRING DOME CAPS TO SUIT AXLE DIAM

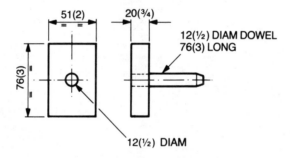

12(½) DIAM DOWEL
76(3) LONG

12(½) DIAM

HITCH PIN ASSEMBLY

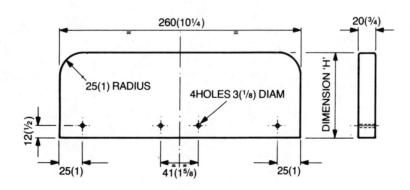

25(1) RADIUS

4 HOLES 3(⅛) DIAM

HEAD AND TAIL BOARDS

HEAD BOARD: DIM 'H' = 95(3¾)
TAIL BOARD: DIM 'H' = 86(3⅜)

HYSTER FORK LIFT

In a world where time is money the very best equipment is necessary to get the quickest possible turn round of ships and trucks at the docks.

The Hyster is the king of fork lifts. These Goliaths can pick up a 40' long steel container, stack it 24' in the air and without pausing for breath dash off to pick up another load.

The combination of a large truck loaded with pallets full of building blocks and a fork lift truck will keep any youngster busy for many years.

This model is tremendously strong and will withstand a youngster sitting and riding on it. I have given the 'mast' a tilt mechanism which is so necessary when trying to lift heavy objects. However, it is a model and will involve some quite involved woodworking. The tilting column is the most difficult part to construct and therefore studying the three-dimensional drawing will be of great help, so familiarise yourself with all the parts before starting.

The Hyster will look best if constructed from a hardwood like beech. As with other models I have combined the timbers to give an interesting colour combination and the fork-lift mechanism of this particular model was made from mahogany.

1 As with all vehicles the chassis is the starting place. The main under-chassis has to be formed to allow the running board to be glued and screwed into place. Cut and drill the axle holes and lower tilt pin hole and the recess for the chrome plated tube which simulates a hydraulic ram.

2 Shaping of the back is done before the engine cowl is screwed on from the underside. Basic shaping of both these components is initially done with a coping saw, then a spokeshave and finish them off with glasspaper.

On the real machine there are two recessed lines on the engine cowl. Two narrow saw cuts are first made, and then cut out with a chisel. This has to be carefully done with a very sharp chisel. Attention to small details of this sort are well worth while. As you will discover it is these that make the finished model look like its larger counterpart. Before screwing the cowl into place shape the back. Attach the cowl to the under-chassis and check final shaping at the back.

3 Mark and cut out a pair of cab walls. You will see from the plan that there is a right and left hand wall to be made. In effect this means that all the chamfers are on the outside edges. Keep the pair of walls together while holes are bored for column tilting handle, lower tilt pin hole, and fork raising handle. Once the cab entry door and recess underneath have been cut individual shaping of right and left hand sides can start. Small chamfers are vital to the finished look of the machine.

4 The walls are held together by bulkheads back and front. The rear bulkhead has a chamfered window at the top. Cut and shape the cab floor.

5 Before the cab walls and bulkheads are glued and screwed together, it is necessary to make the column tilting handle as it is only possible to fit this before the cab unit is fixed together. This handle should be made in beech. To get the column to tilt and stay fixed in position, two notches are cut in the underside of this lever. These must be a tight fit over the

steel bar otherwise the tilt mechanism will not work well.

6 Fit the column tilting assembly and now screw and glue the cab together.

7 Before fixing the roof make the control console, driver's seat and gear lever. A little felt glued onto the driver's seat and the floor will greatly add to the quality look of the machine.

8 Cut and fit the perspex windows back and front.

9 The roof is secured using chrome-plated raised-head screws fitted with cups. Wherever screws are used on this model I have incorporated the chrome plated cups as this makes rather a nice feature.

10 The mudguards can be made in one of two ways:
   a steaming
   b cutting from a block of wood.
I used the second method and it is not as daunting as it may seem at first. The hand saw for this job is a bow saw. After marking out the mudguards the first cut to make is the inside of the curve. Obviously a fairly large chunk of wood is necessary to hold in the vice while the cutting operation is going on.

After cutting out the inside curve remove the saw cuts with a spokeshave or glass-paper. Now cut the outer edge of the mudguard. Adopt this procedure for both back and front mudguards.

Remember that there are left and right hand mudguards when you come to chamfer the outer edges and cut the angles on the back mudguards. Nothing is worse than making a mistake after so much work. Check twice – cut once!

After final shaping, glue the mudguards onto the chassis.

11 The exhaust stack is formed by planing the edges off a rectangular length of hardwood. The plane marks are removed with glasspaper. To add a touch of realism a small dowel rod is fixed in the top, and over this is fitted a length of black rubber tube. This is both decorative and functional as it prevents a child scratching his or her legs on the top of the exhaust stack.

12 The only way into the driver's cab is up the ladders. Perhaps the simplest method of ladder making in miniature is to fix together two lengths of hardwood, mark the position of the rungs and drill the holes, with both sides still fixed together. Make a simple jig and cut all the rungs to the same length. Glass-paper a small chamfer on the end of each dowel rod. The chamfer makes it possible to assemble the rungs into the holes with ease.

Glue all the rungs into the holes on one side of the ladder, put a spot of glue on the ends of all the other dowel rods and fit the other side of the ladder on. Now put the whole assembly in the vice and gently apply pressure until all the dowel rods are flush with the sides.

After the glue is dry, plane the edges to remove surplus glue etc. It is obviously simplest to just make one length of ladder and then cut off the required amount.

13 The ladder is fixed to the roof by two long strips which are fixed onto the two last rungs. The top edges are screwed onto the cab roof.

Fork lift mechanism
How it works
The lifting mechanism consists basically of three parts, tilting column assembly, raising column assembly and fork frame assembly.

When the handles are turned to raise the fork mechanism, the raising column starts to rise in the tilting column. As the raising column travels upwards it raises the fork mechanism, which travels at twice the speed of the raising column and reaches the top as the raising column is fully extended. This does sound a little complicated, but when you get into the job it is not really as daunting as it sounds. The hydraulic ram does not actually push anything in the model but without it there is no realism. The steel rod 'telescopes' inside the chromed steel tube when the fork mechanism is operated up or down.

14 First construct the tilting column assembly. Basically this consists of two sides joined together by sections of hardwood. These cross pieces have notches cut in them to allow the nylon cord to operate without interfering with the raising column as it slides inside the tilting column. The plan shows exactly where these notches are.

A specialist hand tool is required for making the tilting column sides. A plough plane is necessary to cut the grooves that run the full length of the columns.

15 In order to reduce friction two pulleys are incorporated. I was unable to find pulleys with a groove in them so I used existing wheels and with a sharp Stanley knife fashioned a groove to take the nylon cord.

16 The pulleys are mounted on steel rod with blocks screwed onto the tilting column. The pulleys are kept in the centre of the axles by plastic tube positioned either side of the pulley.

17 Now construct the raising column assembly. You will notice that the bottom former is notched to allow room for the chrome-plated tube. Also a hole is drilled in this former and takes the length of nylon cord which actuates the raising and lowering process. The cord goes over the upper pulley, down around the lower pulley and onto the winding shaft. This piece of cord is not connected to the fork lift guide block in any way.

The other length of cord in the mechanism is attached at one end to the top of the tilting column assembly, through two screw eyes and onto the fork lift guide block.

18 The fork lift guide block has to be made carefully and the various slots cut accurately.

19 The guide block has to be fitted inside the raising column assembly. Quite obviously a good sliding fit is essential. A little candle wax will help tremendously.

20 Now assemble the raising block and tilting column together. It is at this stage that a good sliding fit is necessary and you may well have to spend a little time achieving this.

21 Construct the fork back frame assembly and glue and screw the fork arms into place.

22 The lower tilt pin attaches the tilting column to the chassis. The tilt pin goes through the bottom of the chromed steel tube (hydraulic ram). It is necessary to drill a hole through the tube before assembling the column.

23 After fitting the tilting column assembly it is then attached to the fork assembly. The position of this is shown in dotted lines on the three-dimensional drawing.

24 The winding mechanism has two handles to 'crank' up the load. The winding cord is attached to a block which is screwed onto the winding shaft with a small screw. The winding handles themselves are made from beech and dowel rods. The winding handles are kept in place by plastic 'sleeves.' You will find that threading the cord and attaching it to the winding shaft is quite a fiddly task as there is not a great deal of room to work.

25 The air cleaner is made from different diameter dowel rods. At the base a plastic tube is fitted and attached to the engine compartment. Attachment of the tube is easily achieved by fixing screws in the positions where you want the tube to go. The tube then simply fits over the ends of the screw heads.

26 If you have used hardwoods throughout, then the model will look particularly fine if it is finished off with matt varnish.

Cutting list

Main underchassis	1 off	502 x 79 x 44mm (19¾ x 3⅛ x 1¾in)	Timber
Engine forward block	1 off	67 x 60 x 60mm (2⅝ x 2⅜ x 2⅜in)	Timber
Engine cowl	1 off	298 x 79 x 44mm (11¾ x 3⅛ x 1¾in)	Timber
Cab wall	2 off	292 x 200 x 20mm (11½ x 7⅞ x ¾in)	Timber
Mudguards	Make from	305 x 67 x 60mm (12 x 2⅝ x 2⅜in)	Timber
Running board	2 off	248 x 108 x 12mm (9¾ x 4¼ x ½in)	Timber
battery	2 off	38 x 25 x 20mm (1½ x 1 x ¾in)	Timber
Cab roof panel	1 off	146 x 95 x 16mm (5¾ x 3¾ x ⅝in)	Timber
Front bulkhead	1 off	140 x 79 x 16mm (5½ x 3⅛ x ⅝in)	Timber
Rear bulkhead	1 off	210 x 79 x 16mm (8¼ x 3⅛ x ⅝in)	Timber
Windscreen frame	2 off	117 x 25 x 9mm (4⅝ x 1 x ⅜in)	Timber
Ladder stringers	Make from	1360 x 11 x 6mm (53½ x 7/16 x ¼in)	Timber
rungs	Make from	460mm(18in) long x 6mm(¼in) diameter dowel	
Air intake	Make from	70mm(2¾in) long x 22mm(⅞in) diameter dowel	
	1 off	117mm(4⅝in) long x 9mm(⅜in) diameter dowel	
Exhaust stack	1 off	241 x 32 x 20mm (9½ x 1¼ x ¾in)	Timber
	1 off	38mm (1½in) long x 6mm (¼in) diameter dowel	
Fork raising handle	Make from	356mm(14in) long x 9mm(⅜in) diameter dowel	
	Make from	140 x 25 x 20mm (5½ x 1 x ¾in)	Timber
	Make from	25mm (1in) diameter dowel off-cut	
Cab floor	1 off	98 x 79 x 6mm (3⅞ x 3⅛ x ¼in)	Plywood
Control console	1 off	38 x 32 x 25mm (1½ x 1¼ x 1in)	Timber
	1 off	38mm(1½in) long x 6mm(¼in) diameter dowel	
Steering wheel	Make from	22mm (⅞in) diameter dowel off-cut	
Seat plinth	1 off	70 x 41 x 20mm (2¾ x 1⅝ x ¾in)	Timber
Seat	1 off	51 x 38 x 38mm (2 x 1½ x 1½in)	Timber
Gear lever assembly	1 off	12mm (½in) diameter dowel off-cut	
	1 off	8mm (5/16in) diameter dowel off-cut	
Column tilting handle	1 off	184 x 28 x 22mm (7¼ x 1⅛ x ⅞in)	Timber
	1 off	76mm(3in) long x 6mm(¼in) diameter dowel	
Column tilting fork	2 off	102 x 20 x 12mm (4 x ¾ x ½in)	Timber
	1 off	146 x 25 x 12mm (5¾ x 1 x ½in)	Timber
Tilting column crossmembers	4 off	119 x 22 x 18mm (4 11/16 x ⅞ x 11/16in)	Timber
verticals	2 off	330 x 43 x 20mm (13 x 1 11/16 x ¾in)	Timber
upper bearings	2 off	41 x 20 x 12mm (1⅝ x ¾ x ½in)	Timber
lower bearings	2 off	76 x 41 x 16mm (3 x 1⅝ x ⅝in)	Timber
Raising column verticals	2 off	330 x 20 x 12mm (13 x ¾ x ½in)	Timber
	1 off	76 x 51 x 25mm (3 x 2 x 1in)	Timber
	1 off	76 x 25 x 18mm (3 x 1 x 11/16in)	Timber
Guide block	1 off	76 x 67 x 41mm (3 x 2⅝ x 1⅝in)	Timber
Fork back frame	2 off	213 x 44 x 18mm (8⅜ x 1¾ x 11/16in)	Timber
	2 off	143 x 35 x 20mm (5⅝ x 1⅜ x ¾in)	Timber
Fork crossbar	1 off	213 x 32 x 20mm (8⅜ x 1¼ x ¾in)	Timber
Fork arms	2 off	184 x 25 x 20mm (7¼ x 1 x ¾in)	Timber
Ancillaries			
Front axle assembly	1 off	273mm(10¾in) long x 6mm(¼in) diameter steel rod	
	4 off	102mm (4in) diameter road wheels	
	2 off	12mm (½in) o/d x 6mm (¼in) i/d x 16mm (⅝in) long spacers	
	2 off	Spring dome caps to suit 6mm (¼in) diameter	
Rear axle assembly	1 off	171mm(6¾in) long x 6mm(¼in) diameter steel rod	

	2 off	102mm (4in) diameter road wheels
	2 off	12mm (½in) o/d x 6mm (¼in) i/d x 12mm (½in) long spacers
	2 off	Spring dome caps to suit 6mm (¼in) diameter
Front screen	1 off	117 x 79 x 2mm (4⅝ x 3⅛ x ¹⁄₁₆in) thick transparent plastic
Rear screen	1 off	76 x 76 x 2mm (3 x 3 x ¹⁄₁₆in) thick transparent plastic
Air intake hose	1 off	9mm (⅜in) o/d x 3mm (⅛in) i/d x 57mm (2¼in) long rubber hose
Exhaust stack	1 off	12mm (½in) o/d x 6mm (¼in) i/d x 54mm (2⅛in) long rubber hose
Fork raising handle	2 off	12mm (½in) o/d x 9mm (⅜in) i/d x 41mm (1⅝in) long spacers
Gear lever	1 off	38mm (1½in) long plastic cover flexible wire x 3mm (⅛in) diameter
Column tilting spindle	1 off	152mm(6in) long x 5mm(³⁄₁₆in) diameter steel rod
	2 off	Spring dome caps to suit 5mm (³⁄₁₆in) diameter
	1 off	25mm (1in) diameter grooved wheel
	2 off	9mm (⅜in) o/d x 5mm (³⁄₁₆in) i/d x 35mm (1⅜in) long spacers
Column lock bar	1 off	117mm(4⅝in) long x 5mm(³⁄₁₆in) diameter steel bar
Lower tilt pin	1 off	127mm(5in) long x 5mm(³⁄₁₆in) diameter steel bar)
	2 off	Spring dome caps to suit 5mm(³⁄₁₆in) diameter
Upper pulley spindle	1 off	127mm(5in) long x 5mm(³⁄₁₆in) diameter steel rod
	2 off	9mm (⅜in) o/d x 5mm (³⁄₁₆in) i/d x 38mm (1½in) long spacers
	1 off	25mm (1in) diameter grooved wheel
	2 off	Spring dome caps to suit 5mm (³⁄₁₆in) diameter
Hydraulic cylinder	1 off	292mm (11½in) long x 8mm (⁵⁄₁₆in) o/d x 6mm (¼in) i/d steel tube
	1 off	298mm(11¾in) long x 6mm(¼in) diameter steel rod
Various screws	6 off	12mm(½in) screwed eyes, length strong cord

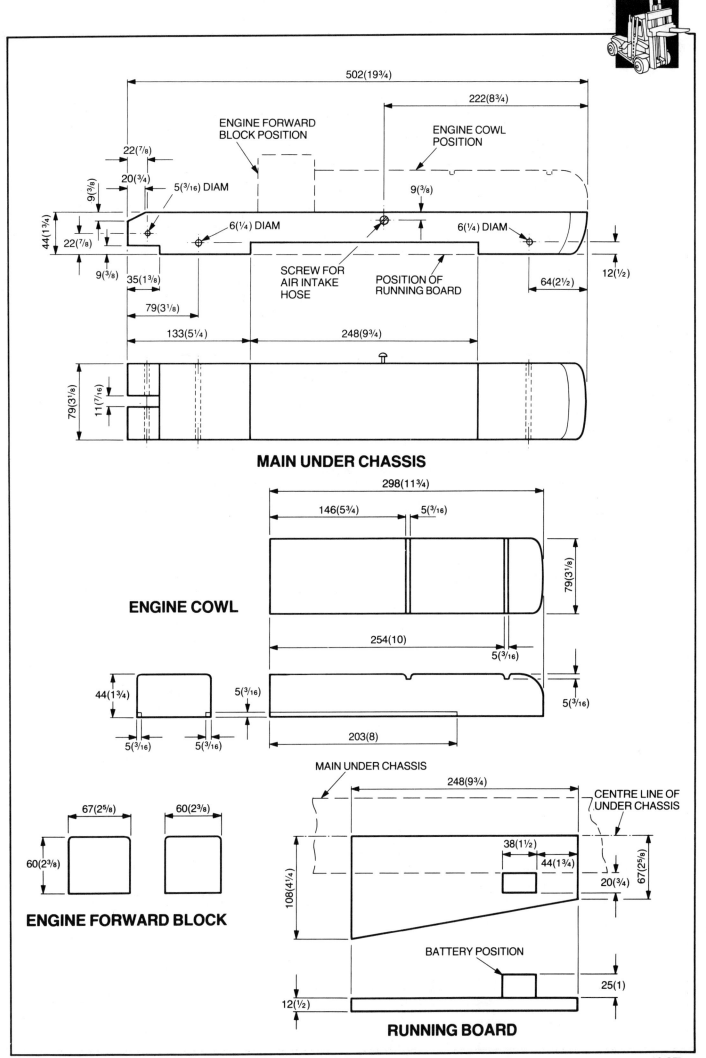

MAIN UNDER CHASSIS

ENGINE COWL

ENGINE FORWARD BLOCK

RUNNING BOARD

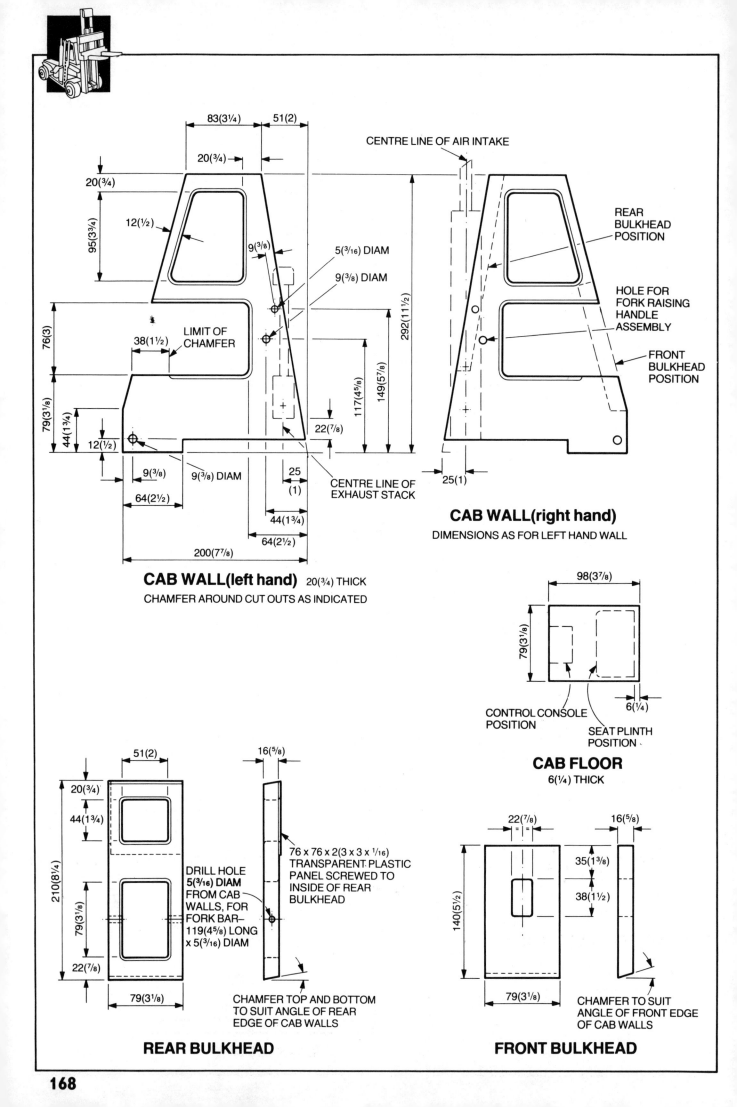

CAB WALL(left hand) 20(¾) THICK

CHAMFER AROUND CUT OUTS AS INDICATED

83(3¼) 51(2)

20(¾)

20(¾)

12(½)

95(3¾)

9(³⁄₈)

5(³⁄₁₆) DIAM

9(³⁄₈) DIAM

76(3)

LIMIT OF CHAMFER

38(1½)

79(3⅛)

44(1¾)

12(½)

9(³⁄₈)

9(³⁄₈) DIAM

64(2½)

200(7⅞)

22(⁷⁄₈)

25(1)

44(1¾)

64(2½)

117(4⁵⁄₈)

149(5⁷⁄₈)

292(11½)

CENTRE LINE OF EXHAUST STACK

CENTRE LINE OF AIR INTAKE

REAR BULKHEAD POSITION

HOLE FOR FORK RAISING HANDLE ASSEMBLY

FRONT BULKHEAD POSITION

25(1)

CAB WALL(right hand)

DIMENSIONS AS FOR LEFT HAND WALL

98(3⁷⁄₈)

79(3⅛)

6(¼)

CONTROL CONSOLE POSITION

SEAT PLINTH POSITION

CAB FLOOR

6(¼) THICK

51(2)

16(⁵⁄₈)

20(¾)

44(1¾)

210(8¼)

79(3⅛)

22(⁷⁄₈)

79(3⅛)

DRILL HOLE 5(³⁄₁₆) DIAM FROM CAB WALLS, FOR FORK BAR— 119(4⁵⁄₈) LONG x 5(³⁄₁₆) DIAM

76 x 76 x 2(3 x 3 x ¹⁄₁₆) TRANSPARENT PLASTIC PANEL SCREWED TO INSIDE OF REAR BULKHEAD

CHAMFER TOP AND BOTTOM TO SUIT ANGLE OF REAR EDGE OF CAB WALLS

REAR BULKHEAD

22(⁷⁄₈)

16(⁵⁄₈)

35(1³⁄₈)

38(1½)

140(5½)

79(3⅛)

CHAMFER TO SUIT ANGLE OF FRONT EDGE OF CAB WALLS

FRONT BULKHEAD

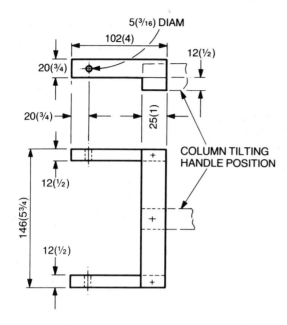

COLUMN TILTING FORK ASSEMBLY

5(³/₁₆) DIAM
102(4)
12(½)
20(¾)
20(¾)
25(1)
COLUMN TILTING HANDLE POSITION
146(5¾)
12(½)
12(½)

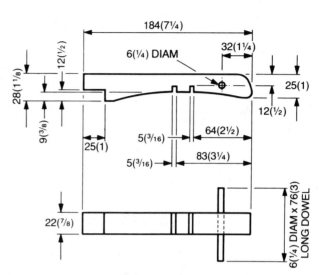

COLUMN TILTING HANDLE

184(7¼)
32(1¼)
12(½)
6(¼) DIAM
28(1¹/₈)
25(1)
12(½)
9(³/₈)
25(1)
5(³/₁₆)
64(2½)
5(³/₁₆)
83(3¼)
22(⁷/₈)
6(¼) DIAM x 76(3) LONG DOWEL

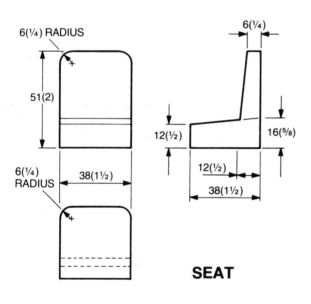

6(¼) RADIUS
51(2)
6(¼)
6(¼) RADIUS
38(1½)
12(½)
16(⁵/₈)
12(½)
38(1½)

SEAT

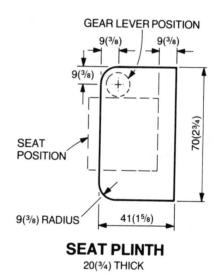

GEAR LEVER POSITION
9(³/₈)
9(³/₈)
9(³/₈)
70(2¾)
SEAT POSITION
9(³/₈) RADIUS
41(1⁵/₈)

SEAT PLINTH
20(¾) THICK

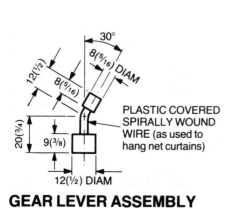

30°
8(⁵/₁₆) DIAM
12(½)
8(⁵/₁₆)
20(¾)
9(³/₈)
PLASTIC COVERED SPIRALLY WOUND WIRE (as used to hang net curtains)
12(½) DIAM

GEAR LEVER ASSEMBLY

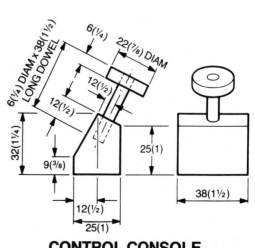

6(¼)
22(⁷/₈) DIAM
6(¼) DIAM x 38(1½) LONG DOWEL
12(½)
12(½)
32(1¼)
25(1)
9(³/₈)
12(½)
25(1)
38(1½)

CONTROL CONSOLE

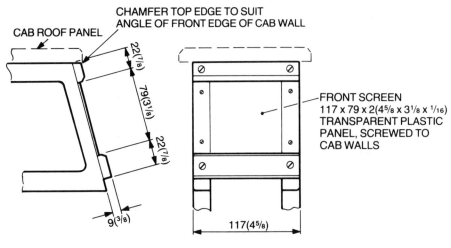

CAB ROOF PANEL

CHAMFER TOP EDGE TO SUIT
ANGLE OF FRONT EDGE OF CAB WALL

22($^7/_8$)

79(3$^1/_8$)

22($^7/_8$)

9($^3/_8$)

FRONT SCREEN
117 x 79 x 2(4$^5/_8$ x 3$^1/_8$ x $^1/_{16}$)
TRANSPARENT PLASTIC
PANEL, SCREWED TO
CAB WALLS

117(4$^5/_8$)

WINDSCREEN ASSEMBLY

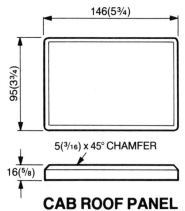

146(5$^3/_4$)

95(3$^3/_4$)

5($^3/_{16}$) x 45° CHAMFER

16($^5/_8$)

CAB ROOF PANEL

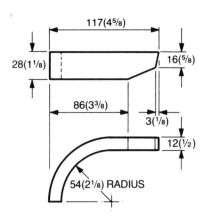

117(4$^5/_8$)

28(1$^1/_8$)

16($^5/_8$)

86(3$^3/_8$)

3($^1/_8$)

12($^1/_2$)

54(2$^1/_8$) RADIUS

REAR MUDGUARD

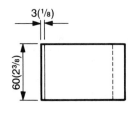

3($^1/_8$)

60(2$^3/_8$)

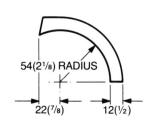

54(2$^1/_8$) RADIUS

22($^7/_8$)

12($^1/_2$)

FRONT MUDGUARD

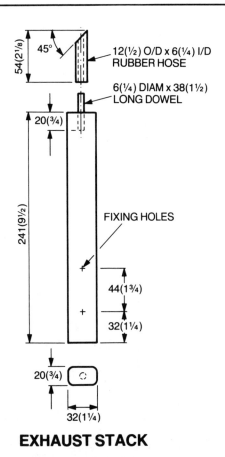

54(2$^1/_8$)

45°

12($^1/_2$) O/D x 6($^1/_4$) I/D
RUBBER HOSE

6($^1/_4$) DIAM x 38(1$^1/_2$)
LONG DOWEL

20($^3/_4$)

241(9$^1/_2$)

FIXING HOLES

44(1$^3/_4$)

32(1$^1/_4$)

20($^3/_4$)

32(1$^1/_4$)

EXHAUST STACK

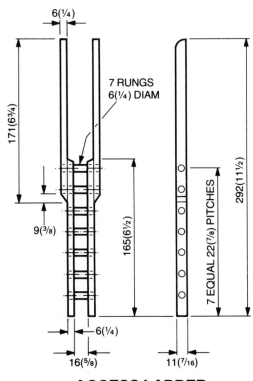

6($^1/_4$)

171(6$^3/_4$)

7 RUNGS
6($^1/_4$) DIAM

9($^3/_8$)

165(6$^1/_2$)

292(11$^1/_2$)

7 EQUAL 22($^7/_8$) PITCHES

6($^1/_4$)

16($^5/_8$)

11($^7/_{16}$)

ACCESS LADDER
MAKE TWO

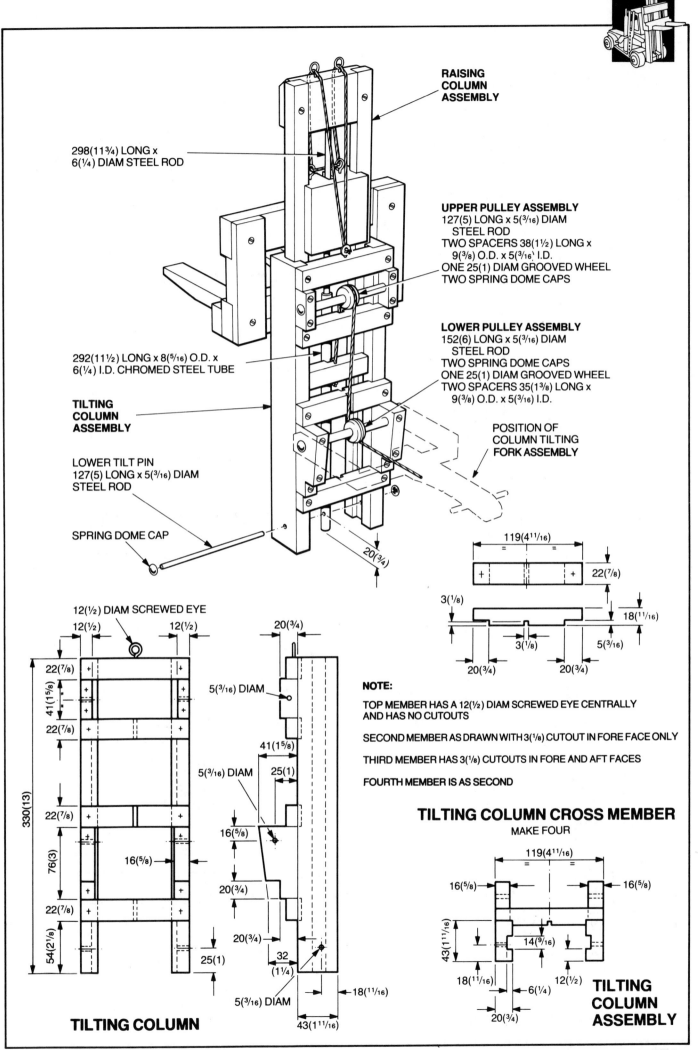

RAISING
COLUMN
ASSEMBLY

298(11¾) LONG x
6(¼) DIAM STEEL ROD

UPPER PULLEY ASSEMBLY
127(5) LONG x 5(³/₁₆) DIAM
STEEL ROD
TWO SPACERS 38(1½) LONG x
9(³/₈) O.D. x 5(³/₁₆) I.D.
ONE 25(1) DIAM GROOVED WHEEL
TWO SPRING DOME CAPS

LOWER PULLEY ASSEMBLY
152(6) LONG x 5(³/₁₆) DIAM
STEEL ROD
TWO SPRING DOME CAPS
ONE 25(1) DIAM GROOVED WHEEL
TWO SPACERS 35(1³/₈) LONG x
9(³/₈) O.D. x 5(³/₁₆) I.D.

292(11½) LONG x 8(⁵/₁₆) O.D. x
6(¼) I.D. CHROMED STEEL TUBE

**TILTING
COLUMN
ASSEMBLY**

POSITION OF
COLUMN TILTING
FORK ASSEMBLY

LOWER TILT PIN
127(5) LONG x 5(³/₁₆) DIAM
STEEL ROD

SPRING DOME CAP

20(¾)

119(4¹¹/₁₆)

22(⁷/₈)

3(¹/₈)

18(¹¹/₁₆)

3(¹/₈)

5(³/₁₆)

20(¾)   20(¾)

12(½) DIAM SCREWED EYE

12(½)   12(½)

20(¾)

22(⁷/₈)

41(1⁵/₈)

5(³/₁₆) DIAM

22(⁷/₈)

41(1⁵/₈)

5(³/₁₆) DIAM

25(1)

330(13)

22(⁷/₈)

16(⁵/₈)

16(⁵/₈)

76(3)

20(¾)

22(⁷/₈)

20(¾)

54(2¹/₈)

25(1)

32
(1¼)

18(¹¹/₁₆)

5(³/₁₆) DIAM

43(1¹¹/₁₆)

TILTING COLUMN

NOTE:

TOP MEMBER HAS A 12(½) DIAM SCREWED EYE CENTRALLY
AND HAS NO CUTOUTS

SECOND MEMBER AS DRAWN WITH 3(¹/₈) CUTOUT IN FORE FACE ONLY

THIRD MEMBER HAS 3(¹/₈) CUTOUTS IN FORE AND AFT FACES

FOURTH MEMBER IS AS SECOND

TILTING COLUMN CROSS MEMBER
MAKE FOUR

119(4¹¹/₁₆)

16(⁵/₈)   16(⁵/₈)

43(1¹¹/₁₆)

14(⁹/₁₆)

18(¹¹/₁₆)   6(¼)

20(¾)

12(½)

**TILTING
COLUMN
ASSEMBLY**

RAISING COLUMN ASSEMBLY

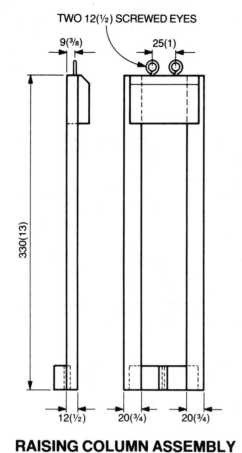

TWO 12(½) SCREWED EYES

9(³⁄₈)

25(1)

330(13)

12(½)   20(¾)   20(¾)

RAISING COLUMN ASSEMBLY

COLUMN TOP CROSS MEMBER

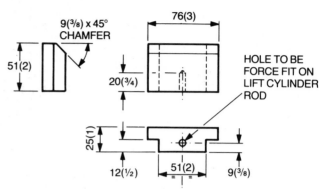

9(³⁄₈) x 45° CHAMFER

51(2)

76(3)

20(¾)

HOLE TO BE FORCE FIT ON LIFT CYLINDER ROD

25(1)

12(½)   51(2)   9(³⁄₈)

COLUMN TOP CROSS MEMBER

COLUMN LOWER CROSS MEMBER

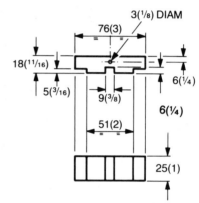

3(¹⁄₈) DIAM

76(3)

18(¹¹⁄₁₆)

5(³⁄₁₆)   9(³⁄₈)   6(¼)

6(¼)

51(2)

25(1)

COLUMN LOWER CROSS MEMBER

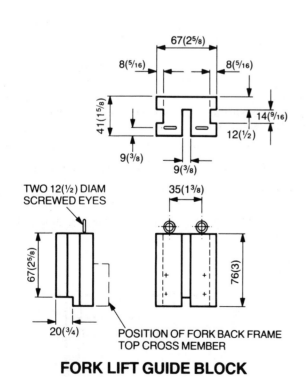

67(2⁵⁄₈)

8(⁵⁄₁₆)   8(⁵⁄₁₆)

41(1⁵⁄₈)   14(⁹⁄₁₆)

12(½)

9(³⁄₈)   9(³⁄₈)

TWO 12(½) DIAM SCREWED EYES

35(1³⁄₈)

67(2⁵⁄₈)   76(3)

20(¾)

POSITION OF FORK BACK FRAME TOP CROSS MEMBER

FORK LIFT GUIDE BLOCK

9(³⁄₈)

FIXING HOLE CENTRES

25(1)

20(¾)

20(¾)   64(2½)   9(³⁄₈)

184(7¼)

FORK ARMS
MAKE TWO

20(¾)   213(8³⁄₈)

32(1¼)   20(¾)

35(1³⁄₈)   25(1) 25(1)   35(1³⁄₈)

FORK CROSS BAR

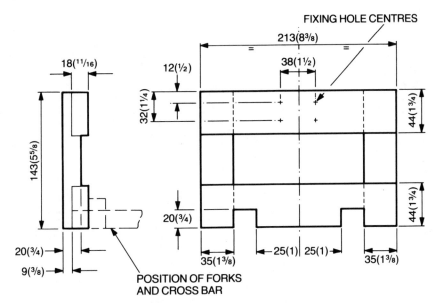

FIXING HOLE CENTRES

213(8³/₈)

38(1¹/₂)

18(¹¹/₁₆)

12(¹/₂)

32(1¹/₄)

44(1³/₄)

143(5⁵/₈)

44(1³/₄)

20(³/₄)

20(³/₄)

9(³/₈)

35(1³/₈) 25(1) 25(1) 35(1³/₈)

POSITION OF FORKS
AND CROSS BAR

FORK BACK FRAME ASSEMBLY

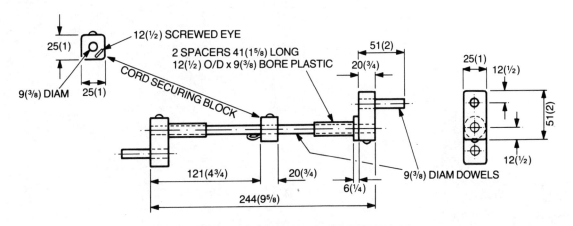

25(1)

12(¹/₂) SCREWED EYE

2 SPACERS 41(1⁵/₈) LONG
12(¹/₂) O/D x 9(³/₈) BORE PLASTIC

9(³/₈) DIAM   25(1)

CORD SECURING BLOCK

51(2)

20(³/₄)

25(1)

12(¹/₂)

51(2)

12(¹/₂)

121(4³/₄)

20(³/₄)

9(³/₈) DIAM DOWELS

6(¹/₄)

244(9⁵/₈)

FORK RAISING HANDLE ASSEMBLY

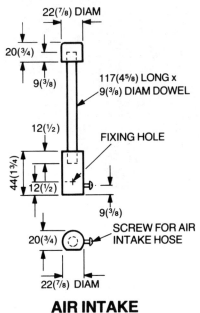

22(⁷/₈) DIAM

20(³/₄)

9(³/₈)

117(4⁵/₈) LONG x
9(³/₈) DIAM DOWEL

12(¹/₂)

FIXING HOLE

44(1³/₄)

12(¹/₂)

9(³/₈)

20(³/₄)

SCREW FOR AIR
INTAKE HOSE

22(⁷/₈) DIAM

AIR INTAKE

The V8 Land Rover represents the most powerful version of this well-known vehicle. The 3500cc engine makes it a superb unit for towing trailers of all sorts over the toughest terrain.

In appearance it differs slightly from other Land Rovers in that the radiator is flush with the front wings and badging is different with an extra logo down the side. Land Rover enthusiasts can distinguish a V8 approaching by the deep throated chuckle of its engine. It is quite simply the vehicle that climbs hills that others can't!

1   The first job to tackle is the making of the chassis. Tape two lengths of wood together and drill the axle holes.

2   Now cut and shape the front bumper and cross pieces. Glue these onto the main chassis.

3   The side panels are next. The first thing to be aware of here is that you need a right and left hand side. The first work to be done is the rebate which takes the front bulkhead and the stopped rebate towards the back.

Mark clearly with a marking knife these two rebates. Using a tenon saw cut along the lines and chisel out the middle portions. Care is necessary to get to the right depth. Take only a little wood out at a time.

4   Once the rebates have been cut, blocks of wood are glued onto the sides of the panels. These represent the front mudguards. To represent the headlamps I bought some chrome plated electrical screw fittings and drilled holes in the front wings to take them.

Now shaping of wheel arches and mudguards can be done. These can be cut out with a coping saw and finely shaped with spokeshave and glasspaper.

5   The radiator recess is cut from a solid block of wood. To take the grill, the front of the block is recessed using a large chisel. Only a shallow recess is necessary. Before cutting, mark with a knife all around the area to be removed. This stops ragged edges developing.

6   Cut and shape the front bulkhead, the central underfloor cross member and the rear bumper bar. The side panels can now be glued onto the bulkhead, the cross member and rear bumper. Fixed onto the bumper is a further cross piece glued in between the side panels. This gives support to the back of the floor. Now fix on the rear number plate.

7   Now cut the tailboard with a fine toothed saw such as a coping saw. The opening section must be cut carefully as the piece you take out will be used again. This piece is hinged. It is necessary to cut recesses to take the hinges. The tail board is kept shut by hooks, eyes and two short lengths of chain.

8   The floor is made from plywood and glued into the cross pieces.

9   Now make the cab foot pedals and gear lever assembly. The gear lever is easily made from dowel rod. A piece of plastic tube pushed over the top and painted black simulates a gear knob.

10   The front fascia is now shaped and drilled to take the steering wheel. It takes a little time and effort to shape and carve the steering wheel.

11   Shape up the rear bench seats. A radius is cut on the outside faces of these to allow the wheel clearance in the arch.

12   The driver's seat is cut from a block of wood. To add a touch of luxury to the seats I covered them with a brown felt. The material texture adds something to the richness of the wood.

13   Cut the bonnet to size and carefully round off all the edges. The bonnet is hinged to the front bulkhead. The spare wheel is mounted on the bonnet. I felt that rather than use a bolt I wanted the top of the wheel to have a nice chrome plated spring cap, so I cut a short length of steel rod, drilled a hole through the bonnet and fixed the wheel in place, securing it either side with a spring cap.

Using a magnetic catch gives a realistic 'click' when the bonnet is closed. I did not put an imitation engine in this model, but if you wish to, refer to the County which has engine details.

14   Now cut out the windscreen panel. The centre bar is fixed in afterwards to simplify the construction. The windscreen is slightly raked. This is achieved by planing a slight angle on the bottom. Glue the windscreen onto the front bulkhead.

15   Now there are many variants on Land Rover bodies. I chose to do the

canvas covered version. If you are building for a young child who wants to ride on the roof then substitute the design and fit solid wood panels.

16   The woodwork to hold the canopy resembles a tent structure (see three dimensional drawing). There are some joints to be cut, but these are all of the halving joint variety. After cutting all the joints, assemble it dry onto the vehicle to check that all the parts fit. If everything fits, glue the joints together.

17   Finding the right 'weight' and colour of canvas was difficult. Finally I bought a stiff denim as used for jeans. This material proved to be ideal as once the seams were folded in, a hot iron was sufficient to hold the material in place without getting involved in threading needles and other technical things.

18   Glueing the denim onto the framework would be rather messy. I therefore used raised head chrome plated screws and cup washers. This makes rather an interesting feature and allows the hood to be removed.

19   The rear fly sheet is fiddly and does need a hem around the opening piece. The window I made from a thick piece of clear plastic. This was glued or stitched onto the denim. The fly sheet is then fixed onto the rear canopy cross member and back frame posts with screws and cup washers.

20   Before the final fixing of the denim takes place, cut and fix the perspex to the front windscreen and side windows. The door window sills are glued onto the perspex.

21   Now drill two small holes both sides of the engine bulkhead. These

are to take the mirrors. The mirror itself is made from plywood. It is attached to the plastic covered spiral curtain wire by a small cable clip (available at electricians). In order that the curtain wire keeps its shape a piece of ordinary steel wire is pushed inside it and the wire bent to shape. The wires are glued into the bulkhead holes with epoxy resin.

22   The chassis and bodywork are now joined together. This is done by four large screws fixing the chassis to the bulkheads.

23   The finish is entirely up to you. If a good quality hardwood is used then varnish is all that is necessary. Wood is beautiful, don't cover it. On the other hand the restrained use of paint can add, and sometimes highlight, the true beauty of the natural colour.

Cutting list

Main chassis	2 off	359 x 30 x 18mm (14⅛ x 1 3/16 x 11/16in)	Timber
	2 off	149 x 22 x 16mm (5⅞ x ⅞ x ⅝in)	Timber
	2 off	83 x 18 x 12mm (3¼ x 11/16 x ½in)	Timber
	1 off	213 x 35 x 20mm (8⅜ x 1⅜ x ¾in)	Timber
	1 off	83 x 16 x 6mm (3¼ x ⅝ x ¼in)	Timber
Side panel	2 off	473 x 79 x 20mm (18⅝ x 3⅛ x ¾in)	Timber
	2 off	146 x 79 x 30mm (5¾ x 3⅛ x 1 3/16in)	Timber
Floor assembly	1 off	311 x 171 x 5mm (12¼ x 6¾ x 3/16in)	Plywood
	1 off	171 x 20 x 20mm (6¾ x ¾ x ¾in)	Timber
	1 off	184 x 28 x 16mm (7¼ x 1⅛ x ⅝in)	Timber
	1 off	171 x 32 x 20mm (6¾ x 1¼ x ¾in)	Timber
Front bulkhead	1 off	184 x 95 x 16mm (7¼ x 3¾ x ⅝in)	Timber
Fascia	1 off	171 x 38 x 16mm (6¾ x 1½ x 1⅝in)	Timber
Steering wheel assembly	1 off	47mm (1⅞in) diameter disc x 6mm (¼in) thick	Timber
	1 off	51mm (2in) long x 6mm (¼in) diameter dowel	
Cab foot pedal and gear lever	1 off	171 x 22 x 20mm (6¾ x ⅞ x ¾in)	Timber
	1 off	51mm (2in) long x 6mm (¼in) diameter dowel	
Wing mirror	2 off	32 x 20 x 6mm (1¼ x ¾ x ¼in)	Timber
Radiator assembly	1 off	111 x 64 x 16mm (4⅜ x 2½ x ⅝in)	Timber
	1 off	111 x 20 x 3mm (4⅜ x ¾ x ⅛in)	Timber
Bonnet	1 off	146 x 140 x 16mm (5¾ x 5½ x ⅝in)	Timber
Driver's seat assembly	1 off	171 x 76 x 9mm (6¾ x 3 x ⅜in)	Timber
	1 off	171 x 38 x 32mm (6¾ x 1½ x 1¼in)	Timber
Rear bench seats	2 off	219 x 35 x 20mm (8⅝ x 1⅜ x ¾in)	Timber
Tail board	1 off	210 x 67 x 9mm (8¼ x 2⅝ x ⅜in)	Timber
Rear bumper bar	1 off	210 x 20 x 16mm (8¼ x ¾ x ⅝in)	Timber
Windscreen panel	1 off	184 x 92 x 12mm (7¼ x 3⅝ x ½in)	Timber
	1 off	57 x 12 x 6mm (2¼ x ½ x ¼in)	Timber
Front door post	2 off	127 x 16 x 12mm (5 x ⅝ x ½in)	Timber
Side window sill	2 off	89 x 20 x 3mm (3½ x ¾ x ⅛in)	Timber
Rear canopy frame post	2 off	127 x 16 x 16mm (5 x ⅝ x ⅝in)	Timber
Canopy lower strip	2 off	191 x 20 x 6mm (7½ x ¾ x ¼in)	Timber
Rear number plate	1 off	171 x 22 x 16mm (6¾ x ⅞ x ⅝in)	Timber
Canopy top side strip	2 off	314 x 12 x 12mm (12⅜ x ½ x ½in)	Timber
Front canopy cross member	1 off	177 x 32 x 12mm (7 x 1¼ x ½in)	Timber
Central canopy cross member	1 off	177 x 25 x 12mm (7 x 1 x ½in)	Timber
Rear canopy cross member	1 off	177 x 32 x 12mm (7 x 1¼ x ½in)	Timber
Ancillaries			
Main chassis	4 off	102mm (4in) diameter road wheels	
	2 off	225mm (8⅞in) long x 6mm (¼in) diameter steel axles	
	4 off	12mm (½in) o/d x 6mm (¼in) i/d x 6mm (¼in) long spacers	
	4 off	Spring dome caps to suit 6mm (¼in) diameter axles	
Side panel	2 off	22mm (⅞in) diameter chromed 'head lamps'	
Cab foot pedal and gear lever	1 off	9mm (⅜in) o/d x 6mm (¼in) i/d x 12mm (½in) long tube	
	3 off	9mm (⅜in) diameter head brass drawing pins	
Wing mirror – arm	Make from	127mm (5in) long x 3mm (⅛in) diameter nylon cover curtain wire	
	2 off	3mm (⅛in) diameter cable grips	
Radiator assembly	1 off	Magnetic catch and packer	
	1 off	Wire mesh from 4 x 2mm (102 x 51in)	
Bonnet	1 off	102mm (4in) diameter spare road wheel	

	1 off	57mm (2¼in) long × 6mm (¼in) diameter steel pin
	2 off	Spring dome caps to suit 6mm (¼in) diameter pins
	2 off	25mm (1in) long brass hinges
Driver's seat covering		Make from 177 × 177mm (7 × 7in) felt
Tail board	2 off	25mm (1in) long brass hinges
	2 off	Screwed eyes
	2 off	Screwed hooks
	2 off	32mm (1¼in) lengths of chain
Windscreen	1 off	168 × 67 × 1·5mm (6⅝ × 2⅝ × 1/16in) thick clear plastic
Rear mud flap	2 off	70 × 38 × 1mm (2¾ × 1½ × 1/32in) thick black plastic
Side windows	2 off	89 × 89 × 1·5mm (3½ × 3½ × 1/16in) thick clear plastic
Canopy		Make from 445 × 356mm (17½ × 14in) canvas
Rear fly sheet		Make from 229 × 152mm (9 × 6in) canvas
	1 off	83 × 57 × 1·5mm (3¼ × 2¼ × 1/16in) thick clear plastic
Canopy fitted with	26 off	9mm (⅜in) long dome headed chrome screws and cup washers

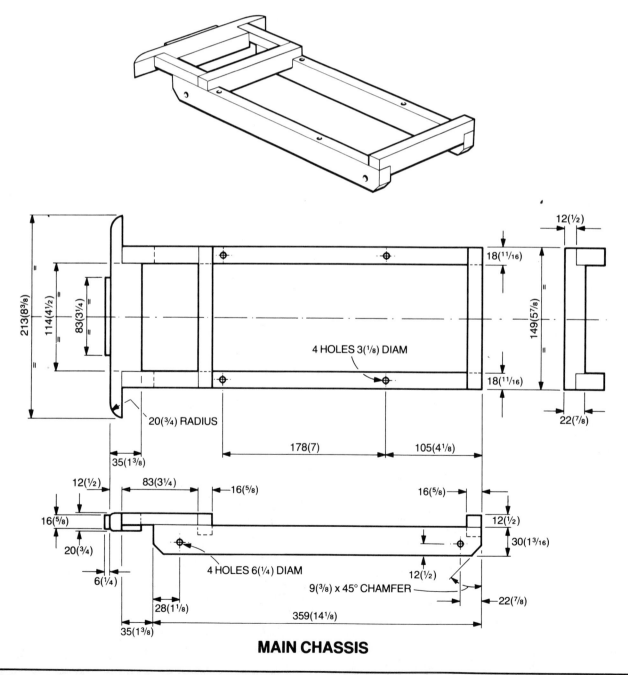

MAIN CHASSIS

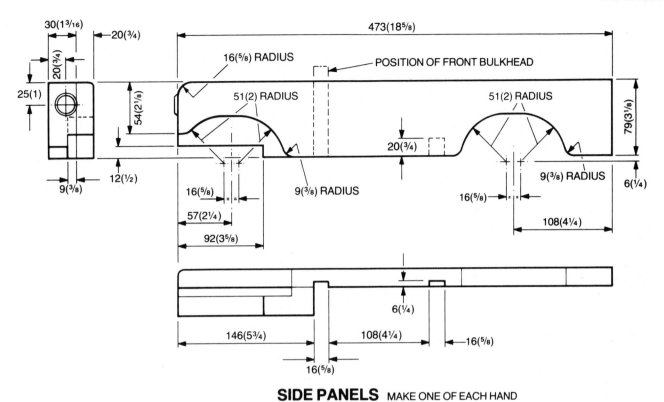

SIDE PANELS MAKE ONE OF EACH HAND

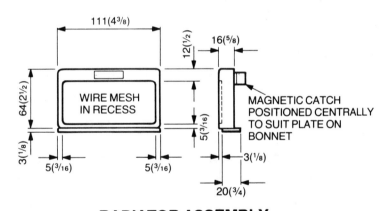

RADIATOR ASSEMBLY

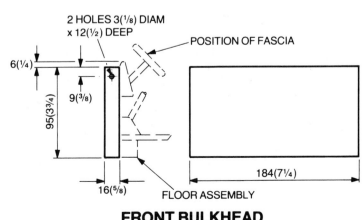

FRONT BULKHEAD

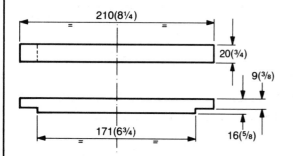

CENTRAL UNDERFLOOR CROSS MEMBER 16(⅝) THICK

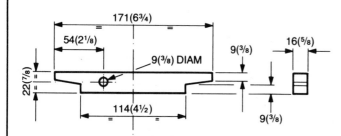

REAR BUMPER BAR

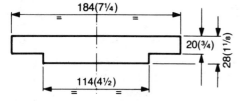

9(⅜) DIAM

REAR NUMBER PLATE

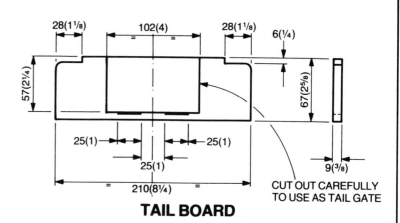

TAIL BOARD

CUT OUT CAREFULLY TO USE AS TAIL GATE

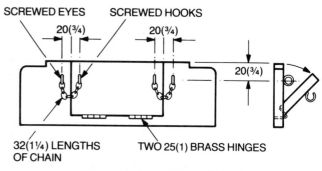

SCREWED EYES   SCREWED HOOKS

32(1¼) LENGTHS OF CHAIN

TWO 25(1) BRASS HINGES

TAIL BOARD FITTINGS

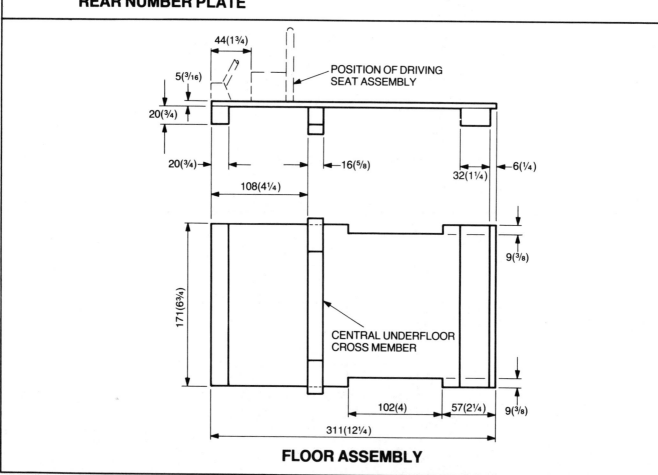

POSITION OF DRIVING SEAT ASSEMBLY

CENTRAL UNDERFLOOR CROSS MEMBER

FLOOR ASSEMBLY

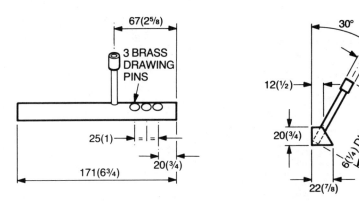

CAB FOOT PEDAL &
GEAR LEVER ASSEMBLY

67(2⅝)
3 BRASS DRAWING PINS
25(1)
20(¾)
171(6¾)

30°
9(⅜) OD x 6(¼) ID x 12(½) LONG TUBE
12(½)
20(¾)
6(¼) DIAM DOWEL x 51(2) LONG
22(⅞)

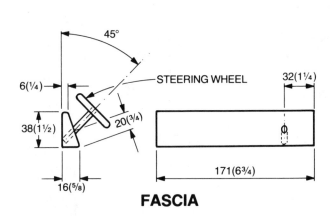

FASCIA

45°
STEERING WHEEL
6(¼)
38(1½)
20(¾)
16(⅝)
32(1¼)
171(6¾)

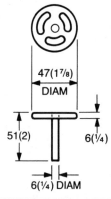

STEERING WHEEL
ASSEMBLY

47(1⅞) DIAM
51(2)
6(¼)
6(¼) DIAM

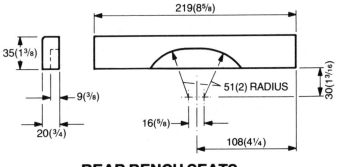

REAR BENCH SEATS
MAKE ONE OF EACH HAND

219(8⅝)
35(1⅜)
9(⅜)
20(¾)
51(2) RADIUS
16(⅝)
108(4¼)
30(1³⁄₁₆)

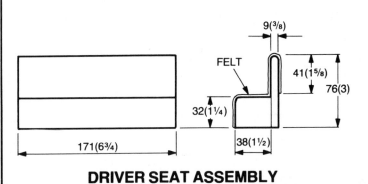

DRIVER SEAT ASSEMBLY

9(⅜)
FELT
41(1⅝)
76(3)
32(1¼)
38(1½)
171(6¾)

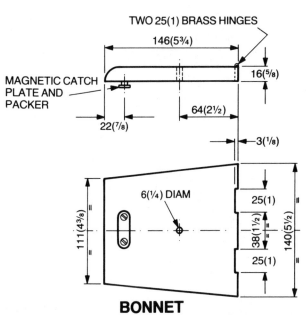

BONNET

TWO 25(1) BRASS HINGES
146(5¾)
MAGNETIC CATCH PLATE AND PACKER
22(⅞)
64(2½)
16(⅝)
3(⅛)
111(4⅜)
6(¼) DIAM
25(1)
38(1½)
25(1)
140(5½)

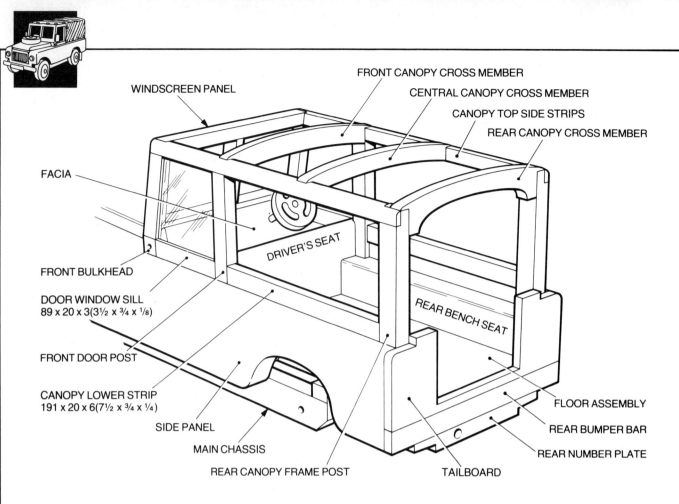

WINDSCREEN PANEL

FRONT CANOPY CROSS MEMBER

CENTRAL CANOPY CROSS MEMBER

CANOPY TOP SIDE STRIPS

REAR CANOPY CROSS MEMBER

FACIA

DRIVER'S SEAT

REAR BENCH SEAT

FRONT BULKHEAD

DOOR WINDOW SILL
89 x 20 x 3(3½ x ¾ x ⅛)

FRONT DOOR POST

CANOPY LOWER STRIP
191 x 20 x 6(7½ x ¾ x ¼)

SIDE PANEL

MAIN CHASSIS

REAR CANOPY FRAME POST

TAILBOARD

FLOOR ASSEMBLY

REAR BUMPER BAR

REAR NUMBER PLATE

CANOPY AND REAR BODY ASSEMBLY

WINDSCREEN PANEL

12(½)
12(½)
90(3⁹/₁₆)
57(2¼)
20(¾)
16(⅝)
6(¼)
6(¼)
6(¼)
16(⅝)
16(⅝)
184(7¼)

1.5(¹/₁₆) THICK PLASTIC
168 x 67(6⅝ x 2⅝) GLUED
TO INSIDE OF PANEL

REAR CANOPY
FRAME POST
MAKE TWO

16(⅝)
16(⅝)
127(5)
12(½)
21(¹³/₁₆)
6(¼)

FRONT DOOR POST
MAKE ONE OF EACH HAND

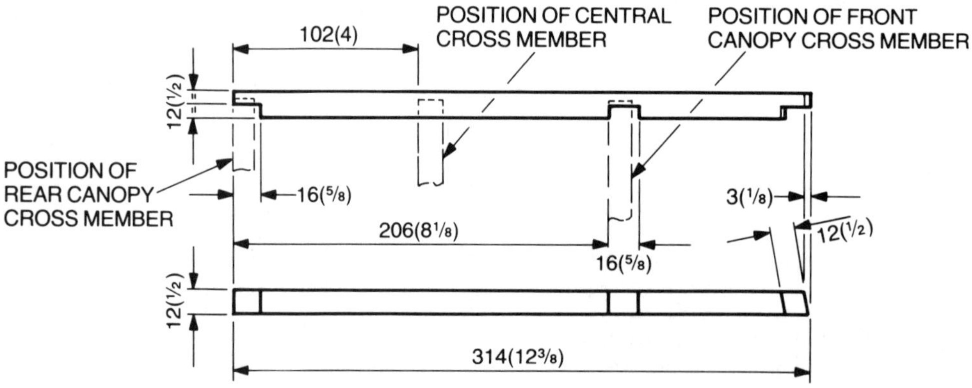

16(⅝)
12(½)
127(5)
12(½)
41(1⅝)
21(¹³/₁₆)
3(⅛)

CUT OUT TO CLEAR
REAR OF DRIVER'S SEAT

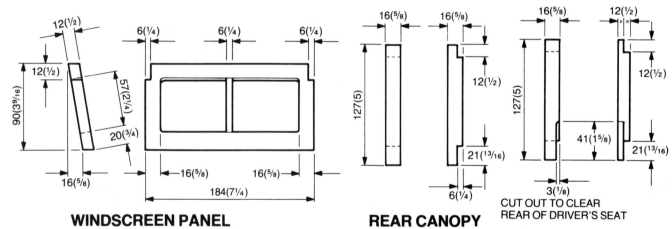

POSITION OF CENTRAL
CROSS MEMBER

POSITION OF FRONT
CANOPY CROSS MEMBER

POSITION OF
REAR CANOPY
CROSS MEMBER

102(4)
12(½)
16(⅝)
206(8⅛)
16(⅝)
3(⅛)
12(½)
12(½)
314(12⅜)

CANOPY TOP SIDE STRIP

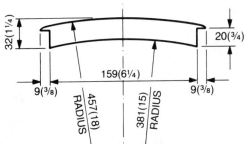

FRONT CANOPY CROSS MEMBER
12(½) THICK

159(6¼)
32(1¼)
20(¾)
9(3/8)
9(3/8)
457(18) RADIUS
381(15) RADIUS

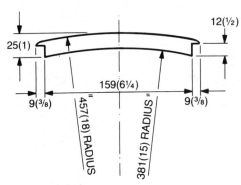

CENTRAL CANOPY
CROSS MEMBER
12(½) THICK

25(1)
12(½)
159(6¼)
9(3/8)
9(3/8)
457(18) RADIUS
381(15) RADIUS

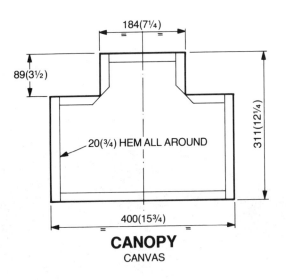

184(7¼)

89(3½)

311(12¼)

20(¾) HEM ALL AROUND

400(15¾)

CANOPY
CANVAS

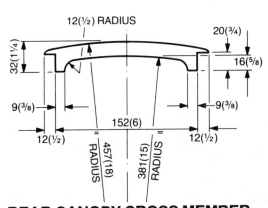

REAR CANOPY CROSS MEMBER
12(½) THICK

12(½) RADIUS
20(¾)
32(1¼)
16(5/8)
9(3/8)
9(3/8)
152(6)
12(½)
12(½)
457(18) RADIUS
381(15) RADIUS

83 x 57(3¼ x 2¼) CLEAR PLASTIC STITCHED TO CANVAS

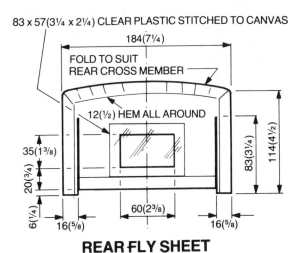

184(7¼)

FOLD TO SUIT
REAR CROSS MEMBER

12(½) HEM ALL AROUND

35(1 3/8)
20(¾)
6(¼)
16(5/8)
60(2 3/8)
16(5/8)
83(3¼)
114(4½)

REAR FLY SHEET
CANVAS

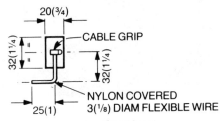

20(¾)
32(1¼)
32(1¼)
25(1)

CABLE GRIP

NYLON COVERED
3(1/8) DIAM FLEXIBLE WIRE

WING MIRROR 6(¼) THICK
MAKE ONE OF EACH HAND

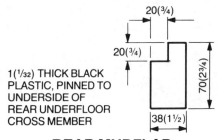

20(¾)
20(¾)
70(2¾)
38(1½)

1(1/32) THICK BLACK
PLASTIC, PINNED TO
UNDERSIDE OF
REAR UNDERFLOOR
CROSS MEMBER

REAR MUDFLAP
MAKE ONE OF EACH HAND

LAND ROVER COUNTY

This latest addition to the Land Rover range is most impressive in appearance, with its two-tone finish. But if you think it's just a face lift look inside and you will find cloth covered individual bucket seats for driver and passengers. The interior is far more luxurious than the usual Land Rover and the acoustic 'kit' inside has deadened much of the noise that one usually gets.

This is one of the most difficult models to build as I have tried to build it, quite literally, like the real thing. From drawings and photographs supplied to me by Land Rover I have tried to copy the real vehicle in miniature. The springs give the model all-round suspension and the use of felt gives the interior a feeling of luxury. The back door opens to give access for passengers. Modelling the engine was quite fun. As I had not put any engine details in the V8 model I thought I should at least try and get this sort of detail in this vehicle. It was perhaps the radiator grill that required the most care and took me many hours to complete.

I was determined not to paint the vehicle, so it was necessary to use mahogany for the lower half of the bodywork and sycamore for the top. The chassis was made in beech.

1 As with the real vehicle start by building the chassis. Make two chassis members, one of each hand (left and right). Note the number of stopped mortices that have to be cut and the stub tenons on both ends of the chassis members that fit into the back and front bumpers. By studying the chassis drawing you will see the importance of a right and left hand side. Note that some stopped mortice holes (blind mortices) have to be cut on either side of the chassis member.

2 Studying the 'general layout' chassis drawing you will see that the main chassis members are held together by four cross members. The cross members have stub tenons cut on the ends to fit into the mortice holes. Make the four outriggers that fit into the stopped mortices (blind mortices) on the outside of the chassis. Make the front and back bumpers. An interesting little detail to include is the rear grab handles and the little step for passengers getting into the back. These were cut from beech and glued on.

3 The spring hangers (brackets) are made from beech. Fix them together in pairs to shape and drill the necessary spring mounting holes. These brackets are tremendously strong and while driving the real vehicle in deep ruts would frequently gouge up the clay as the vehicle progressed. The hangers in the model are glued onto the chassis.

4 Although this book is basically about wood there are inevitably some metal parts required in the models we build, the most difficult of these being springs. The only tools necessary to make the springs are a six inch smooth cut file, drills capable of drilling mild steel, round nosed pliers and a small hack saw.

Start by cutting to length the spring steel. Holding the main leaf and using the round nosed pliers, bend the hook on each end. A bush (tube) is necessary to take the pin that holds the spring in the hanger. The inside diameter of the tube needs to be the same as the pin that goes through the spring hanger. Fit the bushes in the ends of the springs and using the pliers

squeeze the hook around them to hold them in place.

Now cut to length the other leaves. These leaves are held together by spring clamps made from the same material as the springs. When the spring is all fixed together a hole is drilled in the middle.

5 Front and back axles are now cut out. Before any shaping takes place to represent the circular shape of axle cases, drill holes to take the axles. These stub axles are glued into the wood with epoxy resin. Drill holes to take the prop shafts. Now shape up the axles rounding off all the edges. The axles are attached to the springs with screws that pass through the pre-drilled holes in the middle of the springs.

6 Make two lower side panels, one of each hand. It is most important that the rebates to take bulkheads are cut before any shaping of the sides takes place. Mark out the rebates and remove the waste wood with a chisel. Check that the bottom of the rebate is of uniform depth. To form the front mudguards, blocks of wood are now glued onto the side panels. Drill holes to take headlamp and side lights.

Now shaping of wheel arches and mudguards can be carried out. To simulate doors and handles carve a small recess or indentation on the outside of the panel.

7 The radiator grill needs a lot of care. Basically it consists of a grill frame from which the basic shape of the radiator has been cut. That's the easy part. The grill frame on the original model was made from mahogany and the 'infill' pieces from sycamore. The important thing is to get contrasting timbers. Cutting out the 'infills' has to be done with an extremely fine saw - a fret saw is ideal. Once all the pieces have been cut, assembling the pieces 'dry' (without glue) is essential to see that everything fits. In effect this is probably the most difficult piece of work to be done. The curved top of the grill carrying the word 'Land Rover' is glued onto the frame.

8 Now shape up the engine and gearbox block. It is important to fit this before cutting the front bulkhead. The front bulkhead has to be cut away at the bottom to accommodate the engine and gearbox. While shaping the engine and gearbox make the small block that houses the front wheel drive shaft.

9 Cut the bulkheads and fit them into the rebates in the side panels. Prepare the bonnet at this stage as it has to be hinged onto the front bulkhead.

10 The cab and passenger compartment floors are made from plywood, but these cannot be glued into place until the bulkheads and side panels are glued together and onto the chassis.

11 The secret of a successful assembly of the chassis and side panels depends on fitting all the pieces together 'dry' (without glue). Only when all parts fit well should any attempt be made to 'glue up'. It can be a very time consuming business but unless all parts fit well, glueing the bodywork together will be difficult and hours of work wasted. You will find two small wood cramps invaluable as the side panels have to be held onto the bulkheads while the glue dries.

12 Once glued up, the floors can be fitted and work can begin on the interior. The dashboard is detailed and miniature dials can be cut out and stuck on. The steering wheel is fitted to a short length of dowel rod and attached to the engine bulkhead by a small block that fits between the front fascia and parcel shelf. The gear levers, selectors etc. are all made from dowel rod. To add realism a short length of plastic tube is fitted to simulate a knob. These need to be painted black, yellow and red. Don't forget to make the hand brake which is fitted beneath the driver's seat.

The cab seats are all made from a block of pine. You can cut them individually, or plane up a long block of wood, rebate it and then cut off lengths of seat as required. Cover the seats with felt. The central console (glove box) is shaped from a beech block. The rear seat rests are made from plywood and glued into place. The passenger compartment floor is covered in black felt, adding a touch of luxury. Spend a little time on the inside, it is well worth the effort.

13 The windscreen, cab walls and roof come next. Unlike the V8 the windscreen is shaped from one single piece of wood. Cut the windows out with a coping or jig-saw. After cutting out, glasspaper all sawing marks off and round off the edges of all the window frames.

The rear portion of the body is made in two halves. The door is made from plywood. The cab roof is made from a solid piece of wood planed down at the front. Once again careful fitting of all joints is essential before glue is applied. The cab must be varnished before it is glued together. Be sure that no varnish gets on the edges to be glued other-wise the pieces will not stick. The perspex must be fitted before the roof is glued into place. The perspex is fitted tight on all edges and in this way only a spot of glue is necessary to keep it in place.

14 Once the roof is fitted the back portion of the body is fixed. Fix the back door on using small brass hinges. Fix a spare wheel onto the back door using a fairly long screw. The door is kept closed with a small brass hook and eye closer. Cut and fit the ventilator covers on the front screen. Now cut the three supports for the 'tropical roof' (roof rack). To make these follow the existing roof line it is necessary to score them on the underside with a sharp knife. This will allow bending without breaking. Now glue them into place. The tropical roof that fits onto the supports is made from thin plywood. Once again the underside of this is scored with a knife to allow bending. Glue the plywood into place, using weights to keep it in place while the glue sets.

15 The wing mirrors are made from plywood and fixed onto the side panels with flexible curtain wire. Once again they are stiffened by iron wire threaded through the flex. Epoxy resin glue is used to fix them permanently into the pre-drilled holes.

16 The indicators are made by sanding down the end of a dowel rod to form a dome shape. Paint them the appropriate colours, and glue into the pre-drilled holes.

17 Now add the final touches to the engine compartment, putting in the radiator, radiator cap, air cleaner, carburettor and battery. If you wish you can add a lot more detail.

18 It only remains to add the spot-lights to the front bumper and attach the number plates.

19 I used matt coat varnish to finish off as I felt that the hardwood itself was so beautiful it was a pity to cover it with paint. This is, of course, a personal choice.

Cutting list

Main chassis	2 off	487 x 41 x 16mm (19 3/16 x 1 5/8 x 5/8in)	Timber
Front bumper	1 off	232 x 20 x 16mm (9 1/8 x 3/4 x 5/8in)	Timber
	1 off	73 x 16 x 5mm (2 7/8 x 5/8 x 3/16in)	Timber
Spot lamp	Make from	54 x 14 x 8mm (2 1/8 x 9/16 x 5/16in)	Timber
First cross member	1 off	142 x 20 x 16mm (5 5/8 x 3/4 x 5/8in)	Timber

Rear spring rear bracket	Make from	165 x 20 x 6mm (6½ x ¾ x ¼in)	Timber
Rear spring front bracket	Make from	191 x 25 x 6mm (7½ x 1 x ¼in)	Timber
Front spring front bracket	Make from	241 x 25 x 6mm (9½ x 1 x ¼in)	Timber
Lower side panel	2 off	476 x 92 x 12mm (18¾ x 3⅝ x ½in)	Timber
	2 off	156 x 92 x 32mm (6⅛ x 3⅝ x 1¼in)	Timber
Second cross member	1 off	156 x 41 x 16mm (6⅛ x 1⅝ x ⅝in)	Timber
Third cross member	1 off	146 x 28 x 16mm (5¾ x 1⅛ x ⅝in)	Timber
Fourth cross member	1 off	142 x 22 x 16mm (5⅝ x ⅞ x ⅝in)	Timber
	1 off	76 x 22 x 9mm (3 x ⅞ x ⅜in)	Timber
Rear bumper	1 off	216 x 25 x 16mm (8½ x 1 x ⅝in)	Timber
	1 off	98 x 16 x 9mm (3⅞ x ⅝ x ⅜in)	Timber
Front outrigger	Make from	83 x 22 x 16mm (3¼ x ⅞ x ⅝in)	Timber
Rear outrigger	Make from	73 x 22 x 16mm (2⅞ x ⅞ x ⅝in)	Timber
Hand grip	Make from	76 x 9 x 6mm (3 x ⅜ x ¼in)	Timber
Step	1 off	22 x 12 x 5mm (⅞ x ½ x 3/16in)	Timber
Front axle	1 off	171 x 38 x 22mm (6¾ x 1½ x ⅞in)	Timber
Rear axle	1 off	171 x 41 x 22mm (6¾ x 1⅝ x ⅞in)	Timber
	1 off	111mm(4⅜in) long x 9mm(⅜in) diameter dowel	
Rear drive flywheel	1 off	38mm(1½in) diameter x 16mm(⅝in) thick disc	
	1 off	25mm(1in) long x 9mm(⅜in) diameter dowel	
Front wheel drive shaft	1 off	44 x 22 x 12mm (1¾ x ⅞ x ½in)	Timber
	1 off	60mm(2⅜in) long x 6mm(¼in) diameter dowel	
Grill frame	1 off	140 x 59 x 12mm (5½ x 2 5/16 x ½in)	Timber
Grill	Make from	381 x 6 x 3mm (15 x ¼ x ⅛in)	Timber
	Make from	76 x 6 x 5mm (3 x ¼ x 3/16in)	Timber
	Make from	76 x 38 x 6mm (3 x 1½ x ¼in)	Timber
	Make from	73 x 11 x 3mm (2⅞ x 7/16 x ⅛)	Timber
Engine block	1 off	187 x 76 x 44mm (7⅜ x 3 x 1¾in)	Timber
Manifold	1 off	64 x 22 x 22mm (2½ x ⅞ x ⅞in)	Timber
Gear lever	1 off	70mm(2¾in) long x 6mm(¼in) diameter dowel	
Select lever	1 off	28mm(1⅛in) long x 6mm(¼in) diameter dowel	
Air filter	1 off	25mm(1in) diameter x 20mm(¾in) thick disc	
Bonnet	1 off	184 x 137 x 16mm (7¼ x 5⅜ x ⅝in)	Timber
Radiator	1 off	108 x 44 x 12mm (4¼ x 1¾ x ½in)	Timber
Radiator filling cap	1 off	22mm(⅞in) long x 6mm(¼in) diameter dowel	
Battery	1 off	44 x 32 x 22mm (1¾ x 1¼ x ⅞in)	Timber
Rocker cover	1 off	38 x 16 x 12mm (1½ x 1⅝ x ½in)	Timber
Skirt	1 off	140 x 22 x 3mm (5½ x ⅞ x ⅛in)	Timber
Cab front bulkhead	1 off	213 x 95 x 12mm (8⅜ x 3¾ x ½in)	Timber
	1 off	187 x 12 x 6mm (7⅜ x ½ x ¼in)	Timber
	1 off	70 x 22 x 9mm (2¾ x ⅞ x ⅜in)	Timber
Instruments	Make from	25mm(1in) long x 16mm(⅝in) diameter dowel	
Front windscreen	1 off	213 x 92 x 12mm (8⅜ x 3⅝ x ½in)	Timber
Ventilator covers	2 off	86 x 12 x 3mm (3⅜ x ½ x ⅛in)	Timber
Fascia	1 off	187 x 20 x 9mm (7⅜ x ¾ x ⅜in)	Timber
Side panel	2 off	295 x 102 x 12mm (11⅝ x 4 x ½in)	Timber
Wing mirror	2 off	32 x 16 x 8mm (1¼ x ⅝ x 5/16in)	Timber
Cab rear partition	1 off	213 x 57 x 12mm (8⅜ x 2¼ x ½in)	Timber
Rear panel	2 off	175 x 106 x 12mm (6⅞ x 4 3/16 x ½in)	Timber
Rear number plate	1 off	32 x 25 x 3mm (1¼ x 1 x ⅛in)	Timber
Rear door	1 off	154 x 130 x 9mm (6 1/16 x 5⅛ x ⅜in)	Plywood

Cab floor	1 off	203 x 70 x 3mm (8 x 2¾ x ⅛in)	Plywood
	2 off	83 x 70 x 3mm (3¼ x 2¾ x ⅛in)	Plywood
	1 off	203 x 38 x 12mm (8 x 1½ x ½in)	Timber
Floor lever	1 off	41mm(1⅝in) long x 6mm(¼in) diameter dowel	
Brake lever	1 off	64 x 48 x 6mm (2½ x 1⅞ x ¼in)	Timber
Cab seat	2 off	83 x 70 x 51mm (3¼ x 2¾ x 2in)	Timber
Steering wheel	1 off	41mm(1⅝in) diameter x 9mm(⅜in) thick disc	
	1 off	60mm(2⅜in) long x 6mm(¼in) diameter dowel	
Control console	1 off	67 x 44 x 28mm (2⅝ x 1¾ x 1⅛in)	Timber
Rear compartment floor	1 off	159 x 140 x 3mm (6¼ x 5½ x ⅛in)	Plywood
Rear seat rests	2 off	146 x 38 x 3mm (5¾ x 1½ x ⅛in)	Plywood
	2 off	146 x 28 x 3mm (5¾ x 1⅛ x ⅛in)	Plywood
Rear seats	4 off	64 x 54 x 51mm (2½ x 2⅛ x 2in)	Timber
Lights	Make from	229mm(9in) long x 6mm(¼in) diameter dowel	
Roof	1 off	279 x 213 x 16mm (11 x 8⅜ x ⅝in)	Timber
Roof rack	1 off	267 x 178 x 3mm (10½ x 7 x ⅛in)	Plywood
	3 off	275 x 9 x 6mm (10¾ x ⅜ x ¼in)	Timber
Ancillaries			
Spot lamp support	Make from	54mm (2⅛in) long x 5mm (3/16in) diameter steel bar	
Rear spring	Make from	1170 x 16 x 1·5mm (46 x ⅝ x 1/16in) spring steel	
Front spring	Make from	920 x 16 x 1·5mm (36 x ⅝ x 1/16in) spring steel	
Spring clamps	Make from	305 x 6 x 1·5mm (12 x ¼ x 1/16in) spring steel	
	8 off	6mm (¼in) o/d x 5mm (3/16in) i/d x 16mm (⅝in) long tubes	
Spring hangers	Make from	305 x 11 x 1·5mm (12 x 7/16 x 1/16in) thick steel	
Front spring assembly	2 off	35mm(1⅜in) long x 5mm(3/16in) diameter steel pins	
	4 off	25mm(1in) long x 5mm(3/16in) diameter steel pins	
	12 off	Spring dome caps to suit 5mm (3/16in) diameter pins	
Rear spring assembly	6 off	35mm(1⅜in) long x 5mm(3/16in) diameter steel pins	
	4 off	9mm(⅜in) o/d x 5mm(3/16in) i/d x 6mm(¼in) long spacers	
	12 off	Spring dome caps to suit 5mm (3/16in) diameter pins	
Front axles	2 off	89mm(3½in) long x 6mm(¼in) diameter steel rods	
	2 off	102mm (4in) diameter road wheels	
	2 off	Spring dome caps to suit 6mm (¼in) diameter axles	
Rear axles	2 off	89mm(3½in) long x 6mm(¼in) diameter steel rods	
	2 off	102mm (4in) diameter road wheels	
	2 off	Spring dome caps to suit 6mm (¼in) diameter axles	
Grill	1 off	Wire mesh 127 x 41mm (5 x 1⅝in)	
Lever knobs	Make from	25mm(1in) long x 9mm(⅜in) o/d x 6mm(¼in) i/d tube	
Radiator hose	1 off	32mm(1¼in) long x 6mm(¼in) diameter coaxial cable	
Air filter hose	1 off	70mm(2¾in) long x 9mm(⅜in) o/d x 6mm(¼in) i/d rubber tube	
Front screen	1 off	187 x 76 x 1·5mm (7⅜ x 3 x 1/16in) thick clear plastic	
Side screens	2 off	292 x 83 x 1·5mm (11½ x 3¼ x 1/16in) thick clear plastic	
Rear door window	1 off	121 x 83 x 1·5mm (4¾ x 3¼ x 1/16in) thick clear plastic	
Rear side windows	2 off	83 x 25 x 1.5mm (3¼ x 1 x 1/16in) thick clear plastic	
Wing mirror arm	Make from	127mm(5in) long x 5mm(3/16in) diameter steel wire	
Rear door hinges	2 off	25mm (1in) brass hinges	
Rear door lock	1 off	Swing hook and screwed eye	
Spare wheel	1 off	102mm (4in) diameter road wheel	
Spare wheel cover	1 off	92mm(3⅝in) diameter x 1mm(1/32in) thick stiff black plastic	
Felt, various	Cut from	457 x 229mm (18 x 9in)	

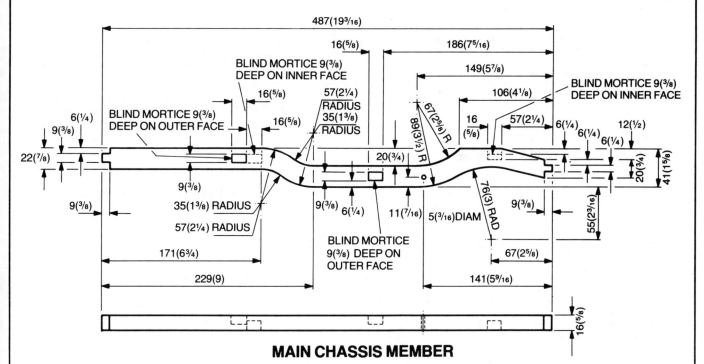

MAIN CHASSIS MEMBER

MAKE ONE OF EACH HAND

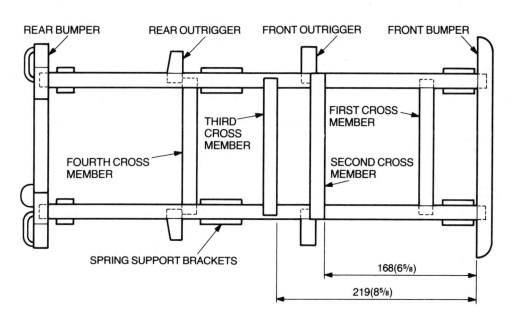

VIEW ON UNDERSIDE OF CHASSIS TO SHOW GENERAL LAYOUT

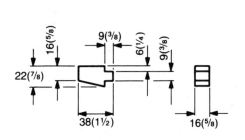

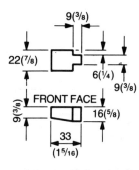

FRONT OUT RIGGER

MAKE TWO

REAR OUTRIGGER

MAKE TWO

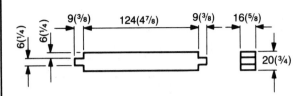

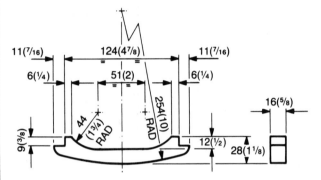

FIRST CROSS MEMBER

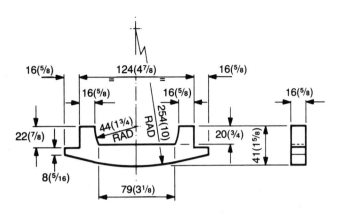

SECOND CROSS MEMBER

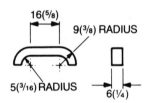

THIRD CROSS MEMBER

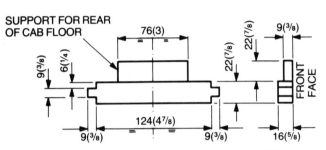

SUPPORT FOR REAR
OF CAB FLOOR

FOURTH CROSS MEMBER

16(⁵⁄₈)
9(³⁄₈) RADIUS
5(³⁄₁₆) RADIUS
6(¼)

HAND GRIP
MAKE TWO

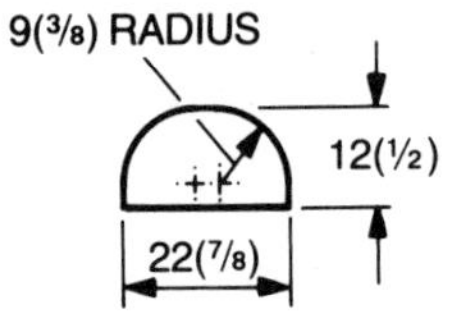

9(³⁄₈) RADIUS
12(½)
22(⁷⁄₈)

STEP
5(³⁄₁₆) THICK

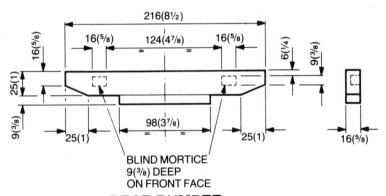

216(8½)
16(⁵⁄₈) 124(4⁷⁄₈) 16(⁵⁄₈)
6(¼) 9(³⁄₈)
25(1)
9(³⁄₈)
25(1) 98(3⁷⁄₈) 25(1)
16(⁵⁄₈)

BLIND MORTICE
9(³⁄₈) DEEP
ON FRONT FACE

REAR BUMPER

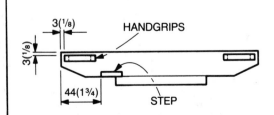

3(⅛)
HANDGRIPS
3(⅛)
44(1¾)
STEP

ASSEMBLY OF HANDGRIPS
AND STEP ON REAR BUMPER

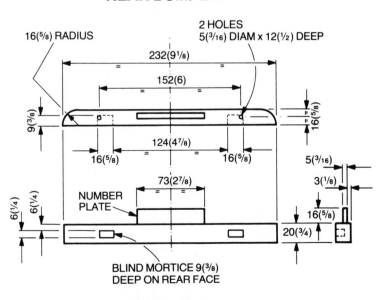

16(⁵⁄₈) RADIUS
2 HOLES
5(³⁄₁₆) DIAM x 12(½) DEEP
232(9⅛)
152(6)
9(³⁄₈) 16(⁵⁄₈)
124(4⁷⁄₈)
16(⁵⁄₈) 16(⁵⁄₈)
73(2⁷⁄₈)
5(³⁄₁₆)
3(⅛)
NUMBER
PLATE
6(¼) 6(¼)
16(⁵⁄₈)
20(¾)

BLIND MORTICE 9(³⁄₈)
DEEP ON REAR FACE

FRONT BUMPER ASSEMBLY

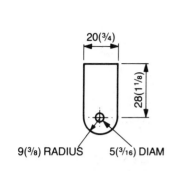

REAR SPRING
REAR BRACKET
MAKE FOUR 6(¼) THICK

20(¾)

28(1⅛)

9(⅜) RADIUS   5(³⁄₁₆) DIAM

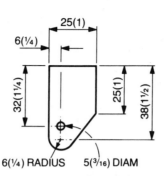

REAR SPRING
FRONT BRACKET
MAKE FOUR   6(¼) THICK

25(1)

6(¼)

32(1¼)

25(1)

38(1½)

6(¼) RADIUS   5(³⁄₁₆) DIAM

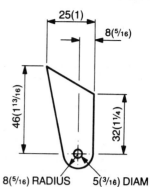

FRONT SPRING
FRONT BRACKET
MAKE FOUR   6(¼) THICK

25(1)

8(⁵⁄₁₆)

46(1¹³⁄₁₆)

32(1¼)

8(⁵⁄₁₆) RADIUS   5(³⁄₁₆) DIAM

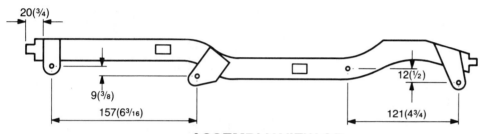

20(¾)

9(⅜)

157(6³⁄₁₆)

121(4¾)

12(½)

ASSEMBLY VIEW OF
SPRING SUPPORT BRACKETS
BRACKETS MOUNTED IN PAIRS

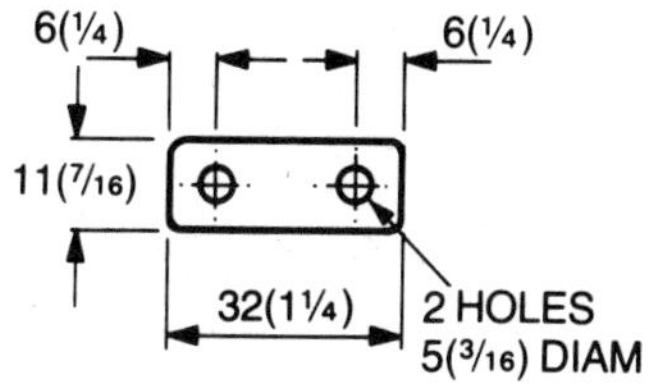

6(¼)   6(¼)

11(⁷⁄₁₆)

32(1¼)

2 HOLES
5(³⁄₁₆) DIAM

SPRING HANGERS
MAKE EIGHT
1.5(¹⁄₁₆) THICK CHROMED STEEL

TO SUIT SPRING
MATERIAL

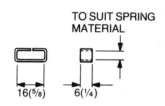

16(⁵⁄₈)   6(¼)

SPRING CLAMP
MAKE EIGHT
1.5(¹⁄₁₆) THICK CHROMED STEEL

117(4⁵⁄₈)

57(2¼)

11(⁷⁄₁₆)

6(¼) DIAM INSIDE   3(⅛) DIAM

16(⁵⁄₈)

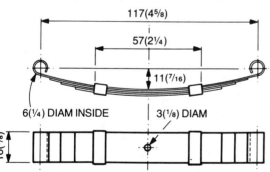

FRONT SPRING ASSEMBLY
MAKE TWO
MAKE FROM – 16(⁵⁄₈) WIDE x 1.5(¹⁄₁₆) THICK SPRING STEEL

2nd LEAF – 108(4¼) LONG
3rd LEAF – 95(3¾) LONG
4th LEAF – 79(3⅛) LONG

ALSO REQUIRED –
FOUR 5(³⁄₁₆) I/D x 6(¼) O/D x 16(⁵⁄₈) LONG TUBES

REAR FIXING

163(6⁷⁄₁₆)

32(1¼)   89(3½)

11(⁷⁄₁₆)

6(¼)

14(⁹⁄₁₆)

25(1)

6(¼) DIAM
INSIDE

16(⁵⁄₈)

76(3)   3(⅛) DIAM

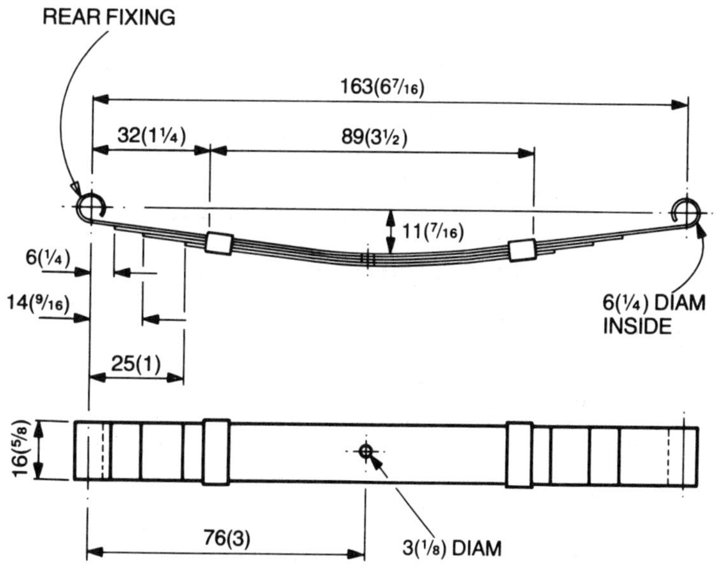

REAR SPRING ASSEMBLY
MAKE TWO
MAKE FROM 16(⁵⁄₈) WIDE x 1.5(¹⁄₁₆) THICK SPRING STEEL

2nd LEAF – 140(5½) LONG
3rd LEAF – 117(4⁵⁄₈) LONG
4th LEAF – 102(4) LONG

ALSO REQUIRED –
FOUR 5(³⁄₁₆) I/D x 6(¼) O/D x 16(⁵⁄₈) LONG TUBES

FRONT AXLE

171(6¾)
140(5½)
6(¼)
22(⅞)
SPRING FIXING CENTRES
57(2¼)
57(2¼)
16(⅝)
38(1½) DIAM
6(¼) DIAM
AXLES – 6(¼) DIAM x 89(3½) LONG STEEL TWO REQUIRED
6(¼) DIAM x 9(⅜) DEEP HOLE – SLIGHTLY OVERSIZE AND INCLINED AS SHOWN TO TAKE FRONT WHEEL DRIVE PROP SHAFT AND ALLOW MOVEMENT AS THE SPRINGS DEFLECT

REAR DRIVE FLYWHEEL

38(1½) DIAM
16(⅝)
9(⅜) DIAM DOWEL x 25(1) LONG
9(⅜) DIAM
HOLE INCLINED TO SUIT PROP SHAFT ANGLE FROM REAR AXLE ASSEMBLY – DRILL SLIGHTLY OVERSIZE TO ALLOW MOVEMENT AS SPRINGS DEFLECT

REAR AXLE ASSEMBLY

171(6¾)
140(5½)
6(¼)
22(⅞)
SPRING FIXING CENTRES
9(⅜) DIAM DOWEL x 111(4⅜) LONG
44(1¾)
22(⅞)
6(¼) DIAM
57(2¼)
41(1⅝) DIAM
16(⅝)
AXLES – 6(¼) DIAM x 89(3½) LONG STEEL TWO REQUIRED
9(⅜) RADIUS
9(⅜) DIAM x 12(½) DEEP HOLE, INCLINED AS SHOWN TO TAKE REAR WHEEL DRIVE PROP SHAFT

LOWER SIDE PANEL
MAKE ONE OF EACH HAND

305(12)
156(6⅛)
12(½)
12(½)
51(2)
16(⅝)
16(⅝)
12(½)
32(1¼)
16(⅝)
5(³⁄₁₆)
476(18¾)
20(¾) DIAM HOLE TO SUIT HEAD LIGHT
16(⅝)
12(½)
12(½) RADIUS
5(³⁄₁₆) RADIUS
35(1⅜)
28(1⅛)
12(½)
92(3⅝)
64(2½)
41(1⅝) RAD
54(2⅛) RAD
57(2¼)
73(2⅞)
16(⅝)
41(1⅝) RAD
54(2⅛) RAD
32(1¼)
2 HOLES 6(¼) DIAM x 9(⅜) DEEP
5(³⁄₁₆)
12(½) RAD
54(2⅛)
76(3)
12(½) RAD
6(¼)
9(⅜) RADIUS
35 (1⅜)
92(3⅝)
8(⁵⁄₁₆)
114(4½)
165(6½)

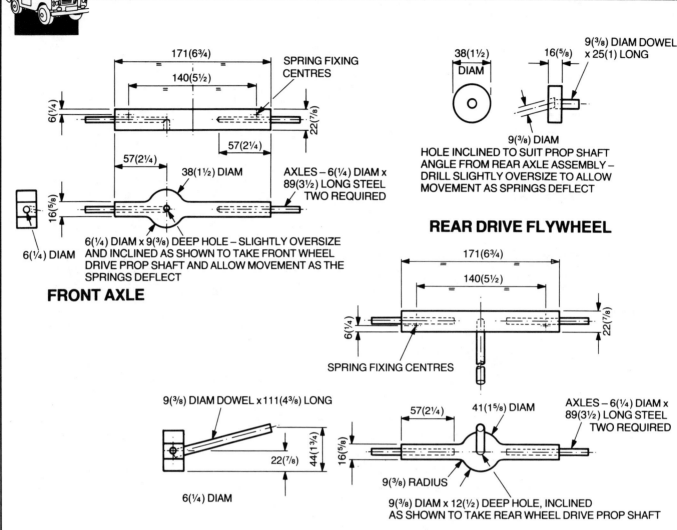

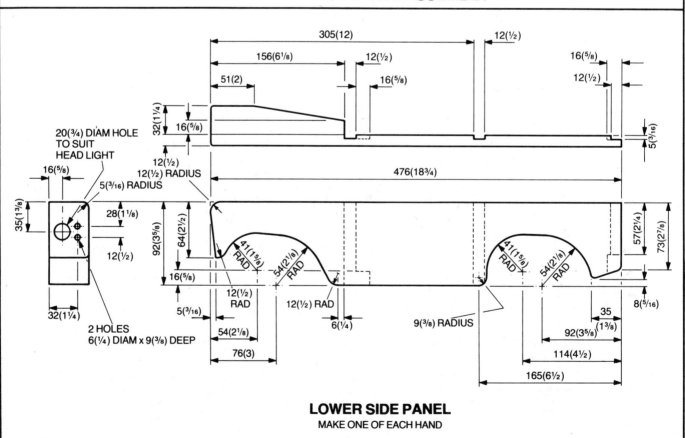

192

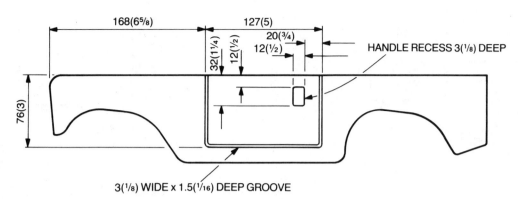

$168(6^5/_8)$ $127(5)$ $20(^3/_4)$ $12(^1/_2)$ $32(1^1/_4)$ $12(^1/_2)$

HANDLE RECESS $3(^1/_8)$ DEEP

$76(3)$

$3(^1/_8)$ WIDE x $1.5(^1/_{16})$ DEEP GROOVE

LAYOUT OF SIDE DOOR INDENTATION

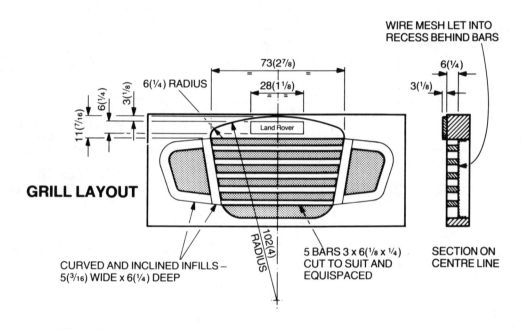

WIRE MESH LET INTO
RECESS BEHIND BARS

$73(2^7/_8)$ $28(1^1/_8)$ $6(^1/_4)$ RADIUS $6(^1/_4)$ $3(^1/_8)$

$11(^7/_{16})$ $6(^1/_4)$ $3(^1/_8)$

Land Rover

GRILL LAYOUT

$102(4)$ RADIUS

CURVED AND INCLINED INFILLS –
$5(^3/_{16})$ WIDE x $6(^1/_4)$ DEEP

5 BARS 3 x $6(^1/_8$ x $^1/_4)$
CUT TO SUIT AND
EQUISPACED

SECTION ON
CENTRE LINE

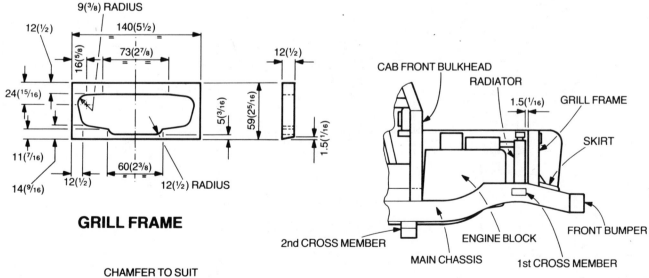

$12(^1/_2)$ $9(^3/_8)$ RADIUS $140(5^1/_2)$ $16(^5/_8)$ $73(2^7/_8)$ $12(^1/_2)$

$24(^{15}/_{16})$ $5(^3/_{16})$ $59(2^5/_{16})$ $1.5(^1/_{16})$

$11(^7/_{16})$ $60(2^3/_8)$ $12(^1/_2)$ RADIUS

$14(^9/_{16})$ $12(^1/_2)$

GRILL FRAME

CAB FRONT BULKHEAD
RADIATOR
$1.5(^1/_{16})$ GRILL FRAME
SKIRT

2nd CROSS MEMBER   ENGINE BLOCK   FRONT BUMPER
MAIN CHASSIS   1st CROSS MEMBER

**SECTIONAL VIEW SHOWING POSITIONS OF
GRILL FRAME AND SKIRT**

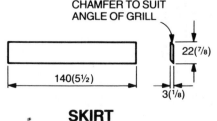

CHAMFER TO SUIT
ANGLE OF GRILL

$22(^7/_8)$

$140(5^1/_2)$ $3(^1/_8)$

SKIRT

193

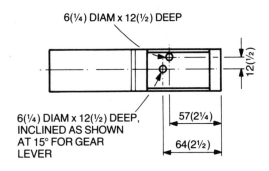

6(¼) DIAM x 12(½) DEEP

12(½)

6(¼) DIAM x 12(½) DEEP, INCLINED AS SHOWN AT 15° FOR GEAR LEVER

57(2¼)

64(2½)

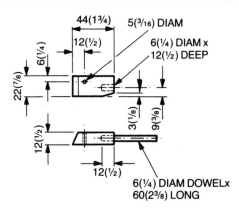

44(1¾)   5(³⁄₁₆) DIAM

12(½)

6(¼) DIAM x 12(½) DEEP

22(⁷⁄₈)

6(¼)

3(⅛)   9(³⁄₈)

12(½)

12(½)

6(¼) DIAM DOWEL x 60(2³⁄₈) LONG

FRONT WHEEL DRIVE SHAFT

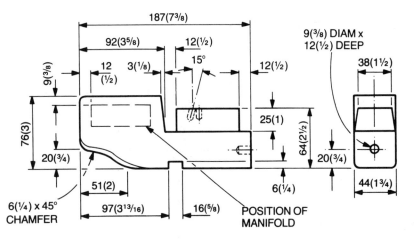

187(7³⁄₈)

92(3⁵⁄₈)   12(½)

12   3(⅛)   15°   12(½)
(½)

9(³⁄₈)

76(3)

25(1)

64(2½)

20(¾)

20(¾)

6(¼)

51(2)

6(¼) x 45° CHAMFER

97(3¹³⁄₁₆)   16(⁵⁄₈)

POSITION OF MANIFOLD

9(³⁄₈) DIAM x 12(½) DEEP

38(1½)

44(1¾)

ENGINE BLOCK

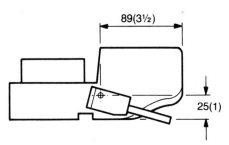

89(3½)

25(1)

FRONT WHEEL DRIVE ASSEMBLY FITTED TO DRIVER'S SIDE OF THE ENGINE BLOCK BUT ALLOWED TO PIVOT ABOUT ITS FIXING SCREW TO ALLOW FOR DEFLECTIONS OF THE FRONT SPRINGS

FRONT WHEEL DRIVE SHAFT POSITIONING

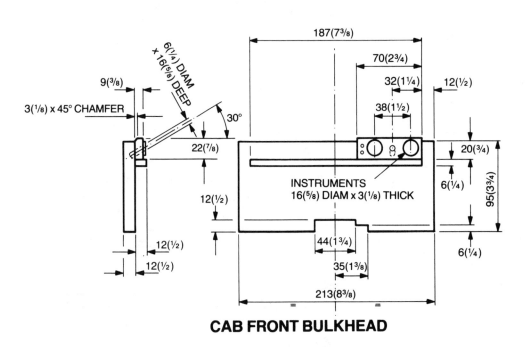

6(¼) DIAM x 16(⁵⁄₈) DEEP

30°

9(³⁄₈)

3(⅛) x 45° CHAMFER

22(⁷⁄₈)

12(½)

12(½)

12(½)

187(7³⁄₈)

70(2¾)

32(1¼)   12(½)

38(1½)

20(¾)

6(¼)

95(3¾)

INSTRUMENTS
16(⁵⁄₈) DIAM x 3(⅛) THICK

44(1¾)

6(¼)

35(1³⁄₈)

213(8³⁄₈)

CAB FRONT BULKHEAD

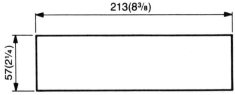

213(8³⁄₈)

57(2¼)

CAB REAR PARTITION
12(½) THICK

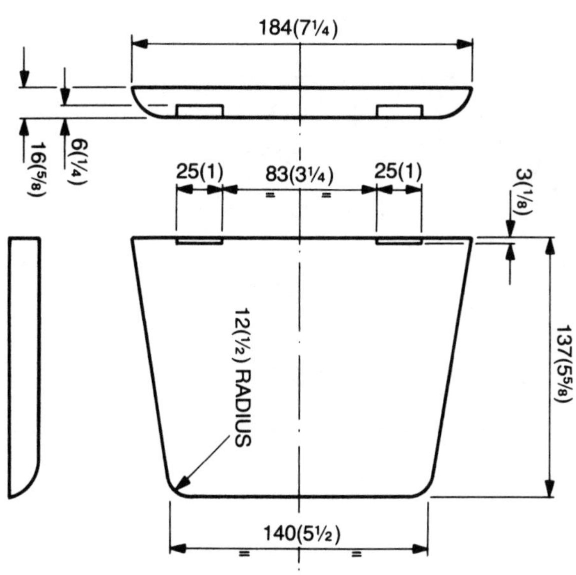
184(7¼)
16(⅝)
6(¼)
25(1)
83(3¼)
25(1)
3(⅛)
12(½) RADIUS
137(5⅝)
140(5½)

BONNET

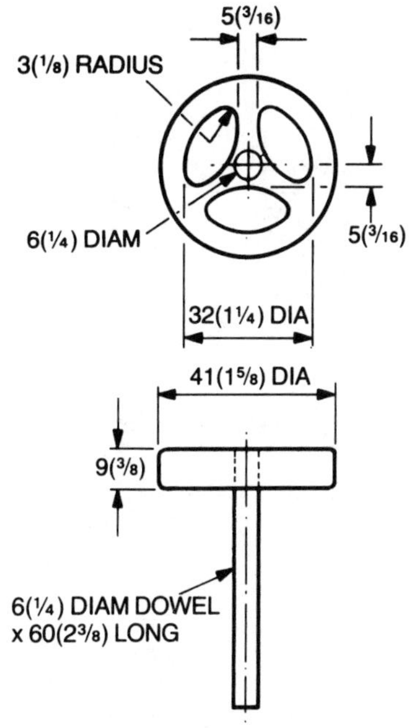
5(3/16)
3(⅛) RADIUS
6(¼) DIAM
5(3/16)
32(1¼) DIA
41(1⅝) DIA
9(⅜)
6(¼) DIAM DOWEL
x 60(2⅜) LONG

STEERING WHEEL

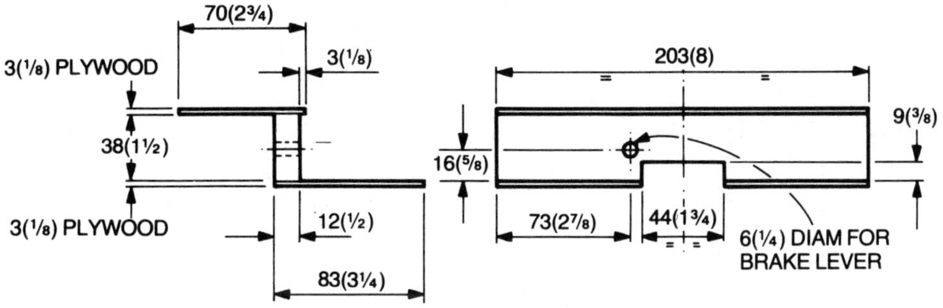
70(2¾)
3(⅛) PLYWOOD
3(⅛)
38(1½)
3(⅛) PLYWOOD
12(½)
83(3¼)
203(8)
9(⅜)
16(⅝)
73(2⅞)
44(1¾)
6(¼) DIAM FOR
BRAKE LEVER

CAB FLOOR ASEMBLY

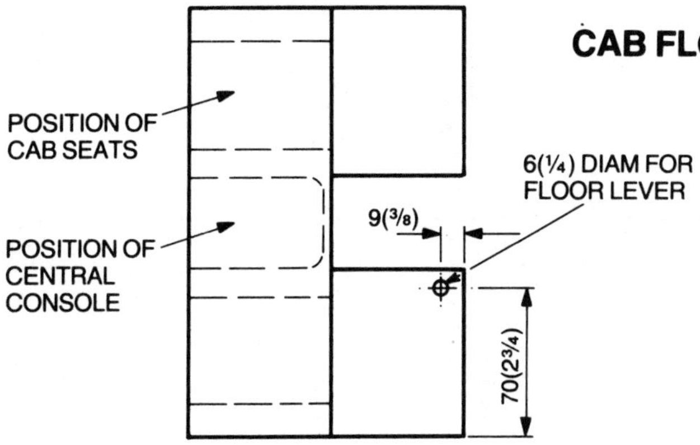
POSITION OF
CAB SEATS
POSITION OF
CENTRAL
CONSOLE
6(¼) DIAM FOR
FLOOR LEVER
9(⅜)
70(2¾)

REAR COMPARTMENT FLOOR

140 x 159 x 3(5½ x 6¼ x ⅛) PLYWOOD.
TOP SURFACE COVERED WITH FELT

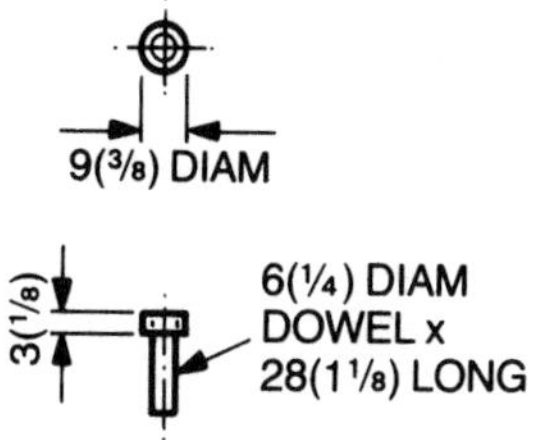
9(⅜) DIAM
3(⅛)
6(¼) DIAM
DOWEL x
28(1⅛) LONG

FOUR WHEEL DRIVE SELECT LEVER

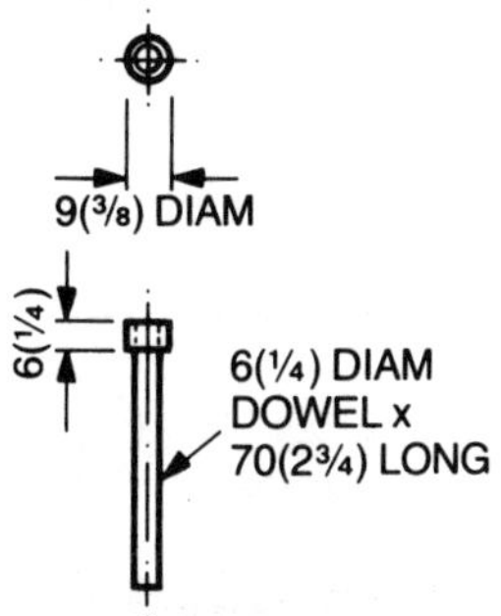
9(⅜) DIAM
6(¼)
6(¼) DIAM
DOWEL x
70(2¾) LONG

GEAR LEVER

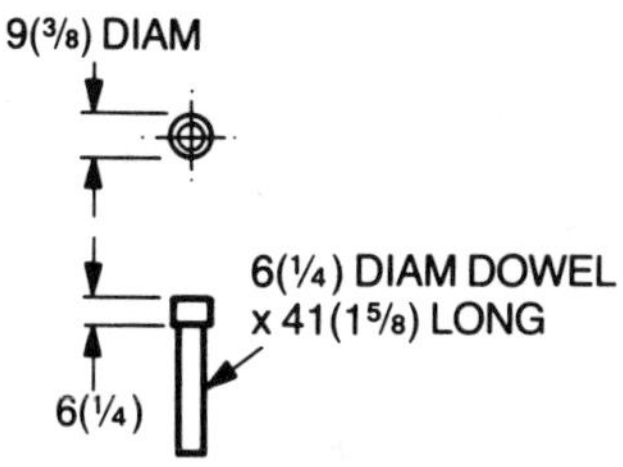
9(⅜) DIAM
6(¼) DIAM DOWEL
x 41(1⅝) LONG
6(¼)

FLOOR LEVER

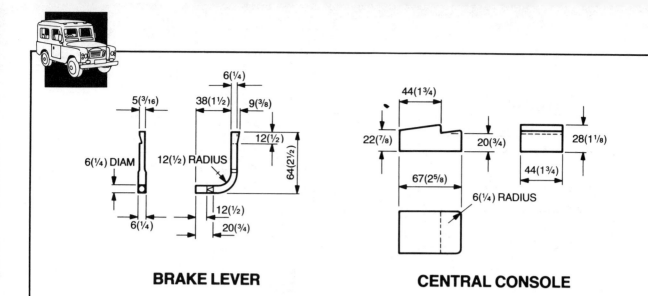

BRAKE LEVER

CENTRAL CONSOLE

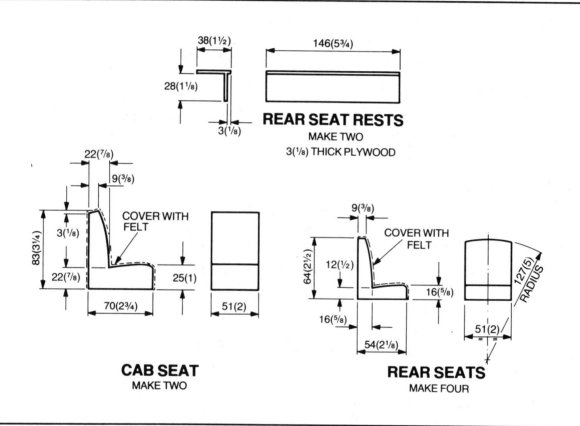

REAR SEAT RESTS

MAKE TWO

3(⅛) THICK PLYWOOD

CAB SEAT

MAKE TWO

REAR SEATS

MAKE FOUR

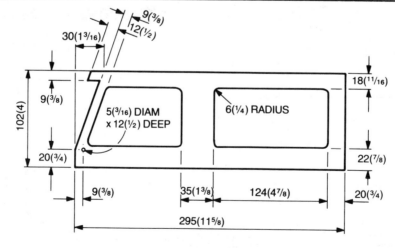

SIDE PANEL

MAKE ONE OF EACH HAND

12(½) THICK

COVER INSIDE OF WINDOWS WITH

1.5(¹⁄₁₆) THICK CLEAR PLASTIC

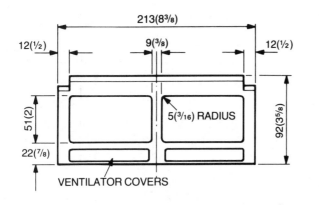

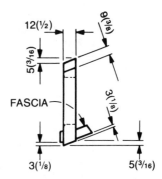

FRONT WINDSCREEN ASSEMBLY

COVER INSIDE OF WINDOWS WITH
1.5($^1/_{16}$) THICK CLEAR PLASTIC

213(8$^3/_8$)
12($^1/_2$) 9($^3/_8$) 12($^1/_2$)
51(2)
22($^7/_8$)
92(3$^5/_8$)
5($^3/_{16}$) RADIUS
VENTILATOR COVERS

12($^1/_2$) 9($^3/_8$)
5($^3/_{16}$)
FASCIA
3($^1/_8$)
3($^1/_8$) 5($^3/_{16}$)

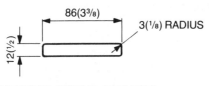

86(3$^3/_8$)
3($^1/_8$) RADIUS
12($^1/_2$)

VENTILATOR COVER
MAKE TWO   3($^1/_8$) THICK

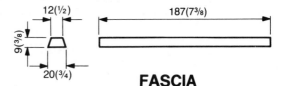

12($^1/_2$)
9($^3/_8$)
20($^3/_4$)
187(7$^3/_8$)

FASCIA

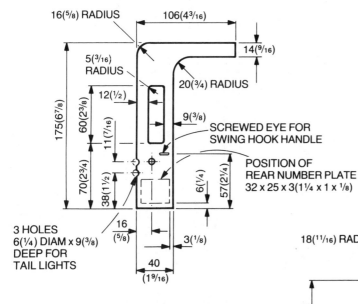

16($^5/_8$) RADIUS   106(4$^3/_{16}$)
14($^9/_{16}$)
5($^3/_{16}$) RADIUS
20($^3/_4$) RADIUS
175(6$^7/_8$)
60(2$^3/_8$)
12($^1/_2$)
11($^7/_{16}$)
9($^3/_8$)
SCREWED EYE FOR
SWING HOOK HANDLE
70(2$^3/_4$)
38(1$^1/_2$)
6($^1/_4$)
57(2$^1/_4$)
POSITION OF
REAR NUMBER PLATE
32 x 25 x 3(1$^1/_4$ x 1 x $^1/_8$)
3 HOLES
6($^1/_4$) DIAM x 9($^3/_8$)
DEEP FOR
TAIL LIGHTS
16
($^5/_8$)
3($^1/_8$)
40
(1$^9/_{16}$)

REAR PANEL
MAKE ONE OF EACH HAND   12($^1/_2$) THICK
COVER INSIDE OF WINDOWS WITH
1.5($^1/_{16}$) THICK CLEAR PLASTIC

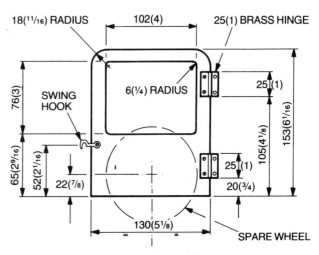

18($^{11}/_{16}$) RADIUS   102(4)   25(1) BRASS HINGE
76(3)
SWING
HOOK
6($^1/_4$) RADIUS
25(1)
65(2$^9/_{16}$)
52(2$^1/_{16}$)
22($^7/_8$)
25(1)
105(4$^1/_8$)
153(6$^1/_{16}$)
20($^3/_4$)
130(5$^1/_8$)
SPARE WHEEL

REAR DOOR
9($^3/_8$) THICK
COVER INSIDE OF WINDOW WITH 1.5($^1/_{16}$) THICK
CLEAR PLASTIC

SPARE WHEEL COVER
92(3$^5/_8$) DIAM x 1($^1/_{32}$) THICK
STIFF BLACK PLASTIC

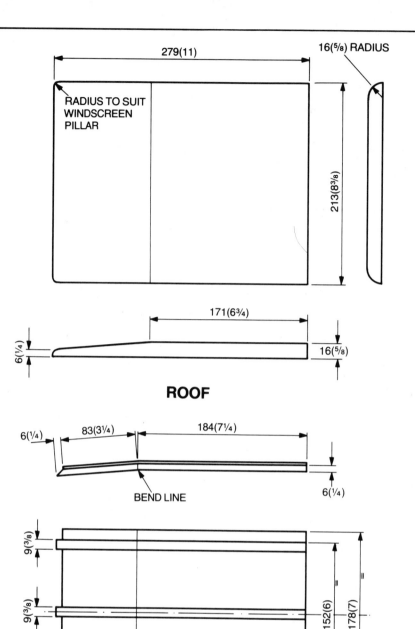

279(11)

16(⁵⁄₈) RADIUS

RADIUS TO SUIT
WINDSCREEN
PILLAR

213(8³⁄₈)

171(6³⁄₄)

6(¹⁄₄)

16(⁵⁄₈)

ROOF

6(¹⁄₄)   83(3¹⁄₄)   184(7¹⁄₄)

BEND LINE

6(¹⁄₄)

9(³⁄₈)

9(³⁄₈)

9(³⁄₈)

152(6)

178(7)

ROOF RACK

3(¹⁄₈) THICK PLYWOOD

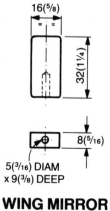

16(⁵⁄₈)

32(1¹⁄₄)

8(⁵⁄₁₆)

5(³⁄₁₆) DIAM
x 9(³⁄₈) DEEP

WING MIRROR

MAKE TWO

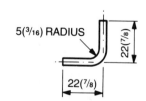

5(³⁄₁₆) RADIUS

22(⁷⁄₈)

22(⁷⁄₈)

WING MIRROR ARM

MAKE TWO

5(³⁄₁₆) DIAM STEEL WIRE

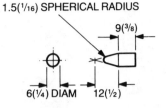

3(1/8) SPHERICAL RADIUS

6(1/4) DIAM 9(3/8)

WHITE FRONT SIDE LIGHTS AND REAR REVERSING LIGHTS

MAKE FOUR

1.5(1/16) SPHERICAL RADIUS

9(3/8)

6(1/4) DIAM 12(1/2)

ORANGE AND RED BRAKE AND INDICATOR LIGHTS

MAKE SIX – 2 RED AND 4 ORANGE

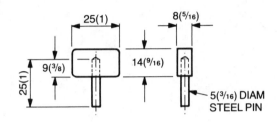

25(1)

8(5/16)

9(3/8)

14(9/16)

25(1)

5(3/16) DIAM STEEL PIN

SPOT LAMP

MAKE TWO

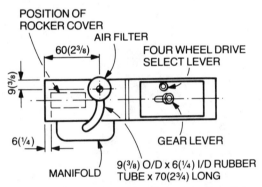

POSITION OF ROCKER COVER

AIR FILTER

FOUR WHEEL DRIVE SELECT LEVER

60(23/8)

9(3/8)

6(1/4)

MANIFOLD

GEAR LEVER

9(3/8) O/D x 6(1/4) I/D RUBBER TUBE x 70(2¾) LONG

BUILD UP OF ANCILLARIES ON ENGINE BLOCK

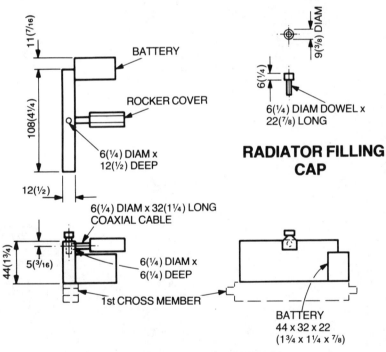

11(7/16)

BATTERY

108(4¼)

ROCKER COVER

6(1/4) DIAM x 12(1/2) DEEP

12(1/2)

6(1/4) DIAM x 32(1¼) LONG COAXIAL CABLE

44(1¾)

5(3/16)

6(1/4) DIAM x 6(1/4) DEEP

1st CROSS MEMBER

BATTERY
44 x 32 x 22
(1¾ x 1¼ x 7/8)

RADIATOR ASSEMBLY

9(3/8) DIAM

6(1/4)

6(1/4) DIAM DOWEL x 22(7/8) LONG

RADIATOR FILLING CAP

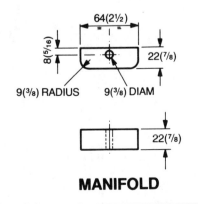

64(2½)

8(5/16)

22(7/8)

9(3/8) RADIUS   9(3/8) DIAM

22(7/8)

MANIFOLD

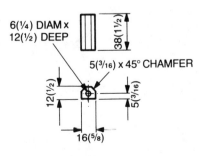

6(1/4) DIAM x 12(1/2) DEEP

38(1½)

5(3/16) x 45° CHAMFER

12(1/2)

5(3/16)

16(5/8)

ROCKER COVER

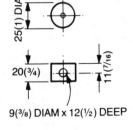

25(1) DIAM

20(¾)

11(7/16)

9(3/8) DIAM x 12(1/2) DEEP

AIR FILTER

199

1907 ROLLS ROYCE

When I was considering the content of my programme, I wanted to feature something that had been designed and made in Great Britain. I wanted to show something that we could take pride in, a piece of craftsmanship in the fullest sense. With these terms of reference my choice fell quite naturally on the Rolls Royce motor car. It was and still is the best. It symbolises mechanical perfection, meticulous attention to detail and a quality that has never been surpassed. It is sometimes a good thing to take stock of ourselves and realise that we 'this island race' are still capable of designing and making the very best.

Things in this world don't just happen. There are the thinkers and the doers; Frederick Henry Royce was both! His father died when he was nine so his teenage years were difficult ones. He worked as a telegraph boy, but quite obviously this work was not going to satisfy this youngster. It was his aunt who came to his rescue when she acquired an apprenticeship for him at the Great Northern Railway Works at Peterborough.

Young Henry found lodgings with a man who had a small workshop at the bottom of the garden. It was here in the evenings that Henry was taught the proper use of tools. So from this humble beginning, one of England's greatest engineers began his career which was, in the future, to prove quite literally the saving of this country. The supremacy of the Rolls Royce Merlin aero engine was to give the RAF victory in the air in the Battle of Britain.

It is true to say that the foundations of the company were laid when the Silver Ghost was built and it was due to its faultless engineering that the company became famous.

When I start building a model I ask the company for outline drawings, photographs etc. In the case of the Silver Ghost none existed. It was therefore necessary to photograph the real car and from these prints work out a set of full size plans from which I could work.

1   Make a start by cutting out the main chassis members. Tape both chassis sides together and 'pencil in' the position of the rear cross member, all the intermediate cross members and the front cross member. Now drill all the holes in the chassis, except the one holding the front spring hanger which has to be done after the sides have been laminated.

2   Cut the joint for the rear cross member which holds the back of the chassis together. The headlamp bar 9mm (⅜in) hole is drilled next. It is from these two fixing points that the whole chassis is assembled.

3   Now that two fixing points have been established, building of the chassis can begin. From the drawings you can see that it curves inwards by the engine bulkhead. Plywood formers are cut to hold the sides together. The chassis can be 'cold bent' while the formers are positioned to shape the chassis. Getting the right shape is fairly critical so be patient and work at it. Once the plywood formers are in place all the intermediate cross-members can be prepared. Note that (**d**) has its ends cut to an angle. Make sure you get this to fit well against both chassis sides. Try the pieces in 'dry' (without glue). Everything should be a push fit and once this is achieved glue all the intermediate cross members in. Don't remove the plywood formers yet. Now cut all the corner fillets and glue them in place. Don't remove the plywood formers for several days because if left, the wood will conform more readily to the curved shaping of the chassis.

4   At the front of the chassis, small pieces of wood are glued on either side. When the glue is set these can be shaped up and the hole bored to take the front spring.
The front of the chassis is a beautiful piece of practical engineering.

5   I used sycamore for the tool box sides and lid. On the real car the tool boxes double up as running boards. The boxes are held to the chassis by forged metal brackets. From the drawings given, cut out six brackets (running board supports) and shape them all up. The brackets are held to the chassis by screws.

6   The tool box/running boards are made so that they can be opened. Plane up the strips of wood that form the box sides and ends. The ends can be glued and butt jointed if you wish, but as you can see in the plan I have cut a small comb joint. It is stronger and looks better.

The bottom of the boxes are made from plywood. A small divider is glued into the box. You will need four pairs of top quality brass hinges to attach the lids to the boxes. The secret of fitting hinges is to make certain that you cut recesses in both lid and box top to take the hinge flaps. Small brass screws are usually supplied in the hinge pack. Check that the screw head fits the countersink hole in the hinge flap. Frequently screws are supplied that are oversize and if these are fitted it will result in the lid not shutting down. Small brass catches are used to keep the lids shut. Use a small carving gouge to recess the hand grips in the sides of the lids.

The spare wheel is mounted on the lid of the box on the driver's side. Holes are drilled through the block to take the leather straps to hold the wheel in place.

An acetylene tank is fitted onto the lid. If you have a lathe then no difficulty will be experienced in turning this up, but if not a large dowel rod will do after a little time and effort has gone into shaping the top and bottom.

7   The tool boxes are fixed onto the supports by screws that pass through from the inside of the boxes. Once the boxes are fixed, work can begin on making the mudguards.

8   The Silver Ghost has very graceful lines and nowhere is this better displayed than in the curvature of the mudguards. From front to back this beautiful line is continued, the thicker mudguard at the front, the tool box in the middle and the much thinner back mudguard tapering to a gentle finish.

Before starting to cut out the mudguards, make cardboard templates

from the plans. You can either cut the mudguards from a solid block of wood as I did, or steam the mudguard into shape. If you are cutting from a solid block of wood, cut the inside curve first. This will enable you to hold the block of wood in the vice while you spokeshave the inside curve. When shaping of the inside curve is complete, cut the outside curve. Obviously holding the pieces while cutting isn't easy and many 'adjustments' of the wood in the vice have to be made as cutting progresses. Finish off with a spokeshave.

The front mudguard has a hole drilled on the inside edge to take the front mudguard support. Be certain to drill this hole extremely carefully otherwise the drill will break through the side of the mudguard and you will have to start again. The rod I used was aluminium, very soft and easy to bend into shape. Fit one end of the rod into the mudguard and the other locates in a hole through the headlamp bar. A recess is carved on the edges of the front mudguards with a small gouge. The carved recess is a small but vital detail and a very sharp tool is necessary to do this fine work.

The front mudguard is held onto the chassis by the small bar that fits into the headlamp bar and it is supported at the back by a small strip of wood screwed into the front edge of the tool box.

Cutting the back mudguard and drilling the metal bar support hole is the same as for the front mudguard. However, the back mudguard being thinner requires a different shaping technique. All the edges need to be carefully rounded, which has the effect of making the back mudguard look thinner than the front one. When fixing the back mudguard to the chassis, the metal bar support fits into the pre-drilled hole in the side of the chassis.

Using an aluminium bar is a great advantage as it is soft and bends easily. Slight adjustment can be made relatively easily when finally positioning the mudguard.

9   The chassis is now complete, the tool boxes made and fitted, the mudguards shaped and positioned onto the chassis. Now some work is needed on the springs, axles and steering gear.

10   Making springs is not as difficult as it may at first appear. The spring steel used was sufficiently soft to allow bending and drilling. The method is the same for both front and back springs.

With a hack-saw cut the two longest pieces of spring to length. Using round nosed pliers form the hook on the end. Do this on both ends and to both pieces. Now cut the other pieces of steel to make up the spring.

To ensure that both front springs are the same length and to put a 'bow' in both of them, a very simple jig is made. Pass a steel rod through the spring hooks at each end. Two short lengths of string are tied onto the ends of the rod. These are then tensioned to give the bow for the spring. Slacken the tension off and using tape attach all the spring leaves. Re-tension the springs and carefully drill holes to take small bolts. Fix the nuts and bolts, remove the string and steel bars from the ends of the springs and you will have two completed springs, each with a gentle curve in them.

You will find that a smooth cut file is of great help to do all the tidying up of edges and general shaping of all the metal parts.

11   The small hook on the end of each spring needs a bush. From a length of brass tube I cut off several bushes. These are then inserted into the hook on the end of the spring. Using a pair of pliers, squeeze the end of the spring onto the tube to keep it in place. All the springs on the model are treated in this way.

One small point to watch is that the inside diameter of the bush must correspond to the diameter of the steel rod that fits into the spring hangers.

All the spring hangers are made from the same material as the springs. It does help to drill the hangers in pairs.

12   The rear springs and transverse spring are all made by the same method. This transverse spring is an interesting feature of the 1907 Ghost. A few years later this was discontinued. For the purposes of the model it does make the fixing of the rear spring to the transverse spring quite difficult. On the real Ghost there is a magnificent arrangement of shackle bolts all fitted with lubrication points. I overcame the problem by shaping up two rear hanger blocks from oak. Study the drawing before starting. The big difference on the model between the front and rear suspension is that the front actually works while the back does not.

The transverse spring is attached to the chassis via a rear spring central support. This resembles a chicken wishbone in shape. It is screwed onto the underside of the chassis. The central hole in the transverse spring lines up with the hole in the spring support. It is onto this piece that the number plate and GB sign are fixed.

When you are satisfied that all the parts fit well, push the steel rods through the spring hangers and push on the spring caps.

13   The front axle is a prominent feature of the car. The axle section (for those technically minded) is an 'H' section. Begin by cutting out a cardboard template of the shape. Transfer the shape by drawing around the template, and cut the axle out. Once again beech or oak is probably the best wood for this job. After cutting out the axle it is necessary to carve a recess along the front. This can be done with a small gouge. It is another of the small details that are of great importance.

Recesses are cut out on the ends of the axles to take the stub axle blocks. The stub axles themselves have to be very accurately made. Basically they consist of a block of wood through which passes a steel bar, the stub axle. Through this passes a smaller diameter bar, the king pin. This pin goes right through the front axle and the stub axle. It is held in place by a spring cap at either end.

The first task is to cut the block holding the stub axle. Drill the block and fit the stub axle. Now fix the whole unit in the end of the front axle. Drill a hole right through the front axle into and through the stub axle. Quite obviously as you can see from the dimensions given on the plan, there is very little clearance for the drill to pass through the stub axle. It is essential that the drilling is done in a vertical drill stand, otherwise it will be impossible to achieve the accuracy necessary for this job.

The steering tie bar is now made and, after drilling, is bolted to the stub axle ends. The front axle is now ready to be bolted onto the front springs.

14   The back axle assembly is far easier to construct. Using oak, cut and shape the back axle. Drill holes to take the stub axles. These are glued into place using epoxy resin glue.

15   Now make the prop shaft, gearbox and engine block assembly. The back axle and prop shaft assembly are held together by two small screws.

16 The rear axle assembly is put together in the following order:

i The rear cross spring central support is first fitted to the chassis.

ii The back axle is attached by screws passing through the axle and cross spring central support into the chassis. The use of stub axles allows the screws to pass through the axle unit.

iii The back springs fit onto the recesses (top of axle) and are held in place by very short screws going into the top of the axle.

iv Torsion bars are cut and at one end glued onto the back axle and at the other fastened by screwing into the side of the chassis.

17 Screw plywood 'decking' onto the top of the chassis.

18 Now make the gear lever and braking system. The Silver Ghost had rear wheel braking and although the model has no brakes, the levers, rods etc. leading the the back of the car are quite a prominent feature.

The transverse rod assembly is assembled with 'tags' on either end. Nylon cord is threaded through the tags and attached to small springs which are fitted onto the back axle. These springs return the lever to the 'off' position. The nylon cord is attached to the brake lever.

The brake arrangement drawings should be studied for details. The gear lever and brake are bolted to the side of the chassis. Spacers are fitted between levers to allow separate movement.

19 The starting handle is bent from a piece of aluminium bar. One end is sleeved with a piece of tube, the other end fits into the hole in the front cross member. The handle is held in a leather pouch when not in use. Cut a strip of leather and tie it to the side of the chassis.

Coachwork

20 This was the age when panels were hand beaten into shape, and the shaping of the Silver Ghost 'superstructure' looks as graceful now as it did 75 years ago. Start by marking out the two sides. After marking out, cut out the various recesses for doors etc. The two sides are then joined together by three bulkheads.

The driver's door is an interesting feature. It does not open but it is detailed on the body panel side. I therefore made a feature of it by

carefully cutting it out then glueing it back in position. The front passenger door is really only half a door. This is hinged to the body by a very small brass hinge. The two rear doors are made only after the seats have been shaped.

21 The spectacular curve at the back of the car starts on the body sides and runs right up through the back seat.

The boot is carved from a piece of solid sycamore. I have allowed myself a little licence here and carved a boot handle. The boot is hinged onto the floor.

22 A massive piece of aluminium forms the front bulkhead on the original car. The distinctive feature of this is the curved section at the top. Cut out the curved section from a solid panel of sycamore. This does require quite a lot of work as a good deal of wood is removed to form the curve. Once this is accomplished the windscreen frame can be made. Now the real ghost windscreen is a mass of tubes, bars and pipes holding the glass in position.

My wooden version of this frame is naturally far simpler. After making the framework I screwed it onto the sides of the bulkhead. Perspex was then cut and fitted. The addition of a mirror is one of the tiny details that makes such a difference.

23 The bonnet is made from two pieces of wood glued together. The top of the bonnet is shaped with a plane.

The radiator for my Ghost was made by Rolls Royce at Crewe (see *Useful addresses* on page 224) but it is not too difficult to fabricate one from plywood or brass. Quite naturally it will not look as impressive as the polished and chromed variety, but with a little effort and time great things can be achieved.

24 Perhaps making the seats requires the greatest skill of all. I cut mine from a solid block of wood but there are other methods of doing this. The sandwich method of glueing pre-cut pieces together would be another way of making the seats.

When removing large pieces of wood from a solid block it is very important that the wood used is kiln dried, otherwise all kinds of distortions may occur later.

It is helpful to think of the block as a cake from which large slices have to be cut. The cutting has to be done with

a bow saw. This tool has a blade that is tensioned by winding the string taut with a wooden peg. It is quite an effective tool but practise on scrap wood to get used to it before starting work on the seat.

A bandsaw would of course be the ideal tool for this work and would cut the seats out in minutes. Schools and technical colleges have band saws and it may well be a good idea to enlist their help.

The first cut to take off the block is the top piece and then the contour off the back of the seat. The last piece to cut out is the seating compartment.

You will now be left with a very rough shape that will require carving into shape. You don't need to buy a vast array of carving chisels for this job, however a small boxed set of six will be of great help. Perhaps the best advice to give here is that you keep all the tools razor sharp and as you work continually offer up the seat to the main body to see how much more has to be removed before it will fit. You will find that you have to keep moving it around in the vice as you work.

Remove as much wood as you can with the gouges and chisels before you use glasspaper. As you chisel and gouge always take light cuts. This is better than taking out great chunks of wood. It is far easier to judge how the shape is progressing by taking only light cuts as you work. Final shaping of the contours will have to be done with a fine grade glasspaper.

You will feel a real sense of achievement as the block of wood begins to take shape. In the final stages you will find it helpful to refer to the photographs in the book. It is at this stage that you must check that everything fits well before going on to the upholstery.

When the seats have been upholstered they are glued onto the main coach body.

25 When the front seat has been finished you will be able to fit it temporarily in place and mark the contour of the back onto card. This is necessary to find the shape of the back door jam. The door jam is then shaped and glued onto the main coach body assembly. The back doors are not fitted until the seats are finally positioned.

26 Upholstering seats is another job that takes time. A thin leather will be best, about the thickness of 'chamois leather cloth'. The main feature to

capture is the raised leather edge on the tops of the seats. From the section drawing through the seat back you will see how this was achieved. Plastic tube was found to be ideal for raising the leather firmly onto the top edge. Great care is necessary when fixing the panel pins into the wood. Make a cloth pattern before cutting any leather. Position it under the plastic tube and wrap it over the tube and down the seat. You will find that a gusset will have to be cut out of the corners to allow the cloth to fit. The cloth pattern will be a good guide for the leather. When it comes to fitting the leather, work very carefully and always try fitting before you cut anything.

26 I found felt an ideal padding to go under all the leather. After upholstering all the 'chairs' cut plywood for the seat cushions. You will have to allow for the thickness of felt and leather. Cover the seats in felt and leather.

27 When you are sure that all fits well, the back and front seats are glued onto the main coach body. The back doors can now be fitted.

28 Imitation dials etc. are fitted to the bulkhead. A wooden box is fitted in the centre of the bulkhead to house the magnetoes. A little time will have to be spent cutting and shaping the steering wheel. The wheel is attached to the bulkhead via a dowel rod and a block of wood.

29 I turned the head lamps on a lathe. The real lamps are very detailed with lots of intricate shapes but I kept mine very simple.

30 The spare wheel is kept in place by a small wooden bracket attached to the side of the bulkhead. The spare wheel itself is made from a standard wheel from which the spokes have been cut out. Small offcuts of leather were used to 'lace' the wheel in place. For the keen model maker there are still many more details that could be added to the car.

Finishing is quite a big task as there are so many separate parts. You will find that some pieces such as tool boxes, mudguards, windscreen frame, seats, chassis etc. need to be finished off and then mounted afterwards. Wheels are always the last things to be attached.

Notes on timber

The Silver Ghost was difficult to envisage without silver paint. However, to give this lightness I decided to build the model in sycamore and rippled ash. Whether I succeeded or not you must judge. The colour of the upholstery can make a big difference. I chose green as this often looks very well with a natural wood finish. The real car has green upholstery so it proved to be a good choice.

With the introduction of air brushes I am quite sure that many car modelling enthusiasts will achieve some quite spectacular Silver Ghost paintwork.

The Spirit of Ecstasy (The Silver Lady)

The Silver lady was not on the 1907 Silver Ghost. The car has on its radiator an AA badge. The Silver Lady only came into being when Henry Royce noticed that owners of his cars were displaying distasteful mascots on the front. In order to counter this he had commissioned the Silver Lady without which no Rolls Royce is now complete.

Cutting list

Main chassis assembly	2 off	768 x 28 x 9mm (30¼ x 1⅛ x ⅜in)	Timber
Side cheeks	Make from	254 x 28 x 3mm (10 x 1⅛ x ⅛in)	Plywood
Corner fillets	Make from	140 x 28 x 16mm (5½ x 1⅛ x ⅝in)	Timber
Cross members	3 off	137 x 28 x 16mm (5⅜ x 1⅛ x ⅝in)	Timber
	1 off	124 x 28 x 16mm (4⅞ x 1⅛ x ⅝in)	Timber
Front cross member	1 off	111 x 28 x 12mm (4⅜ x 1⅛ x ½in)	Timber
Rear cross member	1 off	156 x 28 x 12mm (6⅛ x 1⅛ x ½in)	Timber
Rear cross spring central support	1 off	168 x 156 x 11mm (6⅝ x 6⅛ x 7/16in)	Timber
Torsion bars	2 off	159mm(6¼in) long x 9mm(⅜in) diameter dowel	
Rear axle assembly	1 off	248 x 60 x 25mm (9¾ x 2⅜ x 1in)	Timber
Prop shaft assembly	1 off	273mm(10¾in) long x 12mm(½in) diameter dowel	
	1 off	41 x 28 x 12mm (1⅝ x 1⅛ x ½in)	Timber
Reinforcing plate	2 off	32 x 28 x 3mm (1¼ x 1⅛ x ⅛in)	Plywood
Front axle	1 off	241 x 47 x 22mm (9½ x 1⅞ x ⅞in)	Timber
Tool box/running boards supports	4 off	114 x 95 x 9mm (4½ x 3¾ x ⅜in)	Timber
	2 off	124 x 95 x 9mm (4⅞ x 3¾ x ⅜in)	Timber
Gear box	1 off	137 x 54 x 44mm (5⅜ x 2⅛ x 1¾in)	Timber
Stub axle	2 off	51 x 14 x 12mm (2 x 9/16 x ½in)	Timber
Steering tie bar	1 off	241 x 20 x 5mm (9½ x ¾ x 3/16in)	Timber
Engine block	1 off	152 x 60 x 44mm (6 x 2⅜ x 1¾in)	Timber
Boot lid	1 off	113 x 67 x 51mm (4 7/16 x 2⅝ x 2in)	Timber
Boot lid handle	1 off	47 x 20 x 9mm (1⅞ x ¾ x ⅜in)	Timber
Cab front bulkhead	1 off	184 x 121 x 22mm (7¼ x 4¾ x ⅞in)	Timber
Instruments	Make from	51mm(2in) long x 12mm(½in) diameter dowel	
Brake lever inner	1 off	159 x 12 x 3mm (6¼ x ½ x ⅛in)	Plywood
Brake lever outer	1 off	143 x 12 x 3mm (5⅝ x ½ x ⅛in)	Plywood
Central console	1 off	57 x 25 x 12mm (2¼ x 1 x ½in)	Timber
	1 off	28 x 25 x 5mm (1⅛ x 1 x 3/16in)	Timber
Steering column block	1 off	51 x 28 x 20mm (2 x 1⅛ x ¾in)	Timber
Backing plate	1 off	38 x 32 x 6mm (1½ x 1¼ x ¼in)	Timber
Central quadrant	1 off	32 x 32 x 6mm (1¼ x 1¼ x ¼in)	Timber
Steering column assembly	1 off	133mm(5¼in) long x 6mm(¼in) diameter dowel	
	1 off	60mm (2⅜in) diameter disc x 9mm (⅜in) thick	Timber
Transverse brake con. rod assembly	2 off	32 x 12 x 5mm (1¼ x ½ x 3/16in)	Timber
Front and rear seats	2 off	184 x 140 x 86mm (7¼ x 5½ x 3⅜in)	Timber
Seat cushion	1 off	127 x 102 x 9mm (5 x 4 x ⅜in)	Plywood
	1 off	127 x 89 x 9mm (5 x 3½ x ⅜in)	Timber
Rear spring rear hanger block	2 off	47 x 28 x 20mm (1⅞ x 1⅛ x ¾in)	Timber
Head lamp	Make from	102mm(4in) long x 44mm(1¾in) diameter dowel	
Oil tank	1 off	57mm(2¼in) long x 25mm(1in) diameter dowel	
Rear door closure post	2 off	105 x 22 x 9mm (4⅛ x ⅞ x ⅜in)	Timber
Main coach body assembly	2 off	460 x 67 x 20mm (18⅛ x 2⅝ x ¾in)	Timber
	1 off	114 x 67 x 16mm (4½ x 2⅝ x ⅝in)	Timber
	2 off	114 x 70 x 16mm (4½ x 2¾ x ⅝in)	Timber
	1 off	114 x 25 x 22mm (4½ x 1 x ⅞in)	Timber
Passenger front door	1 off	102 x 47 x 9mm (4 x 1⅞ x ⅜in)	Timber
Rear doors	2 off	98 x 92 x 16mm (3⅞ x 3⅝ x ⅝in)	Timber
Bonnet	1 off	191 x 105 x 73mm (7½ x 4⅛ x 2⅞in)	Timber
	1 off	191 x 105 x 22mm (7½ x 4⅛ x ⅞in)	Timber
Windshield and frame	2 off	219 x 40 x 9mm (8⅝ x 1 9/16 x ⅜in)	Timber

	2 off	203 × 9 × 5mm (8 × ⅜ × ³⁄₁₆in)	Timber
	1 off	203 × 5 × 5mm (8 × ³⁄₁₆ × ³⁄₁₆in)	Timber
Driving mirror	1 off	32 × 16 × 8mm (1¼ × ⅝ × ⁵⁄₁₆in)	Timber
Spare wheel front support arm	1 off	60 × 16 × 12mm (2⅜ × ⅝ × ½in)	Timber
Front mudguard	2 off	254 × 130 × 51mm (10 × 5⅛ × 8in)	Timber
Rear mudguard	2 off	241 × 130 × 51mm (9½ × 5⅛ × 2in)	Timber
Spare wheel lower rest	1 off	70 × 22 × 20mm (2¾ × ⅞ × ¾in)	Timber
Acetylene tank	1 off	60mm (2⅜in) long × 35mm (1⅜in) diameter dowel	
Lamp clamps	Make from	51 × 22 × 9mm (2 × ⅞ × ⅜in)	Timber
Tool box/running board	4 off	330 × 22 × 9mm (13 × ⅞ × ⅜in)	Timber
	4 off	60 × 22 × 9mm (2⅜ × ⅞ × ⅜in)	Timber
	2 off	41 × 22 × 9mm (1⅝ × ⅞ × ⅜in)	Timber
	2 off	47 × 9 × 5mm (1⅞ × ⅜ × ³⁄₁₆in)	Timber
	2 off	41 × 9 × 5mm (1⅝ × ⅜ × ³⁄₁₆in)	Timber
	2 off	330 × 60 × 5mm (13 × 2⅜ × ³⁄₁₆in)	Plywood
Head lamp support bar	1 off	162mm (6½in) long × 9mm (⅜in) diameter dowel	
Number plate	1 off	60 × 16 × 6mm (2⅜ × ⅝ × ¼in)	Timber
Tool box lid	4 off	164 × 60 × 16mm (6⁷⁄₁₆ × 2⅜ × ⅝in)	Timber

Ancillaries

	2 off	152mm (6in) diameter road wheels
	2 off	92mm (3⅝in) long × 9mm (⅜in) diameter steel stub axles
	2 off	Spring dome caps to suit 9mm (⅜in) diameter axles
Front spring assembly	Make from 1220 × 16 × 1mm (48 × ⅝ × ¹⁄₃₂in) spring steel
	4 off	12mm (½in) long × 3mm (⅛in) diameter bolts, washers and nuts
	2 off	25mm (1in) long × 3mm (⅛in) diameter bolts, washer and nuts
	2 off	41mm (1⅝in) long × 9mm (⅜in) diameter steel stub axles
	2 off	152mm (6in) diameter road wheels
	2 off	Spring dome caps to suit 9mm (⅜in) diameter axles
	2 off	54mm (2⅛in) long × 5mm (³⁄₁₆in) diameter steel pivot pins
	4 off	Spring dome caps to suit 5mm (³⁄₁₆in) diameter pins
	2 off	25mm (1in) long × 3mm (⅛in) diameter bolts, washers and nuts
Front spring rear hanger outer	2 off	44 × 16 × 1mm (1¾ × ⅝ × ¹⁄₃₂in) steel strip
Front spring rear hanger inner	2 off	36 × 16 × 1mm (1⁷⁄₁₆ × ⅝ × ¹⁄₃₂in) steel strip
	4 off	22mm (⅞in) long × 5mm (³⁄₁₆in) diameter steel pins
	8 off	Spring dome caps to suit 5mm (³⁄₁₆in) diameter pins
	2 off	6mm (¼in) o/d × 5mm (³⁄₁₆in) i/d × 16mm (⅝in) long tubes
	2 off	6mm (¼in) o/d × 5mm (³⁄₁₆in) i/d × 3mm (⅛) thick spacer
Front spring front hanger	4 off	35 × 16 × 1mm (1⅜ × ⅝ × ¹⁄₃₂in) steel strip
	4 off	22mm (⅞in) long × 5mm (³⁄₁₆in) diameter steel pins
	8 off	Spring dome caps to suit 5mm (³⁄₁₆in) diameter pins
	2 off	6mm (¼in) o/d × 5mm (³⁄₁₆in) i/d × 16mm (⅝in) long tubes
Transverse brake control rod	1 off	168mm (6⅝in) long × 5mm (³⁄₁₆in) diameter steel rod
Side lamp	2 off	20mm (¾in) diameter × 0·5mm (¹⁄₆₄in) thick steel disc
Rear spring assembly	Make from 1270 × 16 × 1mm (50 × ⅝ × ¹⁄₃₂in) spring steel
	4 off	12mm (½in) long × 3mm (⅛in) diameter bolts, washers and nuts
Rear spring front carrier	1 off	194mm (7⅝in) long × 5mm (³⁄₁₆in) diameter steel rod
	2 off	6mm (¼in) o/d × 5mm (³⁄₁₆in) i/d × 16mm (⅝in) long tubes
	2 off	9mm (⅜in) o/d × 5mm (³⁄₁₆in) i/d × 3mm (⅛in) thick spacer
Rear transverse spring	Make from 2050 × 16 × 1mm (80 × ⅝ × ¹⁄₃₂in) spring steel
	4 off	25mm (1in) long × 5mm (³⁄₁₆in) diameter steel pins
	8 off	Spring dome caps to suit 5mm (³⁄₁₆in) diameter pins

	2 off	6mm (¼in) o/d × 5mm (³⁄₁₆in) i/d × 16mm (⅝in) long tube
	1 off	25mm(1in) long × 3mm(⅛in) diameter bolts, washer and nut
Rear spring rear hanger	2 off	35mm (1⅜in) long × 5mm (³⁄₁₆in) diameter steel pins
	4 off	Spring dome caps to suit 5mm (³⁄₁₆in) diameter pins
	2 off	6mm (¼in) o/d × 5mm (³⁄₁₆in) i/d × 16mm (⅝in) long tubes
Transverse spring hanger	4 off	38 × 16 × 1mm (1½ × ⅝ × ¹⁄₃₂in) steel strip
Seat covering	2 off	Pieces of soft leather 457 × 152mm (18 × 6in)
	2 off	Pieces of soft leather 229 × 229mm (9 × 9in)
	2 off	Pieces of felt 457 × 152mm (18 × 6in)
	2 off	Pieces of felt 229 × 229mm (9 × 9in)
	2 off	Lengths of 9mm (³⁄₈in) diameter plastic tubing 457mm (18in) long
	To suit	Dome headed pins to form buttoning effect
Brake lever assembly	1 off	32mm(1¼in) long × 3mm(⅛in) diameter bolt, washer and nut
	2 off	35mm(1⅜in) diameter × 0·5mm(¹⁄₆₄in) thick steel disc
Passenger front door	1 off	12mm (½in) long brass hinge with screws
	1 off	Swing hook and screwed eye
Rear doors	2 off	25mm (1in) long brass hinges with screws
	2 off	Swing hooks and screwed eyes
Radiator	Make from 610 × 28 × 1·5mm (24 × 1⅛ × ¹⁄₁₆in) thick steel	
	1 off	105mm × 76 × 3mm (4⅛ × 3 × ⅛in) thick lined black plastic
Windshield	Make from 102 × 184 × 1·5mm (4 × 7¼ × ¹⁄₁₆in) thick clear plastic	
Mirror arm	1 off	51mm (2in) long × 5mm (³⁄₁₆in) diameter steel wire
Spare wheel	1 off	152mm (6in) road wheel with hub and spokes removed
Front mudguard stay	Make from 330mm (13in) long × 5mm (³⁄₁₆in) diameter steel wire	
Rear mudguard stay	Make from 280mm (11in) long × 5mm (³⁄₁₆in) diameter steel wire	
Lamp arm	Make from 203mm (8in) long × 5mm (³⁄₁₆in) diameter steel wire	
Starting handle	Make from 165mm (6½in) long × 5mm (³⁄₁₆in) diameter steel wire	
	1 off	9mm (³⁄₈in) o/d × 6mm (¼in) i/d × 12mm (½in) long steel tube
Tool box/running board	8 off	25mm (1in) brass hinges with screws
	4 off	Swing hooks and screwed eyes

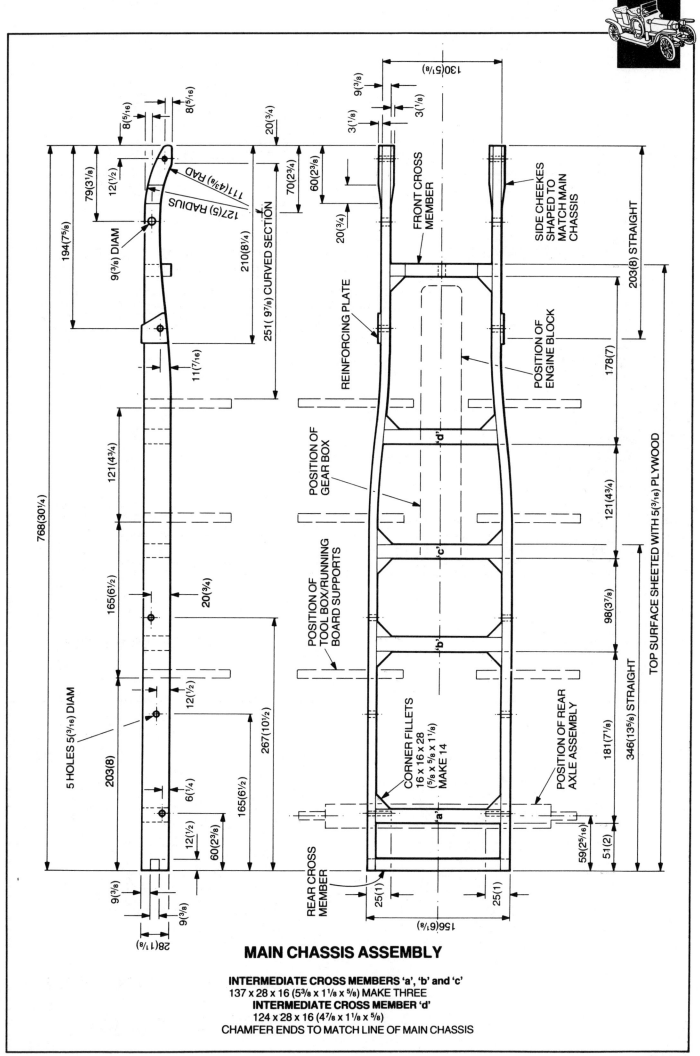

MAIN CHASSIS ASSEMBLY

INTERMEDIATE CROSS MEMBERS 'a', 'b' and 'c'
137 x 28 x 16 (5³⁄₈ x 1¹⁄₈ x ⁵⁄₈) MAKE THREE
INTERMEDIATE CROSS MEMBER 'd'
124 x 28 x 16 (4⁷⁄₈ x 1¹⁄₈ x ⁵⁄₈)
CHAMFER ENDS TO MATCH LINE OF MAIN CHASSIS

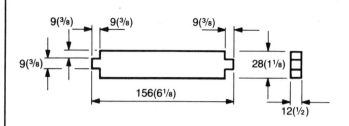

REAR CROSS MEMBER

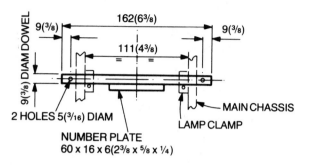

HEAD LAMP/ FRONT MUDGUARD
SUPPORT BAR

BAR THREADED THROUGH MAIN CHASSIS WITH LAMP CLAMPS
BETWEEN CHASSIS MEMBERS. BAR GLUED CENTRALLY IN POSITION.
LAMP CLAMPS GLUED TO BAR AND CHASSIS MEMBERS WITH LAMP
ARM HOLES VERTICAL. NUMBER PLATE GLUED CENTRALLY TO
LEADING EDGE OF SUPPORT BAR.

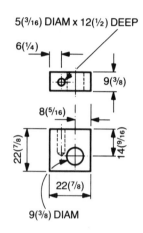

LAMP CLAMPS

MAKE TWO

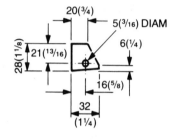

REINFORCING PLATE

3($\frac{1}{8}$) THICK PLYWOOD   MAKE TWO

POSITION ON MAIN CHASSIS SUCH THAT
5($\frac{3}{16}$) DIAM HOLES LINE UP, THEN
TRIM LOWER EDGE TO SUIT CHASSIS SHAPE.

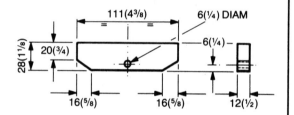

FRONT CROSS MEMBER

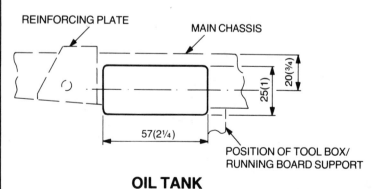

OIL TANK

POSITIONED AS SHOWN ON
PASSENGER'S SIDE OF MAIN CHASSIS

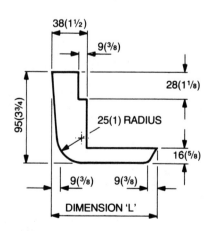

TOOL BOX/RUNNING BOARD SUPPORTS

9($\frac{3}{8}$) THICK

MAKE FOUR - DIM. L = 114(4$\frac{1}{2}$)- REAR PAIR
MAKE TWO - DIM. L = 124(4$\frac{7}{8}$) - FRONT PAIR

210

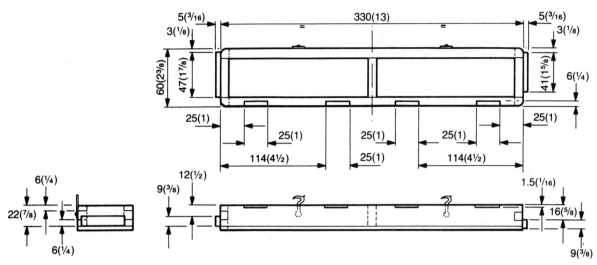

TOOL BOX/ RUNNING BOARD   MAKE ONE OF EACH HAND

BOX WALLS – 9(³⁄₈) THICK AND BASE – 5(³⁄₁₆) THICK PLYWOOD

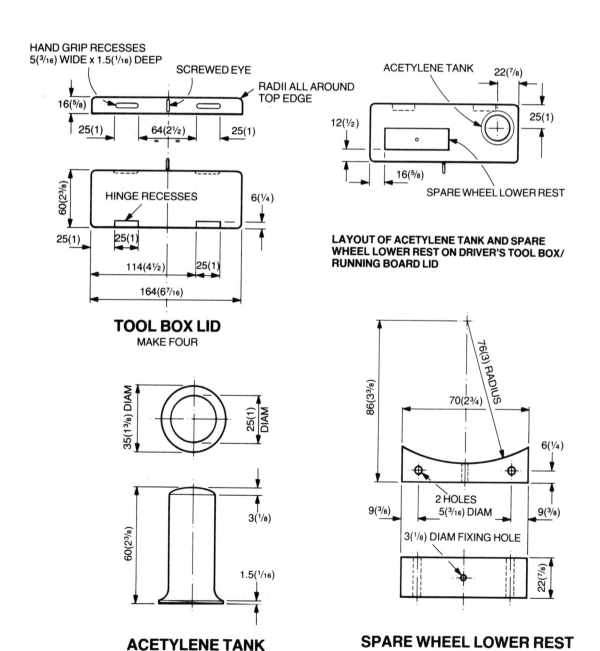

HAND GRIP RECESSES
5(³⁄₁₆) WIDE x 1.5(¹⁄₁₆) DEEP

SCREWED EYE

RADII ALL AROUND
TOP EDGE

HINGE RECESSES

TOOL BOX LID
MAKE FOUR

ACETYLENE TANK

SPARE WHEEL LOWER REST

LAYOUT OF ACETYLENE TANK AND SPARE
WHEEL LOWER REST ON DRIVER'S TOOL BOX/
RUNNING BOARD LID

2 HOLES
5(³⁄₁₆) DIAM

3(¹⁄₈) DIAM FIXING HOLE

ACETYLENE TANK

SPARE WHEEL LOWER REST

211

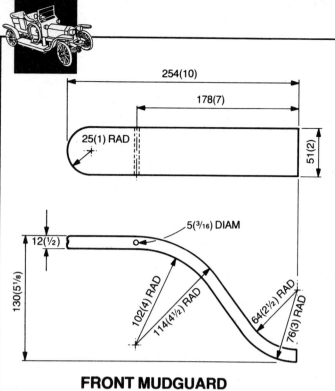

254(10)

178(7)

25(1) RAD

51(2)

12(½)

5(³/₁₆) DIAM

130(5⅛)

102(4) RAD

114(4½) RAD

64(2½) RAD

76(3) RAD

FRONT MUDGUARD

MAKE TWO

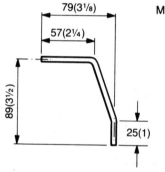

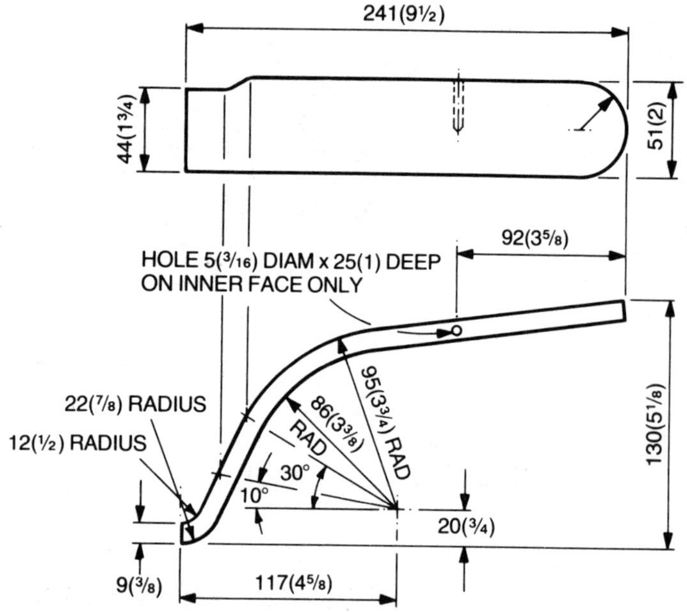

241(9½)

44(1¾)

51(2)

HOLE 5(³/₁₆) DIAM x 25(1) DEEP
ON INNER FACE ONLY

92(3⅝)

22(⁷/₈) RADIUS

12(½) RADIUS

95(3¾) RAD

86(3⅜) RAD

130(5⅛)

30°

10°

20(¾)

9(³/₈)

117(4⅝)

REAR MUDGUARD

MAKE ONE OF EACH HAND

28(1⅛)

73(2⁷/₈)

28(1⅛)

76(3)

REAR MUDGUARD STAY

MAKE TWO

5(³/₁₆) DIAM STEEL WIRE

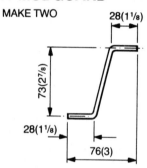

79(3⅛)

57(2¼)

89(3½)

25(1)

FRONT MUDGUARD STAY

MAKE TWO

5(³/₁₆) DIAM STEEL WIRE

FRONT SPRING
FRONT HANGER

1(¹/₃₂) THICK STEEL
MAKE FOUR

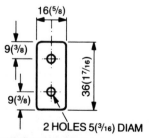

16(⁵/₈)

9(³/₈)

35(1⅜)

9(³/₈)

2 HOLES 5(³/₁₆) DIAM

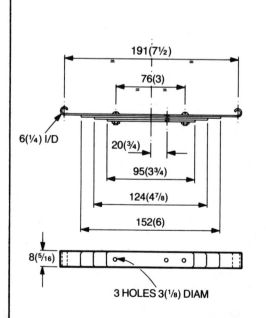

191(7½)

76(3)

20(¾)

95(3¾)

124(4⁷/₈)

152(6)

6(¼) I/D

8(⁵/₁₆)

3 HOLES 3(⅛) DIAM

FRONT SPRING ASSEMBLY

MAKE TWO   1(¹/₃₂) THICK SPRING STEEL

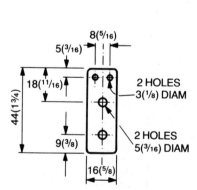

8(⁵/₁₆)

5(³/₁₆)

18(¹¹/₁₆)

44(1¾)

9(³/₈)

16(⁵/₈)

2 HOLES
3(⅛) DIAM

2 HOLES
5(³/₁₆) DIAM

FRONT SPRING REAR
HANGER OUTER

1(¹/₃₂) THICK STEEL
MAKE TWO

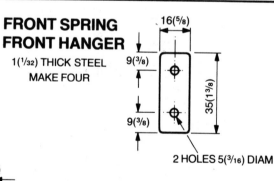

16(⁵/₈)

9(³/₈)

36(1⁷/₁₆)

9(³/₈)

2 HOLES 5(³/₁₆) DIAM

FRONT SPRING REAR
HANGER INNER

1(¹/₃₂) THICK STEEL
MAKE TWO

212

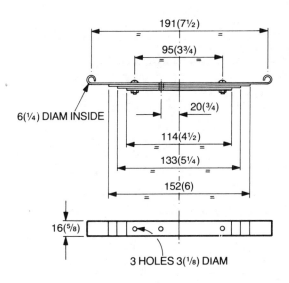

6(¼) DIAM INSIDE

191(7½)

95(3¾)

20(¾)

114(4½)

133(5¼)

152(6)

16(⅝)

3 HOLES 3(⅛) DIAM

REAR SPRING ASSEMBLY

MAKE TWO

FABRICATE FROM 1(1/32) THICK SPRING STEEL

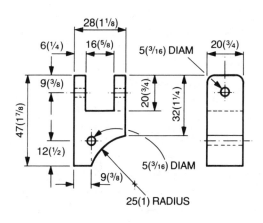

28(1⅛)

6(¼)

16(⅝)

5(3/16) DIAM

20(¾)

9(⅜)

47(1⅞)

20(¾)

32(1¼)

12(½)

5(3/16) DIAM

9(⅜)

25(1) RADIUS

REAR SPRING REAR HANGER BLOCK

MAKE TWO

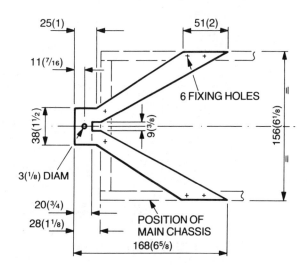

25(1)

51(2)

11(7/16)

6 FIXING HOLES

38(1½)

9(⅜)

156(6⅛)

3(⅛) DIAM

20(¾)

28(1⅛)

POSITION OF
MAIN CHASSIS

168(6⅝)

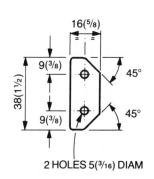

16(⅝)

9(⅜)

45°

38(1½)

9(⅜)

45°

2 HOLES 5(3/16) DIAM

TRANSVERSE SPRING HANGER

MAKE FOUR   1(1/32) THICK STEEL

REAR CROSS SPRING CENTRAL SUPPORT

11(7/16) THICK

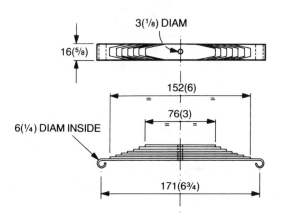

3(⅛) DIAM

16(⅝)

152(6)

76(3)

6(¼) DIAM INSIDE

171(6¾)

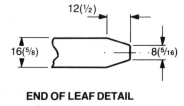

12(½)

16(⅝)

8(5/16)

END OF LEAF DETAIL

REAR TRANSVERSE SPRING ASSEMBLY

FABRICATE FROM 1(1/32) SPRING STEEL.
INTERMEDIATE SPRING LEAVES INCREASE IN
LENGTH BY 12(½), GIVING 7 LEAVES IN TOTAL.

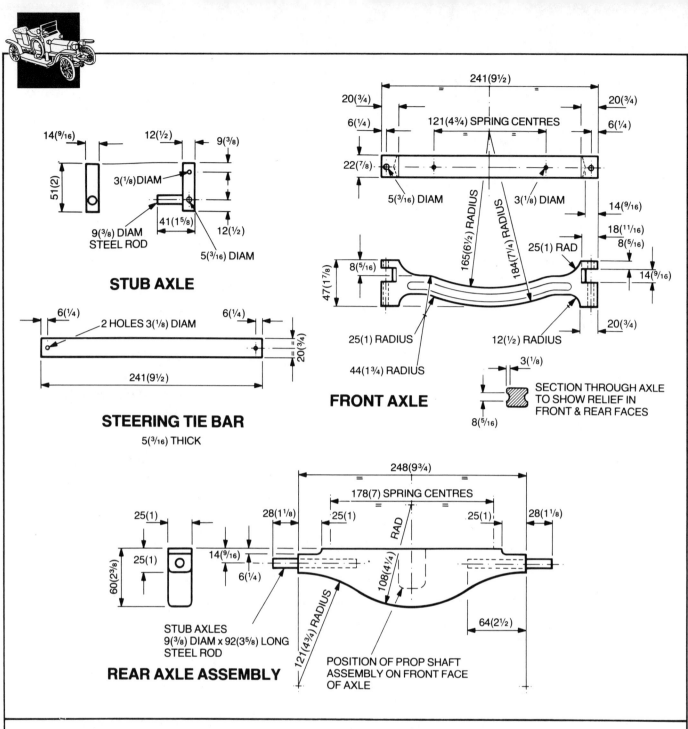

STUB AXLE

STEERING TIE BAR

5(³/₁₆) THICK

FRONT AXLE

SECTION THROUGH AXLE TO SHOW RELIEF IN FRONT & REAR FACES

REAR AXLE ASSEMBLY

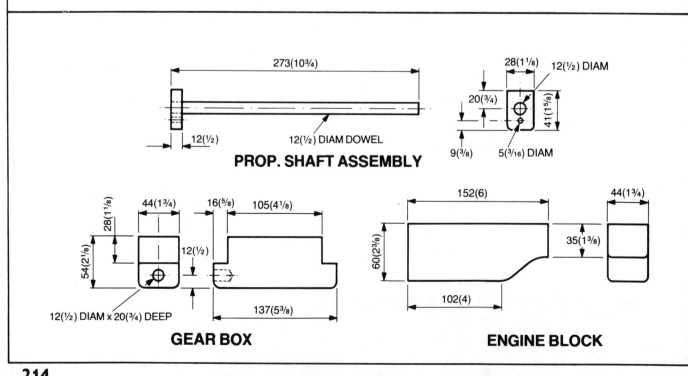

PROP. SHAFT ASSEMBLY

GEAR BOX

ENGINE BLOCK

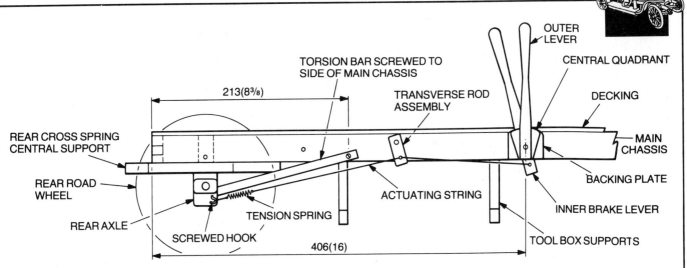

ARRANGEMENT OF BRAKE SYSTEM AND TORSION BAR INSTALLATION

WHEEL, SPRINGS, MUDGUARD AND TOOL BOX
OMITTED FOR CLARITY

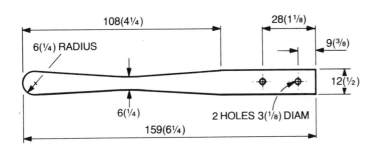

INNER BRAKE LEVER

3(¹/₈) THICK

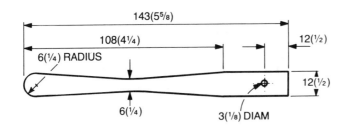

OUTER LEVER

3(¹/₈) THICK

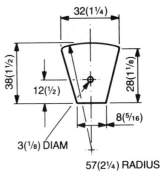

CENTRAL QUADRANT

6(¹/₄) THICK

BACKING PLATE

6(¹/₄) THICK

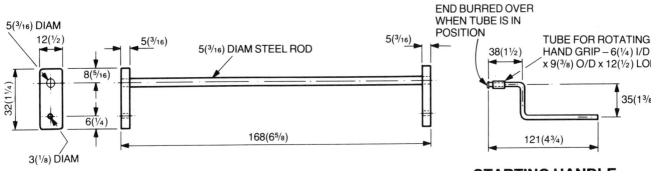

TRANSVERSE BRAKE CONNECTING ROD ASSEMBLY

SECOND END LEVER TO BE GLUED IN POSITION ONLY AFTER
ROD HAS BEEN PASSED THROUGH THE CHASSIS

STARTING HANDLE

MAKE FROM 5(³/₁₆) DIAM STEEL WIRE.
FIT THROUGH HOLE IN MAIN CHASSIS
FRONT CROSS MEMBER WITH END
ABUTTING ENGINE BLOCK

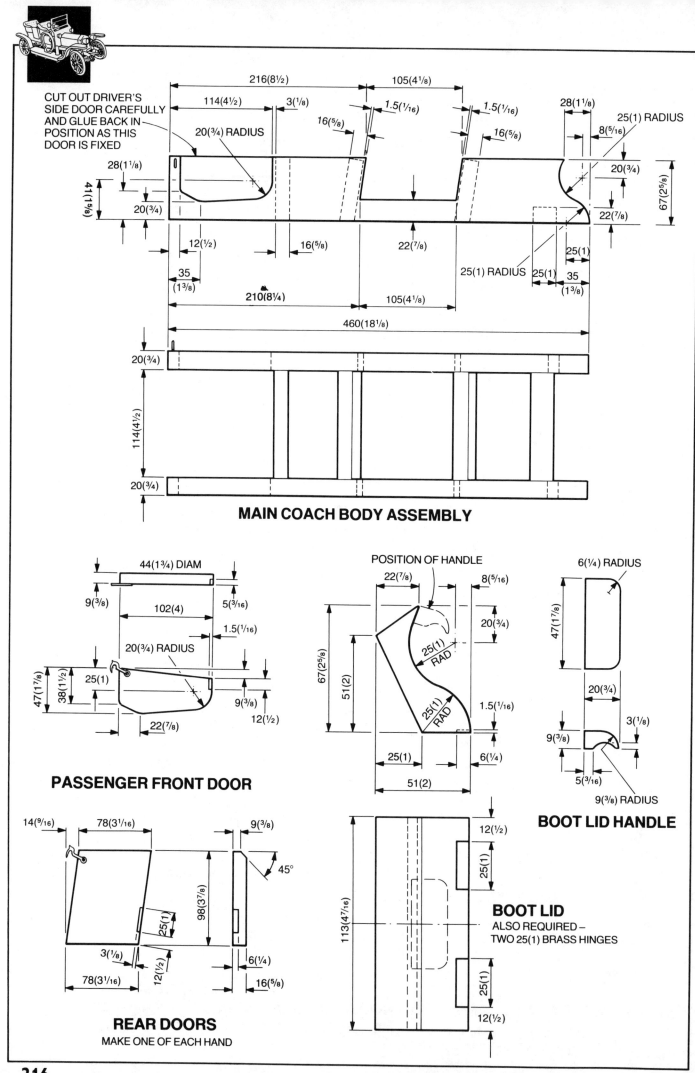

CUT OUT DRIVER'S SIDE DOOR CAREFULLY AND GLUE BACK IN POSITION AS THIS DOOR IS FIXED

MAIN COACH BODY ASSEMBLY

PASSENGER FRONT DOOR

POSITION OF HANDLE

REAR DOORS
MAKE ONE OF EACH HAND

BOOT LID HANDLE

BOOT LID
ALSO REQUIRED –
TWO 25(1) BRASS HINGES

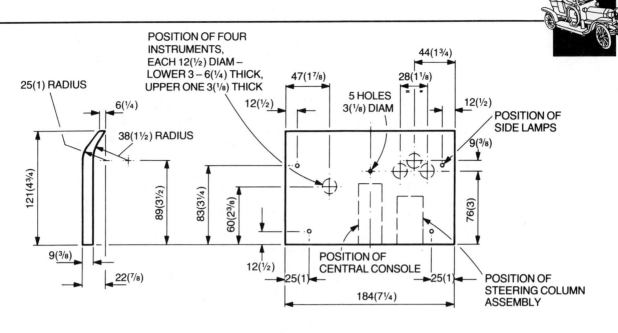

CAB FRONT BULKHEAD

POSITION OF FOUR INSTRUMENTS, EACH 12(½) DIAM – LOWER 3 – 6(¼) THICK, UPPER ONE 3(⅛) THICK

25(1) RADIUS

6(¼)

38(1½) RADIUS

121(4¾)

89(3½)

83(3¼)

60(2⅜)

9(⅜)

22(⅞)

12(½)

12(½)

47(1⅞)

5 HOLES 3(⅛) DIAM

44(1¾)

28(1⅛)

12(½)

POSITION OF SIDE LAMPS

9(⅜)

76(3)

25(1)

184(7¼)

25(1)

POSITION OF CENTRAL CONSOLE

POSITION OF STEERING COLUMN ASSEMBLY

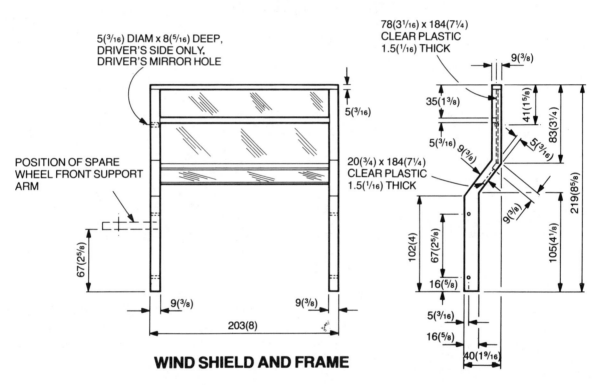

WIND SHIELD AND FRAME

5(³⁄₁₆) DIAM x 8(⁵⁄₁₆) DEEP, DRIVER'S SIDE ONLY, DRIVER'S MIRROR HOLE

POSITION OF SPARE WHEEL FRONT SUPPORT ARM

67(2⅝)

9(⅜)

9(⅜)

203(8)

5(³⁄₁₆)

78(3¹⁄₁₆) x 184(7¼) CLEAR PLASTIC 1.5(¹⁄₁₆) THICK

20(¾) x 184(7¼) CLEAR PLASTIC 1.5(¹⁄₁₆) THICK

9(⅜)

35(1⅜)

41(1⅝)

83(3¼)

5(³⁄₁₆)

9(⅜)

5(³⁄₁₆)

219(8⅝)

105(4⅛)

102(4)

67(2⅝)

9(⅜)

16(⅝)

5(³⁄₁₆)

16(⅝)

40(1⁹⁄₁₆)

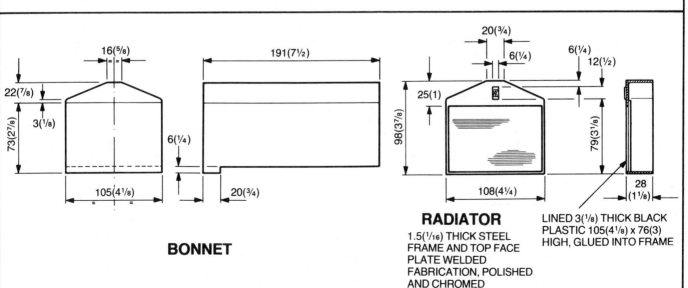

BONNET

16(⅝)

191(7½)

22(⅞)

3(⅛)

73(2⅞)

6(¼)

105(4⅛)

20(¾)

RADIATOR

1.5(¹⁄₁₆) THICK STEEL FRAME AND TOP FACE PLATE WELDED FABRICATION, POLISHED AND CHROMED

20(¾)

6(¼)

6(¼)

12(½)

25(1)

98(3⅞)

79(3⅛)

108(4¼)

28 (1⅛)

LINED 3(⅛) THICK BLACK PLASTIC 105(4⅛) x 76(3) HIGH, GLUED INTO FRAME

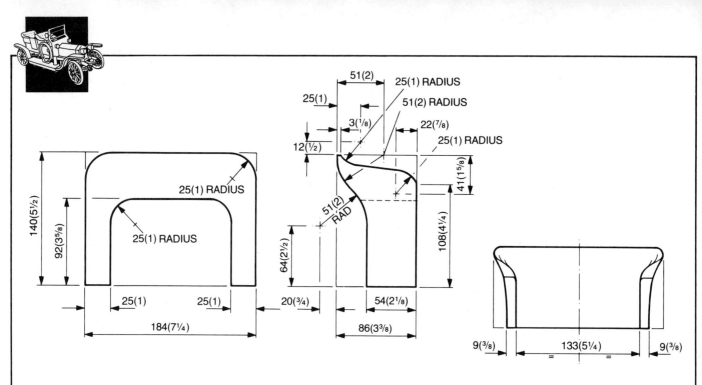

25(1) RADIUS

140(5½)   92(3⅝)

25(1) RADIUS

25(1)   25(1)

184(7¼)

20(¾)

51(2)

25(1)

3(⅛)

12(½)

25(1) RADIUS

51(2) RADIUS

22(⅞)

25(1) RADIUS

41(1⅝)

108(4¼)

64(2½)

51(2) RAD

54(2⅛)

86(3⅜)

BASIC SHAPE OF FRONT AND REAR SEAT ARMS AND BACK

MAKE TWO

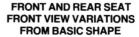

9(⅜)   133(5¼)   9(⅜)

FRONT AND REAR SEAT FRONT VIEW VARIATIONS FROM BASIC SHAPE

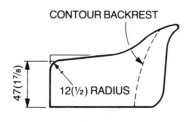

CONTOUR BACKREST

47(1⅞)

12(½) RADIUS

FRONT SEAT ARM VARIATION FROM BASIC SHAPE

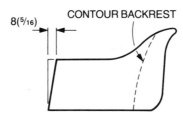

8(5/16)

CONTOUR BACKREST

REAR SEAT ARM VARIATION FROM BASIC SHAPE

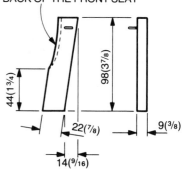

CONTOUR AND CHAMFER TO SUIT SHAPE OF THE BACK OF THE FRONT SEAT

44(1¾)   98(3⅞)

22(⅞)   9(⅜)

14(9/16)

REAR DOOR CLOSURE POST

MAKE ONE OF EACH HAND

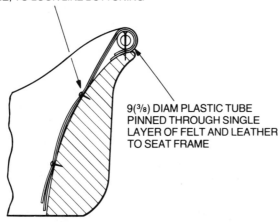

FELT LAID UNDER LEATHER TO GIVE SOFT SPONGY FEEL – BOTH WRAPPED OVER THE TOP OF THE PLASTIC TUBE AND PINNED IN A PATTERNED LAYOUT TO THE SEAT FRAME, TO LOOK LIKE BUTTONING

9(⅜) DIAM PLASTIC TUBE PINNED THROUGH SINGLE LAYER OF FELT AND LEATHER TO SEAT FRAME

SECTION THROUGH SEAT BACK

TUBE EXTENDS ACROSS BACK AND ALONG BOTH ARMS. SEAT CUSHION COVERED WITH FELT AND LEATHER BUT NO TUBE

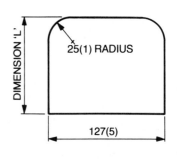

25(1) RADIUS

DIMENSION 'L'

127(5)

SEAT CUSHION

MAKE TWO   9(⅜) THICK
DIMENSION L – 102(4) ON FRONT SEAT
DIMENSION L – 89(3½) ON REAR SEAT

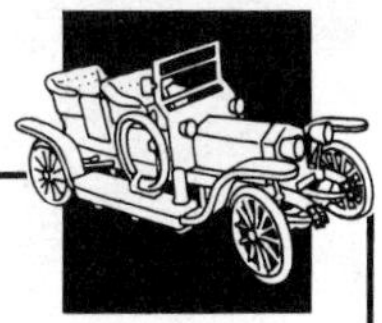

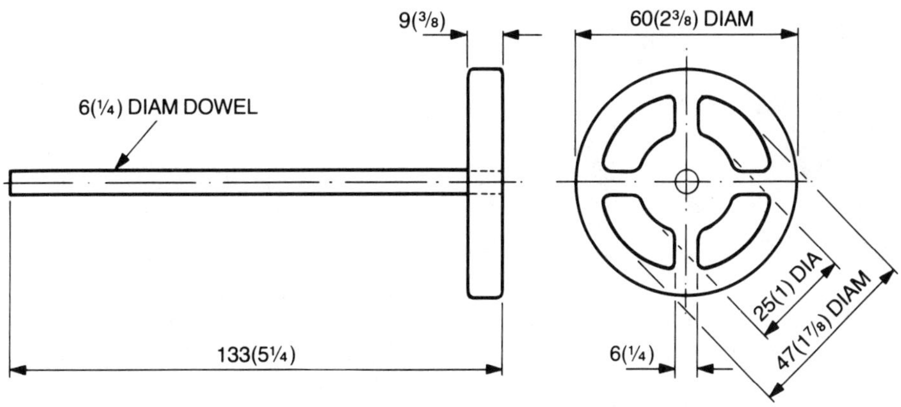

9(3/8)
60(2 3/8) DIAM
6(1/4) DIAM DOWEL
25(1) DIA
47(1 7/8) DIAM
133(5 1/4)
6(1/4)

STEERING COLUMN ASSEMBLY

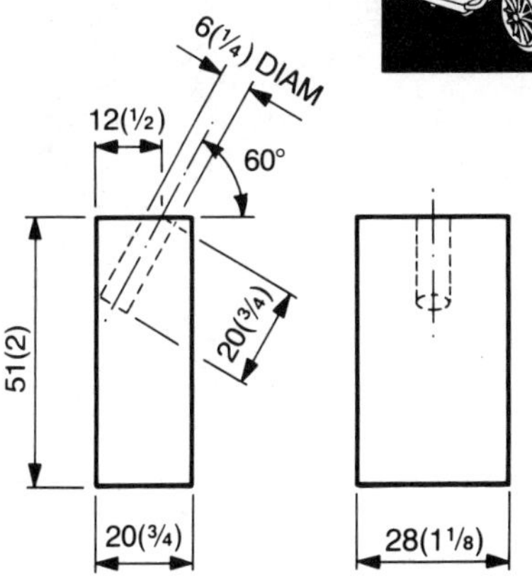

6(1/4) DIAM
12(1/2)
60°
51(2)
20(3/4)
20(3/4)
28(1 1/8)

STEERING COLUMN BLOCK

HEADLAMP
MAKE TWO

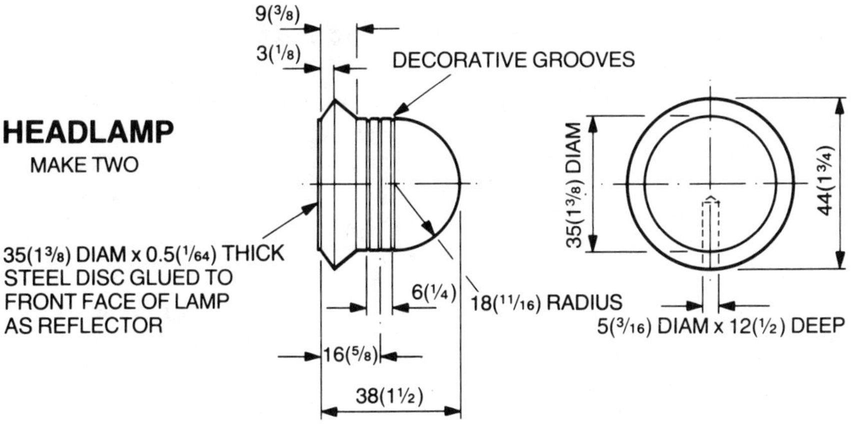

9(3/8)
3(1/8)
DECORATIVE GROOVES
35(1 3/8) DIAM x 0.5(1/64) THICK
STEEL DISC GLUED TO
FRONT FACE OF LAMP
AS REFLECTOR
6(1/4)
18(11/16) RADIUS
16(5/8)
38(1 1/2)
35(1 3/8) DIAM
44(1 3/4)
5(3/16) DIAM x 12(1/2) DEEP

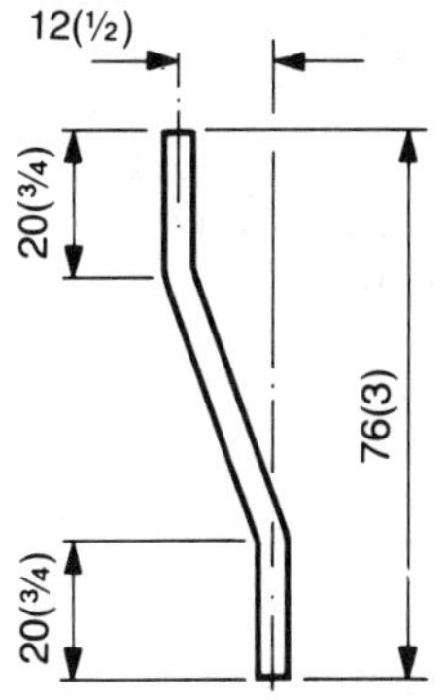

12(1/2)
20(3/4)
76(3)
20(3/4)

LAMP ARM MAKE TWO
5(3/16) DIAM STEEL WIRE

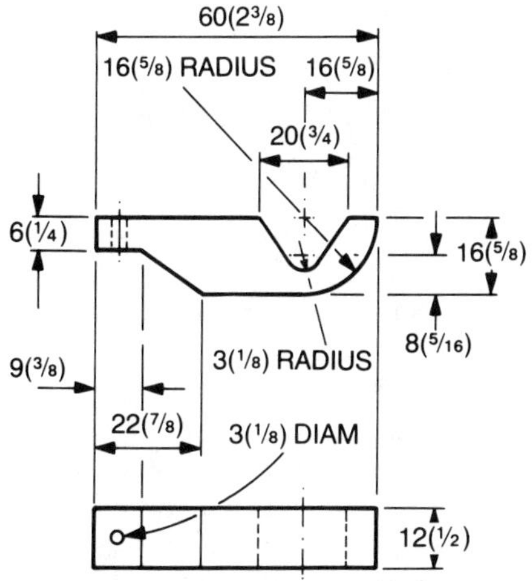

60(2 3/8)
16(5/8) RADIUS
16(5/8)
20(3/4)
6(1/4)
16(5/8)
8(5/16)
3(1/8) RADIUS
9(3/8)
22(7/8)
3(1/8) DIAM
12(1/2)

SPARE WHEEL
FRONT SUPPORT ARM

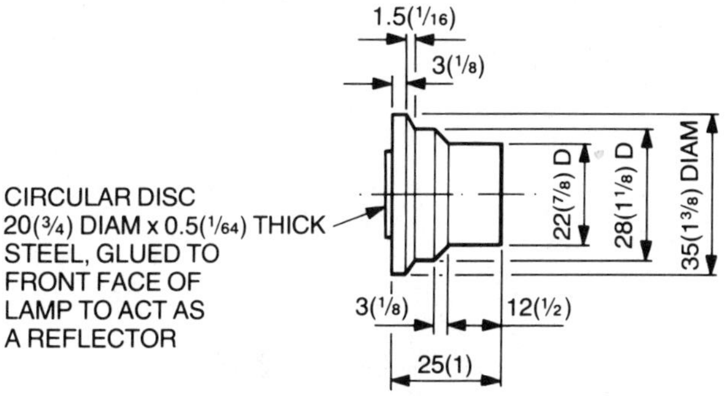

1.5(1/16)
3(1/8)
CIRCULAR DISC
20(3/4) DIAM x 0.5(1/64) THICK
STEEL, GLUED TO
FRONT FACE OF
LAMP TO ACT AS
A REFLECTOR
22(7/8) D
28(1 1/8) D
35(1 3/8) DIAM
3(1/8)
12(1/2)
25(1)

SIDE LAMP MAKE TWO

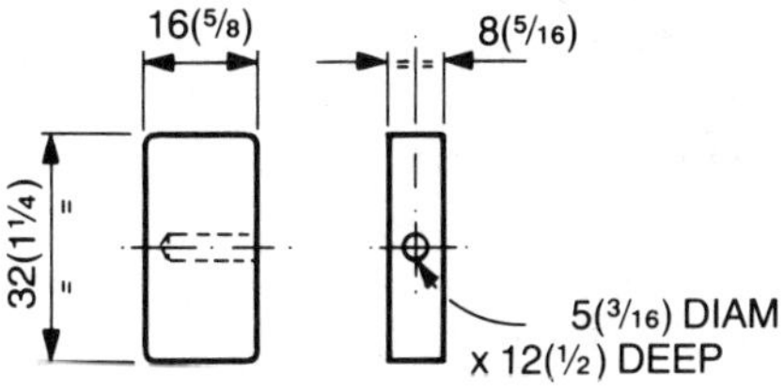

16(5/8)
8(5/16)
32(1 1/4)
5(3/16) DIAM
x 12(1/2) DEEP

DRIVING MIRROR

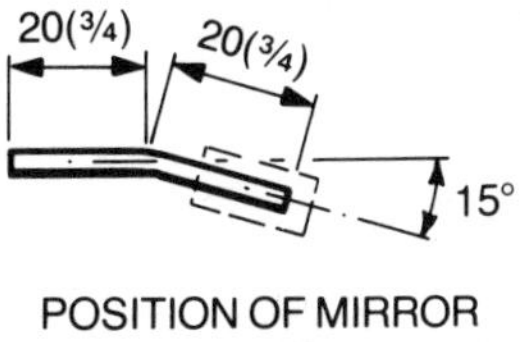

20(3/4)
20(3/4)
15°
POSITION OF MIRROR

MIRROR ARM
5(3/16) DIAM STEEL WIRE

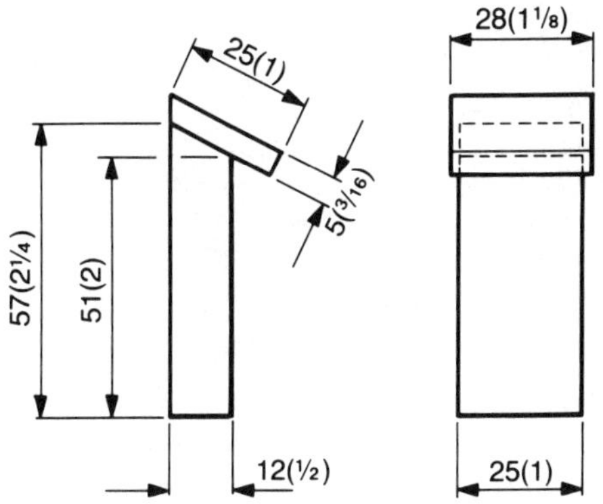

25(1)
28(1 1/8)
5(3/16)
57(2 1/4)
51(2)
12(1/2)
25(1)

CENTRAL CONSOLE

I am often asked the question 'What tools should I choose in order to start a basic tool kit?'

The vast range of hand tools available, the different types of tool, tool patterns and sizes make the task seem intitially daunting. However it is possible to identify the most frequently used tools and I have tried to give you a guide to help you select those basic tools.

Marking out tools
Marking gauge
This is used for all basic marking out work, specifically marking lines parallel to an edge with the grain.

Try square
Available in various sizes (the most popular being 6 inch) the try square is used for testing surfaces and laying out lines at 90° to each other.

Marking knife
This must be used before cutting the marked out work. It cuts the wood fibres cleanly before sawing begins.

Saws
Coping saw
This saw is ideal for small curved work and can be described as the bow saw's little brother.

Bow saw
The bow saw is used for sawing along a curved profile. It has a beechwood frame through which variable tension is applied by twisting the twine. The handles rotate through 360°, allowing the frame to clear the workpiece or bench when sawing deep or complicated shapes.

Tenon saws
A tenon or back saw is a thin bladed, cross cut saw with a heavy brass back to give rigidity and weight for controlled cutting. It is used for tenoning, dovetailing, fine joinery, cabinet work and model making.

Hand saws
The most common of all wood saws, they can be identified by two specific types:
a the ripsaw which is used for sawing with (or along) the grain of the wood.

The teeth of a ripsaw are shaped like chisels which sever the wood grain.
b the crosscut saw which is used for cutting across the grain of the wood. The teeth, usually smaller than those of a ripsaw, are like knife blades which score the wood fibres before sawing to give a clean cut.

Quality saws have solid wood handles with taper ground blades (the steel blade is thinner at the back than at the toothed edge). A tapered blade makes a saw easier to use.

For general work a 24 inch or 26 inch ripsaw with six or seven points to the inch, and a 24 inch or 26 inch crosscut saw with ten points to the inch are the most widely used.

Bench planes
There are basically three types of bench plane: smoothing planes, jack planes and fore or jointer planes. The smoothing plane is the most popular plane as it can be used for final finishing and is ideal for general purpose work.

Spokeshaves
A spokeshave is a handy shaping tool for curved surfaces. There are two types available, flat base for use on convex curves and round face for use on concave curves.

Clamping tools
G-cramps
These are the most popular type of portable clamping tool and are designed with the woodworkers many and varied clamping jobs in mind. The light weight pattern with 2 inch, 2½ inch and 3 inch capacities, is the most useful for the handyman.

Bench holdfast
Work on difficult shapes that cannot be held in a vice for example wood carving can be performed easily with the bench holdfast.

Woodboring tools
Flatbits
The flatbit is todays most versatile bit for use with an electric drill. It bores quickly, cleanly and safely in all types of timber – hardwood, softwood, cross

grain, end grain – and many other materials, such as plastics. The most popular sizes are ⅜ inch, ½ inch, ¾ inch and 1 inch.

Countersink
A countersink is used for shaping the top of a screw hole permitting the screw head to sit flush.

Wood chisels
The use of bevel edge chisels has changed considerably over the last thirty years. What was once a specialist tool is now manufactured with enough strength to be a general purpose chisel as well as the jobs for which it was originally intended – fine cabinet work, dovetailing and chiselling in angled corner joints. It is the most frequently purchased type of wood chisel.

The purchase of a set of wood chisels is a good idea for the beginner as these are often priced below the total price of the individual components.

Cabinet screwdrivers
These are the traditional pattern screwdrivers prefered by many craftsmen. The oval shaped handles with their bulbous ends are designed for positive grip and increased torque.

Bradawl
A bradawl is used for starting screw holes to prevent splitting of the wood. Square section bradawls, drawn down to a fine point, allow quicker penetration with a twisting action and easier withdrawal than a cylindrical blade.

Hand drill
The hand drill is used when small diameter, accurate holes are to be drilled in wood.

Joiner's mallet
This is usually manufactured with a beech head and ash shaft. The wedge shape of the shaft results in the head actually tightening on it as the mallet is swung. The mallet faces are flat but slightly angled to strike the work or chisel squarely.

Carving tools

The extensive range of carving tools with literally dozens of different patterns and hundreds of sizes would astonish any hobbyist. However the average professional uses only two or three dozen on a very regular basis.

Briefly the basic carving tool shapes and uses are as follows:

Chisels

Chisels are flat bladed tools with no curvature and are either square or skew (that is with the blade edge ground to an angle). Chisels are used for outlining, reaching acute corners and cleaning up recessed backgrounds. Spoonbit chisels are tools whose ends are shaped like a spoon and used for fine work that would be impossible with a standard chisel.

Gouges

Similar to chisels but with a curvature to the blade, gouges are used for grooving or, when turned over, for carving convex shapes. Bent gouges are standard gouges but with a long bend in the blade. They are used for cutting hollows in rounded shapes or for removing large amounts of wood when carving bowls.

Parting tools

Often called 'V tools' because of their cutting shape, parting tools are used for outlining, lettering, finishing corners and cutting sharp edge grooves.

For the beginner the ideal way to build up a carving tool kit would be to purchase a set of six of the most popular shapes.

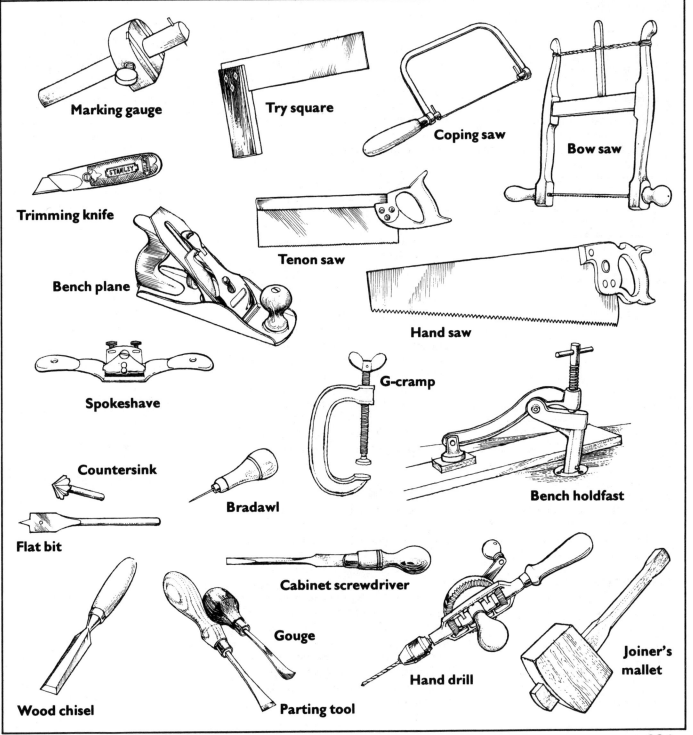

Marking gauge

Try square

Coping saw

Bow saw

Trimming knife

Tenon saw

Bench plane

Hand saw

Spokeshave

G-cramp

Countersink

Bradawl

Bench holdfast

Flat bit

Cabinet screwdriver

Gouge

Hand drill

Joiner's mallet

Wood chisel

Parting tool

POWER TOOLS

The introduction of power tools into any workshop will speed up many of the basic woodworking operations. It is perhaps sawing that is the most arduous task and any electric sawing device that can be introduced must be of benefit.

Electric drills

These will do a great deal more than bore holes. Any tool catalogue will show you just how many accessories are available.

Jig saw

Perhaps the safest of all portable electric saws is the jig saw. Its name implies that it only cuts intricate shapes but in fact it is capable of cutting all shapes including internal cuts in wood. If I had to choose one saw only in my workshop then I would go for a jigsaw with a pendulum motion blade. It will do everything other saws can do only it will take a little longer.

Vertical drill stand

This stand holds the electric drill and makes it possible to accurately drill holes at 90° to the ground line.

Router

This tool basically consists of an electric motor with a chuck holding a cutter. The height of the motor is adjustable. These electric tools work at extremely high speeds (18 000 – 20 000rpm) and make very clean cuts. A large range of shaped cutters are available which makes an extremely versatile machine.

It is capable of cutting most woodworking joints very quickly and makes light work of housing joints which are always tedious to cut.

Band saws

As the name implies a band of steel with saw teeth is stretched around either two or three wheels. The saw is very useful for cutting all curved work quickly. In the past few years small bench top machines have been introduced and are very popular with toy and model makers. Some

machines have incorporated a sanding disc, which is very useful.

Universal woodworking machines

For the very keen amateur who intends to do a lot of woodworking, it is worth considering these machines.

Basically you can get a bench onto which is mounted a circular saw, planer thicknesser, spindle maker and wood boring attachment. Usually one moter powers all the machine through a system of belts.

Buying a machine like this saves a great deal of space in the workshop.

Holding devices

Under this heading comes a whole range of tools designed to hold the work firmly. The point to stress here is that whatever degree of wood working you intend to go to, if you don't hold the work firmly you will hurt yourself.

The simplest of these 'tools' is the G-cramp which will hold timber firmly to the worktop. Slightly more advanced is the 'jobber', a table top mounted work bench. Its two powerful jaws hold work firmly. The 'workmate' is a self standing work table and is a very useful piece of equipment not only for model making but for all jobs around the house.

However nothing beats the purpose made work bench fitted with a powerful vice. It is a very worthwhile investment.

Planing machines

Anyone faced with hand planing a rough plank of wood to a smooth surface will know that it is time consuming and hard work, and unless you have a little skill the plank may well finish smooth but different thicknesses.

The traditional planing machine is very expensive but the introduction of the hand held planer has been a boon to the handyman. Many different brands of planer are available and are well worth considering as there are great savings to be made in planing your timber.

Basically the machine consists of an electric motor that drives a circular drum. Fitted into the drum are two steel blades which rotate at high speed. The blades remove small chips of wood as the machine is pushed along the plank. Provision is made for adjusting the depth of the cut.

All manufacturers of machine tools give clear instructions how their particular tool is best used. Familiarise yourself with the machine before starting it. If you are not confident how it should be used ask the tool supplier for a demonstration.

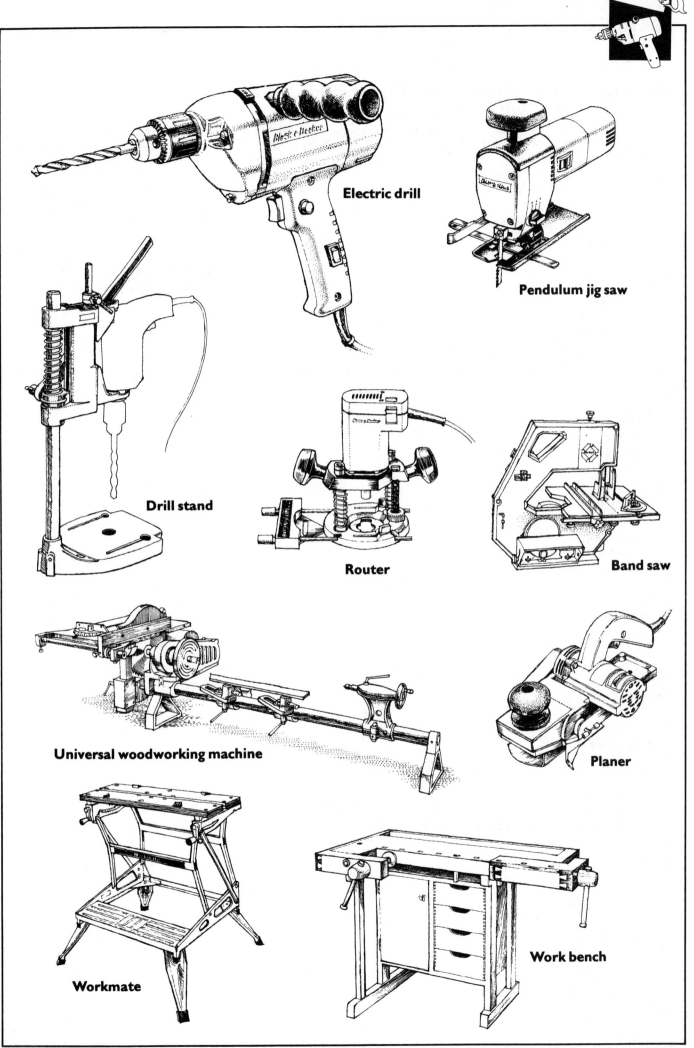

Electric drill

Pendulum jig saw

Drill stand

Router

Band saw

Universal woodworking machine

Planer

Workmate

Work bench

Wheels, axles, spring caps and accessories

Frequently model and toy makers experience difficulty in obtaining the correct wheels for their toy or models. We can supply the wheels, steel axles and the necessary spring caps to keep the wheels on.

In North America, the above mentioned items are available from:

Ortus Marine Inc.
2190 Quest, Boul
Dorchester B/Vd
West Montreal, Quebec
Canada H3H 1R6

Rolls Royce radiators for the Silver Ghost

These genuine hand made stainless steel radiators are made by Rolls Royce craftsmen at Crewe. They are made in the same factory as the cars especially for the model featured in this book.

Accessories

To add a touch of realism to the wooden models, Scania, Land Rover and Hyster Fork Lift trucks have made available complete badging sets.

On receipt of a large stamped addressed envelope prices for all the above mentioned items are available from:

Sterling Publishing Co., Inc.
Two Park Avenue
New York, New York 10016

Index